DATE DUE

0

SUNSET AND TWILIGHT

From the Diaries of 1947-1958

B.B. in Conversation, 1956. *Photo David Lees, Life*

SUNSET AND TWILIGHT

From the Diaries of 1947-1958

BERNARD BERENSON

Edited and with an Epilogue by Nicky Mariano

Introduction by Iris Origo

A Helen and Kurt Wolff Book

Harcourt, Brace & World, Inc., New York

First edition

Library of Congress Catalog Card Number: 63-15313
Printed in the United States of America
Designed by Stefan Salter

ILLUSTRATIONS

EDITOR'S NOTE

The selection from the diaries was made by me in collaboration with Kurt and Helen Wolff. Our joint purpose was to give, in contrast to selections from the diaries previously published, a more personal aspect—Bernard Berenson as he experienced and evaluated his life in his old age. I would have preferred fewer references to myself, but my collaborators overruled me.

Nicky Mariano

This is the diary of the last eleven years of Bernard Berenson's life, between his eighty-second and ninety-third years. By that time, however vital and eclectic a man may be, a process of selection has taken place. With every year, the holes of the strainer become finer, and less is allowed to pass through them. What, in this man of quite exceptional intelligence, vitality, and self-awareness—living a life conditioned to shelter and protect him, physically and metaphorically, from every chilling blast—what remained at the bottom of the bowl?

In this diary, kept almost daily, a few dominant themes soon become apparent: an enjoyment of beauty which old age, far from diminishing, had only rendered still sharper and more subtle, an unquenchable intellectual curiosity, a great many personal relationships (though not all satisfying), an almost uncanny self-awareness—and one dominant, indispensable human affection. These form the leitmotifs of this record of old age—but before attempting to follow them, it is perhaps already necessary, four years after his death, to say what Bernard Berenson was, and what he and his legend signified for his contemporaries.

No one would more freely have admitted this necessity than Berenson himself. As early as 1949, he was already writing: "I seldom open a book published today . . . without finding something that increases my feeling of having survived my world, of having been left behind, of being a tolerated ghost in a society 'that knew not Joseph.'" And he went on to reflect that if he, while still alive, already felt himself to be an unwelcome guest how great an illusion it is for any of us to believe that we would have been happy in the Athens of Socrates or the France of the eighteenth century. Perhaps, indeed, it would even be true to say that the values of the world which B.B. created at I Tatti are already as remote today as those of Athens or Versailles—and for this reason, too, it may be interesting to inquire what their nature was, and what sort of man could spend over seventy years of his life in defining and preserving them: the last true humanist, perhaps, of Western Europe.

The external outline of his life falls naturally into three phases: the period of youth and ascension, the years of achieved success, during which the legend also took shape, and finally, in the period covered by this diary, the rediscovery, always lucid and sometimes merciless, of the true figure, as a tree sheds its leaves, leaving the tracery of its branches bare against the winter sky. In the words of one of his greatest contemporaries, Yeats:

> I made my song a coat
> Covered with embroideries
> Out of old mythologies
> From heel to throat;
> But the fools caught it,
> Wore it in the world's eyes
> As though they'd wrought it
> Song, let them take it,
> For there's more enterprise
> In walking naked.

In his first years in America, the Lithuanian Jewish boy, whose family had emigrated to Boston in 1875, when he was ten years old, went through Harvard as the pupil of Barrett Wendell and William James, the friend of Santayana and Charles Adams, and the protégé of Mrs. Jack Gardner, whose collection later on owed its greatest masterpieces to him. Then, returning to Europe at the age of twenty-two, he found in "the glamorous adventure" of his first visit to Italy the inspiration which set the pattern of his future. The books which first made him known—*The Venetian, The Florentine,* and *The Central Italian Painters of the Renaissance,* and the monograph on Lorenzo Lotto—all appeared between 1892 and 1901, before he was thirty-six. Then came the profession of *expertise* and the partnership with Duveen; soon, in the great international art market, the value of an Italian picture came to depend upon its authentication by Berenson. With the very considerable profits, he transformed a rustic villa of the Quattrocento near Settignano into his famous villa, I Tatti—as pure and exquisite a quintessence of Tuscan architecture, art, and landscape as only a non-Tuscan could have conceived—and this, for the rest of his life, became his home.

It was at this point that the myth began to be woven, and its protagonist to become, with his house, its pictures, and its library, one of the "sights" of Italian travel. Here came disciples, friends, and (in his own phrase) "enemy-friends" from every part of the world: poets and painters, philosophers and historians, the elegant world of Paris, London, and New York and the royalties whom he felt to be a little different from other mortals, the pretty and silly fashionable women whom he desired and who made him talk better than anyone else, old friends from Boston and Harvard and uncouth young students whom he pronounced to be "un-Salonfähig"—unfit for polite society—and yet to whom he gave the free run of his photographs and his library.

And meanwhile the myth was taking shape: of Berenson's brilliant talk—witty, merciless, exhibitionist, but always "life-enhancing"—of his encyclopaedic memory for all that he had ever read in seven languages—of his exquisitely cut pale grey suits and the dark red carnation in his buttonhole—of his indulgence with the young, his ruthlessness with his equals—of his love affairs, his travels, his fabulous art collection—of summer nights in his jasmine-scented garden. The habitués of the house covered a very wide range. There were Logan Pearsall Smith and Bertrand Russell (Mary Berenson's brother and brother-in-law); there were writers as diverse as Robert Trevelyan and Lytton Strachey, Gide and Valéry, Santayana and Vernon Lee, Percy Lubbock and Edith Wharton. There were Italians of such widely different types as Croce and D'Annunzio, Ojetti and Salvemini, Don Guido Cagnola and Francesco Papafava—and, later on, Umberto Morra, Guglielmo Alberti, Giovanni Colacicchi, and Arturo Loria, Vittorio Cini, Elena Carandini, and Clotilde Marghieri; there were the varied and often bizarre owners of the villas which crowned the neighbouring hills, among them the two connoisseurs whom B.B. prided himself on having "brought to

xi

Florence," and who subsequently enriched that city with their collections, Charles Loeser and Herbert Horne; and there were, at different periods, the young men who acted as his secretaries or architects, and who owed to his influence much of the future shape of their life: Cecil Pinsent, who rebuilt his house and designed his garden, Geoffrey Scott, who wrote *The Architecture of Humanism* in his library, John Walker and Kenneth Clark, who wrote of him after his death: "I owe him far more than I can say and probably more than I know."

What was it that attracted to I Tatti so many different kinds of men? Just as there are what Salvemini used to call *"libri fecondatori,"* so there are men who have the gift of sharpening the faculties of everyone who comes near them. Perhaps in B.B. (apart from his wit and culture) it was largely a question of sheer vitality, which gave spice to his talk, even when one disagreed with every word he said. "What we admire, enjoy, and even love," he wrote, "is creative energy, imagination, courage, determination, even if misunderstood or misdirected."

It was these vital qualities that drew the most gifted men in Europe to B.B. and that we still find in this diary. "The life of Berenson," wrote a critic after his death, "is the story of a mind"— and it is the full maturity of this mind that these pages reveal. But which of the threads that had made up so intricate a pattern was gradually discarded and which remained part of the woof until the end?

The enjoyment of beauty was perhaps the chief of the pleasures that never failed. "While everything else physical and mental seems to diminish," he wrote in his eighty-third year, "the appreciation of beauty is on the increase. . . . I enjoy looking not only with ecstasy, but like a wine- or tea-taster." He prided himself, too, on having at last acquired a painter's eye, on seeing objects "in their three dimensions, not . . . in two only. And colours, every day I see more and deeper."

When he went for a country walk, he said (and anyone who has accompanied him knows that this is true), he walked not only with his legs but his eyes, and when he could not go out, he found an almost equal enjoyment in the view from his window. His descriptions of landscape were often formulated in terms of a familiar work of art: the convent of Vallombrosa at sunset, "looking through the grand entrance on the right at the tunnelled road leading down to Tosi," reminded him of "Velasquez's Villa Medici sketches, but ever so much finer"; the landscape from his room at Portofino at dawn appeared to him "exactly as in Giorgione" with the foliage above the cove "feathery yet exquisitely massed," while the coast near Amalfi recalled to him Mantegna, "to such a degree that one could almost believe he had sketched and reproduced it." On another day, when a white fog had veiled the Val d'Arno, the scene looked to Berenson like "a landscape more of foreplan even than a Pompeian, more *estompé* than a Chinese one. Almost like a denser Seurat."

In comparison with this persistent delight, his enjoyment of the other arts was comparatively flat. He read, or was read to, omnivorously, but his literary comments were often commonplace and his references to poetry (in his last years) almost entirely confined to Shakespeare, Goethe, and the nineteenth-century English poets. As for music, he himself wrote that though he often listened to it (and with such chamber music in his own house as that provided by Menuhin and Cassadò) he honestly doubted "whether my ear is very good" and admitted that after a comparatively short period "the music served mostly to liberate various trains of thought in 'free and fantastic' association." The admission shows an agreeable absence of humbug—but this is not how a musician listens.

An unfailing source of pleasure, however, was his pride in his library. He had been building up, he wrote, "a library where a student of White Man's civilization would find every essential book at hand. I hoped to leave it to American students who would grow by using it. Any book is worth while . . . if it has even one illustration not to be found elsewhere, one text not easily to be had in other books."

Yet at times he had misgivings—and so also had his friends. Sometimes, in visiting I Tatti, it seemed to me as if B.B., by his gift of his house to Harvard, were deliberately turning it, like one of the Pharaohs, into his own mausoleum, and many passages in the diary show a similar doubt. In moments of optimism, indeed, he would picture the house after his death as a "lay monastery for leisurely culture" in which "a number of students between twenty-five and thirty" could "enjoy the leisure to mature their talents, their gifts as talkers and writers"—a nest, in short, for dozens of fledgling B.B.'s. But at other times he foresaw the fate overtaking it which, sooner or later, affects most institutions, when the spirit which animated them has fled: "Gardens neglected, indoors necessarily institutionalized. All the odds and ends, the flowers, the trinkets that gave intimacy to a room, will have disappeared. . . . A dreary abstraction will reign. . . . And who will preside, what kind of biped will replace me and mine? . . . Unimaginable! How little one owns, how quietly it goes over to others who make use of it. . . ."

One other pleasure never failed him: that of asking questions. In talking to his friends, as in his diary, the subjects for speculation were unending. How many works of art (such as the Romanesque churches in Aquitaine) owed their preservation merely to the fact that they stood in a region too poor to adopt a new style swiftly? (He would have liked the story, told me by an Italian archaeologist, of the sacristan of the Cathedral of Otranto who, when complimented on the remarkable preservation of the fine mosaic pavement, replied: "It has been saved by poverty. Worshippers in this church, for centuries, have not worn shoes.") Was it true that in generations of men, as in crops, there were good seasons and bad? Why did he himself prefer upper-class to middle-class people? Was it pure snobbery or only that contact was easier? Why do "the great Unworthies" (such as Byron, Napoleon, Alcibiades) make us insatiable for information about them, while the Worthies only obtain lip service? How did Socrates, as an old man, keep clean?

"So my idle thoughts wander to and fro through time and space, asking questions," and vainly trying to reach, in every field, "beyond, *jenseits, au delà.* . . . I recall vividly how as a little boy I wore out my thin legs running as hard as I could to get beyond the horizon."

And he described (wishing that he had Dante's pen to render it) a dream he had recently had, in which he had found himself struggling in a dark, deep wood. Some of the great trees in it, which were pushing out smaller ones, "were topped with crooklike growths, some ending in a mitre, and others curved like a question mark." He stumbled about, entangled in the undergrowth and terrified by the darkness and by the sound of great trees creaking and breaking, and became "aware that there was a desperate struggle going on . . . between the question-mark and the mitre trees . . ." until at last only the question marks remained. "They replaced all other growths, an infinity of question marks, nothing, nothing but question marks—questioning what and questioning whom?"

One subject for speculation to which he constantly returned was the character of his own people, the Jews. "Peter Viereck," he wrote, "asked who and what was a Jew, and at last I think I have an answer. A Jew is the product of being cooped up in ghettos for over twelve hundred years. His conditioning from within and without, the outer pressure driving more and more to defensive extremes, the inner clutching to rites, to practices, to values making for union and for safety, the struggle for food and survival, the lust for pre-eminence and power: all have ended in producing the Jew, regardless of what racial elements originally constituted him."

Originally, he wrote, he himself used to be anti-Zionist, being by nature an assimilator and seeing "no reason for establishing a Jewish ghetto anywhere, and least of all in a hornet's nest like the Holy Land." But gradually his mind was changed by his awareness of his people's need, not only for security, but self-respect. "The fact that contempt is felt for them by the majority of non-Jews makes them not only resentfully unhappy or cringingly eager to be good bourgeois, toeing the mediocre line in every land, but also to feel this contempt for themselves. . . . The remedy may be found in statehood plus . . . military glory. . . ."

As old age crept on, it was an aged Hebrew patriarch or prophet that his visitors would find—wrapped, over his elegant grey suit, in the soft woollen shawl that lay always upon his shoulders, and with a little cap of burgundy-red velvet upon his head. He described an old friend who came to see him, after a separation of six years, "changed from a still youngish Frenchman to a white-haired elderly Jew"—and soon afterwards remarked that not only was a similar transformation overtaking himself, too, but that he enjoyed it. "How easy and warm the atmosphere between born Jews like Isaiah Berlin, Lewis Namier, myself, Bela Horowitz, when we drop the mask of being goyim and return to Yiddish reminiscences, and Yiddish stories and witticisms! After all, it has been an effort (no matter how unaware) to act as if one were a mere Englishman or Frenchman or American, and it is something like home-coming and reposing to return to 'Mother's cooking.'" The significant word in this sentence is "mere."

Among the visitors to his house in the last few years, some of those whose company now gave him the greatest pleasure were Yehudi Menuhin, "the sort of person I could wish to have access to every day," Walter Lippmann, and Isaiah Berlin, of whom he wrote: "We come from the same kind of ghetto, came under similar Anglo-Saxon conditioning, and have both been readers, writers, thinkers. Yet . . . he is a Fellow of All Souls, and I have never belonged anywhere. He is idolized in official society, and I have no place in it. Whence the difference?"

A few other old friends, too, were unfailingly welcome: Hortense Serristori, a friend of sixty years' standing, Salvemini, Harry Coster, Hamish and Yvonne Hamilton, Freya Stark, Francis and Katherine Biddle, and above all Judge Learned Hand, the only man whose photograph, showing his leonine features and bushy eyebrows, was permitted to strike an incongruous and refreshing note in the impersonal little sitting room in which guests waited before meals. His attraction for B.B. was partly one of contrast. "He can clown, mimic, sing like a lively and entertaining youngster. . . . Free from inhibition too. How different from myself, not only held in by all sorts of snobbish habits, but by a psychophysiological economy which scarcely affords to go round and certainly has nothing left over to play with."

Yet on the whole, it was not his intellectual equals whom he most enjoyed seeing. Salvemini, indeed, he described after his return from exile as "one of the brightest, sunniest, as well as best-intentioned to be fair and just" of all his friends; yet even in him he "smelt the smoke and stench of animal competitiveness." Bertie Russell and Santayana, he complained, never really listened to what he was saying, and besides Santayana had no sense of humour, and "kept his heart on ice"; Croce, though undoubtedly a great man, "never has asked me what *I* felt, what I thought." "He was much more the *Duce* in matters of the mind than Mussolini ever was in politics." Gide was too solemn, too unwilling "to recognize me as an equal," while on his side B.B. refused "to submit to him as to a master."

xvi

The audience which B.B. really liked to address was of a very different kind: young people, students, experts in an entirely different field, royalties—and, as indeed he had already admitted in his *Self-Portrait,* admiring women, young or middle-aged, sophisticated or innocent. "Interlocutors with better brains," he wrote, "do not stimulate but intimidate. . . . For my part it is the adolescent mind . . . that stimulates me and . . . with rare exceptions, [women] remain adolescent-minded through all ages." Moreover he frankly confessed that, whereas in his youth he had often been puritanical, at eighty-four he had become "painfully aware of the sex or lack of it in all women except septuagenarians," and desirous of their caresses—*"pourvu que tout se passe en douceur,* and with a touch of nostalgia"—conscious of "the never diminishing hold that sex has on us—sex, its derivations and disguises." But above all, it was to brilliant flights of talk that women stimulated him—and talk he must. "At the end of talks with friends, talks that have gone well, I find that I have enjoyed them far beyond the value of what was discussed. . . . It was the satisfaction of physical need and call of nature to chatter. . . ."

Not until his last years did he admit that he no longer felt that "call." "At my age I know that my words are no longer winged, and that there is little profit in trying to correct the nonsense, the absurdities, the malice, the calumnies, the self-assertion, the challenging dogmatism of one's younger fellow bipeds. . . ."

These comments refer to only one aspect of the general process of dissatisfaction with most human relationships, which the latter part of this diary plainly and painfully reveals. It was not that the flow of visitors decreased: there was indeed scarcely a day in which the visits of old friends or new pilgrims to the shrine were not recorded—and among the latter it was the most exotic, or simply those most unlike himself, who caught his interest most: Katherine Dunham, "looking like an Egyptian queen . . . dressed in stuff that clings to her . . . draping rather than clothing her . . . a work of art, a fanciful arabesque," or a young beautiful Greek woman with "the build, the breasts wide apart, the articulated profile," of Classic Greek sculpture—or, at the other end of the scale, President Truman, "as natural, as unspoiled by high office as if he had got no further than alderman of Independence, Missouri. In my long life I have never met an individual with whom I so instantly felt at home."

Such encounters satisfied his unfailing appreciation of whatever he felt to be completely genuine, first-hand, and first-rate of its own kind, such as the "impression of integral innocence" given by certain American young women, who "look as if no material feeling could prevail, no unseemly, no evil thought approach them. . . . It is not a look void of experience only, but as of a veil of gentle goodness over the features. . . ."

But far more frequent passages record encounters which, at least on his side, held neither purpose nor warmth. In particular, he noted how difficult it was to get into touch with strange young men. "They come for the first time with a lump in their throat and trembling with awe to encounter the myth the old man has become." He was well aware, too, that sometimes it was not only his age but his own manner—too cold or too flowery, too dogmatic or simply too finished—that prevented his guests from being natural with him. Some "spread the butter of adoration too thick," others defended themselves with "stupid dumbness, or flushed impudence and bluffing." Often he wondered why such visitors came at all. Perhaps, he concluded, they felt him to be "the last survivor of a former civilization, a former way of being. . . . Perhaps I have become a Curiosity."

Throughout the diary, the dichotomy continued: the complaints that all these stray contacts were barren and exhausting— and yet the realization that he could not do without them. "*Vorrei e non vorrei* . . . I feel worried, harrowed, besieged by people who want to have a look at me, who ask me for articles, and even books, for prefaces, for recommendations, etc. Yet I am sure I should feel neglected and forgotten if I really was left alone. I feel for instance an infinitesimal moment of resentment against anybody of mark, or any budding art historian, who comes to Florence and does not 'ask for an audience.' "

Perhaps part of the spiritual isolation of his later years was caused not only or even chiefly by his awareness that much of his art criticism was now considered outdated, and that many of "*les jeunes*" thought him "superficial, lacking in depth, ignoring the problems that they sweat to solve, and totally out of sympathy

with their caterwauling," but above all by his own incapacity—
stated with bloodcurdling frankness—to find any comfort in old
friendship just for friendship's sake, when a friend had become
dull, prosy, or out of touch.

"A friend is somebody who stimulates me and I can stimulate
to talk. . . . When the stimulation no longer occurs, it is a
spent, an exhausted friendship, and continues as a burthen and
a bore. . . . Unfortunately, in a long life one gets barnacled
over with the mere shells of friendship, and it is difficult without
hurting one's self to scrape them off."

Even the death of friends, he now openly admitted, moved
him only in so far as it could affect himself. "Am I then utterly
heartless, or am I simply the average man? Are there individuals
who love others for the others' sake without reference to themselves? . . . The human heart is a quicksand, and one sinks into
it. . . ."

What then, in human terms, was left? Above all, one vital,
necessary affection—that of Nicky Mariano, who had come to
work in his library as a young woman forty years before and, after
his wife's death, had become his inseparable companion. Of all the
pages of the diary, those which bear witness to her goodness and
his gratitude make the most agreeable reading. In them she is "the
necessity, the solace, the happiness of my life," his counsellor,
his nurse, his almoner ("I am not hardhearted, but I do not instinctively think of the wants and wishes of the people in need"),
his collaborator, his partner in "a union that could not be nearer
perfection." When for a few days she was laid up, the house
seemed "like a reel of thread when the reel is taken away"; when
he was ill, she hovered over him "with a face beaming with love
to give me courage," and slept beside his door. "She works with
me, she thinks with me, she feels as I do, she is the complete
companion . . . she takes every material burden off my shoulders . . . and yet . . . makes the time to read to me, to edit
what I write, to housekeep . . . to tolerate my flirtations. . . ."
"I cannot imagine life without her."

Eventually he came to feel that "my ideal would be to settle
into a life of almost complete solitude à deux, with Nicky keeping
me company, reading aloud to me. I then could get the calm
and repose which would allow me to think things out and bring

xix

them to black and white. I know . . . that writing is the only self-indulgence, the only satisfaction, left me."

Again and again, this desire is repeated—a nagging, driving need to fulfill himself in writing, and to achieve at last the clarity and conciseness of expression that he so much admired in others. "I am humiliated," he wrote, "exasperated at my impotence in finding words and phrases. . . . It makes me suffer from a kind of spiritual constipation." Later on he complained of a constantly diminishing vocabulary. "I never had one adequate to my purpose, and it has been a handicap." (This, strange as it seems in a man of such wide reading, was true.) Sometimes he wondered whether the reason that he went on writing at all, in spite of "derisory profits, annoying misprints, and malignant reviews," was not merely "to justify my claim to be still a useful member of so-ciety . . . in short, that I am still able to pay passage on the ship of life. . . ." But in truth, he knew that it was to *himself* that writing was still essential, "almost as necessary as eating and drinking, certainly as much as love-making in the past." Even when the great success of his *Self-Portrait* had brought some satis-faction, he was still goaded on by the merciless taskmaster within. "What I have written, what I have stated, counts as nothing. What I still want to do, what I still want to write . . . absorbs my thoughts, my daydreams to the exclusion of any self-com-placency with my own past."

This, surely, is not the self-criticism of a man dissatisfied with his own articulacy, but rather of a writer thoroughly aware of the intricate difficulties involved in the attempt to translate one art into the terms of another, and passionately eager to convey to eyes less sensitive and less trained than his own what he himself had been able to achieve. "A letter congratulating me on the success I had in life. It hurt me because I now realize how much I could have done and said. . . . Almost from infancy I have had a feel-ing about self, about life, and later on and for the last seventy years about art, which I have not remotely communicated to others. . . ." This, from a man who had dedicated so much of his life to the transmission of knowledge and ideas, is surely a remarkable admission, and it was by an equally exacting standard that he measured the actual content of his mind, firmly repudi-ating the reputation for deep and universal scholarship which his library and the brilliance of his conversation had foisted upon him. "How limited," he exclaimed at eighty-eight, "is culture. . . . My own culture, how limited without Russian, let alone Chinese!" "Except in the very small and narrow acre of Italian painting of the fifteenth and sixteenth centuries, where I have wider knowledge than anybody now living, I feel anything but self-satisfied." But he added, too: "How few are as aware as I am of all they miss!" And at ninety-three, he was still eagerly questioning a nuclear physicist about "where science is going," and admiring his modesty and the strictly defined limits he set to his knowledge. "How I envy the scientists, and how I wish I were one of them, and not the magician I am taken for, because of my disreputable profession!"

Here we find a standard similar to that which, when he was over ninety, made him feel it worth while to revise his list of Florentine pictures only on condition that each decision and attribution should be reconsidered afresh, as if it had never been reached before. And it was in a similar spirit that he embarked upon the last task he had set himself—the study already begun in his *Self-Portrait,* but now pursued far more ruthlessly. For so many years he had been considering the attribution of works of art: now he was studying a last one, the one best known to him—himself.

In a sense, it might be said that his whole life had been a preparation for this task. "As I attempt to look back," he wrote about his youth, "I want to note how much . . . I have thought of becoming, of being, rather than of doing. In the vocabulary I use today, I wanted to become and be a work of art myself, and not an artist." The ideal he held before himself—and in this one cannot fail to be aware of the two major influences which had shaped him in his youth, Goethe and Pater—was one which had much in common, he claimed, with "the *kalos k'agathos* of the Greeks, the knight of the Middle Ages, the French *honnête homme* of the seventeenth century, and later on the English gentleman, and above all the Goethean *gebildeter Mensch.* I need no other myth. . . ."

It is the story of his attempts to fulfill at least a small part of this ideal, and finally of the divestment of all the trailing clouds of glory that success had brought, to lay bare, lucidly and mercilessly, the true persona—in so far as he could find and

xxi

fathom him—that is the true achievement of this remarkable document of old age.

The question that he asked himself was the one that sooner or later troubles all highly self-conscious human beings: "Who is the real *I*, where does he hide from ME? I know who he is not, but how and what and if at all HE is, I have never discovered although for more than seventy years I have been looking for him." Among the many strands of which the tapestry of his mind was made up, the many societies in which he had moved, which was the one to which he really felt he belonged? The answer was, not any. There was no single phase of his past to which he could go back "and say, 'This is Me.' . . . Not the ghetto I emancipated from, not the New England where I spent the most formative years of my youth; not England and France, nor even Italy, although I have resided there for sixty years. None of these entities would have me on my terms, nor indeed any church. . . . *Ich bin ein Fremder überall*." Yet still the long, haunted journey into his own consciousness continued, and he sought for the fit epithet to describe it. Rejecting "self-absorption," "self-interest," and "self-awareness," he decided that "My case is well described with the words 'self-curious.'"

Egotism? Of course—but an egotism of singular lucidity and frankness. "*Alle denken an sich. Ich nur denke an mich. Me first* is the instinctive cry of little ones, and I for one at eighty-nine am still there." Even the small, mean faults which we are most disinclined to admit are here laid bare: the grudges and resentments "which steam up from the depths." The admission of vanity, of having reached "the Age of Boasting," of being unable to talk about his own past "without fabulating, exaggerating, idealizing, and outright lying," like "the trills and sequences of sopranos," of his deficiency (which he believed to be common to his race) in the quality which "the Greeks lacked and envied the Romans for having, *gravitas*." And then "every kind of *lâcheté*, meanness, pettiness, cowardice, equivocal business conduct (due more to ignorance and the ethics of art dealers than to my own nature), humiliations, furtiveness, ostrichism, etc. Yes, all these and more and worse that rise and denounce me in the hours of the night. . . ." Once again he might have taken for himself Yeats' words:

"... and not a day
But something is recalled,
My conscience or my vanity appalled."

And meanwhile, Time's chariot was drawing near.

The very first page of the diary holds an entry about time, flying "swifter and ever swifter. I dare say if I live long enough, perhaps another twenty years, time may cease to exist for me. . . . The longest day is so quickly followed by the equinoctial one and that by the shortest. . . . The single days slip between my fingers." Each birthday marked—partly according to that particular day's state of health and mood—a stage in progress. On his eighty-second birthday he was asking, "Shall I still be alive a year hence? I am resigned to not being," but by the eighty-fifth he was "less surprised to be alive, and looked forward to this birthday with less questioning than the one of a year ago. . . . *Encore une année, Madame la Mort.*" By the eighty-sixth, "It is an adventure keeping alive against all the powers of destruction that beset me," and on the eighty-eighth he exclaimed, "I want another and another. . . . There is so much I still want to do and could write, so much in nature and art and people I still could enjoy." But twelve months later, the year that had just passed was recorded as "one scarcely worth living. . . ."

Gradually, lucidly, the ravages of time to each organ of his body were noted, with a scientist's precision: difficulties of digestion, ever increasing deafness, shorter and shorter walks over the hills, then only in his garden, and then—as he became more sensitive to hay fever and to cold—complete relegation indoors, "an indweller in a well." And worst of all, the constant sensation that he was losing hold, that any serious work led quickly "to utter exhaustion, to oversensitiveness, to bitterness, despair, and dissatisfaction with everyone except Nicky. I live out of regard for her." But the perpetual tiredness was the worst. *"Je suis bien fatigué.* Not what I do now, but life, living, has used me up." There were bronchial attacks, one or two alarming falls, and on Christmas Eve, 1955, a frightening attack of vomiting and collapse during which both Nicky and Emma—his devoted maid and nurse—sat by him all night long, and kept on smiling. "Their smiles . . . somehow seemed rouged on their faces rather than

xxiii

real. . . . I caught [Capecchi, his doctor] giving a desperate look at the others. I laughed out loud and said, 'Why do you try to hide from me that you despair of keeping me alive? If you think I am dying, tell me so, for I have various matters to attend to. . . .'" On the next day he added that the expectation of immediate death, "perhaps because I did not believe in it," did not frighten him at all. "The whole drama . . . took place in less than twelve hours. At the time I felt as if years were passing, and slowly. I could not have believed in the subjectivity of my feeling. On the contrary, I *knew* it was real DURATION."

From that time, however, the awareness of death's approach was always with him. "Serious illnesses," he wrote, "are to the individual what wars are to the public. They are as it were landmarks, that cannot be changed or moved . . . not merely calendar dates."

There were, of course, better days and weeks, and then worse ones, each bringing with it a change of mood. Sometimes he had whole days of complete relaxation, without either physical discomfort or mental stress. "I was not questioning. I was not dozing or dreaming. I was enjoying perfect bliss. . . . Did the Fathers who developed the Christian idea of Heaven know like experiences, and erect them into the condition of the Saved?" Certainly what are commonly known as the consolations of religion were not within his reach—indeed, far from drawing closer to the Catholicism to which he had adhered for a short period of his youth, he felt less and less in sympathy with any theological dogma or metaphysical theory. "The vaccination"—as his wife had dryly remarked at the time—"did not take." He believed that there was something in the very structure of his mind which rendered it averse to what he called "Beginnings and Endings." "Hence my hostility to Christian theology in general and to Catholic in particular. It overshadows ritual, which in all churches has found in the course of ages the way for the poor human heart to cry its anguish. . . ."

In the bad days he would be so oppressed by nausea and gloom that he longed "for easeful death." He would then be overcome by a sense of the vanity of all he had done, all he had made. "I have made a home for myself, furnished it for my comfort and pleasure. Some supreme pictures, some real works of art from China . . . I have got together a library. . . . I have built up a garden. . . . If I had a deliberate purpose it was to enjoy it all with a sense of timeless leisure in my old age. . . . Now . . . I am like the peasant in . . . *The Good Earth,* who, owing to his passion for tilling the soil . . . becomes a great landowner, and deprived of the one occupation that gave him satisfaction: digging and tilling. . . ." Often a wave of longing would sweep over him for the places he had once seen, "from Upsala to the Sahara, from Gibraltar to the Euphrates. . . . Not only would I see again all I have seen, but read again all that I have enjoyed, all that has fed my spirit. . . . I long to hear again all *die alten Weisen.* Infinite yearning."

And still, as he lay back in bed, his restless, yearning, eternally curious mind roamed to and fro—sometimes haunted by what he called the Furies, sometimes aware that neither the torments nor the joys of memory were any longer important. "If only one could call up all that in the past was absorbing and what it meant, and how each in turn was replaced by another—if one could look at the landscape of one's whole past, what would it add up to? What am I but a leaf on the Man-tree? The leaf falls and has had all it can, if it has weathered storms and enjoyed sunshine and is allowed to fade and fall to the ground. Why, what, has given me the presumption to believe that I am worthy of being put under glass?"

So, one by one, each spurious garment was discarded: the motley of the cosmopolitan man of the world, the universal scholar, the irresistible lover, and the sage. We are left with the outline of a man of infinite vitality and sensitivity, endowed with talent and knowledge of the very first order in one strictly defined field, and of intuitions and perceptions covering a far wider range, but which he himself felt he had never succeeded in fully developing or expressing: a man haunted, like the rest of us, by a nagging sense of failure, by remorse, fear, and loneliness, but upheld by one tender affection—a man who had outlived his time. A figure who, just because he knew all this and set it down, has gained in stature.

> "For there's more enterprise
> In walking naked."

Iris Origo

1947

January 1st, I Tatti

Time flies swifter and ever swifter. I dare say if I live long enough, perhaps another twenty years, time may cease to exist for me. The seasons seem so short. The longest day is so quickly followed by the equinoctial one and that by the shortest. As for moons, I scarcely measure their flight any more. The single days slip between my fingers. Perhaps because I live fairly in the forenoon alone. The rest of the day I exist merely, unless some very stimulating person rouses me out of invading torpor.

January 2nd, I Tatti

Perfect winter weather, scarcely a breath of wind. Crystal skies, exquisitely lovely sunsets with soft pastel colours, peach and violet, besides refulgent gold. And yet, though I enjoy it as a spectacle more than ever, it is no longer a friend. Mild and gentle, it is nevertheless more than my organism can stand.

I have become so delicate, so fragile, so susceptible to lowered temperatures that I feel the passing of somebody near to me as a chill draft. If I sit with my head uncovered I soon begin to sneeze and cough, and if I shiver then I am in for a bad cold. But this time I recall no shiver. I have often thought since my youth that our bodies were nuisances, which from the moment of their conception all the forces of the universe were doing their utmost to get rid of. So these bodies have to be nurtured and cared for until grown up. They then for ten or fifteen years can hold their own like a besieged fortress and even make sorties. From forty on the hostile—not hostile, not even deadening, but levelling, smoothing out, equalizing forces begin to get the better, to make

3

breaches, which at first are reparable. But these breaches get wider and wider and at last the cosmic steam roller triumphs, and smoothes us out of the way. The nuisance that we were disappears.

January 8th, I Tatti

During my Mary's * last years, and most particularly last months, I used to find her not asleep but not reading, and I would wonder but dared not ask whether she was bored. Now I do the same. Between midnight or so and 6:30 A.M., when tea comes, I lie half awake and again between tea and breakfast at 8:15. Frequently I do not think at all. I am not unconscious but nothing goes on in my mind, unless you call it mental that I am aware of existing and feeling comfort or discomfort. And by the way what is bodily comfort—how to analyze it?

January 10th, I Tatti

In connection with what I said about passing so much time dozing, and merely existing without restlessness and conscious boredom, I recall what happened many years ago. In the course of sight-seeing in Rome I was taken to a dilapidated conventual building at the foot of the Janiculum. There in the cloisters were sunning themselves old men in every state of raggedness and destitution, with nothing to look forward to except the end. I was horrified. Committing the pathetic fallacy of identifying myself with them, I ached and tried to turn away, feeling how bored and listless and dispirited they must be. I should think differently now. They were reduced to mere existence and did not mind it.

January 12th, I Tatti

I ask myself why I am not more at one with the people who at home are making such a strenuous effort to raise funds for restoring buildings here that suffered war damage. It is a fact that

* Mary Whitall Smith (1865–1945), born in Philadelphia of Quaker parents, sister of Logan Pearsall Smith, married first to Anglo-Irish politician Frank Costelloe and, after his death in 1900, to B.B.

4

I have a distaste for "drives" and the publicity and pumped-up enthusiasm that go with them. There is something else, as I wrote at length to Elena Carandini,* when in Rome, soon after the "liberation," a society was being proposed for the restoration of this or that building. I wrote that those would be cared for sooner or later. What seemed more urgent was to take steps to see that the hundreds of ruined villages and scores of small towns were not being hastily rebuilt—hastily yet permanently—in the shoddiest, ugliest, most utilitarian yet showiest way possible. In the Italian landscape the villages looked as little manufactured as the trees, the rocks, the sky itself. They were as much a natural growth of the soil. Now, as I foresaw, they are geometrical excrescences roofed with tiles that will not weather and will never be assimilated by the natural surroundings. It is that which makes me relatively indifferent to the drive for restoring the historical buildings. They will take care of themselves.

February 13th, I Tatti

Everything frayed, worn: clothes, curtains, chairs, sofas. It would have horrified me seven years ago, me with my passion for meticulous order, daintiness, in things about me. Now the contrary has taken place. I feel as if a touch of vulgarity clung to the spick-and-span and a certain charm, a tender, affectionate homeliness to the worn, the show of wear and tear, to the slightly musty, dusty, and rag-fair feel of things.

February 14th, I Tatti

Mary would be eighty-three if she were alive today, and alive she might be if she had not drained two thirds of her strength through an operation twelve years before the end and had not in those and in previous years stuffed herself with medicine and drugs. Even the apothecaries ended by protesting against her fantastic consumption of both. It all came from her intolerance of

---

* Countess Elena Carandini, daughter of Luigi Albertini (1871–1941), editor of *Corriere della Sera* 1900–25, then dismissed by the Fascist regime. Both the Albertini and the Carandini households were rallying points for the opposition to Fascism.

discomfort let alone pain and the conviction that there must be a something to give immediate relief. She seems to have felt any physical disturbance ten times what an ordinary mortal felt.

February 17th, I Tatti

My barber tells me that in 1890 he was eight years old and earning two soldi a day at a carpenter's. For his midday meal he brought a chunk of bread from home and spent one soldo on nuts or raisins. It was a hard life for a small boy of eight, but he recalls it with *Wehmut,* as we all do whatever we did or were done to when we still were living in the world of magic. In a sense we never get out of it, but a time comes when we try to pretend that we have outgrown it.

February 18th, I Tatti

In my diary of the war years I wrote of how important it was to avoid making enemies by rudeness or any other form of bad conduct. I had an instance today. L. C. brought her brother. He seemed not only physically but mentally a vigorous youngish man. He talked forcibly and with no little logic, but to my amazement I found him defending the Nazis against the Anglo-Saxons, the British in particular, and implying that there was little to choose between them, and if there was he might prefer the Germans. It turned out that this young man had been prisoner of war in India for four years. He had not been starved or physically ill-treated, but the way the British rubbed in their "damned superiority" got on his nerves to such an extent that although previously he had often visited England and liked the English he was now full of bitterness and resentment amounting to hatred. I have encountered the same in all Italian war prisoners returned from British camps, and I fear their mood will communicate itself to others, ready as Latins to be anti-British, and produce ill effects in Italian international relations.

February 24th, I Tatti

Three Italian friends to lunch. Talk almost entirely of who was married to whom and what descendants and in same objective tone of who was the mistress and lover of whom. Then who, married or not, left whom or was deserted by whom. And all enjoyed it, including myself, who did not know most of the people discussed. Why did we enjoy it? Only because chatter we must, and such talk is the next-to-anthropoid unsemantic use of what in our case have become organs of speech.

After such talk the easiest and zestfullest is about medicines. With what heat we praise those that have helped us.

February 28th, I Tatti

Some days ago I had a happy thought. It was to write about the vogue now (or recently) enjoyed by Piero della Francesca and to explain it. I meant to brush aside the various culture snobbisms that have led to the mass admiration of Piero, to come to the fact that it was to a great extent owing to a need for justifying a similar cult of Cézanne, and to come to the bottom fact that besides technical qualities which pedants only could appreciate to the full, and tactile values and movement, which with much effort they might be made to understand, there remains the bottommost fact that they are impressed by his unfeelingness; his inexpressiveness, the indifference of the figures not only to what was being done to themselves. I wanted to say that Piero exemplifies to a degree unusual and perhaps exaggerated the arts which avoided the expression and even the show of emotion, the arts in which the figures are content to exist, and exist only, making no effort to explain, to justify their presence, to attract interest or sympathy, just to *exist*.

A hundred years ago Jacob Burckhardt * spoke of certain late Bellini altarpieces as *Existenzbilder*. I scarcely dare to use the term now for fear that it will be connected with Existentialism,

* Swiss humanist, historian, and art critic (1818–97). Author of *Cicerone, Civilization of the Renaissance in Italy*. Greatly and wistfully admired by B.B.

7

a philosophy I make neither head nor tail of. Yet that is what the greatest figure arts are. I meant to go on and speak of the calm, the repose, the strength that is *transpired* (breathed across) from the inexpressive as well as feelingless works of Antiquity, from earliest Mesopotamia and Egypt down to Scopas, and that inspired—no, not inspired—that characterizes the best of Romanesque sculpture and Giotto, the greatest Medieval painter and greatest Romanesque artist.

The grandest, most impressive portraiture too is of this existential nature, making no appeal, existing and nothing more, *selbstverständlich,* none more so than the portraits of Degas, who by the way seems to me to have been one of the greatest portraitists of all time. His people are so free from pose, from uncertainty of look, from any quality but their own existential one, with no slightest touch of inflation on the part of the painter.

Of all this I started writing. Went on bravely for a few pages, and then got stuck and remain so.

March 8th, I Tatti

Zulfaquar Ali Bokhari* dined yesterday, brought by Lionel Fielden.† Except that his hair was more concentratedly black and that his eyes had a certain gleam he would pass for a Southern European. Spoke faultless English with a charming voice. Must not forget to mention well-shaped white hands. For an Indian he was relatively reasonable but behind it all he remained a MUSLIM squire eager to perpetuate Mogul rule over natives. The British have been nothing but pirates, looting and robbing and carrying the proceeds to enrich a distant island. The Mogul rule had been humane and beautiful and he would wish it restored. He regretted it had not converted all India to Islam. A sad disintegrated man, too Europeanized for India and at once dreaded as well as longed to return there.

* Pakistani politician.
† For many years English head of Indian Broadcasting Service. Served in the army during World War II, came to Florence and I Tatti after the liberation, and then settled in Tuscany.

8

March 11th, I Tatti

I listen to music often with pleasure, at times with ecstasy, then again with boredom, august or commonplace. (There is so much jigging in Classical composition, and so much convention in all.) I never talk about music. I am diffident of my own judgment. In the first place I do not know enough. To judge one should know the subject as I know verbal or visual art. Then I doubt whether my ear is very good. Besides, I have no vocabulary in which to express what I might try to say about what I think or feel after listening to music.

March 14th, I Tatti

Finishing Stefan Zweig's *Balzac*. What a bounder this Balzac is, and how infinitely inferior to the artist who wrote the many fine novels and stories going under his name. No parallel in history to the thesis that there is little connection between the man and the artist. In life as lived Balzac is more often than not gross, excessive, intemperate, vulgar, and perhaps never lyrically poetical as for instance in the *Lys de la Vallée* or *Louis Lambert* or *Les Deux Jeunes Mariées,* and elsewhere. His love declarations in his lived life are as rhetorical as they are genuine in his books—and yet Balzac's fault may come from his being so possessed by his creations that he cannot help living them, failing to keep life and art separate, and basing actuality on what in literary art, guided by imagination, is easy to construct, but in life encounters unsurmountable difficulties. Hence his repeated financial disasters, and hence too no doubt something caddish in his relations with women. No, no; the less we know about an artist the better. Blessed be Shakespeare.

March 18th, I Tatti

Robert Penn Warren's *All the King's Men*. Perhaps as narrative, as presentation of character, not superior to many others written today; although scarcely inferior to any. What makes it original is that the supposed writer is one who is deeply imbued with the latest scepticism about man's place in the universe, his destiny, his duties, his urges, his motives. He breathes nihilism

9

and indifference, mere intellectual curiosity to see what will happen if he or others in given conditions do or fail to do certain things. Yet he has an animal side as well, inevitably, and that tends to take its irrational course under compulsion of physiological greeds, satiation, urges, calls—all cutting across his nihilistic indifference, and bringing him back to courses of conduct based on bringing up and traditional values.

The book falls down in that it ends without indicating any good reason for living, for acting; for preferring this rather than that.

After nihilism the only impulsion that is reasonable is to take life as a fine art of which we are the practitioners, all engaged upon producing a masterpiece and a completely humanized mankind.

March 20th, I Tatti

Habent sua fata libelli. Yesterday a young visitor spoke of a film taken from Oscar Wilde's *Dorian Gray* and called this book epoch-making.

On the morning of its publication Oscar came to my room in North Street, Westminster, and handed me a copy, saying it was the first from the press. I took it with appreciation of the gift. The next day Oscar came to lunch, and I did not hesitate to tell him how loathsome, how horrible the book seemed to me. He did not make the slightest attempt to defend it but explained that, he being hard up, the publisher gave him a hundred pounds for a story. But Oscar had it in him, and now after fifty years it is admired and counted as epoch-making.

March 24th, I Tatti

I hear from New York that there is no sale for my *Italian Painters.* The other day I happened to reread parts of it first published in 1897. Sufficient time has elapsed so that I could read "Central Italian Painters" as if I had nothing to do with it. To my surprise I discovered that all I said there expressed all I should want to say now, but I said it better, then, than I could say now. Full of thought, clarity, courage, and ideas. And now in America as well as in England nobody wants to read me. I no longer appeal to a public supposed to take an interest in what hitherto has been regarded as art. Now that people with no mustard seed of native feeling for art constitute the overwhelming majority of the public, they can be bamboozled into taking for art cubism, surrealism, abstract art, and put it on the same level with the artists of the Renaissance, or even of ancient Hellas. For them, what can I mean? I who defend certain relative absolutes or canons in art, and exclude most of what is done today as mere artifact and not art at all; what can I mean to the public of today! So all my efforts of fifty years have served to what purpose? They have amused me at least.

March 29th, I Tatti

A paper in *American Journal of Archaeology* on who were the Philistines. It tries to make out that they were Dinari from Illyria—the same who colonized much of pre-Mycenaean Greece and various parts of Italy. To me doubtful. Why do I retain such eagerness to read about any problem connected with origins in our Mediterranean-Atlantic world? I can give no other reason than a curiosity implanted in me as a very little boy by the genealogical tables in the Book of Genesis. I must have half doubted them as everything in the Old Testament as merely Jewish, and was comforted to discover, when I began to read "gentile" lore, that they were confirmed.

April 4th, I Tatti

Yesterday evening Bach's *St. Matthew Passion* on the radio. Enjoyed it more than ever before and for the first time realized how much Berlioz owed to it, and how much Wagner. Yet it was the first hour only that I gave undivided attention and tried to concentrate on following the music as music. The second hour, the music served mostly to liberate various trains of thought in "free and fantastic" association, at times sordid and workaday, but more often of far away and long, long ago. What a power of transport music possesses, how it excites moods and states of feeling—as no other art whether visual or verbal.

April 10th, I Tatti

Freya Stark * brought an Arab girl to tea. This girl spoke faultless English, fresh from London where she had been taking art courses at the Courtauld. She seems to belong to the top drawer of her world, intimate with ruler of Trans-Jordan and Farouk of Egypt. Well, I should not have known her from a Jewess of a certain class. She had the same golden rusty brown hair, and rusty red complexion. Her smile as well I have seen on the lips of young Jewesses. Likewise in Jerusalem the Grand Mufti looked more Jewish than outright Jews. No difference in blood, yet the bitterest of enemies—*frères ennemis*. What but material interests wrapped in dogma separates them?

April 11th, I Tatti

Marquand's *The Late George Apley,* which I have read just now, long after everybody else, turns out to be an original performance in method as well as content. The method is that of a serious biography, intercalated with correspondence, all having the air of a well-documented history, with no odour of fiction. Yet behind it all there is an irony so free from malice that many a reader may not feel it. At times one wonders whether the author himself does not forget to be ironical and falls into describing his character with complete approval and sympathetic gusto.

What the book proves is that in America there exists a class which regards itself as separated from the rest of the community and holds tight to its own limits and exclusiveness. It is democratic politically but not socially, although endlessly kind and "condescending" and really at the service of the community in so far as this last is subservient to its own ideals—the which it holds as ideals pure and simple, without the least awareness that they may mask self and class interests. Pathetic the hero's eagerness to be boon companion with his son and friends with his daughter, both rebelling (no doubt momentarily) against class tradition.

* English author of fascinating travel books, among them *The Southern Gates of Arabia, The Valley of the Assassins, A Winter in Arabia, Travel-*

April 22nd, I Tatti

Iris Origo's * *War in Val d'Orcia,* an exciting account of everyday doings in the centre of a big estate. First rumours, then Fascists and Partisans, and finally German occupation and retreat. Vivid, human, an intellectual, cultured background; events and characters are drawn with genuine individuality. One cannot help wondering at the courage, the resourcefulness, even the humour of the Anglo-American wife and Italian husband and the way they handled the bluster and brutality of Nazis and Fascists as well as ordinary human nature.

April 23rd, I Tatti

Trevor-Roper's † *The Last Days of Hitler* the first English book known to me [on that subject] written with historical perspective and courage, designating, defaming, and classifying. A pitiful and by me scarcely expected story of intrigue, pushing, struggling for favour as in the court of Siam of old. A horrible story of folly, sheer madness, suicidal obstinacy and recklessness of those who prefer complete destruction to failure in ruling the world. That a great people, as great as any in history, should have submitted to this is terrifying. What happened to them might happen to us.

April 28th, I Tatti

Lunched with wealthy friends and came away poisoned. Why? Everything about their display of wealth, of luxury, of opulence not only rubbed one the wrong way, but seemed to

lers' Prelude, and other volumes of reminiscences. When not travelling, she lives in Asolo, near Padua.

* Iris Origo, daughter of American diplomat W. Bayard Cutting and of Lady Sybil Cuffe, married to Marchese Antonio Origo, knew B.B. from her early childhood. Author of *Leopardi, A Study in Solitude; The Merchant of Prato, The Last Attachment, The World of San Bernardino,* etc.

† Hugh Trevor-Roper, English historian, met B.B. in 1946 through Mary Berenson's sister, Alys Russell. Now Regius Professor of History at Christ Church, Oxford.

13

inject one with noxious elements. Surely nobility has been well defined as ancient riches. It takes generations for people to learn how to use money; how to deal it out to others even at the table, how to avoid offending friends with condescending generosity, how to keep measure and tact; all this is hard to acquire if one has not been brought up to it since infancy. The vulgar *nouveau riche* distresses me as no other human being.

April 29th, I Tatti

The Morgan Walk [so called because of its going through what was formerly the property of a Mr. Morgan]. A day of spring in all its Tuscan beauty, and late afternoon of that same day, as vibrant and inspiring as the morning. The distances pale grape-purple, denser or lighter, magical, nostalgic, calling one, yearning to receive, to calm, to soothe, to dissolve one into their own evanescent substance. Near at hand the sensation of one's feet firmly touching ground, grassy or stony, but as it were with a flitting caress of the soles. Wild orchids, self-sown crocus, bright translucent blue or dazzling white. In mid-distances oblongs of blanched ivory that I know are buildings.

May 4th, Siena

Yesterday afternoon to San Leonardo al Lago. Searching our way to the entrance to the refectory, a small boy I judged to be about twelve and turned out thirteen led us. His head was as finely modelled as a Desiderio and he looked at once intelligent and thoughtful. He had stopped school and was training as a toiler of the earth. A feeling sprang up instantly between us, devotion on his part, love on mine. I yearned to take him away, to give him his chance, to allow him to fulfill the promise of his features. But assuming that he succeeded and became a prominent member of society, would he be a better, a happier man? I feel a strange uncertainty of the outcome.

May 6th, Rome

It was a grey afternoon—took Stephen Spender and his wife to San Paolo and then Via Appia, my original intention having been Hadrian's Villa or Ostia. San Paolo looked big and empty, and the Via Appia drearily unevocative. From Spender I got no response, although I poured out my ointment box of epithets. If he were not an Englishman I should have thought him insensitive to visible things. True enough, they were not looking their best. And yet? Was it my fault? I was feeling out of sorts and snappy, and did I communicate my mood and not my doctrine?

May 8th, Rome

It occurs to me now only within weeks of eighty-two that one of the reasons why old people fall out of the running is that they cannot get free of the problems that absorbed their youth and were then perhaps of great importance, yet have been displaced by others more urgent to the younger generation. They still fight for them or against them and cannot act as if they already had been discarded. This is as true of social and political as of intellectual or artistic matters. Our enemies have never been heard of, our doubts and fears do not exist for the active and effective generation of today.

May 12th, Rome

Dined with Sylvia Sprigge.* A thin, old man addressed me, reminding me that I called on him twenty-five years ago and sat by his bedside when he was laid up with a broken leg. It was Einaudi,† the great economist. I was truly startled that he remembered so well the visit of a person whom, as I recall, he had never

* Both she and her husband Cecil Sprigge (1896–1959) were correspondents of English newspapers in Rome between 1920 and 1930, and again after the liberation, and had many friends in Italian political circles. Author of *Berenson: A Biography* (London and Boston, 1960).
† Luigi Einaudi (1874–1961), foremost Italian economist and liberal statesman, Governor of the Bank of Italy and second President of the Italian Republic, 1948–55.

15

heard of before. On every side people coddle and flatter. Is it my age, that I have survived so long and am now too feeble to stand in anybody's light? Or is there some touch of real recognition? By older people like Einaudi, like Sforza * (who also was there) I am treated as an equal, which goes beyond what I expect—and I am delighted.

May 15th, Rome

I used to look forward to a long stay where I should gather together the threads I had spun during sixty years of sojourn. Here I am—true, after seven years of absence—and now my only wish, my only hope is to disentangle the threads, eliminate the broken ones and strengthen the enfeebled. Now it is reduced to a matter of recapturing from the wastebasket of memory this or that which still retains some vital element of recovery, something that for an instant transports me into the heart of a state of body and mind I enjoyed here years and years ago in this or that spot— or before this or that object. So it comes down to my old conclusion that at a certain age one begins and continues to look back to the time when one looked forward.

May 16th, Rome

Formal but not stiff luncheon at Schwarzenberg's.† Sat by Mrs. D., pinched, no, not pinched but self-consuming, rather pathetic, veiled with pride, likewise appealing. Kathleen Schwarzenberg dissolved in the hostess. Princess A. beautiful, slightly languishing, manifestly not too happy. Got into intimate talk. I happened to say that Italians, poor at most psychology, were good at love analysis. She protested violently, declaring they even did

---

* Count Carlo Sforza (1872–1952), Italian diplomat, in exile 1923–43; Minister of Foreign Affairs after the liberation until 1950.
† Prince Johannes Schwarzenberg, Austrian diplomat, during Nazi occupation of Austria attached to Red Cross in Geneva. Returned to diplomatic service in 1946 as Austrian Ambassador to Italy, then Austrian Ambassador to London. Met B.B. first in 1925 in Vienna. Married to Belgian-born Kathleen Spoelberg.

not know how to begin a flirtation! Cerruti * [with his wife] to tea, she exuberant, talking all languages with an Hungarian accent. He stern and cold-looking, but blue eyes softened and smiled as he got warmed up talking. [At dinner] Jacques Ibert † recounted his adventures during war, victim of revolting accusations. Stayed till midnight, loud in praises of American Henry Miller, to me utterly unknown author.

May 21st, Rome

How difficult it is to foretell what a writer one has admired as author will turn out as a person. I have greatly enjoyed Silone's books, and so much more than he is appreciated by his literary countrymen. I have read him in English only. Perhaps his prose is not good enough for his countrymen. I now have seen him two or three times and cannot bring him to talk. If I intimidate him why does he accept my invitation? Yet he must open his mouth with others or Sylvia Sprigge (for instance) would not be so devoted to him. Do I represent the unclimbable, impenetrable Pharisia, so that he thinks it useless to talk? I cannot make it out, but am more baffled than offended.

May 29th, I Tatti

Lunched with Iris and Antonio Origo at La Foce. In the desert of the badlands they have created a palace with every up-to-date luxury, and gardens of real beauty. All so willed and so little of it the flowering of the earth's energies on the spot. I wonder how long it will survive its creator. Our talk about agricultural conditions drifted to politics. I expressed my dislike of the word "democracy" because it means such different and even opposite things. What we Anglo-Saxons mean is parliamentary government. Origo asked whether it was possible in Latin countries. It took England two and more centuries to learn to use it. Here it is not one century old. Give it another century. "And meanwhile what is to become of me?" cried Origo.

* Vittorio Cerruti, Italian Ambassador in Paris, 1934–36.
† Composer (1890–1962), head of the French Academy at Villa Medici, Rome, before and after World War II.

May 30th, I Tatti

Walked in my own garden. "My own"—what am I saying; I have little if any sense of my own, and least of all with regard to what I own here. A bit more perhaps for my American investments—perhaps, because almost abstract. Here fields, houses, pictures, books—yes, I enjoy them as what cannot be immediately snatched away from me, but which are but temporarily mine— *verliehen* like a prized decoration in Prussia. Perhaps if I had inherited my possessions I might feel differently, but twice uprooted, first to U.S.A. and thence to Italy, how can I feel the fixity of possessions? Perhaps if I had heirs of my body.

May 31st, I Tatti

How in her last years my wife used to annoy me with her choking cough, her flusters, her tottering step. Why, because convinced that they were controllable and if she would she could get the better of them. Now my own experience tells me I did her wrong, that she could not help it. And what walks and climbs I used to make her do! Now that I too have to count my steps I recall with remorse the way I used to whip and drag her on. How is one to understand without experience, and how is one to procure the experience before body and mind have been matured for it? And real conviction in things human comes from experience and almost never through dialectics.

June 4th, I Tatti

People who have not seen me for years congratulate me on looking unchanged, looking so well, with such a fine complexion. They do not seem aware that by doing so they express surprise that despite age I am still about. The facts are that actually I feel tottering in carriage and gait, that I am good for only about an hour of concentration, that I feel exhausted after forty minutes' walk, that I get tired to such a degree that I could cry; that I cannot touch myself anywhere without hitting a sore spot; that intestines and bladder function irregularly; that I suffer from changes of heat. In short, I feel the machine going to pieces. And yet for the hour that it is alive, my mind is clearer than ever.

June 5th, I Tatti

Putting head out of window at 11:15 P.M. noticed sky to east was lighting up. It was moonrise, beginning of third quarter. The cloudlets nearest the horizon were taking on colour, and a minute or two later, so did heavier dark-coloured ones. What I had never observed before was that rose, the flushes of sunrise were entirely wanting. Instead the colours were metallic, opaque, brownish, tawny, and finally the full disk rose like a golden platter over the horizon—golden but not refulgent, circumscribed, not tinting the sky, not lighting it up with streamers.

What a spectacle if, as Heine said, we saw it once in a century. It can be had half the month and for nothing. So we pay as little attention to it as Italians fifty years ago to their own works of art.

June 7th, I Tatti

Thatcher * to lunch. Announced his coming some time ago and more recently came a letter from Johnnie † recommending him highly. He is one of the two or three most important of the younger (now middle-aged) Foggists; indeed, he may be one to follow me at I Tatti when I am gone. Had been here before, years ago, but I did not recall him. Began by conventional praise of Edward Forbes ‡ (to whom he owed initiation in art study) and of Robert and Mildred Bliss.§ These last had been a liberal education—through contact with them, being with them. My eyes must have sparkled with malice as he was ladling out this

* John Thatcher, head of Dumbarton Oaks Foundation, Washington, D.C.
† John Walker, sent to I Tatti in 1930 from Harvard, pupil and devoted friend of B.B.'s; now head of National Gallery in Washington, D.C.
‡ Creator of Fogg Museum, Cambridge, Massachusetts, together with Paul Sachs; took a great interest in B.B.'s plans for leaving I Tatti to Harvard University.
§ Americans of means, furthering cultural and artistic activities; founders of the Dumbarton Oaks Center of Byzantine Studies in Washington, D.C.

turtle soup. Little by little I prodded him into agreeing with me that much of the art study (so-called) carried on at home (U.S.A.) was sheer pedantry. If he returns I may unvarnish him enough to touch something real and get words that sound real.

June 9th, I Tatti

Flemish Exhibition at Palazzo Strozzi. Van Eyck alone wholly satisfactory. In the small *St. Francis Receiving the Stigmata* he gives us a contemporary portrait instead of an attempt to imagine how the saint must have looked on earth or should look in Heaven. Magical landscape as enchanting and evocative as can be. From this to Roger a drop, from Roger to Memling, from Memling to Gerard David a third. Then Mabuse, Matsys, Provost less and less creative. Series interrupted by the overpowering Van der Goes with his searching convincing presentation of actual shapes, yet charged with eager fervour and suppressed passion. To compare great with small he was in the fifteenth-century Netherlands what Caravaggio was in Italy a century later. A contrasted study of both would lead to interesting conclusions about differences between Netherlanders and Italians.

June 15th, I Tatti

A crowd to tea. Among them Fokker and Hutton.* Was horrified by the way they had aged, by their almost spectral reduction to skin and bone. What horrified me? Was it that they had been so reduced, or that I feared I also was equally brought down from my ancient state? Were they as startled by what they saw in me as I by what I perceived in them? No wonder old people prefer to frequent younger and young ones. They then go on deluding themselves that they are in aspect like their juniors or at least that they are not like their own exact contemporaries. Yet how much more sympathy and attention we get from the last, and how many more topics for talk. We can ask "Do you remember?" and expect an answer.

* T. H. Fokker (1881–1956), Dutch art historian established in Rome; Curator of Doria Gallery, 1945–56.—Edward Hutton, English man of letters; author of a number of guidebooks for Italian towns and regions.

20

June 17th, I Tatti

After tea, a drive to the very top of Monte Senario. I took a few steps and enjoyed the air, and gazed around, at hills and knolls and upland meadows where I used to tramp on foot, leaving no hummock unexplored. Distance scarcely existed, mile on mile, up hill down dale. Now the grasshopper is a burthen, and it is hard to believe that I was not so very long ago so muscularly alert, so resistant to fatigue. I do not let regret get the better of me. There is a certain sweetness in being what one is now—not reduced but contracted—so appreciative, so enjoying, so grateful for what has been, and for what is now. It means something to be able to rise above aches and pains, and inertias, and to glory in the world as displayed to one's experienced senses and ordered mind.

June 18th, I Tatti

Dined at Le Fontanelle.* The sun was at its furthest north before setting. Recalled watching in 1943–44 how it travelled day by day to its furthest south, the terrace of Le Fontanelle furnishing a perfect platform for watching the skies. Then how beautiful were the airplanes at night marking the heavens with signs we did not understand.

I have little if any sentimental feelings for places where things of crucial importance, good or evil, have happened to me. On the contrary, I yearn to revisit places which appealed to me for their visual beauty and nostalgic contemplation of the kind of life they enjoyed. I never tire of Rome, of Athens, of Luxor, of Jerusalem, of Paestum, and least of all of noble ruins in unsordidized landscapes—e.g., Hadrian's Villa.

---

* Villa near Careggi on the outskirts of Florence, belonging to Marchese Filippo and Marchesa Gilberta Serlupi Crescenzi, where B.B. and Nicky Mariano spent the year 1943–44. See B.B.'s war diary, *Rumour and Reflection*.

June 20th, I Tatti

Until a few years ago I began my day with Greek and Latin, German and other poets, thinkers, historians in their own languages. Now I read nothing but periodicals, chiefly of the day and about the day. What do I get out of it for myself, and what use is it to others? I enjoy no authority on current affairs, I do not write about them. Nobody effective consults me. My talk about it counts for mere gossip. Why then do I go on, when I know I should be rereading the poets and thinkers of all times? But the present fascinates me, and then it is relatively easy to follow, if harder to understand than the past.

June 23rd, I Tatti

Vissons to lunch, both Ukrainian Jews, but to my expert eyes betraying no Semitic touch. He would pass here as a native, and she looks Tartar. He bursting with energy and sparkling with intelligence. Is reputed to be the leading spirit in *Reader's Digest,* and seems to be very much in everything social and political in Washington and New York. Asked intelligent questions about the Italian situation, and ready to listen and try to understand, not like most journalists, and politic-agents sent over with minds so made up there is no use talking to them. She inarticulate, and I gather with dubious taste in matters of art, yet chief person in *Gazette des Beaux-Arts.* She must have ability and judgment, but did not display them.

June 25th, I Tatti

Wölfflin's * *Prolegomena zu einer Psychologie der Architektur,* presented for doctor's thesis in 1886 (a year before my graduation), contains in essence and more than in essence my entire philosophy of art. Strange that it was never published in his lifetime, nor does its spirit animate his future writings to anything like its expression here! He was only twenty-two and I groped my way till

* Heinrich Wölfflin (1864–1945), Swiss, greatest among German-language art historians after Jacob Burckhardt, whose pupil he was.

I was nearly thirty before seeing clearly a similar approach to art problems. He, however, had Burckhardt and Volkelt * as teachers and generations of German thinkers, while I had what? Only Pater. For I had not read anybody else who wrote of art, and Norton's † interest was only historical and illustrative.

June 26th, I Tatti

Eighty-second birthday. I am no more sentimental about anniversaries than about places. Shall I still be alive a year hence? I am resigned to not being, to the inevitable exhaustion of animal function; if there is more, I cannot conceive it, and therefore let it alone. Luckily, the day passed without too much ceremonial and entertainment. Instead of clubbing the overaged to death, we now feast them into the grave. At Brussa nearly twenty years ago the woman who had kept the inn for many decades was having a ninety-second birthday. We saw her sitting a queen at high festival with between twenty and thirty persons to toast her. She was dead at dawn the following morning. How much anthropology still dominates us!

June 28th, I Tatti

[Giacomo] Devoto to lunch. One of twenty professors, including Russo and Fiocco,‡ just returned from a show of select exhibits in Poland. Brings back conviction that U.S.A. is preventing settlement of German situation so as to give time to train a German mercenary army to attack the Soviets and Co. Devoto was not allowed by U.S.A. to leave train while crossing territory occupied by them. Devoto is a glottologist and historian of Latin literature and in that field weighs evidence minutely and with accuracy. How explain his falling an easy prey to believing what he saw with his own eyes and heard with his own ears during an

* Johannes Volkelt (1848–1930), German philosopher (aesthetics).
† Charles Eliot Norton (1827–1908), author and educator, who held the Chair of History of Fine Art at Harvard from 1873 to 1898.
‡ Luigi Russo (1892–1961), Professor of Italian Literature at the University of Florence, then head of the Scuola Normale of Pisa.—Giuseppe Fiocco, recently retired Italian Professor of Fine Arts at the University of Padua; excellent connoisseur of Venetian painting.

23

official tour? Unfortunately, he is very active and has great influence. No doubt the other nineteen professors were equally converted to Soviet gospel.

June 29th, I Tatti

Drove to San Clemente and as I had nothing on but thinnest underclothing, silk trousers and jacket, I had to walk briskly not to feel chilled by the *tramontana* that was blowing strong. Did not prevent contemplating the landscape. Every feature had been so familiar and frequented, many now half indistinguishable, and with names forgotten, but visually more poignant as well as more beautiful than ever before. How is it that I feel the beauty of nature (so-called) more and more each day of life? Shall I ever again take the long walks from the Guadagni estate to Santa Brigida? Drove down to Gricigliano, to the house with harsh profiles, with moat full of running water and an elegant entrance hall resting on columns and open to the air. An impressive and suggestive sight.

July 2nd, I Tatti

Addie Kahn,* now staying here, is pro-Soviet and pro-Arab. How account for the first is a problem, for she resents every infringement of her right to do as she pleases with her own, and would not readily merge with a national pool her immense income. We avoid discussion, the more so as her tether is short and one quickly reaches the stake to which she is tied. So we spend our togetherness in gossiping about friends, acquaintances, and people known only by hearsay. Is there any profit in it as distinct from recuperative relaxation or killing time? Perhaps. Each individual mentioned is the first sketch of a story or a picture, and gives a momentary flash into an Otherness. These flashes combine into imagining outlines of a world beyond our workaday one, into which we tend to sink deeper and deeper, losing finally all sense of how big the world is beyond.

* Adele Kahn (1876?–1949), born Wolff, married to banker and financier Otto H. Kahn (1867–1934).

July 3rd, I Tatti

"Morgan Walk" with Addie. Came across fawn and ivory cows and calves and shepherding them a slender young creature who turned out to be a little girl all but naked. She was delicately slender, with lovely limbs and proportions and intelligent look. She was eleven, she had finished school, and now, now she was going to work as a *contadina*. This with a tone of regret. What else would she like? To study. That at most would make a school-teacher of her—a sorry lot. My heart melted with regret that she must end as a peasant, but my head questioned whether it was not the far better lot! I cannot get the better of my hanker to select promising things and give them a chance—a chance for what?

July 9th, I Tatti

Kika M., a flirtatious young girl, after being engaged for two years with son of an English peer, acting as Gurka commander and omnipresent intelligence officer, who kept assuring her of his ardent desire to marry her, then courted violently by a young New York Israelite, as well as by a wealthy Christian from Leghorn, met less than three weeks ago at a café an American lad from Minnesota, about whom nobody knows anything but what he said himself, and yesterday married him. He seems the right thing but brought to the wedding three chums who did not look it. I could not refuse attending, having been pushed gently but persistently into position of patriarchal counsellor for the family. It seemed funny to see wild Kika veiled and garlanded like a victim for sacrifice. She may be that but not through the bridegroom's intention. He seems to mean well enough, and is charming. But what corroborative evidence of who and what he is?

July 12th, I Tatti

[Daniel Catton] Rich, the Director of the Chicago Art Institute, only just over forty, alert, energetic, talked of art matters at Chicago, and of how at its university the cranky President wanted art history reduced to philosophy on one hand and ordinary history on the other. Rich wants to make Chicago an art

25

centre for the Middle West. Lyrical over six months spent in South America, revelled in its Spanish architecture adapted to place and people, and enthusiastic over a school of painters he discovered at Cuzco where Spanish art was continued through a son of Murillo and others, but is shot through with native traits. Told of encounters with local swells at Lima who battened off great estates neither they nor their fathers had visited, and let them be worked by peons little better than slaves, etc. All in all, Rich left the impression of keenness, utility, and open-mindedness.

July 18th, Vallombrosa

A red-letter day, with no visitors, no callers. Called at 6:30. Four days ago the sun was already gilding the hill opposite. Now no longer, but a few minutes later each day. Then it lights up trees seen through west window. Morning stroll with view over Florence seen as through smoked glass or antique recently dug up. Many trees cut and pines ill with a kind of rust. Then young chestnuts growing like candles, the craterlike stump from which they grow forming a sort of Romanesque candelabrum. A longer walk in later afternoon. In evening Strauss's *Tod und Verklärung* on the radio. *Quel souffle*—how would one put it in English?—Strauss retains despite his naughtiness *à la* T. S. *Eliot*—and his vulgarity, "Lift up your heads, O ye gates, and be you lifted up." This is true of German as of no other school of music—lay music, I mean. It is exalting and liberating as no other.

July 19th, Vallombrosa

First time in years rereading Tacitus' *Histories*. Horrified and almost frightened by parallel if not identity with conduct of individuals and masses in first century of our era and the Italy of the last ten years. The same cowardice, opportunism, treachery, happiness in servitude, and love of catchwords, and even same acts of heroism or humanity, although, alas! rare enough. Perhaps in one respect only is there an improvement. On the whole Italians nowadays are not so subject to panic fears, or at least to such frantic manifestations of them.

26

July 24th, Vallombrosa

Paolo Guicciardini * and wife. She had never heard the story of David's getting old, and finding no warmth except in the body of a young girl. She asked for more of the same kind and I referred her to the Bible, which she had never looked at, being a conventional Catholic. I happened to quote in talking with him: "Unto every one that hath shall be given" etc. He pricked up his ears and asked where it came from. When I told him it was a saying of our Lord and Saviour's out of the Gospels he was startled. Evidently he had no acquaintance with them. What a different mental and moral background from us brought up on Old and New Testaments, and having them deeply embedded in our minds.

July 26th, Vallombrosa

I am becoming a tyrant at my own table. If we are many I submit and suffer. I have never enjoyed *tête-à-têtes* at the table, where so often the talk one overhears right and left seems so much more interesting than what one carries on with one's neighbour. But when we are few and two pair off to talk to each other, no matter how softly or for that very reason, I cannot follow the conversation I am trying to carry on. Partly it is due to a real confusion of sounds, but in no small part to impatience with people who cannot for even a few moments tolerate general conversation. Of course in that I get most of the innings, although I am as good a listener as a producer of talk.

July 27th, Vallombrosa

What I wrote yesterday proves that I cannot concentrate so well as to be impervious to what is going on around me. "I run after interruptions," as William James used to say. I have never been able to write, to do any work, and scarcely to read in the presence of others. They are (no matter how familiar) too attrac-

* Count Paolo Guicciardini (1880–1955), descendant of the Florentine historian Francesco Guicciardini (1483–1540); author of various publications concerning his family and his house. The Guicciardini Archives were organized and made accessible to students by him.

tive, too exciting. Their mere presence is stimulating but not to my own private occupation. I cannot write while travelling. Happily, I can read, and dash off notes and even letters, which I do more when not at home than at home.

July 28th, Vallombrosa

In late P.M. to Secchieta, up through mangled but still beautiful forest and embosoming shade. At end of road walked on springy ground from miniature grove to miniature grove of stumpy storm-tossed beeches, serving as sheepfolds. Toward south as through smoked glass La Verna and the Mandrioli pass. On the opposite side, the Arno shining like diamonds way below. Before we left a rainbow appeared in southern sky and held its own till we left. Encountered handsome bright shepherd lad, and a party of pleasantly behaved picnickers come in two cars from Perugia. Warm up there too, but air somehow with more ozone as indeed is the case of Vallombrosa compared with Florence.

August 1st, Vallombrosa

Why do I feel more attracted to the Englishman than to the American of the same abilities, equal achievement, and success? It can only be because the Englishman is more of a work of art to be enjoyed as such particularly, whereas the American with rarest exceptions can be admired only. In other words it is a question of breeding, and when we say of someone "he is thorough-bred" we mean it much more in a merely artistic sense than any other.

Men and women as works of art are products not of business and certainly not of wealth alone, but of generations of inherited culture.

August 2nd, Vallombrosa

This cottage * is placed halfway between the Consuma-Vallombrosa highroad and the torrent way below at bottom of ravine

* Casa al Dono, formerly one of the farms belonging to the Abbey of Vallombrosa, bought by the Peruzzis about a hundred years ago and enlarged by Marchesa Peruzzi, William Wetmore Story's daughter. Since 1940 the property of Nicky Mariano.

that separates us from Campiglioni opposite. Above us are ledges of rocks with firs growing out of them. The sunlight filtering through them tends to shimmer and shine as if filtered through still water. The rocks are so ribbed as to give an effect of tactile value and movement. Their colour changes with the procession of the sun, and just before sunset is bronzed gold and golden green under the trees. It seems made of no material more gross than light itself, but light subdued, without dazzle, without glitter—approaching light of precious stones.

August 3rd, Vallombrosa

Sartre's *Age de Raison*. His bag of tricks here is to let people talk, while he tells us what they are thinking. The proportion of latter to former same as that of commentaries to texts in puritan edition of Book of Job. He tries to describe their sense of self in inanimate terms, as of the objects surrounding them. Then his world is a squalid, sordid one, with almost no humanized men and women and numbers of subsocial ones. I greatly prefer Céline's * *Au Bout de la Nuit,* where one touches bottom and yet finds it not too bad to live in. If Sartre meant this novel to be an illustration of his "Existentialism," I should feel more puzzled than ever to understand him.

August 7th, Vallombrosa

Moravia has sent his *Agostino* and insists on my reading it. Admirably written no doubt and well characterized. The youngish mother presented so that you feel her physical attractiveness, her amorousness, and at the same time a gracious if not deep motherliness. Good too is innocence of thirteen-year-old son who is vaguely troubled by what goes on between men and his mother. He makes the acquaintance of a band of low-class boys who do their best to enlighten him. They are commanded by what in U.S.A. some decades ago was called a yegg. They are bestial, they are brutal, they are cruel, they are foul. What a different world from *Tortilla Flat,* not to speak of *Huckleberry Finn* and *Tom Sawyer.*

* Louis-Ferdinand Céline (1894–1961), French physician and man of letters, author of *Journey to the End of the Night.*

August 9th, Vallombrosa

I discover that I do not take kindness, good attentive service, affection, love for granted and as due to me. On each occasion I take them as if unexpected, as if an act of special friendliness or devotion. That makes me feel a glow of wonder and gratefulness. It makes me happy to encounter goodness, love of work, humane intelligence, and people no matter at what kind of job, be if ever so humble, or ever so exalted, who do it well and *con amore*.

August 13th, Vallombrosa

Call on Orlando * and find a *smala* † of sons, daughters, relations, connections.

I try to get him to see the danger of Communism and the necessity of uniting against it. He pays no attention but returns to rage against England for allowing the Russians to have their way with Italian reparations, fleet, etc. I try in vain to tell him that England was not strong enough to impose its will on Stalin, and besides we Americans were at least as much at fault as the British. He would not have it. Then I realized why. It was because he in his eighty-eighth year cannot get rid of the conviction that in matters international England is omnipotent, and therefore alone responsible for all the woes of the world. Hard for age to realize new horizons and new forces.

August 16th, Vallombrosa

Paul Bonner ‡ expressed great hope that considerable quantities of oil would be discovered in the Ferrarese, and as water power might be made to yield as much again, the industrial

---

* Vittorio Emanuele Orlando (1860–1952), Sicilian jurist and statesman; Prime Minister of Italy, 1917–19.
† *Smala*—Frenchified version of Arabic *zmala,* meaning settlement of tribe around important chief.
‡ American author (*The Art of Llewellyn Jones,* etc.); special adviser to U.S. Ambassador to Rome on economics of peace treaty, 1947–51.

30

future of Italy promises to be bright. What of the human future? Italians in their greed for wealth, in their lust for power do not think of the harm successful industrialization would do to Italy and Americans can see in it nothing but the condition for a better life. Is the American expectation likely to be fulfilled? To begin with, industrialization will ruin the landscape, the towns and the countryside. Then industry to Italy, encountering no organized capitalism, will produce its first fruits, Communists who will try to run the country straight to Moscow. Will it raise the standard of life? From an American point of view, perhaps. The factory hand may eat more butcher's meat, he may have fewer working hours, etc., etc.; but he will not have as nourishing and appetizing food as when a farmhand, enjoying in Tuscany fresh vegetables the year round, fresh fruit half the year, and dried the rest, and wine. Nor will he have work that he either loves or at least understands, and therefore does dutifully. Our Consul here, [Walter] Orebough, spoke with contempt of the way farming is carried on here—so much by hand, so little with machine. I tried to make it plain to him that methods successful on flat land could not be applied on the terraced horticulture to which farming is reduced here, every ten furlongs having a different climate, etc. He looked surprised as if such contradiction had not occurred to him before. Yet he has been with the Partisans and knows conditions here. Perhaps he took American methods for granted as the only ones.

August 25th, Vallombrosa

Left to myself and my strongest tropism, I would not leave this summer cottage until cold drove me down to I Tatti, from which I would not budge till I returned here next July. I was almost shocked when Nicky gave me a detailed plan of what she means me to do. In the first place she wants us to leave the 22nd instead of the 25th, depriving me of three precious days. Then she proposes a trip of ten days constantly on the move from place to place. We could not stop to enjoy but merely ascertain whether churches, palaces, paintings still did or did not exist. I could think of nothing but of how tired I should get every day, every hour perhaps, and what an agony of fatigue I should suffer from on home-coming. She thinks ten days would be enough to rest me before proceeding to Rome. I fear neither she nor others believe how unfit I feel for any serious effort, whether physical or mental.

August 26th, Vallombrosa

During dinner, a tablet replacing a tooth gave way, and made me feel dejected and humiliated. Curious it should have that effect every time it happens. Partly it is the thought of going to the dentist, but it is not that alone. Is it because it is so tangible a sign of disintegration, of falling away, while more serious decline is not so palpable and not so strikingly brought home to one? Far more alarming symptoms of decline can be argued away, but you hold the bit of cement in your hand, and can't deny it. Yet it is cement only, and not ivory, and one scarcely felt as bad when the real teeth were extracted.

August 31st, Vallombrosa

D'Annunzio's * La Città Morta is far too discursive, too spun out, with images and metaphors at times farfetched and disturbing, and an excess of everything. The atmosphere of moral sultriness is not as well conveyed as of physical distress over the surroundings; yet the one is supposed to be the exact equivalent of the other. The one really fine scene is how Lionardo gets himself little by little to confess the passion for his sister. Characters described, and overdescribed, and for that very reason perhaps not convincingly there on the stage, fully alive before us.

I believe I saw the first performance of La Città Morta with Duse.† I recall being puzzled, not having read the text.

* Gabriele d'Annunzio (1863–1938), Italian poet, dramatist, and novelist. Played prominent part in World War I as an aviator and melodramatic leader of the Fiume expedition. Lived for several years in the villa La Capponcina at Settignano, near I Tatti.
† Eleonora Duse (1859–1924), world-famous Italian actress, especially celebrated for her roles in the plays of Ibsen and of D'Annunzio, whose inspiration and companion she was between 1897 and 1904.

I wonder whether it was criticized for the fact that Lionardo took it as his manifest right to kill his sister so as to get rid of an incubus. D'Annunzio does not so much as seem aware that he is up against the question. His idea is that the man of genius has a full right to do whatever is necessary for the full realization of himself.

Of course there are beautiful sentences and phrases, and descriptions, throughout, but on the whole the effect is more pictorial than dramatic. Indeed it is the least dramatic of D'Annunzio's plays.

Additional note dictated in 1958:

What I have said about D'Annunzio as a dramatist has made me remember how I met him first. It was at the end of the century, in the Doney restaurant above the famous Doney pastry-shop, so much frequented by the smart Florentine society. It was probably a friend we had in common, perhaps Carlo Placci,* who finding us both there invited us to his table. Of course I had noticed him before getting to know him. One could not help being struck by the way he looked and behaved, always over-dressed, very much aware of being taken for a remarkable man, and by the timbre of his voice.

We had a very good time talking about words and about the strange things that happen to words and which we ended by calling *détournements de mineurs*. I recall our laughing over the English word "kerchief," originally *couvrechef*, which then was changed into "handkerchief" and finally into "pocket handker-chief."

After 1900 we became neighbours and the road leading from the Capponcina to I Tatti is one of those described so admirably in his preface to the *Cola di Rienzo*. At that time D'Annunzio was enchained by the love and the caprices of a great lady. More than once they came together to see me and I noticed how this

---

* Carlo Placci (1861–1941), cultivated, musical, witty, cosmopolitan, B.B.'s oldest friend in Italy.

33

exceptional woman made him feel small and unworthy of her, perhaps resentful of her social superiority. I much preferred seeing him alone or in the presence of other men. The presence of a woman, or worse still of several women and the atmosphere of adulation they created, brought out something boastful, cheap, and vulgar in him. And yet women found him irresistible. In the presence of their husbands I have heard the most respectable women declare that should D'Annunzio try to make their conquest they would be unable to resist him.

Like so many Latins, he was more of a monologist than a conversationalist. With his voice, his gestures, the sequence of the words he used he created a sort of magic spell. Politics did not preoccupy him yet. Philological, grammatical, stylistic problems provided him with admirable subjects of conversation. I almost never talked to him about my work, as he lacked all sense of quality for the visual arts. He had exquisite taste for handling words but none for art or for how to furnish a house. To the beauty of nature and of landscape he had a more direct and genuine reaction.

His financial disasters and his flight to France separated us and I did not see D'Annunzio again until in 1926 at the Scala, during a cycle of Beethoven symphonies conducted by Toscanini, I recognized his profile in one of the boxes. He was talking to an attractive-looking dark woman. Friends told me that it was the pianist Baccara. After all his megalomaniac adventures I did not feel the slightest wish to approach him.

I wonder how much of D'Annunzio's work will be still considered as living literature in fifty years, I mean as literature that can still be enjoyed. I suppose above all his poetry, of which as a foreigner I would not be able to make a fair appreciation. An anthology of his best prose passages (the description of Villa d'Este, of Strà, of Murano, of the Abruzzese coast, of the slum world of Guardiagrele, of the pilgrimage to Casalbordino, the preface of the *Cola di Rienzo*) may go on being included in high-school programs. To me it seems not unlikely that some of his dramas will be revalued in the course of time.

September 6th, Vallombrosa

Henry Miller's *Tropic of Cancer* is the most indecent, most scatological book I ever waded through, yet not the dirtiest. Why? Saved by something genuinely Dionysiac, by the conviction that somehow through enough dissipation one reaches Cosmic Consciousness. On the way thither the author often falls by the road, and suffers every kind of *Katzenjammer* which to him takes the aspect of philosophy. It is commonplace enough, and to be answered with the schoolboy "What would you rather or go afishing." Nothing constructive—"No language but a cry."

September 7th, Vallombrosa

Hare,* whose recollections we are reading—Ouida † for abroad and aristocratically puritan at home—happened to be in Turin when Ruskin ‡ was there. The great rhetorician urged his new admiration of Paul Veronese in terms that amused Hare. Little did the latter realize, and much would he have been excited had he known, what was going on in Ruskin's soul at that time. It is revealed in letters he wrote to Charles E. Norton, in which he describes his agony of doubts about all his precious attitudes toward art and the way he treated it as an adjunct to religion. He was discovering Diogenes as Paul had discovered Christ, and for a time with as revolutionary a vehemence.

September 11th, Vallombrosa

Aesthetically I love the Baroque world with its pomp, magnificence, and splendour. I love ritual order and all that highly efficient rulers exploiting vast territories can do for the elegance and refinement of living, and for the beauty of their surroundings. I even confess to a certain admiration not only for the Petersburg

---

* Augustus Hare (1834–1903), English man of letters and traveller; author of *Walks in Rome, Walks in Florence,* and many other guidebooks, and of his own *Reminiscences.*

† Pen name of Marie Louise Ramé (1839–1908), prolific English novelist.

‡ John Ruskin (1819–1900), English art critic, first Slade Professor of Art, Oxford; author of *Stones of Venice.*

35

of Catherine and Alexander, but perhaps for the Berlin of Hitler (at least I fear it). At the same time I am an ultra-individualistic liberal, hating the state, and regarding it as a necessary evil, without which we cannot exist as a society. And without society no individual could live a life worth living—certainly not I.

September 12th, Vallombrosa

The way the Soviets have twisted the meaning of the word "democratic" to mean the exact opposite, and the success they are having in imposing it, has in history no parallel but one. It is when the Church Fathers took Old Testament prophecy and promises obviously intended for the Jews, and snatched, grabbed, and clutched them for themselves, insisting that they and not the Jews were the real seed of Abraham and the only true Israelites. The Soviet ground was prepared by Poles and other reactionary governments who called themselves democratic this or democratic that.

September 14th, Vallombrosa

Carlo Levi * has been here for a few days. Nose with Etruscan curve, Jewish nostrils. Fine brow, reddish-brown hair combed back. Eyes light blue, yet sometimes turning deep blue. When listening intently his smooth-shaved face takes on a look of intellectual serenity. Dresses as a Bohemian, scarlet checkered jacket, brown cotton trousers. When not tired talks brilliantly, continuously, copiously, almost never about himself (at least not in my hearing) but about politics, people, and writings. Is a good listener as well and quick on the uptake. Scarcely understands English by ear, but well enough by sight to translate some of Donne's sonnets. A painter, yet never talked about his painting, having heard perhaps that I don't care for it.

* Italian painter and writer, as anti-Fascist banished to Basilicata in Southern Italy; author of *Christ Stopped at Eboli*, etc.

September 15th, Vallombrosa

Instinctively I am in opposition to whatever threatens freedom; and every entity that gets powerful enough does threaten it. For freedom is found only between forces contending nearly on equal terms. I am instinctively against any government that threatens to monopolize control, any institution that gets more than its share of authority, any individual who exercises too much influence. I must confess, though, that I am more inclined to dread the Roman Catholic than other churches, other governments more than England's and America's, labour organizations more than capitalists. Not that I love the last. I cannot forget their favouring Mussolini almost always and Hitler for years.

September 19th, Vallombrosa

Leaving in two days and already agitated, worrying what to take by way of clothes in October between seasons, unable to decide what books and other reading matter to take along, eager to finish up odds and ends before leaving—in short, "journey-proud" as I always have been when preparing to leave home for any length of time. But now haunted as never before by fear of getting tired, returning home half collapsed, finding there too many letters to answer, too many books and periodicals to attend to, and too many chores piled up while away. Ah, to wander as a youth when one had no ties and no responsibilities, and no worries to return to—and no fear of fatigue!

September 20th, Vallombrosa

So many "youngs," as Edith Wharton * used to call them, read and look and listen to everything up-to-date, the latest Sartre, the latest Picasso, the latest composer, and seem genuinely to enjoy them and live by them. Nor should I disapprove if only the latest came as the fruition of love for all that was best in the past. But their past is an air-blown plant, not rooted in their souls, as shallow as the Western culture put on with Western clothes

* Well-known American novelist (1862–1937), close friend of both Berensons from 1910.

37

by some Easterners, and by the newly cultured in our midst. That is why the admiration of such people withers so quickly and craves so much for fashion—the which is change impelled by a satiety of poor assimilation.

September 23rd, Rimini

[Before the] Tempio Malatestiano [I am met by the] Superintendent [of Fine Arts], the Bishop, the Mayor, the librarian, the master of works, all for different reasons hinting and then urging that the community was impatient to worship in their own cathedral, the Mayor that his fellow citizens while grateful for such generous American aid feared we might change the wonted aspect of their cherished temple. (As if the people cared a damn!) The Superintendent and the master of works feared taking the building down stone by stone might lead to these blocks turning out so crumbling and brittle that they could not be put back. In short I got the strong impression that none of these people wanted much done, and I began to suspect that they wanted to use for their own purpose, e.g., the rebuilding of the adjacent Franciscan convent, the sum of fifty thousand dollars allotted by Mr. Kress * for the express and only purpose of restoring the temple.

September 24th, Ravenna

With Superintendent [of Fine Arts] all day long. We see San Vitale, where he tries to explain the cupola and other technical matters which interest me little, and he and the master of works (a much abler man) prevent my looking all I want at the mosaics at San Vitale as well as in the tomb of Galla Placidia. Rather bored and even exasperated because I cannot always distinguish between what has been and what has not been restored. Sant' Apollinare Nuovo in squalid state, the Baptistery likewise. There the stuccoes within the arches strike me as centuries later than the mosaics. All interiors suffer from the fact that their floors have had to be raised, so that the space effect is no longer the same. As the shades pluck Dante by the sleeve (as it were) everybody

* Rush H. Kress, head of Samuel H. Kress Foundation; died 1963.

dragged me to see what interested him. At Dante's tomb a dear canon told us he had been ordered to send the grandest sarcophagus to serve as coffin for D'Annunzio.

September 25th, Bologna

An hour in the Pinacoteca. Trecento native painters vulgar and boring—curious, seeing that the [illuminated Bolognese] pandects of the early fourteenth are in elegant Cavallinesque style. So-called great Bolognese School is beyond me, except for Guido, whose *Samson* and whose *Massacre of the Innocents* suggest what an artist he might have been. The Caraccis bore me. Some of the women portraits took my fancy. As for non-Bolognese, Raphael's *St. Cecilia* (a favourite of my youth) still holds first place, despite its deplorable condition. Perugino disappointing, Vivarini of archaeological interest only. Quaint Nicolò d'Alunno still charms me. Reward of visit was finding the Piero della Francesca [fresco] of Malatesta [before the Emperor Sigismund] there, and could look at it eye to eye as it were. What a masterpiece of drawing, installing, and colour!

September 27th, La Gazzada * (Varese)

Was enjoying morning radiance in this paradise I love and frequented so much nearly fifty years ago. As I flung open windows there was the entire range of Monte Rosa with its highest peak all dazzling white like a sugar loaf with fresh fallen snow. Was looking forward to timeless forenoon with the rest of the world shut out, when lo! letters belated and requiring immediate answers were brought. Again for the many thousandth time I could have cried, *"Du hast sie zerstört, die schöne Welt."* How will-o'-the-wispy; a breath dissipates it! The paradox of life. Had I lived it as an idyll, world-forgetting and world-forgot, I should

* La Gazzada, fine villa with vast park near Varese in the Lombard lake district, now belonging to the Vatican, formerly to Don Guido Cagnola (1862–1954), art connoisseur and collector, one of B.B.'s earliest and closest friends in Italy. La Gazzada in earlier days was frequently the centre of B.B.'s and Mary Berenson's Lombard sight-seeing expeditions.

39

have had to become the little personage in a landscape as we find it in sixteenth-century drawings and engravings. Yet all my years I have longed for the idyllic life.

September 28th, La Gazzada

Dawn in clear sky, palest of peach colour. Then the chain of Monte Rosa waking with a blush as if feeling the kiss of the sun, and blushing deeper and deeper until the full refulgence of the light on the snow-covered peaks turns the entire chain into dazzling white. The lake at our feet beyond the peak begins to be covered with mist that rolls toward us like bales of cotton wool, and when all is covered takes on an aspect of hummocks on a field. What trees! Twice the height and girth and leafage of any seen further south—cedars, beeches, hornbeams, oaks, sequoias, weeping beeches, all of giant size and awe-inspiring. Man-designed time-made "nature," destined to be man-destroyed.

September 30th, Milan

Yesterday with Fernanda Wittgens * to Sant'Ambrogio, then to San Lorenzo, and finally to the Brera. There Piero della Francesca's Altarpiece, Raphael's *Sposalizio*, and Bellini's *Pietà* had been unpacked and placed in the open air of the courtyard for our inspection. The Piero, besides its marvellous architecture, spaces the figures in a matchless way. Never anything more tridimensional as they stood out. Literally one felt as if there was plenty of space behind them for one to walk in although seen too close at hand they scarcely seemed detached from the wall against which they might be thought to stand. Along with this greatest delicacy of touch, the Madonna's hair is nature itself, and the pearls on the foreheads of the angels as refulgent as real ones. Raphael's space effect is all I ever expected, and the figures (charming in themselves) help to constitute it. Not likely that Raphael was conscious of what he was doing, but subconscious no doubt. Then there is a virginal freshness about it! Bellini's *Pietà* sublime in its grandeur, its heroic silence! The Madonna rather Flemish.

* Italian art critic (1905–57), from 1945 to 1957 head of Brera Gallery, Milan, and superintendent of other museums in Lombardy.

40

Left Milan before three and yet did not reach Genoa before nine, having to go around by way of Mortara and Alessandria to find crossings over the Po. Enjoyed beauty of prosperity in look of fields.

October 2nd, Portofino

If only I could describe what I saw with my body inside and out as well as with eyes and mind at dawn this day. The sky was already alight and sunrise at hand. At the same time the moon, nearly full, was still above horizon. Rose and purple, and straw-colour and buff cloudlets all gilt splashed the sky. The cove way below fast asleep. The foliage exactly as in Giorgione, feathery yet exquisitely massed and each mass delicately drawn. Something almost miniature in Japanese fashion about promontory and rocks and sea inlets—so restful after the expanses of places inland and wide horizons toward sea.

October 3rd, Viareggio

Left *das Phaeakenland* of Portofino—and why have we no equivalent in English, why has the story of Alcinoüs and Nausicaä appealed so little to our poets?—and drove along lovely shore and wild mountain until we declined to the suburbia into which the Mediterranean coast has been turned—and all since I have been here—almost to the gates of Rome. Happily above Lerici Phaeacia remained intact and a very up-to-date Nausicaä * built herself a palace of delight now dwelt in by her surviving husband, Percy Lubbock.† For most of the year he lives there alone; for only company the clouds, the waves, the sea's sunshine and sorrow, and books, embattled complete works! How I envy his leisure based on a capacity for being alone. I need the stimulus and caresses of women and the talk of real men.

* Lady Sybil Cuffe (1879–1943), first married to American diplomat W. Bayard Cutting, then to English man of letters Geoffrey Scott (B.B.'s secretary for several years), and after her divorce from Scott, to Percy Lubbock; owner of Villa Medici, Fiesole, and of Gli Scafari near Lerici.
† English man of letters, author of *Earlham, The Craft of Fiction, Portrait of Edith Wharton*, etc.

October 4th, Viareggio

Yesterday at Pisa, exhibition of thirteenth- and fourteenth-century sculpture and paintings. Mysterious how it was they excelled in first and were so poor in second. My conclusion is that except for students and the merely curious exhibitions are to be discouraged. The truly sensitive person gets surfeited and overfed with food that is both boring and indigestible. If at all, exhibitions should be made not as now for the benefit of the superspecialist but selected for the enlightened dilettante. He then with good conscience could defend what was, and show and try to teach those nearest him in sensitive preparedness.

October 5th, Viareggio

At Lucca for the day. Just the light and temperature wanted. Worshipped the cathedral with its sumptuous black and white, its cubic axes, and its juicy, succulent Romanesque carvings. Few Italian exteriors if any make such a cathedral effect, helped on no doubt by surroundings kept low and at right distance. What a town in its garland of walls, and how much more beautiful still sixty years ago when I first saw it rising out of the deep meadow grass instead of the suburbs that now besiege it. Walls were not only a protection but the frame to a picture, a definite conclusion to a composition—suburbs are patternless and anarchic.

October 8th, I Tatti

Why at my advanced age do I let myself get agitated, driven, fussy, still eager to write and worse still to publish, still wanting to enjoy *Freude am Ursache sein*? And I can be so happy when, away from home, I wander carefree, sight-seeing and enjoying the beauties of art and nature for which seventy years of experience (trial and error) have so well prepared me. I should give the example of disinterested attainment beyond the itch for transitive activities. I should let myself be dominated by my strong feeling that in some mystical way enjoyment like mine benefits society more than anything that could be achieved by further publications.

42

October 10th, I Tatti

Raymond Mortimer * has been reading the preface to my diary where I declare myself to my own eyes a failure, and why. He questioned me whether I could have come out different. It then occurred to me that from the point of view of transitive activity, production, etc., I may have done far less than I might have, yet owing to that I may have in myself (intransitively so to speak) become more of a personality, more of a human work of art. That would explain that I radiate (it seems) authority and influence, which on grounds of objective achievement I have not earned. "Man as a Work of Art." What a subject! If only I had the energy.

October 13th, I Tatti

Rather stern, melancholy, youngish-oldish James Lees-Milne, † secretary of society for the preservation of country seats. The fabric can be preserved, and even the furniture in great part; but the soul is gone out of them when occupied by private persons whose standards and habits are different, and entirely so when given over to public uses, as schools, or convalescent homes and the like. It is impossible to prolong a past that is ours, because the life that created it has ceased. Yet what to do? Let the great country houses fall into ruin? Surely the best solution (artistically considered), for then we enjoy their picturesqueness, and can indulge in nostalgic romances about the kind of people who once lived in them.

October 14th, I Tatti

Heard Handel's *Rinaldo*—what magnificent colonnades and strings of sound, what cascades of song! Yet how recapture the way contemporaries felt about it? Not only did they know much

* English man of letters and literary critic. Met B.B. first in 1923, but joined the circle of intimate friends at I Tatti only after World War II, during a lecture tour in the spring of 1945.
† English architect and man of letters. Active in the promotion of "The National Trust," established to save historic country seats in England.

43

less about what preceded but nothing necessarily of what followed. We hear it with the music of Mozart and Beethoven and Wagner and Brahms and Strauss and even Stravinsky in our ears, and therefore give it a value of relief from turmoil, and the blast of our orchestras and the cacophonies of the latest composers, yet without recapturing the serenity of Handel's auditory.

October 15th, I Tatti

Kenneth Clark * dined and recounted in a bland voice the saga of the woman who came with her husband to tea the other day. Looking at her, who would have thought that she was such a woman of destiny that she could not be resisted nor resist? No doubt she was good-looking, perhaps a bit alluringly so, yet it remains for matter-of-fact me a mystery that a mere picture woman should be so fatal and even drive rational men to suicide. And the husband ready to stand by her through thick and through thin, ready to help her return. Her own sex tropisms seem to have been anything but well guided by a refined instinct. I return to wonder whether the attraction between sexes is not chiefly *chemical*.

October 16th, Arezzo

Arezzo, Piero della Francesca's frescoes—awkward in action, almost deliberately inexpressive, they yet are of such a saturation of colour as in fresco is achieved, but with less discretion, only by Titian at Padua. But in sturdy tridimensionality, in the power given to the joints, the way hands grasp and feet stand, those compositions are unsurpassable. Yet the greatest achievement remains to be mentioned. It is the luminosity of the sky, which not only is reflected radiantly from the figures and objects, but is in itself as positive, as deep, as transversal, as in Cézanne and beyond. Paolo Veronese wanted such skies and tells you so in all his paintings, but does not realize, only promises. Then Piero's un-, nay,

* Sir Kenneth Clark, prominent figure in the British art world, Director of the National Gallery, London, 1936–46; author, art critic, and lecturer. From 1925 in close touch with I Tatti, first as pupil and assistant, later as friend.

44

anti-romantic landscape, but so convincing. The reflection in the representation of the Tiber!

October 17th, Assisi

Overcome, overwhelmed by the beauty of the place, as a place apart from its works of art indoors. Even more intact, far less demedievalized, than Siena. The winding lanes between towering fortresslike palaces, the openings, the views revealed of the spacious yet so well-composed, so easy to embrace Umbrian valley, the façades of the Romanesque churches, the variety of Gothic elements, give the town as it climbs steeply its mountainside an heroic ✓ beauty not surpassed by any town I can recall in the world known to me. Perhaps in Armenia and its approaches, in Persia, in Afghanistan, there are even more grandiose, more picturesque, more romantic sites. Then the patina of warm grey that dominates everywhere. All that, yet according to all accounts its denizens are among the least reliable, least agreeable in Italy.

October 18th, Rome

Drove as not for many years past Spello, recalling exploration of that little town, the Romanesque cippus in the cathedral, early Peruginos and view at San Girolamo; then Foligno grazing the Albergo Posta where for years was my centre for exploring Umbria. Under Trevi to Spoleto, giving time for cathedral, where Fra Filippo's frescoes made a better impression than hitherto, particularly landscape and effects of sunrise and sunset; and San Pietro, where "movement" was revealed to me. Through varied, wooded landscape up hill, down dale, to Terni, now a dreadful proletarian sprawl of a town instead of the sleepy one I first knew nearly sixty years ago. Restaurant with ceiling resting on corrugated glazed columns, Città Castellana with its elegant Cosmata porch, and Soracte changing shape as we drove, and finally the sordid suburbs, and Babylonian tenement houses between Ponte Molle and Piazza del Popolo.

45

October 19th, Rome

Crowds pushing through one door of St. Peter's, and streaming out from another, yet inside look like small groups scattered about here and there. This lets one infer the vastness of the interior, and standing at the great Bernini tabernacle and looking toward the entrance the nave, while seeming foreshortened or rather telescoped, has arches that diminish rapidly in height and above them a cornice that dips sharply. People milling around aimlessly looking vaguely at the papal monuments, the which by the way retain to the very last pope a certain monumentality. Penitents kneeling at the confessionals. Little girls of two and three and four playing and climbing up the balustrades of the chapels. Excepting the dazed, incompletely humanized peasants, all seem at home as much at least as they would out of doors. St. Peter's remains the place where one meets others, where one takes one's ease, not as in the New England "meetinghouse" but as in the Antique basilica and Medieval cathedral.

October 22nd, Rome

The early morning sun gilding the house opposite cheers me a hundred times more than if it tried to warm the wall of the room I was occupying. Forenoon spent mooning in quarter of SS. Giovanni e Paolo and San Gregorio al Celio, now so changed (although one of the least changed) from the silent dignified rusticity of the past. Two dusty playing fields, the old approaches barred, trams rumbling thunderously by and in the space between SS. Giovanni e Paolo and the Mattei gardens, the dregs of an installation for the scenario of a film. The grounds of this monastery, formerly so gardenlike, torn up, jumbled over with brick and stone and iron for new buildings. Yet enjoyed the interior of SS. Giovanni e Paolo, a charming *petit salon du Bon Dieu*, the Pompeian murals underground and in one of the chapels adjacent to San Gregorio a fresco by Domenichino anticipating Poussin and all that is best in French historical painting of the seventeenth century.

46

October 23rd, Rome

With Raymond Mortimer to the Vigna di Papa Giulio. It was a lovely day and the great court, the intermittent curving colonnades, the nymphaeum, the frescoes on the barrel vaulting of the circular corridors were looking their most inviting, their most gracious—the right setting for the humanist ideal of the good life. For all those reasons I felt as never before a certain resentment as if I deliberately had been deprived of it. Instead of being born in conditions obliging me to struggle to attain it, I should have had it as my birthright. Yet had that been the case, should I have yearned for it as I have since I first felt it (almost before seeing it) more than fifty years ago? People take for granted what they are born to and are apt to use it as a springboard.

October 28th, Rome

Yesterday morning a young woman, a student of art history, joined us to see the Cavallini frescoes at Santa Cecilia. She had never seen them before and began at once to point out inequalities and different hands that must have taken part in the execution. The fault of teaching art history. The student is inclined to analyze and dissect the moment he encounters the object, instead of letting it soak into him as he gazes and looks, and dreams for hours together, the way I used to when young, and still should if I had youth's leisure. I recall writing in the same vein about the contemporary student's approach to literature. He is not encouraged to live and muse and ruminate over his reading but to precipitate himself with scalpel and microscope. I wonder whether the arts gain by being taught in schools.

October 31st, Rome

The cupola of St. Peter's—it is as inexhaustible as a human face. It blushes with the first flush of sunlight, and changes expression all day long, and is as poetical, as dramatic before the last rays of the sun leave it, as just after sunrise. It changes with the sky, with the clouds, grey against darker and light, or rose-coloured, against pale rose, or rosy red. It is in such complete re-

47

pose on its drum, and its curve is of a swanlike elegance. One could easily fall into Oriental dithyrambs writing about it.

Mooned strolling on Palatine. It is years since I had last been there. Once upon a time I was familiar with every stick and stone and up-to-date with what was known. Since then much has been discovered, reaching out beyond my curiosity. I no longer care insistently to know just what these terraces, these substructures, these ragged piles of masonry were when in use, and how many were going up at the same time. I was enjoying it all as classically romantic landscape, vaguely recalling the many hours spent there in my early twenties. One thing struck me as never before: the immense height of the uppermost terraces as you look down from them to the Forum below. Thence the pile of the Palatine must have looked overwhelming in its majesty.

November 7th, Rome

To dine: a youngish Austrian Jew, well made, with sparkling deep brown eyes and beautiful hands, with no touch of Jew in appearance, except faintly in the curve of the nostrils. Mattioli * had been startled by what this young man had read of Mattioli's character [in his handwriting]. He read mine. It was far too flattering and yet I could not believe that he meant to flatter. I wonder therefore whether what he told me he actually descried in my handwriting, or whether he was not reading into it a flattering myth that has been shaped around me; for I have become a myth, or rather two myths, a kindly flattering one and a hostile, damaging one. In the last I find it difficult to discover much likeness with what I know of myself.

November 14th, Rome

British ex-diplomat whom I had not seen since '40 dined. The name of Cyril Connolly † occurred and he had never heard it.

* Raffaele Mattioli, Director of the Banca Commerciale, friend of Benedetto Croce, active in promoting cultural activities.
† Anglo-Irish man of letters, editor of *Horizon* magazine, author of *The Unquiet Grave*. Was first introduced to the Berensons in 1926 by Logan Pearsall Smith.

Made me realize again for the how-manieth time since my youth how tiny was the world we, the real intelligentsia, live in. Here is a man of the solidest and on the whole most civilized circle in England, and perhaps of the world, and yet he has never heard of a writer who has been so much read and talked about in recent years. Perhaps in the course of time the name will reach his class as those of Yeats and George Moore. We intellectuals row feebly a small boat in a vast ocean which knows us not.

November 16th, Rome

Indiscretion not always indiscreet. A couple of days ago we sauntered into San Luigi dei Francesi. A High Mass was going on with vocal music. When it was over we tiptoed toward the chapel with Caravaggio's paintings. Found an elderly man quietly sitting in a corner. Looked as if he were there to worship. Then what seemed a boy of fifteen joined him and both began to look at photos and compare them with the paintings. The seeming boy turned out to be a youngish woman, obviously the man's secretary. Curiosity got the better of me, and as politely as possible I approached and asked what he was there for, and who. He was Walter Friedländer,* whom I had been wishing to meet; told him who I was. Asked what made Caravaggio, and he could only repeat Longhi's † guess that Caravaggio had studied Lotto and Savoldo. Unlikely, for Caravaggio came too early to Rome; and besides, artists of that time took what was going and did not look out for the unusual.

November 18th, Rome

Tea with Prince and Princess Filippo Doria ‡—he a strangely unexpected product of his subtle, refined, but far from saintly

* German-born Professor of Fine Arts at the Institute of Fine Arts of New York University; authority on seventeenth-century schools of painting.
† Roberto Longhi, Professor of Fine Arts at the Universities of Florence and Bologna. Considered by B.B. the most gifted among Italian art historians and critics.
‡ Prince Filippo Doria (1886–1955), head of Roman branch of the Doria family, passionately opposed to Fascism, banished to Southern Italy from 1941 to 1943, first Mayor of Rome after the liberation.

49

mother, and a putative father who never grew up and to the end of his days remained an unconscious self-indulgent man of pleasure. Filippo is austere, opinionated, philanthropic, devoted to what he thinks his duty, utterly un-Italian even to his hurricane of a laugh. They still nestle in the spacious grandeur of the seventeenth century surrounded by great masterpieces of painting, magnificent tapestries, furniture—what will become of it all in a generation or two? Not even a dreary museum. More likely a school, or at best offices retaining vague traces of past magnificence, interesting nobody.

November 21st, Rome

Have taken both the Dunns * to sight-see several times, and discovered that they appreciated works of art for their intrinsic qualities chiefly, although he in particular had a certain interest in the archaeology of what he was seeing. Finding people so able to understand, feel, and enjoy is so rare among my acquaintances, particularly of the well-to-do "governing classes," that it strikes me as a miracle. As a rule they care for the work of art only out of sheer curiosity, or because they are plotting to acquire it. I suppose that a real love of art is as much a gift as creating it, and may be due to the same source in the mind.

November 23rd, Rome

The Farnesina—there is a "princely residence"—building of perfect proportions, halls and rooms of harmonious space, and paintings by Raphael, by Sodoma, by Peruzzi, by Sebastiano del Piombo. Agostino Chigi was happy in being rich at a moment when such artists were there to be employed. Had our wealthiest bankers desired to do as much, they would not have found the painters. The shell-like crispness of the Peruzzis, the sensuous charm of the Sebastianos, the incomparable invention of Raphael, and their contrast with the voluptuousness of Sodoma, the scene painting of Peruzzi again, and his friezes—what a synopsy, and yet on the scale of livable life.

* The Hon. James Dunn, U.S. Ambassador to Italy from 1946 to 1953.

50.

November 28th, I Tatti

Have just read Scott Fitzgerald's *The Great Gatsby* more than twenty years after its publication. It may have been the first or one of the first novels about the flashy, tinsel life of the American suddenly enriched adventurer. It pictures an amoral, if not in every individual, a criminal society. Yet the atmosphere of the whole is romantic and deeply nostalgic. Cheap if you like, but not cheaper than fairy stories of all lands, and Aladdin of *The Arabian Nights*. Gatsby, no matter by what devious ways, victim perhaps of wholly antisocial forces, is a Dante in his way, longing for reunion with his Beatrice, and all else is but instrumental in the hope of attaining that end.

November 29th, I Tatti

Very well-meant essay on "Mr. Berenson" by Linklater *
in a book he just sent me. On the whole the least objectionable I ever read. His visit was hurried, scarcely an hour, and I did most of the talking. Extraordinary how much of it he carried away. Description of my physical appearance not flattering, nor his comparing me to a fox rather than a lion. I descry nothing foxy either physically, morally, or mentally in myself. Of reported conversation again and again he loses the point. He omits names of many authors I read during my occultation, and makes it seem almost as if I read more German than other writers.

November 30th, I Tatti

Former English officer and his newly married wife dined yesterday. She is smallish, fresh-looking, serious, and with a look as if she had a will and could assert herself decisively. Rumours run that he has married her solely to pay off debts which his extravagance has piled up. His former mistress tells me he still loves her, and that she cannot help loving him back although she has not forgotten what a heavy drinker, womanizer, and spendthrift he has

* Eric Linklater, English man of letters, author of *Private Angelo, Juan in America*, etc.

51

been. He has been all that to such a degree that I got disgusted and did not want to see him any more. The pity of it, for he is a handsome, manly creature, of best Nordic type, and a genuine musician, with a feeling for literature. Keen interest in politics, and at the same time a fine organizer. It was he who shaped and controlled the local press as the Allies fought their way up from Salerno to Milan. It was he who with the profits of the same press started symphonic concerts everywhere. While at it he was a prince and spent and lived like one. Demobilized, he discovered that he was a sorely indebted nobody who met resentment from the people who felt obliged to lick his boots. Now he is leaving Italy and expects to journalize in Moscow! In this role he has no preparation I can discover, except a sympathy with the Soviet experiment. As he is arrogant, impatient, and critical he may not stay long in Russia. And then? If his young wife can keep him away from drink and lechering he may take to serious work, for he has brains, constructive intelligence, and great gifts as an organizer. He is a Viking, a Northman pirate, up-to-date. He has their self-disintegrating and politically constructive capacities and gifts. I may never hear of him again or he may still turn out one of the master-builders of the coming years.

December 5th, I Tatti

Every human and perhaps all other beings, say higher animals, have implicitly, if incapable of becoming aware of it and explicating it, a philosophy. The poet, who is such a being, has his philosophy, his *Weltanschauung*. To assume, as so much of contemporary writing on poets, that it is their philosophy which is the most interesting thing about them, that their philosophy gives them importance and value, seems absurd. Surely philosophy as such is most comprehensively, most intelligently, and most systematically stated by technical philosophers. I suspect that to seek philosophy in the poet means that the critic does not know how to approach his poetry, to feel it, to isolate its quality, to communicate it, or at least to describe it to others.

December 14th, I Tatti

How fragile I have grown. I was feeling fairly well yesterday, and enjoyed my morning and evening strolls in the garden. Then a long visit *en tête-à-tête* from Hortense Serristori.* We never pose with each other or make an effort to entertain. We can be comfortably silent for minutes together, so I was not particularly indisposed or overtired. But I vaguely became aware that it had grown cooler in the room, and all of a sudden I began to sneeze. It got worse and worse. I had to dismiss the lady rather curtly, and hurried to undress and get to bed—to the alarm of all and sundry. I was feeling ill enough, but the cosy comfort of bed began to have its effect and soon I was well enough to eat, and later to allow Nicky and Freya Stark to sit by me. Aspirin and other remedies before going to sleep—slept, and this morning I feel no worse than usual.

December 16th, I Tatti

Freya Stark, now Mrs. Perowne, left this morning after a stay of ten days. Never had a more stimulating, more companionable, more discursive visitor, ready to talk about everything from the hyssop growing out of the wall to the stars in their courses. She glows with physical warmth, and she never touched me without my feeling a thrill. Never should take her for an Englishwoman, nor indeed a Northerner. She must have gypsy blood in her veins, no matter from what distant source, and it is that which gives her the passion for travel, real travel, not being transported but wandering in remote, untrodden, dangerous lands. And God has given her the gift of words, of the evocative epithet, of the poetical image, of rhythm in her prose so that she can make us live and pant and risk and rush with her.

* Countess Hortense Serristori (1871–1960), Spanish-born wife of the Florentine Count Umberto Serristori. Met B.B. in the early nineties through Don Guido Cagnola, and remained one of his closest friends for life.

53

December 18th, I Tatti

[Francis] Steegmuller's *States of Grace,* a burlesque comic operetta about inside working of Irish-American Catholicism. Comforting as showing that in the first place it is already more American than Irish Catholic. Then that it is beginning to disintegrate, getting smart, worldly, dissipated, and losing its character of a minority on the defensive not only without but within. If U.S.A. succeeds in Americanizing its Catholics, the Irish in particular, then its future spiritual unity is secured to the extent at least that is desirable. If Catholics begin to see the merely human, too human working of their religiosity or hierarchy, then we are on the way to safety.

December 19th, I Tatti

Tried hard to *converse* with a young man of twenty-one and a girl of nineteen. Hard and profitless task. Too much interested in each other, or was it merely chemical attraction? Would have been much better in a room by themselves. It may be self-indulgent and irresponsible on the part of older people to leave the youngsters to their own devices, but it certainly makes for comfort. As a rule the young ones care not for our conclusions regarding our experience. They want their own and blast the consequences. So youth and crabbed age had better keep apart, except of course when youth has something to get out of age, and stimulates age by its acquisitive eagerness and zest.

1948

January 1st, I Tatti

Bright and wintry, the New Year begins with seasonable cheer. Shall I outlive it? What can we expect of it? It promises to be a year of crisis, of decisions such as the world has perhaps never been called upon to make, such as history has not recorded. How will the tussle between Tartary and Europe end? By Tartary I mean a polity based on usages formed in North Central Asia, which exclude the individual except as a drop in the ocean of the mass. By Europe I mean all descendants of the tradition and aspiration of the Judeo-Greco-Roman world as continued by the Latin Church and so-called Western civilization, its successor. I am passionately, patriotically for Europe and against Tartary. But once pushed back on its own, I am willing to let it stew in its own juice until it is ready to play a supernational game and join loyally a Europe united in cultural values and ideals.

January 3rd, I Tatti

Victor Emmanuel III died a couple of days ago. Early in his reign Richard Norton, then head of the American Academy in Rome, went to the Quirinal to see him and found him furiously kicking the wall. He stopped and explained that he was letting off steam because as constitutional monarch he had just been obliged to sign the appointment of a batch of senators most of whom he regarded as utterly unworthy of the honour. Starting out as an idealist, and called upon to approve measures he detested, he may have settled down to take his office cynically and to play the part of constitutional monarch in a way that reduced him to a mere rubber stamp, and leaving him as a human being to think of nothing but the future advantage of his family.

January 9th, I Tatti

Buying books has become a disease. I have much less time for reading than I used to because I have to waste so much in resting and in bodily care. Then I want to read ever so many more reviews, weeklies, monthlies, quarterlies, with the result that the leisure for books is small. Yet I order them from New York, from London, from Paris, from Bern, not to speak of the Italian ones I get here. And if Germany were publishing and exporting I should get floods of books from there. Here I scarcely dare enter a bookshop, I feel such an inclination to buy up everything. Almost I find myself ready to carry away volumes in editions that I know I have. So book-buying is all but a monomania with me, and it is getting more and more of a problem to house them.

January 10th, I Tatti

Tea with Miss Wilson, an elderly American spinster whom long, long ago I knew as a young girl, daughter of a lawyer from Washington, D.C. She now is grey-haired, dressed in black, bespectacled, and not interesting in talk, or even vitalizing with the remains of animal spirit. No, the way she is, the way she lives, her anxiety to serve tea like a dainty, yet appetizing, a most sacramental ritual, turn her and her surroundings into a conversation piece, a picture of refined, exquisite genre like, say, Terborg. Women like her, and they are not uncommon among Americans of her age, are masterpieces of art, untheatrical, perpetual *tableaux vivants*. I enjoy them not for what they say, nor for what they achieve, but for just what they are as existences.

January 13th, I Tatti

How little does one discuss sex relations seriously. There is the fact that after a limited time they become a mere matter of animal contact or worse—even ending in incapacity to find satisfaction. Not only can this still be had with others, but these others retain glamour, romance, novelty in short, which the legitimate or usual partner has lost. Seeing that the sexual urges continue to operate, it would seem that the traditional French and Italian way

58

is the best, namely: marry young, and let the wife produce two or three children. By the time she is thirty she will have had enough of husband and children, and sigh for romance and satisfaction elsewhere. This she is allowed to have, provided she keeps up appearances. Indeed she can, and more often than not does, remain on the best of terms with her husband, who on his side is some other woman's lover; and the children are protected.

January 21st, I Tatti

Van der Meersch, *La Petite Ste. Thérèse*—the life of the young female who ended as Ste. Thérèse de Lisieux. Theology and vocabulary apart, her search for selfless goodness, the struggle to get rid of the ever interfering, deviating, poisonous ego, its vanity, its self-regard, its hates and loves, its fears and greeds, its failures and successes, its constant outlook for its own prestige and advantage—all, all are shared by me. But with the difference of determination, of uninterrupted intensity of pursuit, and so little transferred to the field of action! When not thinking and acting for my own petty purposes, I remove myself to pursuits in which my ego is not immediately engaged but of doubtful efficiency in improving myself, and of no use (or very problematic use) to others. She ended as a saint; how far from that am I.

January 22nd, I Tatti

To tea, a boy of twenty-two, named Boselli, son of a modest Piedmont-Lombard father and an English mother. Has been eight years in England, and four at Wadham, Oxford. Except for his looks, nothing left of the Italian about him, in speech, in deportment, in clothes. He had become completely English, and incidentally very conservatively English. If he had spent those eight years in Italy would he not have become as completely Italian, excepting of course for a certain ferment acting like a *vis a tergo*? What would have become of me had I remained in a Lithuanian ghetto, or as an emancipated Jew living in Russia? Or if I had stuck to America, never leaving it except for short excursions abroad? No doubt I should have become more absorbed in specifically American problems, but perhaps never felt

59

more American. The twelve years between my eleventh and twenty-third years shaped my mind and furnished it with "prejudices" I have never discarded.

January 25th, I Tatti

In the middle of the fifteenth century a Brescian could insist on being tried by Lombard law. At the same time a Mohammedan on his tombstone in Sicily boasts that he has stuck to his faith and his race. Both are instances of individual freedom scarcely permissible in our time. The first certainly not. The second when you reflect that he was descended from alien conquerors, perhaps oppressors, and now almost isolated. Imagine a parallel case in Soviet or even in any Western land. It would be interesting by the way to investigate whether the beautifully carved Arabic tombstone was or was not made in Sicily, as can be told from the stone and the lettering. If in Sicily, it would imply that Arabic tombstone makers must have been able to make a living there, and that therefore the Arab-speaking population was large enough to support them.

January 27th, I Tatti

A Genoese gentleman brought me a little Annunciation he wanted me to see because he thought it was by the same master who painted a small Crucifixion in my house. I did my best to explain to him that while there was a superficial likeness, particularly in the architecture, there was a different spirit, a different purpose in each. Mine was still of the epic, the heroic, while his was already sentimental, almost expressionistic. I could not persuade him. No wonder. Has it not taken me sixty years to learn to feel, to analyze, and to understand the intimate spirit of a work of art, and to realize what differentiates it from another? Many words won't effect what a long self-analyzing experience alone can bring—sensitiveness, awareness, and understanding.

January 30th, I Tatti

An entire issue of the *American Archaeological Journal* taken up with the question of the relation in early Antiquity between Egypt, Crete, and the Aegean world. Important in so far as commercial [relations are discussed], for pedlars of wares are also pedlars of ideas. But from an artistic point of view the interchanges and influences interest me less and less. Not whence nor how things came, but what artists did with them is now my chief concern. From that point of view, how little Crete and Egypt affected each other, the latter seeking the massive, the static, the bulky even, while the former wanted the quick, the nimble, the suspended. Its pillars and columns diminish in girth as they reach the ground, as if to say, "We only are touching it with our toes."

January 31st, I Tatti

One reason why I write so little (and now talk less and less) is that I have always been unable to shut out the other side, the side that invalidated or cancelled the conclusion to which I was gaily running. So I would stop short and "go on saying nothing." This is particularly true in my chosen field, the field of criticism, where almost anything one says can as easily be disproved as proved, where one can as it were look at the same geometrical drawing and read it off as concave or convex. How often I have a happy run with an idea, enjoying my own functioning as well as what I see and hear, am carried away, until something happens, a flash from a clear sky, and the idea has vanished like a figure in a faint mist dispelled by the sun.

February 4th, I Tatti

I cannot overcome a feeling of absurdity when people come to—shall I say—worship me. Of course worship is the extreme to which their attitude toward me does not attain, but nevertheless partakes of. No doubt mere curiosity is mixed up with it, the triumph over others who have not succeeded in seeing me, a few minutes' subject for conversation. Yet when I come down, a certain hush comes over visitors who see me for the first time, and a faint, a very

61

faint look of something like awe on their faces. All so comic! Have not numberless persons felt as I do, people with endlessly more claim to admiration? In history I recall Vespasian only who must have felt the ludicrousness of his being worshipped as a god.

February 5th, I Tatti

Mr. and Mrs. [Arthur] Koestler. She rather washed-out blonde, physically (to me) uninteresting. He dark, nut-brown, jet-black hair, fine head, arresting eyes. Features not Jewish. Perhaps a touch of gypsy. His speech impeded by a successive word or phrase leaping on the back of one he has not yet uttered. His English would be almost perfect but for his pronouncing W's as V's, and "th" as Z. Spoke of experiments proving scientifically the existence of telepathy, and of mind influencing inorganic matter, as in case of dice. Yet why not? We have for thousands of years made an absolute division of *mind* and *matter* as if they were two distinct orders of things that did not know each other. But in pre-Socratic, prescientific ages it was not so. Man felt that all in him was of the same nature as all else, inanimate as well as animate, and was more in touch with reality than those who inscribed the geometrical in reality, and forgot that they were only figures and not reality itself.

February 8th, I Tatti

Have glanced at Shaftesbury's essay on *Hercules at the Cross Roads,* forgotten because replaced by Lessing's *Laokoon,* which not only cuts deeper, but with less quaintly archaic locution. His philosophizing on art, as indeed all art criticism, bores me. Yet I write it. Can I expect others to be interested? Scarcely. The fact is that I write because it is my only way of functioning transitively, producing obvious results. And I have a physical need of such activity, as physiological as the digestive functioning of my body. I get as painfully constipated when my mind does not produce matter for print as when intestines do not function healthily. The exercise of function is behind the urge of action, rather than "purpose," which is only a glare or mirage or myth, which however seems to be a necessary accompaniment.

62

February 14th, I Tatti

The last number of the *Illustrated London News* to reach me has picture of the Dean and Chapter of Westminster Abbey depositing the ashes of Beatrice and Sidney Webb.* Startling in a way, but intelligible when one recalls that this honour is granted to those of her children whom England represented by her government regards as having given the utmost they could and that of universal value, regardless of party quarrels. Anything more hostile to, more destructive of all that Westminster Abbey stands for is not easily imaginable. And yet! So was Shakespeare, in his historical plays, ready to receive all fair combatants, though they cut one another's throat, grimly enough. In Shakespeare as in the Abbey I discover the same generous, affectionate attitude toward their fellow countrymen who have borne the utmost in a cause. There is no such thing on the Continent, where partisanship is too fierce to do justice to or to feel proud of adversaries.

February 22nd, I Tatti

"Europe, Europe, Europe" filled my eyes and was dinned into my ears all through my undergraduate days at Harvard. After sixty years of Europe, propaganda in its favour during my formative years is still operative. Apart from material considerations—for example, the relative ease of living here with ample space in and out of doors, abundance of servants, etc.—I cling to Europe as the seat of all I hold most precious, namely, what Europe has produced in all intellectual pursuits, and all creative activities. True, I regard European settlements overseas with an overwhelming majority of white population as equally European. But the background there is not the same, and besides I feel that in all matters of literature and art (except possibly the short story) geographical Europe is still likely to be more creative than the Americas or the Austral England.

* Sidney Webb (1859–1947) and wife Beatrice (1858–1943), leading English Socialists, co-founders of Fabian Society.

February 23rd, I Tatti

Why are people, Anglo-Saxons especially, so suspicious of self-awareness, of self-analysis, "self-consciousness" as it is generally called? Because it spends energy required for action? Perhaps. Yet possibly owing to a deep (and of course unanalyzed) feeling that the effort of introspection not only is futile but harmful. The fact seems to be that the more one delves into self the less one finds. It seems to exist only through the activities of an intransitive (it is true) more than transitive, I mean productive, kind, and through the reflection and repercussion of effect upon others more than by isolated search into self. I for one have never touched bottom in self, nor even struck against the surface, the outlines, the boundaries of this self. On the contrary I feel the self as an energy only which expands and contracts.

February 27th, I Tatti

Just before sunrise I saw the sky dappled with varying, swiftly changing shades of rose. It was an enchanting spectacle, and what would not conspicuous wasters pay to admire it, if it cost a huge sum to see it. But as it costs nothing, few take the trouble to look out of the window for it. The fact is that what costs nothing in cash or effort does not count. The Italians never take into account that they enjoy so much more sunlight all the year round than the Northern people they envy, not to speak of beauty of landscape and of art.

February 29th, I Tatti

Robert Gathorne-Hardy, semidetached secretary of my brother-in-law Logan Pearsall Smith,* is staying with me and we spend the evenings reading an account of his relations with Logan. It brings out Logan's physique, his humour, his wit, his malice, his childishness, his cantankerousness, his sentimentalities, his prejudices, his passions and ambitions and ideals, his petty vices, his

* Brother (1865–1946) of Mary Berenson, essayist, contemporary of B.B.'s at Harvard.

64

follies, the whole man in short, as I can recollect no other account of a person. I wonder what the effect will be on those who have not known him, whether they will care to read so much about him. Some certainly, but perhaps not many in this world, so busy on the one hand and so trivial on the other.

March 3rd, I Tatti

My dreams are as commonplace in detail as the workaday events, even if somewhat absurdly placed or timed. As a rule they deal with the matters that happened on the previous days, or are going to happen the next. No phantasy. Moreover I dream but rarely now—when young (but I seem to recall having written this already) I used to see marvellous Giorgiones and Correggios, but even more wonderful than the actual ones seemed in my waking hours, although even then I saw them through a golden glamour that made them far more marvellous still. I must be at bottom an earth bubble pure and simple, with no fancy, bound down to facts and factlike conclusions.

March 4th, I Tatti

Walked over to Villa Gamberaia, found it neglected, unkempt, grass not mown, trees with branches broken looking like elephants with broken tusks, the house burnt out with the beautiful court-yard fallen in, vases and stone animals on parapet thrown down and broken—and yet the place retains its charm, its power to inspire longing and dreams, sweet dreams. Its beauty though so uncared for is still great enough to absorb one almost completely, the terraces, the ponds, the great apse of cut cypresses, the bowling green as you look at it from the grotto toward the south like a great boat sailing through space, the view over the quiet landscape of the Chianti hills and further over domes and towers to the snow-capped Apennines and the Arno glimmering in the plain.

March 5th, I Tatti

Fifty years ago I began to frequent this paradise, then belonging to a narcissistic Rumanian lady who lived mysteriously in love with herself perhaps and certainly with her growing creation, the garden of the Gamberaia. With her was an American friend, Miss [Florence] Blood. She painted not too well, yet it was she who copied Egisto Fabbri's * Cézannes to such perfection that it made me wonder. I did not make love to her. As I look back now I wonder whether she did not resent it. I recall outbreaks of hostility on her part for no accountable reason except nerves. Be that as it may, for years Gamberaia remained one of the *fari* [beacons], one of the haunts of my life, well into this century, till 1910 at least.

March 11th, I Tatti

I fight against indifference regarding my possessions here, not fields and houses, but library, garden, etc. At all but eighty-three, with perhaps days only to live, why should I go on worrying about difficulties, annoyances, not to speak of cost of books for my library. . . .

True, it has been my sole ambition apart from self-improvement. For fifty years I have worked with my limited means to build up a library where a student of White Man's civilization would find every essential book at hand. But I have hoped to leave it to American students who would grow by using it. Now with possibilities of Sovietism or chances of civil war that hope at times fails me. Yet I go on accumulating books, improving the garden —out of habit?

March 12th, I Tatti

The Goncourts were right in laying it down that after them their art treasures should be sold at auction so that others should enjoy the same pleasure of acquiring and treasuring them that they themselves had had. Pictures hanging on walls may possibly be respected by my successors. What will happen to all the tiny odds and ends in bronze, in jade, and others bigger in hard stone?

* Wealthy Italo-American (1865–1933), established in Florence, owner of a group of Cézanne paintings which he later sold to create the school of Gregorian chant, according to the G. B. Ward method, in the Casentino valley.

They will either be put away in cupboards or suffer the ignominy of being shown in glass cases. I never look at them now because the enjoyment is half spoiled by the inquiry as to what will happen to them the moment I am gone. What a pleasurable excitement it was to acquire them one by one.

March 16th, I Tatti

I am often worried by doubts as to the civilizing effect of the arts. The Germans wallowed in music as no other people, not arias such as Italians and other people love, but grave and exalting symphonic music and their own spacious and uplifting chorales; yet have they not turned out to be as a mass capable of every horror, every revolting bestiality? The Tsarist and Turkish aristocrats, so refined, so up-to-date in all the arts—who more inhumane? William James used to say that every gush of feeling should be followed by adequate action, or (he implied) the feeling turned to poison. That must be the reason why wallowing in music and poetry does not humanize, does not civilize. And are not barbarous people more musical?

March 18th, I Tatti

Yesterday a Dominican Père Philippe from Fribourg. We discussed Thérèse de Lisieux and world matters in a way that might have made him believe that I was as fervent a Roman Catholic as he. I did not pose as one. I sincerely sympathized with his point of view and accepted it all—all but a miracle he described of the favourite novice of Thérèse, who felt the dead saint's hand gripping hers when they touched. All Christians, as would all Jews, all Mohammedans, etc., etc., find me as responsive, as ready to accept their attitude toward actualities. When they learn how I combat their theology, their hagiology, their metaphysic, they "softly and silently vanish away." Shall we never get rid of these empires of nonsense that waste and divide us, use up time and energy, and turn us into packs of howling wolves?

67

March 22nd, I Tatti

Trevor-Roper's *Last Days of Hitler* is written in a more Tacitean style and with more Tacitean spirit than any other historic or politic writing that I can recall. Yet he, now thirty-three, assures me that he read him only as a schoolboy and that he had not been impressed by him. How account for this? Was it so to speak inculcating his subconscious to come out when he found a suitable subject or is it a mere coincidence, namely, that he is so Tacitean? In any case it should caution one against ascribing influences or derivations. On the other hand if either or both are nearly contemporary with the source we are justified in concluding that by osmosis if not by a more conscious process the younger contemporary was influenced by the older and continued in his wake, even if with a protest.

March 23rd, I Tatti

Mary died three years ago. I think of her often and at times with a tender pity. Her life was in many ways based on mistaken premises. Literature, art, people were only adolescent curiosities. Later they were mere condiments. Her dominant and deep concern was for her daughters and their children. Little thought of their happiness but passionate eagerness for their having an expensively good time. So she was always heaping presents, piling luxuries on them. For their friendship she did not care—nor indeed for anyone's. She cared only for in-love relations. The last war, which she would have spent more happily if less comfortably in England, deprived her of communication with her offspring, atrophied her only real interests, and must have left her lonely and bored. For I had ceased to stimulate her long ago, and my two daily visits to her bedside during her last years bored her. The one relief was her writing about her daughter Ray Strachey.*

* Daughter (1886–1940) of Frank Costelloe and of Mary Berenson; author of several biographies, active in political and social work.

March 24th, I Tatti

Poland to the greatest degree, Hungary next, then Rumania have always hated Russian dominion, and the Czechs have not loved it. I counted on that to bring about ultimate revolution in those countries against the Soviets. I did not count with the factor of conditioning and *bourrage de crâne*. The Quislings in those lands will see to it that children and young people are indoctrinated with the catchwords and misinterpretations of the Soviets and made impenetrable to Western ideas. The only hope is in the Catholic Church, the only organization keen enough and strong enough to resist and to combat Soviet doctrine. Thus everywhere on the European continent we are brought back to the Church as the ally of people like myself who can fight along a great way with her in defence of humanistic values which the Soviets are out to destroy.

March 28th, I Tatti

Until thirty I lived in a magic world. First it was the fairyland of childhood. From thirteen or at least fourteen it was the excited and participating interest in the progress the U.S.A. was making in every direction, quantitative chiefly, and privately the acquisition of knowledge, or rather of information of every kind. Current beliefs and aspirations sufficed, and the taking for granted that the order of things rested on solid foundations. After thirty I began very slowly to want not only to be informed, but to understand. It is the problem with which I have been increasingly occupied ever since. The more I try, the less I succeed, and even knowledge is dissolved and doubt prevails over everything. I now feel that I know little (except the quantitative matters universally accepted) and understand nothing—positively nothing.

March 29th, I Tatti

Dined yesterday a young Austrian couple. He was Czech Chargé d'Affaires to the Vatican, and publicly resigned after Sovietization of his government. Neither very intelligent, yet informed, cultivated, and interested. That is not the interesting thing about them. It is that they are manifestly, impressively aristocrats. The women particularly of the Austrian *erste Gesellschaft* have a *Rassigkeit,* a distinction that makes them into fascinating works of art. At bottom and for us (if unhappily not for themselves) it suffices that they exist. That is what I enjoy about them, and not what they say or do, even when delightful. What they say and do may be no more than my pretext for remaining with them and enjoying their presence. Or they may be far from me in all that to me is most dear, yet I cannot help admiring and lingering over them.

April 2nd, I Tatti

I cannot keep from wondering how old people of the past, in Antiquity and the Middle Ages particularly, kept clean. Their beards must have got into a horribly filthy condition, and there was no toilet paper. Their undergarments too must have got lousy, and can have been washed but rarely, and their clothes spotted, blotched, and stained in loathsome ways. They themselves stank no doubt, and unless very rich could not afford perfume to counteract this. As late as Dr. Johnson's time, "clean-shirt day" was an event in his circle. All this is one of the many instances where all but the poorest today can attain a standard of life that the highest and wealthiest of the past could not achieve. That at least is to the good.

April 4th, I Tatti

But for my own comfort and the wish to hand over my property for purposes of culture, why am I so opposed to Sovietism, seeing I believe that in the course of time mankind assimilates any kind of doctrine and reduces it to an eternal average, regardless of the ideals and abominations of its start? Look at Buddhism, look at Christianity. The history of the latter during its first few centuries was filled with faith and hope and charity, swindles, treacheries, violences, bestiality, but now Christianity is a civilization rather than a religion, and a civilization based on what could be saved of Judea, Greece, and Rome. What makes me dread Sovietism is that if it prevails it will not shake down in the end to those values as Christianity has, but to utterly unhumanistic ones, to merely quantitative, mechanical, purely zoologically practical ones.

April 11th, I Tatti

I am so much, very much more easygoing in attributing pictures to "great masters" than I used to be—long ago. Why? I recognize now that at times even they could be careless, slovenly even; that the present state of an "old master" is rarely what it should be, and an adverse judgment of authorship may be based on passages in his paintings which have altered considerably since he left them. All that, but I fear part of the reason for being more kindly is that I have less and less daily contact with the "old masters" whether in original or reproduction, and therefore less searching judgment in analyzing a given work of theirs. I have become more generalizing, more easygoing, more indulgent— through indolence, and perhaps senile indifference.

April 13th, I Tatti

When young I used to flare up with envy and jealousy of any superiority that I recognized or any public success encountered. The last leaves me cold personally, although I may regret it as a symptom of something rotten in the state of society. Superiority, now and since many a day, makes me feel humble and grateful; humble because it obliges me to recognize my own inferiority (the which I am now so ready to admit), and gratitude for insight, or beauty that was new, at least to me, and of a kind that enriched life, and made it more worth while. If there is anything that calls out worship in me, it is the recognition of creative genius in others!

April 16th, I Tatti

I begin to wake after four, at most five, hours of sleep, feeling as heavy as lead, and unable to pull myself out of a lethargy that holds me tight. A smoky sensation in a rough throat. Nose

71

swollen, I struggle till tea comes. I take it and begin to revive. Eyes lotioned. Gums iodined. Nostrils opened up with drops. I start reading and for about three quarters of an hour with clearness of mind. Then I drop into a doze, of which I cannot get rid, although I do not sleep. I bestir myself. Take Swedish exercises. Return to bed and relax, feeling at last taking possession of me a delicious repose, a balm of Gilead, a physical happiness. What is it, what are its physiological causes, how is it that glands and viscera are so coddling? Why did I wake, or rather begin to wake, so tired, as if instead of sleeping for five hours I had been working like a hod carrier through the night? But the deliciousness of the bodily harmony that follows repays for it all.

April 17th, I Tatti

Ingres inveighed against the artists of his own time in terms, word for word, that in *petto* and even in *talk* I have used against those of today. But he had in mind Delacroix, and I the distortionist, contortionist, difformist, inflationist, deflationist, unrepresentationalist, abstractionist, etc., etc., etc., of the last twenty years. What vocabulary could an Ingres find for them, seeing that he exhausted all the reserve of vituperation against the mild rebels of his own day? Or, like me in most cases, would he have ignored what lately has been and still is being produced nowadays as either anti-art, or having no relation to art?

April 25th, I Tatti

As I watch the *clouds* I see them taking shapes not only of mountain ranges, almost illusive, but of various animals and even of human profiles, at times of one's acquaintances, thrown as it were on a cosmic screen. I watch them forming and gradually dissipating. And it occurs to me to wonder whether a dreamy Deity may not look at what goes on in the universe as we do at clouds, watch occurrences and characters shaping and dissolving in the same way, and from Deity's timelessness free from any idea of direction and passing with speed to us unimaginable across an infinite horizonless sky. Often the time factor amuses me, as if it were an accordion to pull out and to press together again.

April 29th, Siena

Lunched with Guido Chigi,* uncrowned king of Siena, who reigns but does not govern. A Restoration figure, a Romantic of 1830, and an exile in the world of today. He lives in a palace which on entering it he restored in pseudo-Gothic style, with the addition of a music room that makes one feel inside a wedding cake. Not clever, nor intelligent, ultra-conservative more out of self-interest than of any well-constructed world-order, now rather living like a lamp at half-cock, he yet exercises a certain charm as of a work of art that calls up a world of its own, a way of life one cannot but fall for. And I enjoy glimpses of him, although aware of how little we have in common in serious matters. Nor does he care to know who I am in myself, half and perhaps more than half believing that as a work of art he is not called upon to take an interest in or understand the spectators.

April 30th, Siena

After many years, I revisited [Villa] Belcaro. What did it not call up in my own past! Vernon Lee's † book, which I read while still at Harvard, invested the name with even more magic than other Italian place names. I walked out an autumn afternoon in 1889, and approached it through a road bordered with over-bowering trees, and sparkling with scarlet arbutus berries. From the *chemin de ronde* of the château I gazed over the soft slopes up and down the landscape, stretching to the horizon on every side except where red Siena barred a small segment. As I looked down my eyes pierced the dense wall of clipped ilex that ringed the castle. Inside the palace, pictures which at that time I worshipped because Italian, because on gold ground, because I wanted to find out why they attracted, fascinated.

Yesterday the palace was inaccessible, and the view grey with

* Count Guido Chigi Saracini, descendant of illustrious Sienese family noted for its protection of the arts; creator of the "Chigiana" Academy of Music at Siena.
† Pseudonym of Violet Paget (1856–1935), English author and art critic; lived from 1871 to 1935 in Italy. Author of *The Eighteenth Century in Italy, Genius Loci,* etc.

73

clouds, shutting out the Amiata and the further sky line. So I concentrated on chapel and loggia, both decorated by Peruzzi and, although completely renovated, still retaining a great charm for me, who love his dainty manner, his elongated, elegantly aristocratic nudes which make his sacred subjects agreeable, and his mythical ones perfectly charming. Some are erotic yet curiously chaste, because the actors are not of flesh and blood, but of pounded shell and similar substances. Curious that Peruzzi as painter and decorator, with the ceiling of the Galatea hall in the Farnesina and the architectural friezes of the upper rooms, should be little appreciated. I always have, from my first glimpses in the autumn of '88, and ever since with keen delight.

May 1st, Siena

Monte Oliveto Maggiore after eighteen years. Approach through badlands with their sharp edges hundreds of feet long cutting off the site of the monastery, approachable by two narrow ways scarcely wide enough for a road. Brick building with gay Veronese architecture contrasting with the severity of the scene. Frescoes by Sodoma as charming, as frivolous, as compact as ever. What an artist he could have been had he had more seriousness to his nature! But how much better than Signorelli as a frescoist, though so inferior a draughtsman and artist. Was recognized by Don Patrizio, who was here as a boy when I spent some weeks or longer in the early winter of '90–'91. I revisited the apartment I occupied then, and recalled the fire we made in the sitting room and how the Abbot Di Negro would tell me stories of his seminary stage in Rome, and all sorts of anecdotes about the clergy of that date.

[Returned to] Monistero, the huge brick building on the Maremma road, a couple of miles out. I used to go there often, and at one time toyed with the idea of buying it and of living there with a few choice spirits in a sort of Thélème. I went there at least once with my brother-in-law Logan Pearsall Smith, and out of this came the sketch concocted by us together about Altamura, printed in the first number of the *Golden Urn*. This series of pamphlets was to contain the purest poetry only, a hundred lines perhaps of each, of a Dante, a Shakespeare even. A few

numbers appeared and encountered the execration of nearly all
our friends. No wonder, for it must have called them up to ask
"What is poetry?"

May 2nd, Siena

When asked who He was the Lord God answered, "I am
that I am." It is perhaps the sublimest saying in the Old Testament. Jehovah does not autobiographize. He does not apologize.
He is and that suffices. He is being in the fullest, completest
way, and has nothing to explain, and nothing to do. Unfortunately,
most Old Testament writers forget that and make Him act like
a sort of centuplicated male. It took the contemporaries of Jesus to
bring Jewish feeling to Deity and pure Being. In our infinitesimal-
ity we should try to imitate our Maker and think less of doing,
acting, and more of being—of becoming works of art. The work
of art alone among finite things approaches pure Being. It just is,
and asks nothing, makes no appeal, knows nobody, yet is there
to absorb us spectators, to allow us to identify ourselves with it,
to become it, even as the mystic yearns to be absorbed by Deity,
and ultimately to be identified with It.

May 3rd, Siena

Yesterday at Campriano with the Dario Neris.* A wood-
cutter on the place (now nearly blind) with a remarkable gift for
sculpture, carving himself in wood, in stone, in marble. He is un-
tutored, and probably never teachable, not interested in looking
or seeing, yet he does things which are startlingly like late Antique, say third- or fourth-century reliefs, or like early-dynasty
Egyptian. Excepting animals, nothing of our own day, I mean in
the visual language of today. It is impossible to get a word out of
him, beyond the declaration that he has it in his head before beginning to work. I cross-questioned him as to whether he had
been to Rome, to Ravenna, to Milan. Never. He thus could have
seen nothing upon which to model himself. Strange, mysterious.

* Dario Neri (1895–1958), Sienese painter and landowner; creator and head
of the Electa publishing house, which brought out almost all of B.B.'s
post-World War II writings in Italian translation.

75

May 4th, I Tatti

How account for my delight in green, grassy slopes, in pastures, in woods, in forests (not jungles), in weather-worn buildings, and *per contra* my distaste for most everything recent, industrial establishments in particular? It comes to my seldom seeing earth turned up for building purposes without asking how long it will be before the ensuing structure will tumble into ruins and be recovered by Mother Earth. Is my feeling innate? I cannot recall. Is it the result of mere habit, the constant contact with things old, and because like Riegl * I find that everything *alt ist schön*? Not quite, for a well-proportioned building of material and colour and relief harmonizing with the structure can still give me real pleasure.

May 5th, I Tatti

What an incisive draughtsman is Van Gogh, and that despite his touch which often is fuzzy as if his line was of worsted. The critics, finding it hard to say much (as we necessarily all do) about the pure art of a painting or piece of sculpture, take refuge in expatiating at length about its "contents," and the creator's *Weltanschauung,* or perchance his secretive and malicious meanings subtly concealed and discovered only by the piercing intelligence and encyclopaedic scholarship of the operating critique. All of which has led to ignoring the plain fact that what really makes Van Gogh into a real artist is not his woefulness, nor his populism, nor even his colour, nor technique, but his *draughtsmanship*.

May 6th, I Tatti

A list of principal handicaps from which I suffer: Jewish origin, American citizenship and patriotism; being a notorious Anglophile, art historian, art "expert," "bourjoui." If I argue in favour of Jews or Americans or British, people discount what I have to say. If I oppose certain art tendencies of today, it is because my

* Alois Riegl (1858–1905), Austrian art historian.

occupations have made me blind to what is being done now. I am accused of making advantageous attributions. If I am anti-Soviet it is because I am a capitalist, etc., etc.

As a matter of fact, these though they are handicaps are not due to blind prejudice. I can see through Jews, Americans, and Englishmen and recognize their faults. Only these faults are rarely those of which they are accused. I know as well that my anti-Sovietism is not due to my economic situation but to my horror of the totalitarian. As for the accusation that I make lucrative attributions, its only shadow of justification comes from the fact that after sixty years of experience I know how a given painter can fail.

May 9th, I Tatti

I lunched yesterday with Captain and Mrs. S. in a villa scarcely a kilometer away which I had seen hundreds of times and never entered. Evidently sixteenth-century, with splendid loggias looking west and south. From either the so-familiar landscape is completely transformed, so that if the cupola of the Duomo did not tower over the one, and Ferragamo's place on the southwest side of Monte Ceceri, one would not have known where one was. Only that yesterday looking at the green meadowlike slopes, the gilt-green yet dark cypresses, the spreading cobweb of the umbrella pines, it was paradise. Almost every villa, every *contadino* cottage, offers an unexpected variation in the view, as indeed every little nook has its own climate, every bit of ground sheltered by a rock has its own flora. If man is made by the landscape he inhabits, no two Florentines should be alike.

May 12th, I Tatti

The *Nazione* brings news of Luli Torrigiani's * sudden death yesterday afternoon. She was zestfully, vibrantly alive some ten days ago on her last visit. She was some years my senior—eighty-seven—and still good to look at with sparkling sapphire eyes, and

* Luli Davis (1861–1948), American-born wife of Anglo-Florentine businessman Dearberg and, after his death, of Marchese Carlo Torrigiani, Florentine aristocrat.

77

a lithe, supple body. I told her a year or so ago how delightful and entertaining I found her. "Ah," she said, "but you do not know how amusing I could be in bed." This from a woman brought up in Cambridge, Massachusetts, a niece of James Russell Lowell. How she drifted hither and married a jolly English bounder named Dearberg, and then ended up as Marchesa Torrigiani, would be worth recounting. As Mrs. D. she entertained people like Algar Thorold, who enjoyed food, wine, cigars, and (as he used to tell her) her naughty stories, incomparable for wit and smut. She still enjoyed telling them. Amoral, heartless, fond of her playfellows while playing, but not longer.

May 13th, I Tatti

I am resigned to the idea that any little cold, any indigestion no matter how slight, any sudden faintness, may be the beginning of a quick end. But I think of what would follow as if I were there to be distressed by the confusion, the red tape, the boredom of winding up the estate till it passes to its heirs, and the intervening suspension of salaries perhaps, and all other financial arrangements. A great sympathy and pity almost comes over me with and for the survivors who will have to deal with all this. For the two or three who really have loved me and whose career it has been to serve me heart and soul, all the fuss following my death may keep them busy enough to prevent their thinking too much about me, and to help them over the loss.

May 17th, I Tatti

How much I need the stimulus of others! Yesterday evening Rosamond Lehmann * kept pumping me about Edith Wharton, and out poured floods I scarcely recognized as coming from me, and yet genuine recollection and sincere interpretation. Now I could try to recall what I spouted, and get Rosamond to help me to remember and write it down, if I had the leisure, the energy, and the determination to put aside for the time being other

* Rosamond N. Lehmann, English novelist, author of *Dusty Answer, The Ballad and the Source, The Echoing Grove.*

schemes for writing which I feel more called upon to carry out. My case is not isolated. Ugo Ojetti * used to come to be stimulated to bring out what was in him when he had to write certain articles. Yet the highest inspiration I ever got in the long, long run, was from the blank sheet of paper, if I had the patience to stare at it for weeks together.

May 19th, I Tatti

Yesterday P.M. I happened to walk from Piazza Santa Maria Novella to Via Tornabuoni by way of Via delle Belle Donne. With wide-open mouth I gazed at the buildings on both sides of the street. Some, as their towerlike shapes showed, went back to the twelfth century, while others looked as late as the seventeenth. Many are faked up to look almost contemporary, yet each betrays what a palimpsest it was, a Romanesque door or window, or only the upper part of one, a recessing, a joint exquisitely carved, a something distinctive in each house. So much of that remains in Florence, yet because I live here I almost never stop to look, regarding Florence chiefly as the place where my dentist has his office. In Siena, in Rome, in Venice, I am always sight-seeing and revel in things that Florence can parallel or surpass. Workaday life can obliterate with dust and ashes.

May 22nd, I Tatti

My step-granddaughter Barbara Strachey,† widow Halpern, recently came across erotic passages in letters written by her parents before she was born. Although converted years ago to Catholicism, she is a free spirit, and besides too grown up to be shocked. I should have been when young. Why? Instinctively we take for granted that we are not animals, and our birth not as of animals. Hence the almost universal tendency in mankind at all times to express their wishful thinking about the way we come

* Italian writer and critic (1871–1946), successor of Albertini as Director of *Corriere della Sera*; founder of the literary and art periodicals *Dedalo, Pan,* and *Pegaso*; author of *Cose Viste,* etc.
† Barbara Strachey Halpern, daughter of Ray Costelloe and Oliver Strachey, granddaughter of Mary Berenson.

79

into life, to create myths about virgin birth, immaculate conception, etc., etc., and thereby to reinforce our instinctive belief in our being not only superior to animals but quite distinct from them. Hence too the cult of chastity, of purity, and the treatment of all sexual matters in Judaism and Christianity as of the very essence, the basis and main structure of morality. The scientific recognition that we are only animals among animals is changing all that.

May 24th, I Tatti

Interlocutors with better brains do not stimulate but intimidate. Hence the mistake of hostesses' inviting celebrities and expecting to hear good talk. They are too shy of each other, too much afraid of giving themselves away. For my part it is the adolescent mind of no matter what sex or age that stimulates me and liberates me from inhibitions so that I improvise and come out with ideas and bright sayings that are a surprise to myself. If it is chiefly women that affect me so, it is not due to sex but that with rare exceptions they remain adolescent-minded through all ages. Of course there are sham-naïve women who to whip up flagging talk will jump in, as Lady Cunard,* with some preposterous question that creates a roar of laughter and starts a hullaballoo of chatter which may evolve into real talk. Give me an aspiring and admiring woman to crank me up for talk.

May 25th, I Tatti

A woman finds it much more difficult to separate sex from a career, in literature especially. Her own dreams, aspirations, romances stick out ever so much more than in a man's work. Yet when she in any career manages to get rid of sex entirely she becomes a monster of implacable activity for her supersexual or unsexual ends. You would think that wife-and-motherhood would be the ideal life for women, seeing it admits full opening for both sex and work. But in many cases (perhaps the majority)

---

* Lady Cunard (1872–1925), American born, married to Sir Bache Cunard, whom she later divorced; noted hostess.

monogamy no more suffices the more vital female than the more gifted male. She is the *trouble-fête* who can wreck not only families but whole societies in her instinctive quest for the combined satisfaction of sex and social activities.

May 28th, I Tatti

Henry Moore lunched here, still provincial in clothes and accent, but one of the most appreciative persons I ever took through the house. We looked at sculpture chiefly, and he dashed forward without prompting to what best deserved attending to. He talked understandingly about everything. Then how account for the fact that his own sculpture is so revoltingly remote from what I feel to be art? Is it due to the obstruction of the channels through which the creative spirit of the last six thousand years has worked? Why does this so sensitive, so honest-minded man produce such horrors of distortion, misformation, and abstraction? More incomprehensible still are his ardent admirers, Kenneth Clark for instance. With them it may be a still further exoticism, along with Negro and Polynesian art.

May 29th, I Tatti

From the parapet facing the ilex wood at the bottom of the garden, looking toward the house, people coming through the orangery, framed in as they came by its great arch, then descending down the steps from landing to landing, to us watching them from below offered a spectacle as theatrical, as operatic as any ever on the stage. Yet I am sure no participant was self-conscious, posing, or aware of how he was looking. The fact is that I have got to see many visual events and things as already complete works of art: landscapes, houses, distances, shrubs, trees, plants, flowers, men and women, children, all animals, and to see them in their three dimensions, and not as most in two only. And colours, every day I see more and deeper. I enjoy them almost as I do smell, with almost equal poignancy.

May 31st, I Tatti

For a week my parish church has been turned into a brilliantly lit drawing room, where the villagers were attracted to come and listen to the eloquence of a Franciscan who harangued them about their duties as Catholics, as men, as Italians. He addressed them in language of their own brew without inhibitions, and from the age of three upward they listened and had their ears filled with the rhetoric they love. Then yesterday a procession with bands, gorgeous garments, flowers, gaiety of every orderly kind, to my private chapel. All in all a work of entertainment going straight to the senses and heart of the villagers (or rather suburbanites), that Communists and similar performers cannot rival. Think of the dreary harangue in Gorky's *Foma Gordeev* whom his fellow picnickers, revolutionists like him, had to stop! No, anthropologically the Church has all the innings.

June 3rd, Bologna

On a beautiful day an Italian town is intoxicating. No matter how well I know it, it is still *herrlich wie am ersten Tag*. More impressed than ever by Nicolò dell'Arca's *Pietà* at Santa Maria della Vite with the wild disfiguring grief of the women's faces rendered aesthetically beautiful because it is so logically the flowering of the motion and vibration of their entire bodies. In San Petronio a marble grille to a chapel with putti over it coming straight from Desiderio's at Santa Croce in Florence, but halfway to Cossa. The so-called "seven churches" * too puzzlingly restored so that one's sense of historical perspective is baffled, and then all the palaces. It was before one of these, fifty-five or more years ago, that as I was gazing a small crowd gathered and one finally spoke out and asked, *"Scusi, signore, cosa guarda?"*—"Pardon, sir, what are you looking at?"!

* Group of Medieval churches and chapels in Via S. Stefano, Bologna.

June 5th, Abano

Padua, teeming with life, elegant shop windows, bookstores with latest French *nouveautés,* occasionally good-looking young women as straight as dies, curious piazzas rather oval, something not Italian about them, palaces with fine gardens, a certain awkwardness of taste after 1550. But the *Giottos* in the Arena! Surely art never achieved anything finer in execution, more jewellike in colour, nobler in composition, and deeper in conception than these interpretations of the Gospel narrative. Of course one must learn the language as one learns Latin even if one's mother tongue is a Romance language. When one has, then it is as intelligible as Raphael's, or Titian's, or Poussin's, and perhaps even more accomplished as artistry than any of them. It is puzzling, however, to link these up with the frescoes of the upper church at Assisi.

June 7th, Maser *

Little did I think when in September 1888 I came here on foot from Montebelluna, and, seeing a man walk up and down furiously with purple face and rabid look, had the courage to ask him to see Paolo Veronese's frescoes, that a day would come when I should arrive here as guest, able to enjoy these same frescoes at leisure. Yesterday afternoon at Fanzolo † I enjoyed the inferior yet delightful frescoes by Zelotti, erotic mythologies, yet in almost each room a sacred subject. Madonna and saints, Christ shown to the people, St. Jerome. To Fanzolo too I came on foot from Castelfranco nearly sixty years ago, and though a complete stranger, an insignificant youthful tourist, was taken in, allowed to look, and kept to dinner—an episode I can never forget. What memories knocking about in Italy calls up! Sixty years of vital contact with its people, its works of art, its thought, its past, its present.

* The villa of Maser was built in the sixteenth century by Palladio for the Barbaro family, and decorated with a cycle of frescoes by Paolo Veronese. Bought in 1935 by the financier Count Giuseppe Volpi for his daughter Marina (married to Count Enrico Luling), who still owns the property.
† The villa Emo (1551) at Fanzolo with frescoes by Battista Zelotti.

83

June 9th, Venice

In golden days like yesterday and the day before Venice has a glamour, a radiance, that are as unreal as a fairy world. One cannot believe it, although one lives it. Such a complete artifact, everything but site and sky man-made, and how supreme a work of art in every detail, even the sordidest. Unhappily, *le esigenze della vita moderna,* even more of a fetish in Italy than elsewhere, are little by little destroying the harmony of the whole, by putting up buildings of a height and bulk that jump out of the design, break the sky line, obstruct the views of churches and palaces. Worst of all, making the town accessible by land has deprived the traveller of the sense of something apart, sacred almost, that he felt when he had to approach it over the water.

June 12th, Venice

Turner at the Biennale, lyrical, romantic, Byronic, but always convincing and absorbing, irresistible. On the other hand Henry Moore, who rejoices boyishly in shaping and polishing surfaces in good materials—arts-and-crafts run as wild in the body of art as a canon in the human frame. Yet it never would have come to that but for the encouragement of critics and patrons without visual convictions, and yet desperately eager to get away from the boredom of their own dull way of seeing. Incapable of transfiguring their vision, they can find satisfaction only in the sensational and extravagant, as indeed is now and for similar reasons the case with the up-to-daters in all the arts.

June 15th, Venice

How account for Paul Veronese! Badile, Primaticcio, Parmigianino, Titian, all may have instructed and influenced him, but at twenty-five at the latest he achieved a serenity, a clarity, a beauty of colour, a form, a composition, nearly perfect and entirely his own. There is a gulf between him and the nearest to him, like Zelotti for instance. He is an instance, an example of sheer genius rivalling Velasquez, and like that great Spaniard springing from a modest provincial source, he from the third-rate Badile, as the other from the even humbler Pacheco. Genius can in no way be accounted for. All attempts merely deal with the circumstances that enable it to flourish, but not to be born.

June 16th, Venice

I suddenly realize that at last after more than seventy years of looking I see things as they are—what a phrase, "as they are"— and not, as in all past years, wrapped in concepts, e.g., man, woman, flowers, trees. I see them now as islands of black and white that move, or spots of colour making an herbaceous border, or a garden of flowers. As for distances, my eye now measures them with diminution of subjects, and as for vertical perspective it sees the Venice Campanile, for instance, tapering not only, but leaning as it were to right or to left. All of which means that at last I see as painters see, and if now I had the manual skill I could paint men and women, and landscape, as my best contemporaries have. Is it because I have assimilated their vision?

June 17th, Venice

Venice was built during centuries when ugliness scarcely could show its head, in architecture at least. So as one floats along the slummiest canals of today one cranes one's neck looking at palaces of splendid proportions, and beautiful detail. It was as easy to do a beautiful as an ugly thing before the machine age. Indeed, what is genuinely hand-made can be only in bad taste, or more or less alive, but never ugly. Real ugliness (from my point of view) can be achieved only by the machine, the mechanized hand, and the mind corrupted by the promises of machinery.

June 18th, Venice

Am rereading selections from Ruskin about Venetian things. An odd sensation to encounter so much genuine feeling wrapped up in such pompous Baroque phraseology. And not like Thomas Browne solemnly gorgeous enough to be a joy in itself.

85

But Ruskin's prose is not, good as it is, good enough to be independent of its contents. It is these contents which his contemporaries fancied they cared for. Now that these same contents are no longer new, the style emerges more and more as out of date and at first puts one off. That is the case with all manners that do not quite succeed in attaining real style. And yet Ruskin remains the greatest writer on art up to date.

June 19th, Venice

At Lili Volpi's yesterday, Princess Aspasia of Greece. Had not seen her again since first meeting her at Palazzo Trabia, Palermo, where Giulia Trabia hoped to get her married to one of her sons.* Lovely then, and now after twenty-two years distinguished but bony, almost scrawny, anxious-looking, and like all fallen royalty, let alone quasi-royalty in a false position, still expecting recognition, yet afraid. And what has she to expect now? A daughter married to a young king in exile! She talked very appreciatively of English behaviour during the Blitz, and yet I did not get the impression that she enjoyed living in their midst.

June 21st, Venice

I have realized here looking at steamers crowded with folk plying up and down the Grand Canal that all my life I have been looking at them conceptually and not visually. What I see is more like an herbaceous border, a crowded one, than individual human figures. Even when in gondolas, I perceive silhouettes only slightly third-dimensional that might be crooked sticks to the mere eye. I see spots of colour that I interpret as faces and darker masses that I interpret as clothes. All this at a pictural distance where tactile values do not count as they do the moment living creatures

* Lili Volpi, French-born second wife of Count Giuseppe Volpi.—Princess Aspasia of Greece, morganatic widow of King Alexander of Greece, mother-in-law of exiled King Peter of Yugoslavia.—Princess Giulia Trabia (1870–1947), born Florio; wife of Prince Pietro Lanza di Trabia (1862–1929), Sicilian aristocrats entertaining lavishly in the Palazzo Butera at Palermo.

View of Villa I Tatti. *Photo R. Papini, Firenze*

Limonaia (Plant House) and Formal Garden, I Tatti.
Photo Soprintendenza alle Gallerie di Firenze

Cypress Hedge in Formal Garden. *Photo Dimitri Kessel, Life*

Formal Garden in Winter. *Photo W. Mostyn-Owen*

Enclosed Garden and Façade of I Tatti in Winter. *Photo W. Mostyn-Owen*

Chapel, Bernard Berenson's Burial Place. *Photo Levi, Firenze*

come near enough for individual third dimension and light and shade. How many see in third dimension?

June 23rd, I Tatti

Mary used to say she had to keep me from meeting my worst enemies, because I was so completely the victim of a present sensation that if these worst enemies happened to make a pleasant impression all my prejudices would vanish, and all defense, exposing me to their hypocritical peace-feelers. And yet how often I harbour strong feelings of hostility toward individuals whose political or social conduct I violently disapprove. When I meet them personally they may appear so differently from my expectation of them that my prejudices vanish immediately, to be replaced by kindly feeling to the human being before me with his too human faults and qualities. That was the case a couple of days ago when I met a Venetian woman of whom I used to hear as a violent Fascist, Francoist, and pro-Nazi.

June 24th, I Tatti

A distinguished and good-looking young woman under thirty of Mediterranean classical type came to interview me. Her name, Zevi, excited my indiscretion, and I asked what it meant. She answered promptly that in Hebrew it means "deer" or "stag." She was a Sephardic Jewess, and had been eight years in the U.S.A., where all-prevailing anti-Semitism seems to have made a Zionist out of her. She told me that nearly every house close to Harvard University was "reserved," i.e., not to be let to Jews. When neighbours discovered that she and her husband were Jews, they made it impossible for the couple to go on living there. So this lady—I use the word deliberately—has been wrenched out of her feeling of solidarity with the Christian world, and shoved back into a ghetto which her people here in Italy have left generations ago. She now is eager to go to Palestine, to be somewhere where she can feel completely integrated. The fate of Israel at times tempts me to believe in Jehovah and His chosen people.

June 25th, I Tatti

Dressed in blue, I drove down to Palazzo Strozzi,* was received and lifted to the halls where I was introduced to a podgy, not significant-looking, youngish man, the Minister of Public Instruction. With him to a hall where the public already seated greeted us with hand-clapping. I sat right of the Minister, to his left Ragghianti, organizer of the congress of art students. He read a long report, most of it without interest to the audience, and was followed by Gonella, the Minister, who spoke less boringly but had little to say. Third, a brief talk about me by Giovanni Poggi, Superintendent of Art, and that really was to the point. More hand-clapping, and I was shoved into a room where soft drinks were meted out. There I was greeted, embraced, and hand-shaked by scores upon scores of people, some of whom I scarcely knew, others whom I had not seen in years. Strange how a festive atmosphere makes people momentarily affectionate while the rest of the time they may be indifferent or even hostile.

June 26th, I Tatti

The congratulations and celebrations for my eighty-third birthday scarcely touch me, certainly do not go to my head. Indeed, they make me wonder whether this occasion is not seized upon because great doubt is entertained whether I shall live to have another birthday. As I look back on my long career it is not praise or any form of recognition that I have craved for, but freedom from calumny and misunderstanding. These I have suffered from, like, I suppose, every other individual who lifts his head above mediocrity. My profession as authority on pictures made me peculiarly vulnerable, and wherever in the world my name meant something, the myth-makers got hold of it. Freedom

* During a Congress of Art Historians at the Palazzo Strozzi in Florence, a medal was solemnly presented to B.B. and speeches in his honour were delivered by Carlo Lodovico Ragghianti, Professor of Fine Arts at Pisa University, by the eminent jurist Guido Gonella (at that time Minister of Public Instruction), and by Giovanni Poggi (1873–1961), the distinguished scholar who for many years was Superintendent of Fine Arts for the province of Florence.

from *médisance* and not praise and celebrations or decorations or honorary degrees is what I wanted.

June 29th, I Tatti

I feel as dissipated as if I had spent night after night in a whorehouse. Since returning from Venice I have done nothing but see people, pet females, and read periodicals. No serious reading, no writing. Positively feel in need of a moral purge. If I do not read, begin the day with something remote from worka-day occupations, which engages the whole of my mind, that day is one that I live through with haunting dissatisfaction. The Greek Classics or something intellectual, which perhaps I but vaguely follow, makes me feel as if I had been to Mass and started well for the ensuing tasks. Habit, is it only that? Or does it give perspective, proportion, even well-distributed light and shade to the ensuing hours?

July 6th, I Tatti

What is the purpose of teaching the young the history of art, and what is the history of art? Assuming it is the story of man's effort to give visual interpretation and statement to his reaction toward the chaos outside himself, how is it to be taught in a way that will make the young student feel and understand each achievement on its own merit? Whence is to come the orien-tation and the standard? And are we out for teaching him *about* art or how to appreciate it? The present approach seems external even when the subject is Picasso. How is it to be done otherwise? Perhaps by Socratic method, by persuading the student to look and try to state what he finds as he looks at a given art.

July 13th, I Tatti

I envy the surplus energy of Learned Hand.* He can clown, mimic, sing like a lively and entertaining youngster, and

* Judge Learned Hand (1872–1961), noted American jurist. His friend-ship with B.B. dates from their meeting in New York in 1920–21 during B.B.'s last visit to the U.S.A.

89

is seventy-six and looks it. Free from inhibition too. How different from myself, not only held in by all sorts of snobbish habits, but by a psychophysiological economy which scarcely affords to go round and certainly has nothing left over to play with. The play element has been lacking in me, and perhaps accounts for my not being more and not having achieved more with the mind and heart nature has given me. Or are my love of talk and my philandering playful enough to be taken for play? In reality my philandering is pure play, or would be if the lady took it for that. But would I enjoy it as much if she did?

July 25th, Assisi

Touched by the humble intimacy of San Damiano, of the refectory particularly, where the tables looked as if toothless time had nevertheless worn them out from within. In church and chapels, frescoes which may have been of no mean order, but now covered with the ashes of the ages. Shall I ever see it again? How resigned I am to the idea that I may never again see places I am now visiting, and persons. All one's life through one has done the same, leaving behind what can never be recalled. One is always, always being parted, separated. Only it is so continuous, so constant that we are not aware of it, or almost as little as of the turning of the earth on its axis. Only that we who are sensitive can sometimes feel separations and partings of each moment.

July 28th, Vallombrosa

In the early nineties of the last century William James was wintering in a pension on Piazza Indipendenza. Mary and I saw him often. I used to take walks with him, and he was always rebelling against walls along these lanes shutting out the view. He was run-down and could not sleep. No pillow on which he could lie back comfortably. I remember wondering how one could be so crazy as to mind pillows. For some years past these same pillows have become a serious matter when I am away from home. To be satisfactory, that is to say to allow of sleep, I want them to support spine, shoulders, neck, and back of head, and they must be neither too hard nor too soft. If all these requirements are not forthcoming I toss about and fight with the pillows as Paul with the lions at Ephesus.

July 29th, Vallombrosa

How bored I get reading about the sources, the origins, of great works of art, whether visual or verbal. I have been perusing monographs on Bellini's *Feast of the Gods*. They try to trace back every figure to a preceding one from somewhere else, or as inspiring some later work. Endless discussion of what artist's first intention was, how he changed it, how much Titian altered it all. I dare say dwelling upon the subject gives one a humanly warm feeling about a masterpiece, and more still toward its author. I doubt, though, whether it does not lead one away from feeling it, living it, identifying oneself with it as a pure work of art, and appreciating it as such.

July 31st, Vallombrosa

Unless for unanalyzable reasons one gets fond of them, few people wear well for more than a few encounters. How often have I been enchanted with a person's presence and conversation when first meeting them; and again and again. Then suddenly something happens, a gap, a yawn, and the earth as it were falls away, and all is gone. I'd rather not see that person again. I wonder too how many times one can lie with the same woman (not as a matter of habit, as mere sex relief) and retain the feeling of glamour, of rapture, of ardour, of zest with the embrace of an unexplored source of exquisite transporting sensations!

August 1st, Vallombrosa

Woke early feeling cosy and free. Projected and saw clearly how to write three papers. One on the Sienese rustic sculptor, which will attempt to state the impression his work makes on me, and its historical parallels without attempting to account for them. The other would be *Caravaggio Today*. Besides being an estimate of his paintings from my point of view, it would be a protest against the universal assumption of today that historical interest and even importance is the same as artistic value. I want to say that a painter or sculptor or architect may have had very great influence, and yet been but an incomplete and even poor artist, and his career a disaster. The third essay I saw clearly how and what to write, would be about actual seeing and the utterly naïf and unconscious interpretation of what we see. So we really do not look but think we see, and the realist painter thinks he touches reality when he reproduces what he is convinced he is seeing. To put down what he actually is seeing would be as confusing as "nature itself," i.e., chaos. Now all art is a compromise with chaos, and the quality of a work of art results from the success of the compromise. Thus Roger van der Weyden gives figures at various distances their various sizes *but* he gives them shapes he could not identify at the extreme distance. Yet it is that granting us the illusion of being able to identify what we in actuality could not identify that is so life-enhancing and delightful.

August 4th, Vallombrosa

Valéry once told me he hated poetry including his own except at the moment of composing verse. So I wonder whether any reader gets the pleasure out of verse that its maker had while forging it. And so with epigrams. They come with a spasm of joy to the writer, and he has a moment of happiness while trimming the idea into verbal shape. The reader seldom shares the satisfaction of the writer. Not only do epigrams tire one after one has consumed a few, but in a fairly large number there are not many one reads with the flash of comprehensive penetration that made the author so happy. That is my experience with Valéry's *Choses Tues*.

August 6th, Vallombrosa

Ernst Seraphim, *Führende Deutsche in Russland*, an interesting book by a stupid Teutomaniac. Yet his story is important, telling of what people of German, generally Baltic, origin did for Russia. Indeed, if one deducts what we all know they did, there was little to tell of what they, the Russians, were left to do.

It aroused their jealousy and envy, and determination to get rid of the Germans. They, the Russian upper classes, succeeded, but this success was perhaps a chief reason for their own elimination that followed so soon. One of the most deplorable events of our time has been the destruction of the high culture built up by the Baltic gentry, even more of a loss than that of the dominion of the Anglo-Irish gentry in Ireland. Both were but the forerunners of what is happening the world over, the overwhelming of our so fragile and so hard-won culture by the natives whom we were dominating and Europeanizing, retreat of English from India and of practically all Europeans from the Near East, resurgence of native elements in Central and South America, retreat of Western influence in the East, and in Malaysia. It threatens to be parallel to the overwhelming of Hellenistic civilization by barbarians from every side. It cannot go so far and will not last so long, because our books exist in too many copies to become ever rare, and because our machinery needs brains to run it, some of which brains will stray into paths leading inevitably toward revival of culture.

August 11th, Vallombrosa

The two women nearest to me seem all of a sudden to redouble, nay to decuple their wakefulness, their solicitude, and above all their affectionate tenderness toward me as if they wanted to expend all the love they have of me during the short interval before my death. I am deeply affected by it, and it will be marvellous if it does not either evaporate or cool off if I go on living longer than they expect. On the other hand, they will be so happy to continue the present situation, precarious as it is, apart from deeply loving reasons. My death will mean the reshuffling of their house of cards—which after all any life is.

August 12th, Vallombrosa

I used to wonder when I went into Mary's room and found her lying there doing nothing, not reading, not even a light novel, I used to wonder how she could. Now I do nearly the same. I lie for half an hour at a time vacuous, empty-headed, and if any idea or thought flickers through my mind it has no more meaning

93

than the dark spots before one's eyes when one is too tired. How much I understand now in my own flesh that used to annoy me in Mary through most of the fifty years we were together, and increasingly so toward the end.

August 16th, Vallombrosa

Sforza's secretary,* a young Jew, culturally heir to all the ages, when asked by me whether he would marry a non-Jewish girl, confessed he had a feeling against it. This hold of tribalism on a person in every other respect so emancipated shocked me. I cannot understand it, for to me, the issue of a ghetto far more backward than his, Judaism has long since ceased to have any but an historical interest. Nearly, nay more than two thousand years ago the nation was merged in the religion. The religion in its turn became a machine for isolating its votaries. If the religion ceases to hold one, as it surely has done in the case of this young man, what remains to keep him from marrying a gentile? Only habit of feeling formed in preconscious years.

August 17th, Vallombrosa

A Sicilian to tea yesterday, as free from any nationalistic or tribalistic complex as Sforza himself. Spoke interestingly of the Cinis, of Volpi, and then came out with the statement that he was a nephew of Pirandello. Touching, his account of Pirandello's last minutes. How he recognized death, regretted it, dozed off, woke up and begged his children to love each other, opened his eyes again and said "Now come" and closed them forever. Made little money with his plays. Nobel Prize found him penniless. Too absorbed in his creative work to have any sense of business or how to keep the little money he made.

August 18th, Vallombrosa

Almost everybody walks with their legs, and most in their better years enjoy it. Few walk with their eyes. They are so ab-

* Vittorio Calef, for a number of years secretary to Count Carlo Sforza, the distinguished Italian statesman and leader of anti-Fascist opposition.

94

sorbed in the muscular occupation that they either have no energy, or indeed little inclination for looking and seeing. I seldom walk with friends, except German and English, and even these rarely, who seem to enjoy with their eyes. Often I stop them, drawing attention to something that delights me in a landscape. They look in a perfunctory way and go on talking almost as if I had not interrupted them. No wonder we are so unacquainted with the shape of things, and so incapable of reproducing them, if we so little enjoy looking at them.

August 20th, Vallombrosa

I get so worked up discussing her future after my death with Nicky, and think of it so much myself and with such absorbing interest, that I get to feel at times I would have it happen soon as if I were zestfully to take part in it. So difficult is it to realize that anything in which one is deeply concerned can take place without one's being its active centre. Its passive centre, its point of reference, one of course may remain for quite a while after one's demise, long after questions connected with one's last will and testament are solved. One's soul goes marching on so long as one remains alive in a living person's heart. Hence in Christian (un-Protestant) and Jewish churches, commemorations of the dead!

August 21st, Vallombrosa

Italians are supposed to be musical. Of course they have had great composers and performers, and the entire people do love a tune which they take up and sing or hum themselves. We have staying with us two women of upper classes, of culture, of ripe years—say early forties. The radio was bringing to our ears a singularly good transmission of Mozart. The women, who see each other often with ample leisure and opportunity for chatting, went on, feeling more lively because of the music but paying no attention to it, except to hum a strain or two when its liveliness penetrated their talk. Unless professional, Italians seem to listen to music seldom for its own sake, but to enjoy it as a condiment, or elsewhere as an occasion for light conversation.

95

August 26th, Vallombrosa

Only now in my eighty-fourth year do I realize in what a magical world I lived in my earlier years, till thirty at least. Horror of the animal in me, of all physiological activities, even of feeding and drinking, and of course getting relief, even sexual. It never occurred to me to think of myself as an animal, and still less of the woman I loved or wanted to love. Nor that I could satisfy lust with a woman I respected—and of course I could not conceive loving a woman I did not respect. Thus I knew desire and lust, but distinguished, separated it entirely from love which was more aesthetic, romantic, nostalgic, than in any way connected with satisfaction of animal appetites.

August 28th, Vallombrosa

Returning to what I was writing the day before yesterday, it is curious to look back to my early years and how very little I was aware of sex in the women I frequented, and how remote the thought that they could serve for sexual satisfaction or that they needed it and might want to find it in me. And this to a certain degree remained the state of my mind the greater part of my life. Only in what might be called old age have I become aware of sex and the animal in women. Is it perhaps that which makes them too on their side so aware of me and so manifestly eager for my caresses? Or is it the feeling they have that caresses between us will go no further, can have no consequences?

August 29th, Vallombrosa

Young Oxonian keen and energetic, wild with curiosity about Italian pictures, knowing the attributions, peregrinations, and changes offhand, has read no word of Morelli's * and scarcely heard of him. And then I recall what Morelli meant to me sixty years ago! Clearly only contemporaries interest. It is a miracle that I still interest a youngster starting to run or to continue the

* Giovanni Morelli (1816–91), Italian art critic, one of the pioneers in the study of Italian painting.

road I have used and extended. So much for immortality and expecting to be remembered. The only reward for work is the zest with which one does it, the happiness of having functioned in a way satisfactory to oneself. Little else counts. Praise is almost painful to receive, and so-called honour silly, for what counts is whether I can do tomorrow as well as I did yesterday.

September 1st, Vallombrosa

Everybody is an artist who enjoys his job and takes pride in making the best of it, putting his whole self into it—having what the Italians call *passione*. It matters not how humble or petty, shopkeeper or the higher occupations, from domestic servant to President of the U.S.A. or Prime Minister of England. It is the zest, the delight in his work, that something extra which he puts into it, that blesses him and those who benefit by him. Contrary to the person who enjoys his task so much that he puts payments, compensations, rewards, honours, last, the man or woman who does not enjoy his work wants to be exorbitantly paid for what he dislikes or even hates doing. So I always have found innkeepers and workmen more exorbitant in their charges the worse they had served me. The more incompetent and lazy, the more they will hold hands to heaven and cry *"Quanto ci ho lavorato,"* like my poor dear friend Donna Laura Gropallo, who without the least gift toiled and moiled to produce stage plays; not that she enjoyed the effort but that like so many writers the stage meant for her fame, success, recognition, and money.

September 3rd, Vallombrosa

From a pig a bristle, and from the chaos inside and outside ourselves the slightest good. We have no claim upon this chaos. It has not like Jehovah promised rewards as Job thought He had and therefore cried out indignantly that he, Job, had kept the contract while Jehovah failed him. There is nobody, nothing we can whimper to, and say you promised and see where you have left us. So every bristle is to the good, and once levelled to that level of expectation how much more we have received than from that same level we could expect! And the end is not yet, for we do not conceive what man may make out of the chaos that begot him and surrounds him.

September 4th, Vallombrosa

So poor Beneš * is dead. I first met him either late in 1917 or early in 1918 at the Baronne Lacaze's. She introduced him as a young Czech student who was working for the freedom of his country. I was living opposite the Trocadéro, where he came to see me, asking to be put in relation with our (U.S.A.) State Department. This, owing to Felix Frankfurter,† I was able to do. Perhaps it was his first direct approach to an Allied government. I kept seeing him off and on until after the Peace Conference in 1919, when he gave a big farewell luncheon to all and sundry who had helped him. He was quiet, modest, gentle, never seemed put out, never said anything extravagant. Robert Cecil ‡ told me that Beneš never asked for anything one had the heart to refuse. Only he came often and in the end got just what he meant to get, whereas the Italians put people's backs up by beginning with exaggerated demands. Beneš openly declared that his spiritual home was Russia, that Russian verse and prose expressed him better than any other. Perhaps he was too inclined to trust the Russians when it meant Stalin and Zhdanov, and this misplaced confidence may have hastened the end of his policy.

September 6th, Vallombrosa

Got a wire two days ago from prominent New York publisher, and asked him to come to tea yesterday. It turned out to be the wife, a slight, ex-vampish, darkish Jewess. She indignantly rebutted accusation of publishing best sellers, and said one of Gide's most talked-of books had only sold some two thousand. I teased her so much that she never came to the point. This almost

* Eduard Beneš (1884–1948), Czechoslovak statesman and patriot; President of Czechoslovakia, 1935–38; head of government-in-exile, 1939–45; President of Czechoslovakia until his death in 1948.
† Felix Frankfurter, noted jurist, professor at Harvard Law School, 1914–39, Associate Justice of the Supreme Court from 1939.
‡ Robert Arthur James Gascoyne-Cecil, fifth Marquess of Salisbury, K.G., P.C., Leader of the House of Lords since 1952.

certainly was to induce me to do something like what I refused Bompiani, namely, an anthology of the world's painting selected by Berenson, with a few epithets under each reproduction. Catch a publisher who wants *my* book. They want me to do *their* book with my name.

September 12th, Vallombrosa

Writers on art, literature, things of the spirit are always writing *sibi et amicis,* inevitably regarding themselves as the paragon, the standard, and writing for others who accept them as standard-bearers. The trouble is that it is a coterie that may impose itself on the large public for a while as Bloomsbury did twenty years ago or the "Wastelanders" later, but only for a while. When the coterie is found out as being for the happy few only, it is jeered out of favour and authority. It is replaced by another, which attracts attention to matters and standards the former sneered at or ignored. If you do not take active part in one of these conventicles, still more if you stand aside and look on at the minnows disporting, you are a back number, a dead man, a mummy!

September 14th, Vallombrosa

How lucky that desires, longings even, quiet down with the growing inability of my age to realize them. Little by little I am giving up travelling for fear of fatigue. Less and less do I think of going as far as Paris or London. Indeed, I feel more like scarcely leaving my house even to sight-see in Florence. Nor have I the spare energy to roam about in my own library or even to look through all the books and reviews I receive. One gets resigned to one's lot in a way that astonishes me, seeing how recently (after all) I still expected to roam far and wide in space and in time, through travel and reading and conning photographs. Even those now tire me.

September 15th, Vallombrosa

Sublime effect of spring clouds over vast sky line, as vast and sweeping as the grandest Patinir in Spain. Such movement of shapes and patterns melting and reshaping and colours! On

99

apple-green and indigo-black background, fiery ruby as of stained glass, and pale blue and a brown as if a varnish over gold. But I feel humiliated, exasperated at my impotence in finding words and phrases and rhythms for what I feel and see. To be so inexpressive when one perceives and enjoys so much. There is no complete joy without the ability to put it into words, or paint or music. I can do none of those things, and it makes me suffer from a kind of spiritual constipation.

September 16th, Vallombrosa

As a boy I used to revel in pushing against the northeaster as I buffeted my way over the West Boston bridge to Cambridgeport. I have retained the love of the onset and roar of the wind and particularly of the west wind. Unfortunately, I now am too old for its embrace. I walked against it yesterday and today I am laid up with a disgusting digestive chill. *Entbehren sollst du, sollst entbehren*—how hard it is to give up walking, travelling, a whole day's work. Instead, I now think first of how any and everything will tire me, and even make me ill. *Nessun maggior dolore.* . . .

September 17th, Vallombrosa

My present is devastated by the dreadful urge to write, write for print, the only occupation that I call "work." If I have not written, or successfully thought out what I want to write, I feel dissipated or worse still inferior to my idea of myself. Yet I know that at my age with no unusual constitution it is almost as absurd to expect capacity for the long hours of concentration required for writing as the virility that would make a woman with child. We who are normal resign ourselves easily to the last, with even pious and manly resignation, but not to the first. Man in the end expects more from mind than from body.

September 18th, Vallombrosa

I find it heartbreaking to read Thucydides. I feel so much that if names were changed, and certain omissions made, his story would be ours to a terrible degree. The same seeing the better so clearly and following the worse, the same outrunning of character by intelligence, although ours perhaps is more outrunning of intelligence by science. The same helplessness in face of mass folly, of individual criminality, of clique conspiracy. The same military incompetence, rashness, and cowardice. Truly for good, and even more for evil, the Greeks have supplied models for ages and ages to come. Things are bigger but scarcely better. Only more and more complicated.

September 24th, Vallombrosa

Here as elsewhere, at I Tatti, for instance, in forenoon I get to feel shut in, no matter how comfortably, how splendidly, in a great Egyptian tomb. Then I go out of doors, here particularly, and see the trees, the sky, the grass, the flowers, and instinctively I stretch up my arms and open the palms of my hands to greet and embrace the beauty I encounter. The ecstasy that overcomes me wafts me away from cares and worries and aches and pains, and for an instant, no matter how brief, I am completely above workaday life. And I take up the rest of the day with less anxiety, less fear of fatigue, of annoyance, of bores, and above all of people who write or come to ask me what they should or do know I must not in conscience do for them.

September 25th, Vallombrosa

How often do I think of demolishing a reputation and go out to curse, and like Balaam remain to bless and—better still— to explain. Thus I am so annoyed by the admiration and exaltation of Caravaggio that I thought seriously of writing to deflate him. Approaching the subject closely, I should prefer to discuss him at length, which would require a monograph and more time than I can spare to prepare and complete it. The three outstanding facts seem to be that his first and last preoccupation was with chiaroscuro, for which he was ready to sacrifice everything. Then he did not hesitate to visualize as the average person does, i.e., in workaday, commonplace fashion. Finally he was indifferent (shockingly so in his day) to dignity and spirituality in subjects requiring both.

September 27th, Vallombrosa

My century, my own, is the nineteenth. I am and remain a mid- or at best a late Victorian—not Edwardian, let alone Georgian. I try to encounter the events of the day, but my attitude toward them, no matter how sympathetic and benevolent, is a nineteenth-century one. On the other hand toward the arts I am neither sympathetic nor benevolent but without understanding and therefore contemptuous and hostile. Yet while I grant that con-ceiv-ably my feelings about events and ideals political are outmoded and I should accept those of today (in moderation), I can admit no such participation in the art of today, really of today alone.

October 6th, Vallombrosa

Maintained against Hugh Trevor-Roper that historians can continue to be read as literature only, seeing that the point of view from which history is written is changing continually as heaps of new documents keep coming up. He protested that besides literary qualities of a permanent appeal they also must have the facts, and cited the case of Hume, whose quality as literature is high, but whose documentation has become too scant. He went on to quote Gibbon, who still is read although his literary qualities are certainly no better than Hume's. I retorted that Gibbon was certainly not better informed than Hume, but wrote of a period regarding which so few new facts have appeared that there is no reason (as yet) for his being superannuated, except perhaps for a change of taste. I mean that his style of writing now rather palls on me. Even as historian Gibbon is a greater favourite with a cultured public (who of course read him as literature) than with those who take a real interest in East Christian happenings. Not that anything like the same fresh material has come to the fore for Western lands, but that our curiosities are wider and deeper than Gibbon's, who for instance scarcely ever touches economic and ethnic questions. A paucity of documents, a restriction of curiosity and interest, keep a writer going through the ages.

October 7th, Vallombrosa

Despondent about my writing. Not so much what I say—although that strikes me as not plumbing deep enough—but the way. I reread and it is like stumbling over a path paved with stones of unequal height, and bumping along somehow. Lacks in spring, in elasticity, and needless to say in elegance. What can I do about it at my age? Why do I go on expecting from myself now what I failed to achieve in earlier, more vigorous years? If only I could put down on paper what still flashes through my brain, and flashes often enough to convince me something is there worth organizing, composing, and expressing in intelligible speech!

October 13th, I Tatti

Coming down from Vallombrosa, lunch with Anreps.* Rarely away from my own table, I enjoy eating out, the change of food, of surroundings, of people. There I rested and was struck by the cosiness and friendliness of the furniture, the way it was arranged and spaced. I feel a certain lack of all that at I Tatti, where everything is more formal, more monumental, but ever so much less homelike. I have little of the interior decorator about me, and even less of the homemaker. I could, if need were, live with little but creature comforts and books and writing materials, the way that after all one does live in hotels, weeks and even months at a time.

October 14th, I Tatti

Thucydides feeds, nourishes, and satisfies me as almost no later historian. Not only because he has a keen sense not alone of fact, but what is important of significant fact, but that he sticks to it and does not use it as springboard to launch out or dive into pools of deep thought. His thinking is strictly about the

* Baroness Alda and Baron Egbert von Anrep, sister and brother-in-law of Nicky Mariano; had to abandon their Baltic home in 1918, established in Florence since 1925. Baroness Anrep was librarian at I Tatti from 1929 to 1961.

matter in hand interpreted in the light of rival, competing interest, tempered (in discussion) by what is considered decent by all Hellenes. Opposed arguments are given in the form of dialogue as clean and fitting, or rather dovetailing, as in Miss Compton-Burnett's novels. These discussions between deadly enemies are carried on as intellectually as if the contending parties were in no way concerned about the result.

October 18th, Geneva

Tea yesterday with Marie-José, young Queen of Italy in exile. One wonders what royalty today thinks about itself. Can it retain a conviction of its call (from where?) to reign, to be an elite apart, to be descendants of the gods? More likely they regard their claims as absurd, as archaic, as liquidated, and do not know what attitude to take toward the world of today. The younger males in numbers take to bourgeois careers to start with and end by making rich marriages. All disappear from the rank of pretenders, except such as the French. It would be amusing to have a heart-to-heart talk with the French pretender, and to try to understand what dope has been injected into him, not by his colleagues, but by the theologians of royalism—not a few in France.

October 25th, Zurich

Yesterday forenoon wandered through the old town of Lucerne, and was amazed to discover that its fine houses were turned away from the lake and the grand view of the mountains, but picturesquely faced each other in Medieval lanes like an Oriental suk, or magnificently across the river as in Venice the palaces on the Grand Canal. It shows that until the nineteenth century and the epoch of the Romantic tourists, town folk took no interest in scenery, did not build to enjoy it, but if they displayed magnificence it was to impress or delight others, or as an act of financial exuberance and artistic taste. All man-made for man to contemplate in a universe where man was the chief, in a sense the only, interest. Since his growing absorption in what he did not create, he began to lose his humanity, and to become more and more abstract, and more dehumanized, and a *Kulturtier*.

November 1st, I Tatti

Cannot overcome, at my advanced age and after so much experience, a certain surprise that anybody should make a profession, one's only means of earning a living, out of writing. In my innermost heart I retain the prejudice that the would-be writer should write only when convinced that he has something to say because nobody else has had the thought or the courage to say it. It is clear that not only publishers, mere men of business, reduce writing to a question of supply and demand, but authors themselves. If an author will not, he is regarded as a freak. Thus I have been urged again and again to make this or that omission, this or that change in a book, so as to make it sell better. My answer is "Then it will not be what I meant to say, but a commercial product." Or they will urge and urge that I write down, and down on my own subjects, for a wide public who could not, nor could wish to, understand what I really wanted to say. I wonder whence this feeling of mine against writing as a profession? I suspect it may go back to a Talmudic feeling against using one's higher functions for sordid ends.

November 2nd, I Tatti

The Greeks were clear-sighted and unhypocritical and on every level called a spade a spade. Thus when a Spartan no longer could pay his quota for the black broth consumed together he was dropped. Economic necessity compels us to do likewise. A friend who cannot keep up with a certain way of living falls out of affection, or becomes a case for charity, as one not of the same standing, able to reciprocate. Thus, as I already may have written down, I once was lunching at Delmonico's [in New York]. At a table nearby sat an attractive couple. I asked who they were, and my host cautiously glanced round and whispered, "They used to be awfully nice but they have lost their money." In highly civilized societies the common standard has wide and elastic boundaries, as in England. In U.S.A. much less.

November 3rd, I Tatti

The process which in babies, in children and young people is growth, is deplored in the mature and increasingly in the aged as decay. Yet it is the same energy, the same activity that propels us from the cradle to the grave. But such is our concentration on the human evaluation of the procedure, on its life-enhancing or life-diminishing emotional reaction, that we think of growth and decay as entirely different matters. In fact growth is an accelerated aging at a pace more rapid than during normal decline. Our feelings, our thoughts, our vocabulary are conditioned by the love of what in the individual encourages the illusion of increasing vitality.

November 8th, I Tatti

Fed up with reproductions whether in books or in illustrated weeklies, even the *Illustrated London News*. Partly it is that they reproduce less and less what interests me, but more than that it is that I really am fed up with every kind of reproduction including photos—excepting always those of a painter I am going to write about. Being fed up, satiety, is a curious thing. That it happens with "carnal pleasure" is easily understandable, but that it should occur likewise to mental operations! I understand brain fatigue, which does not give me headaches but backaches. Mental satiety is more mysterious—how the mind ceases to react toward certain matters, objects, or problems that have occupied it too much. Perhaps the mental is as physiological as the "carnal."

November 10th, I Tatti

I wonder what will be the effect of teaching little children that we are only animals among other animals, superior mentally no doubt, but yet made of the same elements and in the same way. We, my generation, were born to or brought up to the feeling, undeliberately, unconsciously, that we were, we humans, of an altogether different category. The animal in us was tacitly ignored, and even the study of physiology (except for special-ists) was discouraged, or bowdlerized. There was so much there that a gentleman or lady should not know. The animal in us was the devil pulling us down to hell, whereas we were heirs to the Kingdom of Heaven, and presumptive gods or angels. Did that go with instinctively aristocratic pretensions, that we were the aristocrats of nature, of the cosmos? Plebeians all now, with all other animals.

November 13th, I Tatti

Walter Lippmann * on a too, too flying visit. Just about thirty years that we first met, both bitter over the way things were preparing to go over the peace treaty with Germany. Since then he has been here a number of times, and more than once we fell out, once over Mussolini, another time over Chamberlain, against both of whom he thought I was too violent. Now I could quarrel with him over his taking far too favourable a view of the near future of Poland, and being far too much disposed to agree with France over the settlement of Central Europe. I am no longer as combative as I used to be; besides, I feel too strong a current of affection between him and me to waste time, the few hours together, over discussions that can only end in assertions.

November 23rd, I Tatti

I cannot see what reason Jews can give for continuing as communities within European communities. Persecution drives them to Palestine. By all means let them form a state, gather to it all the Jews who want to go there, and end as a Greece, or at best a Turkey. But what good can the Jews in other countries do by remaining recognizable and so consciously separated from others? I know of no mission of theirs to justify separatedness. The only possibility would be the argument that by keeping their blood pure they produce more gifted individuals. It is doubtful. Surely what gift they may be able to hand on would be as operative in the long run no matter how mixed with blood of non-Jews.

* American author and editor, columnist on national and international affairs. His friendship with B.B. dates from their meeting in Paris during the 1919 Peace Conference.

December 1st, I Tatti

Until the relatively recent attempt to laicize the ghetto, no East Central European Jew thought of Palestine as anything but the land, the home, from which he had been exiled. His greatest and deepest desire was to return there. From his point of view therefore he goes there not as an intruder but as a homecomer. The London *Spectator*-minded Anglo-Saxon is indignant with the same Jew for violently dispossessing the Arab in Palestine. But how did his Celtic, Saxon, Jute, Danish, Norse ancestors come to England? As suppliants begging to be admitted (as indeed the Jews in Palestine for decades)? They came with fire and sword, sparing no one. And how about America? What of our invasions in every part of the "New World"? Brutality, treachery, violence, assassination—no doubt the Jews are practising them nowadays against the innocent, helpless Arabs. But in history is there a people who has come to nationhood and still less to statehood without every kind of reprehensible conduct on all sides? What even of our American revolution where the individuals engaged were of the same blood and, what counts more, of the same religion and civilization? As a matter of fact the most active—no matter how inhuman, how unfair—are those who now count as heroes in the epic myths of every country. The most abhorred of the "Stern Gang" recently raging in Palestine may one day have the most magnificent status.

December 8th, I Tatti

I have observed often that Jews are seldom at ease in society, seldom take themselves as a matter of course, seldom forget that they are not quite "in" or "of." That tends to make them either too polite to the point of cringing, or too amiable, too ready to be obliging; or on the other hand to keep gloomily, sulkily aloof until their superiority is amply recognized. That makes them behave like strangers, like newcomers in their own lands, where perhaps they have been living longer than the "nations" now possessing them. There is also the self-consciously free-and-easy Jew, who bluffs it out, like Henri Bernstein * or Maurice de Rothschild.

* Henri Bernstein (1876–1953), popular French playwright.

December 11th, I Tatti

The things that embitter my old age are the intellectual Communists or "fellow travellers," the versifiers and the sculptors and architects and above all painters and "poets" up to date. Then I kick myself for caring. Why? I have had and am still having my own world. When it was in the making I was proudly delighted with being too good for all but the happy few. Now I am grieved to be of the few and not at all happy. Is it because I feel that I have been tried and thrown over, abandoned? Is that my real grievance, rather than what appears on the surface, my distress over the disruptive politics, the drivelling verse, the anti-art of most visual artifacts of the day?

December 12th, I Tatti

At tea yesterday I was trying to talk German to the Wolffs, Italian with Calef, and French and English with others.* Scarcely anyone present could speak to another who spoke his own language. The result is not only fatiguing and annoying, but distressing. For none of us could say all he wanted to say in another language, and ended by saying only what he could in the interlocutor's language. If he used his own he soon felt that the other was not grasping his full meaning. I incline to believe that even when one expresses oneself fluently and grammatically and idiomatically in another language, it is as it were changing one's own voice and natural expression of face and features.

December 13th, I Tatti

Denis Mahon's † *Studies in Seicento Art and Theory* I read as others do a novel, because it gives me so much gossip about

* Gerhard Wolff, German Consul in Florence, 1939–44. Did what was in his power to protect, warn, and help whoever was threatened with imprisonment by the Germans or the Fascists.—Vittorio Calef, see p. 94, note.
† Anglo-Irish art connoisseur, critic, and collector, chiefly of Italian seventeenth-century paintings.

people of the seventeenth century and their intellectual pursuits. Infinitely pedantic and silly, yet I enjoy closer contact with them, at least most of them, than I had previously, contact with them as human beings despite their pedantic philosophizing about the Beautiful. Some of their names were familiar enough, but I enjoyed giving them substance. Indeed, names are magnets that have the will for anything they can attract, facts, gossip, comment. That is why after all stuffing names into our memories has its uses.

December 15th, I Tatti

I wonder what gives all foliage these long-drawn autumn hues, hues of various kinds of amber, from deep purply brown to pale yellow. All remaining vegetation likewise. And the clouds —those nearer the sky line have a horizontal tendency and higher up in the sky wispy, flimsy, gay, like Chinese screen decoration. And the colour of the clouds, never in my recollection surpassed for beauty and splendour. Thus yesterday driving down from Castel di Poggio the west looked as gorgeously mysterious as the choir of a great cathedral transfigured by its epiphany of stained glass. Why all this display, what in earth and sky to account for it?

December 21st, I Tatti

Reduced to snatches of activity between hours of sleep, hours of dozing, and hours of vacuity. In short, working hours now take the minor role that hours of rest and play used to have. Of real sound sleep I enjoy an average of three and a half hours only. Yesterday at luncheon I could scarcely keep awake till the short meal was over, and afterwards I dropped off again and again, struggling to keep awake. Just now (it is 8 A.M.) I had the intention of starting an essay on Caravaggio but drowsiness overcame me and I remained in a light stupor for an hour or more. *Ach das Alter, das Alter,* as said the old Goethe.

December 22nd, I Tatti

Bittersweet—even *ein schmerzlicher Genuss*—to come across writing that expresses one's own so original, so intimate thought and feeling far better than one has managed to do. On the one hand it is a joy to discover in this ocean of turbulent nonsense in which we now try to keep our heads above water, other heads engaged in the same effort. We are momentarily less isolated, less tempted to fear that one is mad in thinking so globularly against that mass. On the other hand it means being convicted of spiritual impotence, to me an incomparably worse distress and exasperation than would be sexual impotence. My lifelong worst suffering has come from inability to express myself satisfactorily.

December 26th, I Tatti

Since many years nobody in my presence starts a conversation but leaves everything to me. To keep talk going I ask one leading question after another, hoping it will lead to easy flow of talk. If it does not, I feel that it is I who must crank it up, and I feel this even in other houses where I have no responsibility. If talk dries up it seems to be my fault and mine only. *Die Welt bezieht sich auf mich.* Another thing and more curious is that it never occurs to the young and younger people to inquire what I am thinking, what I am planning, what I am doing. I interview them, and give them the advantage of my experience, and comfort them, and encourage them. It never occurs to any of them so much as to think of doing the same for me. Is it shyness on their part, a certain awe, or the feeling that I either do not need sympathy, or am beyond profiting by it? In a sense I am glad they do not bother me. Yet it is a proof how "in the sea of life enisl'd . . . we mortal millions live alone." All the same I prefer their absence of interest to the polite society ladies (French as a rule) who ask what I am now writing with as little desire for a real answer as people who say "How are you" expect detailed accounts of your health.

December 30th, I Tatti

At lunch yesterday enjoyed myself hugely clowning because there was a chic youngish Parisian woman to draw me out to talk, to tease her, to say anything that happened to slip over my tongue to my mouth. And I was in a good vein for I had surprising command of French and memory served me in recalling persons and subjects to the fore in Parisian society and its set of intense but so flattering excitements. In short, for two hours I was or felt that I was one of them, as I never do here in any company. Compared with Parisians, Italians do not understand frivolity, verbal play that is not punning. Above all Italians do not understand teasing and being teased. They are at once rhetorical and literal.

December 31st, I Tatti

What counts in life is what takes hold of the imagination, and particularly with regard to other persons and other living things. Without it life seems all but impossible. For most people after pairing and its imaginative illusion what counts is children. They love them as projections of themselves about whose brilliant future they can dream and let their imaginations work, or as playthings to watch zestfully. Lacking offspring, they take to animals. I have known sterile couples or elderly celibates who seemed to live entirely for their dogs, their canary birds, a pet monkey, or most unexpected of all a hare. One couple of my acquaintance suffered agonies of grief for the death of their hare, and the husband of this couple was one of the most learned and most cultivated of my friends. The instinct to love some living thing seems as strong as any other of the less urgent ones. Indeed, an individual without something to cherish, to fondle, to dream about, to long for when absent, scarcely exists. Perhaps no one is so hard of heart. Yet "realists" have great followings and success when they represent humanity as heartless, brutal, cruel, malignant, and incapable of a tender feeling. Why, then? Is it possibly mere Otherness, a reaction from presentations too sugary, too incredibly altruistic, too romantically pretty, too gushing? I can think of no other explanation.

1949

January 1st, I Tatti

What do I want this year? To live for Nicky's sake, and to write. To finish the supplementary essays on which I am engaged and to start writing the book on Man and His Society as Works of Art. I think of this in my waking hours at night, and when alone in daytime. Happy thoughts come in shoals, but shall I be able to marshal them into a book? Of course I shall enjoy my friends, enjoy gulping information, enjoy nature, enjoy works of art. These, however, like poetry, are no longer a craving. I now am my own artist and see in nature what no painter can reproduce. If only I don't get too invalid, keep my head and a certain capacity for work!

January 3rd, I Tatti

Sleepless, then dozing followed by sound sleep, then dozing again, but disagreeably heavily. Tea, frictions, inhalations calm me, so that I doze pleasantly or gather strength to read or even to write. Finally comes breakfast, and coffee alone seems to do the trick to fit me for the day. But my day is short and checkered. I write, I am read to, I walk in the garden, and chat, or discuss, or gape and gaze. I then go up to my study and write till lunch. Generally there are guests, and if they stimulate me I talk, and even brilliantly, till it has turned three. Then I lie down and sleep for half or three quarters of an hour, followed by a doze as long. After which I walk again in the garden, or farther afield on the hills. Tea and talk, followed by perusal of papers, reviews, and learned journals. Dinner and talk or music until eleven. After three life is difficult.

January 4th, I Tatti

When I think of all the care it takes to keep me in condition, the trouble, the expense, the time, I cannot help shuddering at the thought of what life must be to the needy of my age, cold, ill-fed, unwashed, unattended to. On the other hand I envy older contemporaries, like Santayana and Orlando, the first now about eighty-six and the other eighty-nine. Each of them shifts for himself. About Santayana I know little, although from what I do know he cannot be receiving the endless cosseting that I enjoy. As for Orlando, he would not submit to it. I doubt whether he washes carefully, let alone frictions, inhalations, attention to nose, to gums, to throat, to ears. And he still works all day at his trade as a lawyer.

January 12th, I Tatti

Sinclair Lewis, more presentable than I expected, having heard so much about his hard drinking and slovenly ways. Tall, slender, fine blue eyes and tolerable pronunciation. Would not have it that there was much difference between novel and short story. Would not allow Edith Wharton's *Ethan Frome* was only a short story, but with the "herd" (my way of putting it) considered it her masterpiece. Greatly admired her work, and felt sure it would come back. Generous admiration of Faulkner and Robert Penn Warren. Inclined to agree with me that in the latter's *All the King's Men* the most interesting figure was the supposed teller of the story. Spoke of a visit to Faulkner, a broken-down farmstead in darkest Mississippi, a small Negress for only servant, impression of uncaring remoteness from life. Said he always thought his last book the best. Works now on a theological subject.

January 20th, I Tatti

I seem to myself like a small glass with a constantly changing liquid. The succeeding knows not what was there before. I get absorbed in a subject until it exhausts me and I it. During that time I reach rational conclusions regarding it and even good catchwords. I seldom write them down, and when I come across them in some writer who has gained authority because he has published, I am not only surprised, a bit regretful that I did not forestall him, but above all happy to be reminded of my own past preoccupation—long forgotten. So I am constantly being reminded of my own submerged conclusions, but they constitute no continuous whole that I can survey and declare, "This has been the logical me, from first to last."

January 22nd, I Tatti

A cousin in U.S.A. has had in his house a fire where disappeared a family tree. Uninterruptedly the pedigree went back fully nineteen centuries, and more sketchily all the way to Solomon. Now the historian that I am laughs at the idea of the possibility that such a backward connection can be established for a family now living even when deeply dug into the soil where it always has been living, let alone wanderers that my forebears must have been through the centuries, kicked about, getting poorer, poorer, and poorer until ending up at long last as mere immigrants at Castle Garden. Yet hearing of this claim gave me a certain satisfaction, as in another realm I feel more hopeful about the coming month if I have seen the new moon not through glass, have made three bows to her, and have turned over three times the loose cash in my pockets. I know the absurdity of it as I do over my reluctance to start anything on a Friday. Yet I remain apprehensive if I do. Also if I sit at a table as one of thirteen. Thus there remains a pull, a drag towards superstition in any and every one who was brought up as hitherto most of us have been in a magical world. I have known people who never were, and bonedry of any superstitious whimsicality, but they have something—how shall I put it—as if they were trees growing out of a ground where there was no grass, no underbrush, out of the desert in short.

January 26th, I Tatti

Cecil Anrep * has just returned from Paris, where he saw [the German industrialist] Johannes Semmler, the same who about a year ago dared to face the U.S.A. authorities and criticize their policy. He told Cecil that when our troops reached the part of Germany where he was they handed him papers for the declaration that he had not been a Nazi. The procedure then took a long time before one was cleared. He got his clean slate in a week or so, and inquired how it happened. He was told that the officer who came with the papers picked up a book of mine with a very friendly inscription to Semmler dated '41 or even '42. The U.S.A. authorities took this as proof that he never could have been a Nazi. But what luck that the officer in charge knew my name. I cannot believe many did, or realized what I stood for.

January 29th, I Tatti

I cannot help enjoying the presence of well-bred, well-groomed people, who look and act as if by inheritance and bringing up they were in the foremost ranks of culture, were in short almost completely humanized. So much so that they even have reached sterility and deserve the description of *fin de race*. I feel more at home with them no matter how many conclusions about the universe we may disagree over. Nothing on the other hand as tiresome as people with whose ideas and ideals we are in agreement while their bodily presence, their ways and voices are rough, incongruous, unharmonious. One is tempted to reconsider and to reject every thought one has in common with them, while ready to make every allowance for those who are works of art in themselves.

January 31st, I Tatti

Memory more and more tricky. I have a flash of an idea and for a second or two I see its possibilities of development and then blotted out completely so that the instant after I cannot

* Cecil von Anrep, Nicky Mariano's nephew.

remember what I was about. In talk I am about to mention a name. It is on the tip of my tongue, and instead of uttering itself it glides back into my throat like a lizard, and is not to be retrieved. Another trick is in recalling whom I saw yesterday, and harder for luncheon than for tea or dinner. Then people come whom I have enjoyed seeing, and not only their faces, but their names vanish forever. I was never good at reporting talk, no matter how good, how impressive.

February 3rd, I Tatti

What a dilettante I always have felt to be! I never thought I had anything like sufficient acquaintance with a subject to write about it. I ended up by making a dash, leaving me wondering whether other people were equally as uncertain of themselves, and whether all writing was not essentially a blind hitting out, with the frightened hope of producing something better than one's vague preparations justified. Perhaps all human knowledge is built up the same way, held together reciprocally until a wind from a foreign quarter blows it away for a time like a torn or merely lifted curtain, or for good. How can one feel sufficiently prepared to conclude about anything!

February 10th, I Tatti

Walking yesterday from Castel di Poggio to Settignano I saw over the ground above the road, oxen slowly dragging the plough between olives and grapevines. It gave me a moment of happiness. Why? The spectacle in itself was beautiful. At the same time it gave me a feeling that I was looking at what has been going on ever since civilization began, and is likely to go on for a good while yet in Mediterranean lands, where, owing to terracing, the agriculture of the great American and Russian plains would be unsuitable. To think of dragging tractors through a Tuscan terraced *podere*! Then this plowing gave me a sense of continuity as well as hopeful projection into the future, and finally there was something domestic, kindly, *à mesure de l'homme* about it, that I could easily encompass, assimilate, and make my own.

119

February 14th, I Tatti

Am I the last European, refusing to condemn any one of its peoples wholesale, the Germans particularly? "Oh yes, they have had plenty of brains, but never used them to a good purpose." Nothing less true. I grant that they are not so integrated as most Western peoples are, and therefore capable of greater extravagances. Moreover like gifted children under ten they can remain in the metaphysical age through the whole of life. But what have they not achieved in the arts, in literature, and in music, surely more than all other peoples put together. How much I owe them for their poets, their more humanistic thinkers, their great scholars. True, all this suffered eclipse under the Nazis, but terrible as that episode was, it was brief, and its aftermath will disappear in a comparatively short time, and the Germans will show their best as well as their worst.

February 22nd, I Tatti

Walter Bosshardt's * *Mongolei,* all about grasslands and pastoral life, delighted me as does any book that brings vividly before me steppes, deserts, all places where patriarchal life still can expand, where one can roam through empty space careless of city life. Why have I since boyhood loved to read about them, and why have I been so happy in empty Asia Minor and in Nubia and in the Aurès? Is it merely the change, the otherness, the newness, or is it possibly something deeper, something hereditary come down from remote ancestors some of whom roamed the Russian steppes and others the Arabian deserts? *La recherche de la paternité est—inutile.*

February 24th, I Tatti

When I glance at the *Literary Supplement* or the *Figaro Littéraire* and all their announcements, reviews, and advertisements, and ditto at Italian and American dailies, weeklies, monthlies, and quarterlies, an anticipated nausea as of surfeit seizes me,

* Swiss newspaper correspondent who spent many years in China.

always has, and gives me a momentary longing for illiteracy, for a society where few read and almost nobody writes. I cannot get over my instinctive feeling that it partakes of prostitution to write for money, worse still to make writing for gain one's profession. Besides, at the present pace the writer before long may end as the slave-scribe that he was in Pharaonic Egypt. Nay, he is that already (in a sense), writing as he does what the Pharaoh of our day, the PUBLIC, commands him.

February 26th, I Tatti

Why do I take the trouble I do to get things published, to get them translated? The profit it brings in is derisory. The satisfaction it gives is generally spoiled by annoying misprints, distasteful ways of putting a book out, foolish or malignant reviews, etc., etc. Is it vanity, habit, that impels me to seek publication? I have delved deep into myself and brought up a possible explanation. It is that, feeling far from sure of my right to exist, I want to justify my claim to be still a useful member of society, and capable in some slight measure of influencing it—in short, that I am still able to pay passage on the ship of life which is carrying us all—whither?

February 28th, I Tatti

When young, whatever one did, whatever one enjoyed, was in the nature of trees growing out of a rich underbrush, the which was hope of the future—activities, realizations, etc. At my age what trees remain grow out of a barren earth, with no underbrush, no forest tangle promising a beyond, a future, an adventure. That is perhaps the greatest difference between youth and crabbed age. Or to change the simile, youth is a music played with a ground bass of expectation and palpitating eagerness for the coming events. Age has little to look forward to, at most to getting no feebler, no less incapacitated for work and play, for work that is play—at least. For it cannot profit.

March 6th, I Tatti

Dreamt that I was arrested in a crowded public place for being a nuisance in following women. I took it as a joke, and the police was friendly. Sat down together for a cocktail, and was being joined by acquaintances when I woke up. The Freudian interpretation would be simple—a common and ordinary sexual ferment. But why this particular incident? I have been little of a dreamer since early manhood. When first in Italy I used to dream of Giorgiones and Correggios more beautiful than any that could be seen. As a boy of ten in Boston for a year almost I passed every night in my Lithuanian home, living there a full and splendid life. I was not unhappy as a young immigrant in Boston, I was full of eager curiosity and enjoyed discovering America and adopting its language and its ways. The dream-life must have had other causes than nostalgia, dissatisfaction, let alone unhappiness.

March 14th, I Tatti

To dine, a Hindu who impressed me as a gentleman and as a person who tried to be sincere. He was an extreme nationalist but not in a political, only in a cultural, sense. For him the Europeanized Hindus are all on a false track, having abandoned their own civilization, based as it is on purely metaphysical premises. All other considerations counted little with him, and clearly he had not thought out the problem of India's relation to England. He uttered Hindu grievances without conviction, and in a rather abstract fashion, and in almost every concrete case had nothing but praise for the English. They are now liked as never before, and their departure was marvellously staged. English probity, English reliability, English sense of responsibility are beyond praise and lacking in Hindus; consequently Hindu government already deteriorating.

March 22nd, I Tatti

Neue Liebe, neues Leben—short of love, a new acquaintance can give one a renewed zest for life. A woman oftener than a man, a youth oftener than a greybeard, a greybeard oftener than a middle-aged male. They must have (for me at least) a desire to enjoy me, to draw me out, to be eager for my words. When they are I become more than my average self. I become more creative, more penetrating, happier in spontaneous epithet and phrase, in short more alive. And in this condition I can feel a gush of affection for the person who does all this for me, and in the case of a woman an unavoidable sexual element creeps in which in the earliest stage has a dawnlike freshness, by itself inspiring. But there must not be a practice of looking out for such acquaintances.

March 26th, I Tatti

While reading I am envious of every word, every phrase, every epithet that I should not have used, and in rapture over an idea that had not occurred to me but that I seize at once. All make me feel so circumscribed, so incompetent in expression, so shallow or unpenetrating in thought. When I read the Ancients, or the later truly great, it does not occur to me to compare myself with them, and their superiority is like great, great wings which carry me on and on—forward. I try to discover why others who do not seem more intelligent than I am are so effective where I am not. Is it my indolence, my lack of gift as a writer, my impulsive tactlessness, my want of technique in all things?

March 28th, I Tatti

A day. Woke feeling my world was coming to a miserable end. This passed away with tea and various bodily attentions. Enjoyed coffee and toast, enjoyed writing and hearing Nicky read Hodgkin * aloud. Walk with Kiki † in garden, and delighted in air, in light, in blossoming trees, in wild flowers, anemones

* Thomas Hodgkin (1831–1913), English banker and historian, chiefly known for his *Italy and Her Invaders*.
† Baroness Kiki Ritter de Záhony, born Fénelon de Salignac, owner of Quarto, the villa near Florence where part of the library and the photographic archives of I Tatti were stored for safekeeping from 1943 to 1944. Cf. B.B.'s war diary, *Rumour and Reflection*.

123

particularly. Work again. To lunch, Montezemolo, * he sharp-featured, Etruscan nose, piercing black-brown eyes, voluble, eloquent, limited but not *boring*, and straight as a die; she massive, silent like a dark sun whose gravity is felt although its shape is unseen. A nap, followed by an invasion; Peggy Guggenheim, silly but not stupid, a good sort despite her financial freedom to do what she likes, a Mr. [Billy] Rose of New York. At first glance not attractive, but turned out to be the quintessence of sheer cleverness. According to his own account (which I dragged out of him), he was one of the clowns in chief to the sovereign city of New York, and enjoyed his job, to which he recently has added that of columnist. Dined with Kiki and she read French aloud afterwards.

March 30th, I Tatti

Raja Rao, a strict Brahmin, sees a great upsurging of spirituality in India and a growing devotion to spiritual values, and hopes for a return to the Brahmanist ideal of the church-state. I could not discuss history, politics, art, literature, philosophy with him any more than with a Sovietist, because we started from entirely different premises, his being of the clouds and mine of the earth. From him I wanted information, from me he seemed to care only for my ear. How can he believe that his dream for India could be realized in the world of today without its being devoured by the Muslim world, whether Pakistan or Afghan, not to speak of the Russian grip? And how can he hope for an administration that would avoid the errors and the sins he ascribes to the British occupiers?

April 9th, I Tatti

Visit of Georges Bonnet,† wife, and a boy of fourteen who looked charming enough to melt one's heart. Bonnet has a rather comically pleasant, friendly face, and in talk he seemed straight-

* General Alberto Cordero di Montezemolo and his wife Lilina, on friendly terms with B.B. after his visit to Tripoli in 1935.
† French politician and diplomat, Minister of Foreign Affairs (1938–39) at time of Munich conference.

forward, not too reserved and diplomatic. This is the person I have regarded as an enemy ever since Munich. Danger of judging people in the abstract for their public conduct, without knowing them personally. Of course their conduct is a test of intelligence as well as character, and while the last can perhaps be exonerated the first cannot. The fact remains that Munich was a tragically stupid affair, for which Bonnet was as responsible as Chamberlain, but the human being on acquaintance makes a kindly, frank impression.

April 12th, I Tatti

I go on wondering that I seldom hear or read of what seems to me one of the most important results of the last war. It has nullified the German effort of seven centuries to push Greco-Roman-German civilization eastward, and allowed the Slavo-Tartar faintly Byzantinized one to flow back to the Elbe. As the Germans are not likely to accept this they will lose no time in beginning to push them back. Of course Sovietization of the German masses may prevent this, but it is doubtful whether any ideological propaganda can make headway against the so easily roused feelings globally known as nationalism.

Peter the Great was the first to stem the Teutonic tide unwittingly. During the First World War a Russian told me his country needed another hundred years of German rule.

April 22nd, I Tatti

To dine, Guy de Rothschild,* slim, alert, keen, intelligent, eloquent, well balanced, [speaks] idiomatic high-class English— I should scarcely have known whether born English or French. It is true that he descends from the best branch of the family, so that his good qualities are less surprising. It does give me pleasure to see any old family continuing to produce good fruit. Not that the Rothschilds are so very old, but that they have made history as if they were centuries instead of generations old. Guy makes the impression of wanting to be a good banker, a good sportsman, a

* Present head of French branch of the Rothschild banking house, son of Baron Edouard de Rothschild.

good society man, a full-fledged citizen in short. To me there was something unusually life-enhancing about him.

April 23rd, I Tatti

Why do I prefer "upper-class" to "middle-class" people? I don't think it is snobbery on my part, nor even the fact that contact with them is easier, if for no better reason than because we are likely to have more conversational topics in common. Most probably it is that they are ever so much more apt to be enjoyable works of art in themselves, "thoroughbreds" as the saying is, and that being with them is in and by itself life-enhancing, as being with representational works of art. Yesterday to tea, several male and female Israelites from Boston, men all Harvard graduates, and yet I could only tolerate them. In themselves they were not yet works of art, but only on the way, although as mere humans worthier perhaps than many that are.

April 24th, I Tatti

The Roman Catholic Church still counts by the hundreds of millions and among its adherents there is probably as large a percentage of fervid and generous believers as ever. If ever there was the relation of cause and effect between faith and money on the one hand and art on the other, art in service of the Catholic Church should be flourishing. It still builds, it still decorates, it still wants statuary and bas-reliefs and paintings, and gets them. Yet the same Church has not produced in a hundred years a single work of art of any high order. It is all—except to a moderate extent the buildings—vapid, unplastic, boneless, *bondieuseries* of St. Sulpice, and cheap chromos. Were one to judge Catholicism by its products one could only declare "presumptive death."

April 25th, I Tatti

I ask myself why I so often suffer from frustration, an acute feeling of inferiority, of not being worth myself, and the only conclusion I come to is that I have neither the brain, the character, nor the systematic industry for being better. I should resign myself with pious humility if I did not so frequently encounter individuals ever so much abler, more efficient, far better known than I am who in talk seem to me so much less intelligent, less vigorous-minded, less clear-sighted than myself. So perhaps what I lack is not brains but ability. My brains, besides, are not good for the highly mechanized thinking of today, being more adapted to historical and ethical thinking.

April 27th, I Tatti

Walking at least once a day in the garden attentive to the processes of growth and decline in the vegetable world, I cannot help being more and more impressed by the unity of all life. "Flesh is grass" no longer seems a metaphor but a reality. Except in degree, their life is identical. We bloom and wither, as grass does. A full-blown rose is an opulent middle-aged bourgeoise. When all vegetation grows wan, loses colour, and tends to grey, it resembles aging mortals. Toward evening wisteria, rosemary, roses, in short all flowers, droop with fatigue as we do, while so proud and erect in the morning. And to an eye that knows how to see there is no growth of garden or field that lacks its individuality, its difference from every other of its own species.

April 30th, I Tatti

The people *en masse* still love royalty. Look how at Naples they crowd to have a look at the young daughter of the only great effective, no, I mean reigning king in Europe. What fascinates them? Is it not that royalty holds up a model of life above workaday contingencies, of a life above the clouds, a hope that someday everyone may realize it, and meanwhile by identification almost lives it? Royal personages appeal to the crowd perhaps as *promesses de bonheur,* the definition given by Stendhal for a work of art. Their abolition deprives the public of a source of innocent communal, pleasurable excitement, which nothing else can replace —perhaps not even military parades.

May 1st, I Tatti

Some fifty years ago I bought a terra-cotta bust of a young woman about half life size, supposed to be by Mino [da Fiesole]. It fascinated me, but from the moment I brought it home the canker of doubt began to haunt me, and one evening Herbert Horne * came and I observed him looking at it with a self-satisfied grin. So I came out and said, "I am no student of sculpture," etc., etc. I could note that he was struck dumb. Evidently he had believed that I pretended to universal connoisseurship and inspired understanding. My confession brought me nearer but on his own level, no longer the superior one he more than half believed was far above him. What if I had bluffed the way a Bode † did about the notorious Leonardo bust, would Horne have continued in unwilling yet awed admiration, and did not my value diminish in his eyes because I declared my own limitations? Be that as it may be, I could not do otherwise, because while I am a mine of faults, bluff is *not* among them.

May 5th, I Tatti

I go seldom to other houses, but when I do I enjoy them, provided they are not too splurgy and extravagantly vulgar or too slovenly. I instinctively insert myself into them, and for a moment I feel like the person who occupies these spaces hemmed in by these colours in the midst of these things, and how he uses them. For this same instant another personality is superposed on my own, the which however does not cease to follow what is happening to me. I experienced this thousands of times when I used to go out. In a vague yet more overpowering way travel used to do that and still does. I am not the same feeling self in Paris that I am in London or New York or Rome or Cairo.

---

* English architect, art connoisseur, and critic (1864–1916), for many years established in Florence. Left his fine Quattrocento palace containing his collection—now called the Museo Horne—to the city of Florence.
† Wilhelm von Bode (1845–1929), German art historian and director of royal museums, acquired for the Kaiser Friedrich Museum a bust of Flora supposedly by Leonardo, which proved to be a fake.

May 8th, I Tatti

Barbara Ward,* slim, girlish, well made, with an oval, rather pointed and longish face, shining brown eyes, and brownish-auburn hair. No touch of self-importance. Easy, gay, we hooked on almost instantly and for an hour and a half strolled in the garden, exploring each other, more antiphonally than inquiringly. She was not looking and smelling as I did. Outer world not so attractive to her as to me. Sexually aware and vibrant, but discreet and under control. Brought up a Catholic and therefore without the convert's cantankerousness. Middle-class family, no antecedents. What a miracle of intelligence, scholarship, and gift of expression she is! What a sport in the biological sense. And so sweetly reasonable with me, but after lunch when Burnham † plied her with sceptical questions about the British government she warmed to pepperiness, and betrayed a capacity for fanaticism. How will she age, and what awaits her who already has achieved so much?

May 11th, I Tatti

Cold, almost icy, a cross wind torments the twigs of the stone pines. My peasants say this nip of frost is bad for the crops, after the long drought. Nature takes its course as if there were no life on the planet, let alone human life. Man inserts his activities into the moments, happily not too few, when nature is favourable. The same with our bodies, which ignore our souls, and go on their way from conception to extinction, regardless of mind and character. We can't do much to make our bodies behave, but they can punish us severely if we rebel, and try to make them work harder or quicker than they choose. Our bodies ignore us almost as much as "nature" does.

* Barbara Ward Jackson, English economist and sociologist, married to Sir Robert Jackson; member of the staff of *The Economist,* author of numerous works on economics and international politics, lecturer on economics at Radcliffe College.
† James Burnham, American economist and sociologist, author of *The Managerial Revolution,* etc.

May 12th, I Tatti

Talk about art and literature as abstract subjects now bores me so that I cannot read anything concerning them. I still am ready to peruse a detailed study of a concrete instance if it promises to be informing and illuminating, although even then I deplore time spent on such reading. It is too apt to take one away from the text, the representation, the musical composition, which one cannot know too well. Every time I read or see, I find something new by myself, which perhaps no interpreter has communicated. I deplore the "machine-age" mentality which urges one to inquire instead of enjoying almost passively and being fed by that enjoyment. Far, far too much writing *about* books and pictures.

May 18th, I Tatti

Catalogue of Kansas City Museum. A selection of fine specimens in every field of great visual art. For whom? How many citizens of Kansas City have the instinct, the training, the leisure even to profit by them, to be fed, to be inspired, to be fecundated by the sight of such masterpieces? Yet if one in a generation can profit by frequenting them, the effort availeth. The gifted everywhere are as few as the just at Sodom, but few as they are it is for them that civilization exists and has value, apart from the joys and sorrows of merely animal life as lived by the rest of us.

May 21st, I Tatti

An American professor of Sicilian origin with a Franco-American wife, angels both, brought a number of Smith College girls to see the house and its Klingsor. Several of them were of Italian parentage, and I was happy to be made aware that the children of Italian immigrants were attaining gentility by going to college. One of the other girls looked like a bright little Jewess, but declared herself a Lebanese. She certainly would be taken for a Jewess everywhere. What a mixture in the Lebanon. Have seen women there as fair and milky-complexioned as Russians, others auburn-haired and magnificent as great French ladies, and still others with Hittite noses, like the "tower that looks toward Damascus." All held together at top by common catchwords, but below do not different ancestral traits ferment and struggle to assert their individuality?

May 24th, I Tatti

Loria * finished reading my *Sketch for a Self-Portrait* in his Italian version. I had thought little or nothing of it hitherto, but as he read it aloud it made a good impression, and there were passages that really struck me. Was it the fact of hearing it in another language objectivated it, and made it seem more like another writer's work, and that I really have formed it so much better than I expected, or is it possible that Italian as a language lent itself better to my *forma mentis* in this particular case, and even to my *forma scribendi?* Yet I wonder how Italians will take it, whether the subject matter itself will not estrange them, and make them ask why I presented it to them. All capable of following could read it in English.

May 25th, I Tatti

Countess Serristori is one of the very few intelligent humans of my acquaintance. Nevertheless she is so encased in prejudices based on being a Spaniard by birth and of the stick-to-your-wealth class, that it is clearly impossible for her to look straight at what is going on in the world. She gives seventeenth-century explanations for everything in the twentieth century as Sovietists give theirs, and is as impenetrable and impermeable to political ideas as they. Conclusion, that we will our world as it is willed for us by our conditioning, after which we use our so-called intelligence to defend it, and to attack others. Or, as in the case of the Serristori, to good-natured resignation and making the best of things. In talk I never can approach certain subjects with her.

* Arturo Loria (1900–57), Italian man of letters, poet, essayist, stylist, and brilliant talker. From 1931 one of the intimates of the Tatti circle.

June 3rd, Milan

How much mood governs us. To enjoy works of art we must be in a state of grace. Otherwise we only appraise them as an auctioneer might. That was my case yesterday, at both Ambrosiana and Castello [Sforzesco]. There were pictures I have adored, worshipped, and written about lovingly. Now "we did not speak as we passed by." I confess leisure and light are responsible for much. If I had had time to give and light to do them justice, I might have enjoyed them, but both were lacking, and besides I was with people who either wanted information or were hurrying through because pictures never spoke or rather whispered solicitingly to them.

June 14th, Verona

What passion, what excitement, what enthusiasm I bestowed on the study of Veronese painting when I was young, came here repeatedly for weeks at a time, and learned to know every bit of paint crumbling on wall or peeling from panel or canvas! What small beer it seems now! Only one great painter remains, but what an artist! * As a town, however, Verona is more fascinating than ever: its endless variety of stately palaces and picturesque market places and odd corners; its fine spacious churches, its very good sculpture through the centuries, far superior to its painting, and then the quality of the air, and the gaiety of the inhabitants.

June 17th, Venice

Corpus Domini at St. Mark's. The crowd so thick that it seemed impossible there should be room for it. People standing packed everywhere, all possessed by same fervour as they chanted the appeal for something superanimal. In all languages since Babylon and Egypt it has been going on until at last it got crystallized into the Christian (preferably Roman or Orthodox) ritual. Since my adolescence I have always felt that in partaking of it I

* Pisanello must be meant.

132

was joining the countless millions who through the ages have chanted these words with a fervour that increases with the volume of sound produced communally. It is irresistible and sweeps one clean away from one's own minuscular self into an *élan vital* from which one returns refreshed and zestful.

June 18th, Venice

That man can get on without art is as foolish a thought as that he does not need religion. "Pitch it out of the window, it comes back through the door." Take art away from him, and either he becomes a dreary puritan who really tries to get on without it, or an addict of all the absurdities of the no-art of today. Man emerges as a Phidias, and unfortunately has ended as a Ford. Unless he recovers, and returns to art related to his physiological, plus mental, plus emotional functions, he will end by losing along with religion (its greatest manifestation) most if not all that distinguished man from any other animal, from the completely socialized insects. He will have like them eliminated all that is not necessary for mere survival even if that is to be on a level of greater comfort than yet attained.

June 20th, Venice

The older I get, the more easily do I succumb, do I melt, to Catholic ritual. No matter how bawled, the Gregorian chants, the mutterings of the congregation, the scanned heroic *récitatif* of Gospel and Epistle, even the overpowering tremolo of the organ, subdue me to a state of happy continuance that nothing else does. The nearest approach is the sound of folk music at a distance.

June 23rd, Venice

As the stream of consciousness never ceases to flow except during sleep (but only partially) it is natural that longing, dreaming, wishful thinking, desire, yearning should go on and on uninterruptedly and leave an ever so much greater wake than the object attained. This is relatively momentary. We look forward to

133

it, and look back to it, but the stream carries us on, and the recollection of the desire realized remains with us while its realization grows dimmer and dimmer. So the past tends to dissolve itself into memories of looking backward toward what one had been looking forward to. And the present all but ceases to be. At my age it is swept away from one almost before it is recognized.

June 24th, Venice

Wandering about following the stream of people, looking to right and left at stately palaces and picturesque rookeries, is one of the most satisfactory ways of spending time (not wasting it) known to me. Then dropping into a church, a confraternity, exploring alleys ending in cloisters or gypsy dens. Or you stumble into San Giorgio degli Schiavoni and find yourself in the midst of the Carpaccios glowing on the walls, and I wish we had a word like the old French *chante-fable* for these so lyrical, so pictorial narratives. What effects with rather sharp, knife-edge lines, and flat colour. Landscape effects worthy of Vermeer!

June 26th, Venice

My eighty-fourth birthday. Should be feeling solemn, but there is little solemnity in me and that little never about myself. The past year has brought decided diminution of energy. I get tired more and more quickly. I have to forget walks of more than forty minutes at the utmost. Forty minutes is the limit of profitable concentration whether on active reading, writing, or enjoyment of conversation. I have to lie up more hours of the day, long rest after luncheon and again before dinner. My real day ends after luncheon; for the rest of the day I feel too tired, too aching, too sleep-oozing to feel comfortably awake. It takes an effort to behave as if I were.

June 30th, Asolo

Communication between persons difficult not only because of the inadequacy of language and our incompetence in using it, but even more because of the lack of faith in the sincerity of others.

In Italy in particular, nobody listens to what you are saying, but to what he imagines you think. So an Italian will persist in acting out his idea of what you are thinking, no matter how much you try to persuade him of the contrary. Misunderstandings follow, and when at last, long last, he must conclude that you really meant what you said, he accuses you of having misled him and henceforward regards you as a bad character—by which he means not only "bad" but obdurate and obstinate.

At Possagno the Doric patio and the dome of the Canova mausoleum command one of the most idyllic views anywhere in Europe, made more enjoyable by being seen through interstices of sturdy columns. From a distance it turns the landscape into a Poussin. What realization of a Classical-minded dream, and how effective it still is, with its esplanade and impressive mass, not to speak of the Pantheonlike inside. All the more delightful as it is little visited, and there are none of the petty vendors and greedy guides to disturb one's moments of self-identification with the vision, and of imaginative sympathy with the genius whose dream is here realized.

July 3rd, Milan

One first travels brimming over with wonder and joy to find out what to see. One returns to look and see what is considered worth study. One comes back to try to understand what one has seen. Finally one comes yet again, but this time to enjoy, pure joy, pure ecstasy. That has been the case with me the last five weeks revisiting (perhaps for the last time) the cities and towns of North Italy. Venice was pure ecstasy. I lived, enchanted. I felt as if I had painted it all myself. Not a nook or cranny that it did not make me happy to look at, and to caress with my eyes. And so with the countryside, particularly at Asolo and its surroundings.

July 7th, I Tatti

Although only two or at most three days that letters have not been forwarded, find a dread pile on returning. Will take hours to read, and days to answer. Many ask for "opinions" of pictures of which they enclose photos. Other mere fool letters. I lack the courage to tear them unanswered, particularly those requesting opinions. Then piles of printed matter, photos, appeals— the thought of them skims the pleasure of homecoming and almost turns it into a dread. And after all I am a very private person. What must it be like with a person in the limelight. Of course they are organized to cope with it and I am not. In fact I am not organized for anything any longer.

July 9th, I Tatti

Ideas swifter than meteors cross my mind and in a flash not only disappear but without the faintest trace in memory. It is of such frequent recurrence that it must be a characteristic of a brain in decomposition, a sort of marsh-light phosphorescence. Literally shooting stars of cerebration, some lighting dazzlingly a vast horizon. Too swift to note down between the flash and the forgetting, even if one always stood or sat like St. John as represented at Patmos, pen in hand waiting for the voice of the Holy Ghost. And may not experience like mine have been the source of the belief in divine inspiration, or of the Muses?

July 12th, I Tatti

My *Sketch for a Self-Portrait* was tossed off lightly in the hours between siesta and tea. It is having a success that nothing I hitherto have written remotely resembles. Reviews come in, all taking it seriously, sympathetically. Of course I am pleased, but nothing like so much as if I had written today a page that satisfied me today, and would be an incentive to what I was to do tomorrow. If I look back it is to sensations, to experiences, to encounters, to states of mind, never to achievements. What I have written, what I have stated, counts as nothing. What I still want to do, what I still want to write, occupies, preoccupies, absorbs my thoughts, my daydreams to the exclusion of any self-complacency with my own past.

136

July 23rd, Vallombrosa

Finished Eckermann on Goethe. He gives the human being, the man, the undress personage, the mere individual as nobody else, but at the same time the man of universal curiosities and ever fermenting creativeness. His book is scarcely inferior to Boswell's, but who would be tempted to write and say, as many now do of Johnson, that Goethe was after all a creation of Eckermann? The answer gives the measure of the difference between the nearest approach England ever had to a Goethe and the real Goethe, the great human being and the greatest German. Compared with him how intellectually limited are all his British contemporaries. The young Emerson was less provincial.

July 27th, Vallombrosa

Acute embarrassment seizes me when I appear in public not as my own mere self but as art critic, celebrity of any kind, no matter how petty. Why? It must be in part at least because I feel something ungenuine, unreal, in being taken and appreciated for what seems to me so little connected with my kernel of self, my own ownness, so to speak. It is an imposed pose, liked perhaps by individuals who feel inferior to the temporary role they are playing, like travellers who during a tour allow themselves a more expensive life than the one they have at home. And just as these strike me as vulgar, so does (I cannot help it) the individual enjoying praise, celebration beyond his real self as a person. Anyway, I feel a contradiction that annoys and bothers me.

August 3rd, Vallombrosa

Autobiography—is it a self-portrait, or is it a chronicle of one's past, a combination of the two, or what? In exasperation most autobiographers of my time have dwelt on their infancy and boyhood or youth, that is to say if they really were writing about themselves and not merely about their careers. To write my own would oblige me to tell of my encounters in a way that would be considered boring, dull, amorous, or hateful—in short not all-for-giving if not all-forgetting. Moreover, as is only too human, I recall burningly the wrongs done me, my own *gaffes,* cowardices, meannesses, and shadiness, more than I do the tenderness and sweetness, lovingness and generosity of others. Not only that, but writing about these tends to be insipid, while the first can be interesting almost without effort. These among hundreds of other reasons why I will not write my autobiography.

August 14th, Vallombrosa

History tells us about wars and conquests. Now it is trying to write about economic conditions. Wars and conquests no longer due to ambitions of Alexander and Caesar but to land-hunger, fear of labour, finance, etc. As yet (to my limited knowledge) no historian has told us not how it was, but how it felt in the "Middle Ages" to be a peasant tied to the glebe, or a small townsman enclosed in his guild. Of even the uppermost class we know little how they felt, for their poets record "wishful thinking" and not what they had to enjoy. Only the students in their Latin or macaronic lay or ribald verses tell us that then as now and probably always youth in the lump enjoys life and not only scampers and kicks and bites like young horses but sings like birds.

August 21st, Vallombrosa

Few if any moments more rapturous than those no matter how fleeting that call up sensations of earliest childhood, babyhood almost. Yesterday looking at a runnel of pure mountain water I suddenly was flooded as it were by the memory of a trough near my home through which flowed water impregnated with iron and sulphur. The memory was as vividly poignant for a second as an actuality, and it made me vibrate with the fullness of the so distant past. Was I peculiarly endowed from infancy, or are most people as receptive to and appreciative of their little universe, and then of an ever increasing one, as I have been? And is all this receptivity trampled down by workaday life and its desiccating demands? I wonder whether there are not more feelers than Philistines.

August 28th, Vallombrosa

Had no idea, I being a normal male, that homosexuality could be so ravaging. Just had a note from a most gifted middle-aged friend saying that his lover's wife has just had a child and that he, the writer, had been through HELL. Not long ago a younger and much dearer friend wrote that he had been in hell because his young lover had proved unsatisfactory, had disappointed, etc. The said youth in turn wrote that our friend had been so possessive, so brooding in the physical as well as the psychological sense, that he the youth could not breathe and occasionally had to break away. Whence all the trouble? I had realized that Lesbianism could be and most often was disastrous, but never as now that eroticism between males could be so devastating.

September 8th, Vallombrosa

There are three kinds of converts to Catholicism: the mystic, the aesthetic, and the theological. I have every sympathy with the first two and abhor the last. These are generally people (particularly if English) who transfer purely metaphysical argumentation into Catholic theology, and although they seek it out as a relief from uncertainty they carry into it the cantankerous self-assertiveness of schoolmen, and have no atom of contrition or charity in their mentality. I knew one who was so outrageously insulting to all Churchmen who did not agree with him that I asked him why he had joined the Church, and he snapped back *pour embêter le Pape*. Scarcely a Christian reason, but I fear he gave away (he was an Irishman married to a Frenchwoman) what is in the head of many converts.

September 9th, Vallombrosa

The first time I can recall a completely sleepless night. I doubt whether I dozed off at all. I had had a worrying day discussing I Tatti after my demise, but got into bed at midnight calm and relaxed, expecting to go off at once. Instead, I kept wide awake, relaxed, not agitated, without a thought of the talks of the day. I thought hard of the two books I should like to write, the one on Functioning as the Basis of Action, and the other on Man as a Work of Art. I thought of any number of things to go into the one as well as the other, but could not find a way of stringing these pearls and making a composed book out of them. Then I fell to translating Jehuda Halevi's "Lament for Zion" into English, and I sought in vain for verbal equivalents that would convey the rhythm of the quatrains, yet carry the exact sense. And so till at 6:30 Emma brought my tea.

September 11th, Vallombrosa

When I come here and for the early weeks of my stay, everything not so much outside as inside myself has a different perspective, and different lighting, a different colour, but it narrows and pales too as my stay here is nearing the end. On arrival I look forward hopefully to the work I shall have done. As the season advances to a close, I grow grey with disappointment. "Out of the day and night a joy has taken flight." I look back on the weeks that have passed, and I feel as if scarcely I had lived them. The mental landscape is so dull and dim, and yet I dread the departure, and the effort to start again, to crank up the rusty and used-up engine expected to work so much harder when in city pent. Strange how much I look forward to coming here, and how little to returning to I Tatti, although I leave here without regret.

September 13th, Vallombrosa

Habitual relations even when hostile are hard to break, and when the connection is intimate as between persons who live constantly together, particularly if in harmony and with love, separation can be almost unendurably tragic. Not so when individuals live at a distance, even a small one from each other, and have not shared daily life together. No matter how much we love relations or friends, if they have not been our daily associates, their loss even though poignant for a moment is soon quieted, and becomes a tender but consuming feeling. Not so for the survivor of those who have lived together. Their wreck is a real wound, a gash, a breaking up of a world, a tearing up of habits, which it takes long to heal, and leaves cicatrices that never disappear.

September 14th, Vallombrosa

I long ago foresaw the inevitability that the U.S.A. should take the lead of (at least) the European white man's world, but I did not expect it to happen so quickly, and over such a prostrate Europe. Shall we succeed better than the Romans in ruling it without corrupting ourselves and completing their ruin? It is very well to say that history does not repeat itself. Nevertheless human nature changes little, and perhaps scarcely at all in the last two thousand years. We are even less prepared for the task than the Roman was. To be sure we start pretty well, but how long will it last before our Senators and our Knights act as the Romans did? If we can retain the sense of responsibility and urgency that seems to possess us before corruption sets in, we may impose a *Pax Americana* that will keep the earth from becoming a desert—just yet!

September 16th, Vallombrosa

No matter how much of a cad, poseur, and swine Byron reveals himself—as he does so revoltingly the way he writes to friends about his relations with the Guiccioli (for instance)—he remains one of the most life-enhancing figures of the past, along with the other Unworthies (Napoleon let us say) about whom we cannot read enough. We are insatiable for information, and what would one not give to know more about the private life of an Alcibiades or a Caesar. The great Unworthies were, apart from strictly political or even ethical considerations, fascinating as works of art, wherefore they remain exciting, stimulating, vivifying when we read or hear about them. The real Worthies, on the other hand, garner our approval, our lip service. Hearts seldom go out to them.

September 18th, Vallombrosa

From my bed I see through the window the sunlit hillside opposite, and all the winding paths by which even ten years ago

141

I could reach the top. Now I can contemplate the view only as a landscape. I no longer can walk in it in all directions, and end up on the ridge, the sky line. And so with travel. I can recall what I have done and that while travelling I believed I only was exploring to find out what to see on my return. I have not returned, and all I retain is a memory picture which only can fade but never be strengthened by renewed experience. So life is a continuously progressive restriction until if I live much longer I am confined to my bed. And yet if free from pain, and above all from nausea, I can believe it worth living, for an infinity of ideated sensations remains in memory to be combined and recombined in charming ways.

September 20th, Vallombrosa

With two or three splendid exceptions the reviewers of my last two books * spoke more of what they knew about me as a person than of the books and what they contained. Indeed, I had the impression that some had not read them through, and few indeed had mastered their contents. Who can blame the hack reviewers? To write a proper review means reading the book at least twice. Given the poor pay of reviewers, who can expect them to give so much time to a book? Then the reviewer seldom understands his task. It should be in the first place to find out and tell what a book contains, and what the author meant to say. Then to discuss whether he has succeeded in communicating his meaning. Finally the reviewer should discuss the value of what the author meant to convey, whether it is something important, revelatory, or at least stimulating and suggestive. If not, he should say so, and warn the public against wasting time or absorbing false doctrines. Instead, the average reviewer censoriously blames the author for not having written his, the reviewer's, book, without taking serious trouble to tell what the author was after.

Mediocre books, mere reading matter, should be pilloried as such, but the journal which did so systematically would soon cease getting advertisements from publishers, and imperil its ex-

* *Aesthetics and History* and *Sketch for a Self-Portrait.*

istence. So reviewing tends to be a racket, and not even a good one, only cheap and sordid.

September 22nd, Vallombrosa

Luck and forethought and money have helped me to save the hills and valleys nearest to I Tatti from suburbanization. Yet I have always trembled for the sky line to the right with its avenue of stone pines and lower and nearer for the slope of farmland that might be sold any day and built over. Likewise further away within sight a most noble stone pine might be cut down. Wherefore I have always hankered to buy up all in sight and save it from deturpation. Will my successors care? Unlikely. Yet I ardently want the landscape looking forever as it does to me. What is my caring but a projection of my will, of my personality into a future where I shall have no hold, being entirely forgotten with perhaps a *meaningless* name surviving?

September 26th, Vallombrosa

My list of Italian painters has got to be common property to such an extent that nobody thinks of me in connection with them. Students come to my library and use my collection of photos, and not only never make the least acknowledgment for the favour, but publish my unpublished material there contained as their own discoveries. As a rule, I am happy to boast, I not only do not resent it, but am proud that so much of what I have done has entered the public domain. What I do resent is the students who, guided by my list of obscure out-of-the-way places where most likely I have not been in fifty years, go and sneer at the attributions I then made, and which I should long ago have corrected if I had seen them again. And such criticism would not be possible but for what they have learned from me. Of course I am cross with myself for such petty resentments, but my animal nature is still strong enough to come out with horns and tail, although I do all I can to humanize it. *Xalepa ta kala* *—and nothing more diffi-cult than to live up to one's standards.

* Beauty is difficult.

September 28th, Vallombrosa

At 6:30 this morning the sun was just gilding the crest of the hill opposite, and quickly it ran all the way down the slope, which shone like a golden shield. My heart leapt up at the sight, as much as it tightens at the sight of the shadows gliding (but not so swiftly) down the same hillside. Strange that ever since my fourth or at latest fifth year, the effect on me of sun and shade has always been the same. The sudden shadow affects my bowels now as it did eighty years ago; while the sun (in our climates, and except in midsummer) makes my "heart" (whatever that may be) glow with comfort and security.

September 29th, Vallombrosa

Peter Viereck * asked who and what was a Jew, and at last I think I have an answer. A Jew is the product of being cooped up in ghettos for over twelve hundred years. His conditioning from within and without, the outer pressure driving more and more to defensive extremes, the inner clutching to rites, to practices, to values making for union and for safety, the struggle for food and survival, the lust for pre-eminence and power: all have ended in producing the Jew, regardless of what racial elements originally constituted him. The Semitic element is, however, seldom quite absent, although not necessarily of strictly Jewish but also of Syrian, Phoenician, Arab origin.

September 30th, Vallombrosa

Annoyed with myself, but amused at human nature, that I resent my ideas, my conclusions, my discoveries being ignored, whether maliciously or out of ignorance, and credit for them being given to others, to others moreover who exploit or plagiarize me. For the youngs read each other only, and although still aware of

---

* American poet, essayist, and historian, professor at Mount Holyoke College, Massachusetts. His friendship with B.B. dated from the spring of 1945, when he went to Florence on the staff of the Psychological Warfare Branch.

my existence do not read me. I am annoyed because I know that my resentment is due to animal egoism. Spiritually I should rejoice that what I have done has been seminal and spread by others, as the sower scatters seed without thinking who first introduced it. At bottom it is the animal fear of being crushed that makes one so jealous in one's own interest, and so indignant at being deprived of the credit one imagines one deserves. Every time I feel this kind of resentment I get indignant with myself.

Even with our nearest and most beloved we keep piling up resentment about little things, and occasionally big things, which when we lose our temper pour out like a filthy stream from our pent-up gall. In the case of people living together these expletives are nearly forgiven although not quite forgotten, and ready lurking for another discharge. But as between less intimate, although devoted friends, it generally ends in a breach, which either is never filled up or is filled in such a fragile fashion that sooner or later it breaks down. But yet "The falling out of faithful friends, renewing is of love."

Can no longer partake in controversial talk. For one thing I can't distinguish sense in the rumble and surge of excited discussion. Then I am bored and distressed to try to follow arguments that are launched to squash rather than to illumine, uttered for the sake of getting the last word, and inspired if not by the puerile desire to come out victorious, more by first principles, by general attitude toward life, than by the specific subject of the dispute. I sit silent, seeing the good points on each side, but aware that my intervening would contribute more heat than light. So that I abstain.

October 5th, Rome, Villa Aurelia

If only I felt leisurely and spacious, as if I were going to spend six months here instead of forty-eight hours—if only, how I should enjoy these golden days of summer tempered by the faintest touch of autumn! How radiant it all looks, how magnificent, how sumptuous. In the Vatican galleries the living faces of tourists excited me so much that I could scarcely look at my so dear sticks and stones. What a variety! After eliminating the dull, the vulgar, there remain Northern visages, English, American,

Scandinavian, so wistful, such palimpsests of writing to me intelligible, yet not intelligible enough, so that I longed to speak to each of them and to find out all they have lived, and what they still yearned for or wanted. The impulse is so strong that I had to restrain myself, in order to look at the objects exhibited. How interest in human individuals has grown on me, me who cared so little and felt so little when young.

October 8th, Naples

Called on Croce.* Had been in his study some time before he arrived. Appeared and looked so congested and flushed that only when he took his hat off did I fully recognize him. Struck by his small, pretty hands. Nicky made what talk there was. I can only get monosyllabic words out of him, but he never has asked me what *I* felt, what I thought. He is even more uninterested in my approach to things than I to his, with this difference—that I enjoy his stories, and greatly admire him as biographer, e.g., of Tanucci, of Caracciolo, and occasionally as literary critic, e.g., in his interpretation of Robert Burns' "Mousie." Truly, "in the sea of [thought] enisl'd . . . we mortal millions live alone," God's little way of preventing our growth.

October 12th, Torre del Greco

With Maiuri † at Pompeii, startled by several tufa capitals that I easily could have mistaken for Gandhara work. Such was the expansive power of Hellenistic art that as far away as present Afghanistan art was produced that resembles closely what was done so near to Greece itself and in a town perhaps largely Greek, or at least under overwhelmingly strong Greek influence. A

* Benedetto Croce (1866–1952), famous Neapolitan humanist, philosopher, and historian. Founder and editor of *La Critica,* he profoundly influenced the Italian and European thought of his time. Met B.B. in 1926 through Nicky Mariano, whose father, Raffaele Mariano (1840–1912), had been a friend of his in the early part of his career.
† Amedeo Maiuri (1886–1963), well-known Neapolitan archaeologist and writer, until recently Superintendent of Classical Art for the province of Naples.

miracle is the perception of superiority on the part of people who have not produced it themselves, yet want it the moment it is presented to their seeing eye. Surely it was the quality of Greek art that appealed directly to the non-Greeks. Who could or would have imposed it upon them!

October 13th, La Quiete,* Santa Maria La Bruna

Few days pass without my being haunted by the caricature made by Thackeray, showing in one sketch a skeletal, doddering old man, on crutches, in a second a superb royal outfit; in the third the outfit is on the senile figure. The first is labelled *"Louis,"* the second *"le Roi,"* the third in all his panoply *"Le Roi Louis."* This haunts me because I keep wondering how much that people show me in the way of respect, regard, affection is due to my outward paraphernalia, my hospitality, the legend on which people have been working for sixty years, and how much to my naked self. Does my myth, do I as a kind of work of art, count ever so much more than as a mind, than as an artist? When I compare myself to Bertie Russell, who is not seen through a mist, who has nothing but his mind and art to offer—!

October 14th, La Quiete

The mature woman needs nothing so much as someone to love and to mother. Becoming a mistress to the beloved is incidental, and undesirable if the preferred object is a younger male. If lucky she has a son or nephew, and if most fortunate these do not exploit her too greedily. Her danger is of giving all her love to a younger male who uses her as a milch cow. So far as I can recall—but I have been no great reader of fiction—the novel has not treated the subject much. Perhaps it is too unattractive material, and scarcely life-enhancing as the subject matter of all art tends to be. It could of course be made beautiful treating of the maternal devotion of younger women for much older men.

* The property, near Torre del Greco, of Clotilde Marghieri, Neapolitan brought up in Tuscany. Met B.B. through Florentine friends. Author of delightful sketches and articles.

October 16th, La Quiete

Never stayed anywhere that made me feel so much as if I still was living in the Antique. Not merely because of the neighbourhood of Pompeii and Herculaneum, but because of the life itself. Half-naked youthful fauns working in the fields carrying on their heads huge baskets of grapes, and retiring for meals and bed to lava cottages as in Antique paintings. Two thousand years ago life could not have been lived for the peasantry differently from what it is now. What is to them the *autostrada* one hundred paces away, and Naples glimmering in the sunlight! Their workaday life scarcely is touched by today's newness, and their holidays are still kept as worship and feast after the ancient pattern.

October 17th, La Quiete

Returned to Salerno, where I was stranded for a few hours on my way to Greece exactly sixty-one years ago. Gaped at the cathedral and then looked for an eating house. For hours talked with all and sundry although my Italian was strictly confined to Dante and perhaps a poem or two by Lorenzo de' Medici and Poliziano. In the end the whole company saw me off at the station toward midnight. A couple of years later an almost similar cordiality occurred between me and engineers who were building a railway (which never was finished) at Macerata. Then never again. I can find no reason for the barrier that then rose between me and the rest of the world, the average Italian particularly. What made me timid, shy, exclusive? I was not so by nature. Was it Mary who cared for nobody who had not been to Oxford or Cambridge, or for her own exact kind, and among women only for expectant mothers?

October 18th, Naples

Light and colour effects of the most delicately evanescent quality, as if to prove that objects had no colour in themselves. For the most part as if on a pure, but mat, marble surface. The sea toward evening was milky, and accounted for the Greek *gala*. This led me to ask what connection there was with Galatea, and then why Pygmalion. How did she become the statue shaped and wor-shipped by Tom Thumb? Driving in to Naples in the gloaming, the lights of the wide-flung town and its shores, on the Sorrento Peninsula, and on Capo Miseno were playing hide-and-seek with the invading mists. Sea and sky afford all the variety, all the change demanded by our spirit, so incapable of enjoying a sensation for more than a second.

October 21st, I Tatti

Enchanted with my garden, although so modest, confined as view, so much more sober as vegetation than what I so rapturously enjoyed at Clotilde's. There man need do nothing, can do almost nothing, for nature has already given him more than he could imagine, or ask for. In consequence he is absorbed entirely by his surroundings and the way they condition him, so that they, men I mean, cannot attempt to compete with nature, and Neapolitans have imported artists but have had few of their own, unless we count the paintings of the seventeenth century, with their ques-tionable appeal to rank as universal art. Art seems to flourish best where man is impelled to improve upon nature, and is not dis-couraged by its opulence.

October 23rd, I Tatti

The trouble if any with Walter Lippmann is that he tends to treat politics as a series of problems almost geometrical, and fails to take into sufficient account that politics consists not merely of abstract good and evil, but chiefly of the human material engaged, whether as executors or public. Ever so much that would be feasible and rational with reasonable beings is anything but possible with inertia, tropism for the immediate advantages, and impulsive greed. They play havoc with the proposals of the noblest legislators, and dispose according to their fundamental urges. In Walter Lippmann again and again I have felt an impatience with such considerations, and indignation with "the fools" who would not attend his behests.

October 27th, I Tatti

Why am I so eager for the post? I do not expect love letters, nor the news of unexpected increase of income. Reviews of my own books leave me indifferent or at most procure but a minimal satisfaction. As for news from friends, little interests me but to know that they are well, and in most cases the sight of their handwriting on the envelope satisfies me. Yet when the post delays, let alone fails, I feel impatient and if it brings few letters I am left feeling flat, although a copious delivery overburdens me. What does it mean—that I am bored, do not know what to do with leisure, am eager for the last news? None of these things. Yet it may mean that the post satisfies the need for more excitement than sedentary life offers.

November 3rd, I Tatti

Who can tell what ancestors of the last one hundred thousand years will be reborn in the child of one's loins? My dearest friend here has a grandson who enjoys at eighteen all the characteristics of a picaresque Spaniard of the seventeenth century, and is the despair of his parents. Among other prowesses he has got a girl of his own class in the family way and has to marry her. What a start in life—I hug myself for never having had children nor a wish to have them. Instinctively I have felt that I was *fin de race*.

November 4th, I Tatti

Mrs. Luce of *Life, Time,* and *Fortune* has never heard of Washington's three famous hostesses, Mrs. Robert Bliss, Mrs. Truxton Beale, and Mrs. Bacon. In London or even Paris it would not be possible for so prominent a person in the worlds of journalism and entertainment to be unaware of who were the great hostesses, not to speak of frequenting them. This division of worlds may lead to a society stratification as in Holland and Belgium, where the aristocracies have mummified themselves and the other classes remain unaware of the refinements that contact with folk who in themselves are works of art can give. The good society can come to be only where classes mix.

150

November 6th, I Tatti

With scarcely a touch of pity I say good night with no "animal faith" in waking up the following morning. I always feared I might never see again the persons I took leave of for even an hour. Now it is almost with an ironical smile that I say *au revoir, arrivederci*; ironical, because those to whom I say it scarcely can imagine how little at the moment I feel a security that I shall see them again. I dare not promise myself or others anything without the mental reserve of "assuming that I am still alive." I was peculiarly obsessed yesterday by this kind of scepticism. Saying farewell to the [Countess Hortense] Serristori, who is off to Rome for the winter, and again when Nicky said good night. Happily, I am going to see Nicky presently, and may it presage that I shall live to see Hortense again.

November 11th, I Tatti

I see people all the time, most of them mean little to me; why, then? Partly because it is difficult to put them off, partly because of a residual hanker to know varieties of men *and*—don't let me fail to confess—to be known by them, and partly because it is exciting. And like the rest of the world, I need a certain amount of excitement in the working day. And yet I go on believing I could get on without people, and be happier. I could concentrate more on "creative work," and the research and hard thinking it involves. That as I know can be exciting enough. The trouble is that such activity is fatiguing, and *now* I should be exhausted for the rest of the day after an hour or two. How to fill the rest of the time? Reading, but there is a limit to what I can enjoy reading in the course of a day. Seeing people fills out the rest.

November 17th, I Tatti

British Minister to Vatican complained of total indifference to art on part of its members. That may help to account for the deplorable fact that Church art is no longer a living thing, but a ghost of the past. The Vatican seems incapable of injecting lifeblood into it to make even the ghost speak.

151

It is an instance of a dead end that was reached centuries ago, in fact around 1700 at latest, a dead end for Christian art as complete as the end of all visual representation that has taken place in the last thirty years. Visual equivalents failed both, and the attempts at renewal of liturgical art will fail more completely than the renewal of the figure arts as a whole. They must return, but Christian iconography not. Christianity is no longer creative in the arts.

November 19th, I Tatti

Boethius,* Swedish archaeologist, whom I saw last more than twenty years ago, then young and fresh and gay, now considerably older, with huge brachycephalic head. But to me what delightful company! He knew the works of Eduard Meyer † and admired them as much as I did. His speciality is Roman topography and housing, and I share his interest in tracing the continuity of housing from Antiquity to the Middle Ages. How pleasant it is to converse with somebody who knows more than one knows, yet shares the same viewpoint! It makes talk like being carried forward on a rolling platform, instead of walking against its advance as too often is the case with people who are too ignorant, or too impenetrable to discover a common approach!

November 22nd, I Tatti

My present writing cannot refrain from harping on contemporary art and its iniquities. Yet what can I do about it? I cannot expect to stop the avalanche, the Niagara. I am sure it will pass and leave few if any traces of its having held the field. Then why vex my soul, why fume with indignation, why denounce the age? Is it mere impatience, that I cannot tolerate its triumph, its almost universal acceptance by people in the know, and to the fore? It certainly is not that I personally resent the worldly success of these perverted artists and their verbal henchmen. I feel about it all as I

* Axel Boethius, for years head of Swedish Institute in Rome; close friend of the Crown Prince, now King, of Sweden.
† German historian (1855–1930), best known for his publications on ancient history.

do about Soviet doctrine and propaganda when it attracts adherents among the so-called intellectuals in our midst.

November 25th, I Tatti

Nothing proves better how little of an isolated individual man is than his anxiety as to what will happen to his belongings and his loves after his demise. Here I worry over not having enough capital to endow this place with fellowships. Without them the institution would be half dead. I worry over not being able to leave enough to those who have dedicated themselves to my service. None of which I could do if I were an individual careless of ought but himself. Of course the *Non omnis morior* comes in and way deep down one does not believe in one's extinction but expects somehow to be present and to watch what happens to one's successors.

December 6th, I Tatti

I seldom open a book published today, let alone a periodical, without finding something that increases my feeling of having survived my world, of having been left behind, of being a tolerated ghost in a society "that knew not Joseph." I wonder what percentage of people nowadays would still recognize this quotation! If I feel so outlived while still alive, still a not unwelcome guest at the table, what an illusion it is to imagine we should feel more at home in some moment of the past. Some of us dream of living in Socratic Athens, others imagine themselves in imperial Rome or in eighteenth-century France. Everything in the people of those days would offend us and we in turn would shock and disgust them.

December 15th, I Tatti

Nicky was surprised to find our guest, a Frenchified American, established in California, sitting in the dark and reciting the Rosary. Holy Church provides occupation for us when not actively engaged. Instead of letting us stray to idle thoughts, we are commanded to recite the Rosary, or if clerics to con the Breviary. Of course owing to use and wont, we can end by doing this so automatically that concupiscent, or otherwise reprehensible, thoughts may arise. Still the utmost is done to canalize, deodorize, and purify the brain vapour graced with the name of thought, the which however is nothing but mere cerebration. The brain goes on functioning, pretty much like the intestines.

December 27th, I Tatti

Praise of my works embarrasses me, and almost never touches me. Yesterday Giovanni Colacicchi * remarked that my books were easy on first reading, but remain heavy on the mental stomach as one ruminated over them. That is praise I enjoyed, for that is what I want my books to achieve, namely, to start people meditating, thinking, pondering on the subject I touch. I say "touch" deliberately, for I seldom discuss, which is the reason no doubt why I am not discussed by the pundits, nor given serious consideration by them.

* Italian painter, since 1957 head of Academy of Fine Arts, Florence. His close friendship with B.B. dated from 1941.

154

1950

January 1st, I Tatti

If some years ago, say twenty or thirty, I had been told I should live to celebrate New Year's, 1950, I should have been sceptical enough to dismiss the promise as of no practical interest. Yet here I am, and enjoying the platinum shining sky, and its brightness with its presage of a good year, so presaged because we are physiologically so conditioned. I make no promises. I shall probably achieve nothing in the coming year but keep alive full of aches and pains, and dreads, and yet enjoying the sunshine like an Homeric Greek, and enjoying friends, and talk, and perhaps above all reading that requires no great yet some effort—and women of course. If I can begin to write on Man and His World as Works of Art, I shall rejoice.

January 2nd, I Tatti

How ignorant, how out of it, how uncouth people of the smart world make me feel with their up-to-date talk of people I have never or seldom heard of, with occupations I know nothing about, but who now constitute "society": dressmakers, shoemakers, perfumers, ballet dancers, cinema people, script writers, song writers, theatre gentry of all and every kind, etc., etc., etc. In short, all who work or are supposed to work for the super-rich, but are saved by the amount of joy they get out of their work, and by the fact that they constitute a society of their own. Indeed, they are a vast super-national family, and perhaps the only one still remaining. Their talk is of each other, full of snap and good stories, with their own learning and knowledge. In their midst I feel like an ignorant and morose bookworm.

January 5th, I Tatti

From friends to whom I have sent my *Sketch* [*for a Self-Portrait*], or who have bought it, I hear that it is being snatched out of their hands by their friends eager to read it. Why do not those go to the length of buying it? People who enjoy a book they have not bought do not realize that by borrowing it, they are diminishing its sales, to the extent perhaps of discouraging publishers from printing the author's next book. Why in all countries including the U.S.A. will people be so reluctant to buy a book, when they are so ready to spend a lot for far more ephemeral entertainment? Is it the facility of borrowing the book, while a good meal, or a theatre performance, or opera, or a concert, has to be paid for in reciprocity or kind?

January 8th, I Tatti

A white but dense fog filled the entire Val d'Arno, turning it into a landscape more of foreplan even than a Pompeian, more *estompé* than a Chinese one. Almost like a denser Seurat. Usually what I see when I look out of doors is a painting. This time it is a drawing. Close at hand the trees are exquisitely silhouetted in sharp outlines against the milkiness of the fog. Further on the cypresses loom tridimensionally but not monolithically out of the fog, more majestically than usual when seen in full colour. Fog and snow as interpretation of landscape.

January 20th, I Tatti

The present Shah's sister with her husband, one of the daintiest, most subtly lovely creatures, dark but not swarthy, delicate, every feature perfect in contour and modelling—"Oriental," a houri if ever. Husband good-looking and might be any Mediterranean, well-groomed, well-bred young man. Her English hesitating and his fluent and nearly perfect, about Persian art. Of this they knew even less than Italians did of their own when I first came here over sixty years ago. As a rule people have to become aware of themselves through others. Even we Americans had Whitman and Melville revealed to us by the English, and Central Americans are made aware of their art by North Americans and Europeans, the Chinese to some extent and the Hindus to every extent by Europeans.

January 21st, I Tatti

Shah's sister sent up photo, which at first I could not recognize as of herself. Then I realized that it was of her, but with a determined, savage look as of a tribeswoman in defence. Does she fancy herself like that? More likely the photographer posed her in that attitude. Strange how few people like their own real looks (if such there be), and how much they enjoy posing as some ideal they have in mind, generally a shoddy and smart one totally unlike their real selves. Or they know their own looks and expression so little that almost anything satisfies them. "Know thyself" is almost as difficult visually as it is psychologically. How many times I have looked and studied my own face, and yet how little I know it now. I could not tell what aspect of it was my realest self.

January 26th, I Tatti

Thinking of good stories that may be lost encourages me to narrate the following: King Milan of Serbia was losing heavily at cards while playing in Paris with a Jew. Losing patience, he threw down the cards and shouted, *"Sale Juif, veux-tu me manger vif?"* *"Sire, ma religion me le défend,"* was the answer.

Another Jew story. At a banquet given by authorities at Warsaw, the Archbishop was sitting opposite the rabbi. Hors d'oeuvres were served, and the rabbi, refusing to take ham and salted pork strips, was ironically asked by the prelate "Why?" The rabbi answered that it was forbidden by his religion. The ecclesiastic replied it was a pity, and that the rabbi did not know what he missed. When it came time to separate, the rabbi asked the priest to be remembered to his wife. The indignant prelate cried, "But don't you know that a priest can have no wife?" "What a pity," murmured the Jew. "You don't know what you miss."

February 1st, I Tatti

Mr. Berenson, Mr. B.B., even "B.B." *tout court* no longer correspond to what I feel to be the real me. With the first, which suddenly, I am sure temporarily, has become an *article de commerce,* I feel no connection whatever. Little with the second, and *au fond* not much with the last, where my most intimate women friends fancy they find me. I am not there, and a good bit more with men friends, real ones, few as they are. But with Mr. Berenson I feel no connection at all, and when he is written about or addressed directly, I scarcely realize that it is I who is meant. Yet who is the real *I,* where does he hide from ME? I know who he is not, but how and what and if at all HE is, I have never discovered although for more than seventy years I have been looking for him.

February 8th, I Tatti

Difficult to begin with young men. They come for the first time with a lump in their throat and trembling with awe to encounter the myth the old man has become. At first he may frighten them into stupid dumbness, or into flushed impudence and bluffery. If they do not meet again, they recall each other—if at all—with detestation. Let the elder be patient and ignore the first impression and elicit the confidence of the younger, and that younger may become a devoted disciple and understanding friend. They may stimulate and draw each other out, and become comrades and forget the decades of difference in age. Such a relation can be as ideal as any which humans can hope to attain, and it can be achieved.

February 11th, I Tatti

The Israelite chroniclers in the Old Testament seem to have regarded their God as the combination of those forces in the universe which made for the health and prosperity of the individual as well as of the community. That was virtue which accorded with this view, and transgression was to ignore its behests. Even apostasy comes under this category, for it would disintegrate the community, and thereby lead to the impoverishment and degradation of the individuals. "Obey my behests, and you will be happy in the land I have allotted to you." This doctrine surely is at the root of Spinoza's teaching, both metaphysically and ethically. God is all the forces of the universe that work in unison for its preservation, and Man can thrive only when he lives and works in harmony with them.

February 13th, I Tatti

Woke up feeling well. Insides quiet, warm, and cosy. No disturbing gasses under the ribs. Muscles distended. No tingling in the feet, no hardness in calves of legs. Throat clear, neither rasping nor smoky. Mouth not sour, gums not aching. Head not heavy or muzzy. In short, a harmony of all functions in tranquillity, and a feeling as if pleasant glow were caressingly warming the whole system, and as if an ichor of the gods were flowing through the veins. For a moment I felt a physiological happiness which I may have had thousands of times in childhood, and youth, but then seldom if ever with the awareness and enjoyment that I have now. And awareness is the compensation that age gives us in exchange for mere action.

February 14th, I Tatti

It is perhaps easy to understand that there is in us an instinctive feeling of awe, of something numenal, about the shedding of blood, of taboo about human life. In my own case there is exactly the same feeling about any other person's individual will. I feel deeply his right to have it, and that I must respect it, and under no circumstances break it. Every persuasion but never force.

That would have made a poor creature of me in business, and still worse in public affairs, and worse still in bringing up children or teaching and training the young. How to impose one's will without breaking that of others—there is one of the problems of social life.

February 21st, I Tatti

Defenders of the hermetic, the cryptic, the unintelligible in all the arts now in vogue, refer constantly to innumerable examples of opposition to newness in the past. But that was always against newness of vision, of feeling, of experience, of penetration. It was opposition to new acquaintance, to unaccustomed food, to outlandish ways and costumes. That is not the case now. The artist of today has no new world to reveal, no new planets to display, no promised land to guide us to. The very contrary. His hermeticism, his crypticism, is to a fabulous extent an effort to cover up his having no vision at all, or such a very commonplace one that they deliberately daub it, smear it over, or chatter and mumble and moan. They have nothing to reveal, and if you make a desperate effort to understand, there is nothing but commonplace.

February 26th, I Tatti

Katherine Dunham,* looking like an Egyptian queen, like Queen Ti, dressed in stuff that clings to her, although of a quite current cut, particoloured green checkered with red, draping rather than clothing her. Whence this sureness of colour and its creative use, positive, bold, and not negative as in most of us, that seems a birthright of the Blacks? Or is it that dark chocolate or dark bronze is a background on which all colours look well, and so encourages the inventive and courageous use of them? Be that as it may, Katherine Dunham is herself a work of art, a fanciful arabesque in all her movements and a joy to the eye in colour. I wonder whether her performance will enhance these qualities for me.

March 1st, I Tatti

So bored with my own face, which besides is not the kind I instinctively admire. I admire the completely Nordic one, and mine is a mixed grill. I can understand the joy of putting on masks as eighteenth-century people did so much. Masks, how-

* American dancer, writer, and anthropologist, creator of famous ballets based on Caribbean and South American folklore.

ever, were most employed by savages who had no looking glasses to see their faces in, and to get bored with them. They must satisfy another postulate. Women can alter, modify their faces not only with the paint but more still with *coiffure* and *hats,* and furbelows. We males enjoy no such advantages as individuals, although as a class, when all get bored with clean-shaven faces, we can take to various cuts of beards, whiskers, and moustaches. If only I looked at myself and discovered I had grown a "Grecian nose," and regular features, and a bright complexion, what would happen!

March 3rd, I Tatti

Reproached for not speaking of my struggles. In the first place my *Sketch* is not an autobiography. Am urged from all quarters to write one. Chief reason why I shall not is that I have seldom felt like struggling, or even pushing, and still less plotting and planning—as Mrs. Arthur Strong * never lost opportunities of proclaiming. Simple fact is that my curiosities made me into an expert whose services were considered indispensable at a moment when collectors wanted Italian masters and dealers were ready to pay me for giving them the security they needed. But for that accident—perhaps more unhappy than happy—I should have remained a poor and probably obscure critic, scholar, writer, but much more in harmony with what was best in me than I am now.

March 6th, I Tatti

Can't get over my surprise that many of the public-school class of English are homosexual to a degree that almost unfits them to be with women. I do not speak of the predestined ones to whom women are repulsive, but of those who would have normal relations if from puberty on their sexual impulses had not been deflected to other males. Among my acquaintance there are many

* Eugénie Sellars Strong (1860–1943), Assistant Director and Librarian of the British School of Archaeology in Rome, 1909–25; author of *Roman Sculpture,* etc.; her husband, Arthur Strong, for many years Librarian of Chatsworth and of Welbeck, did much to build up the history of the collections in both these great houses, and drew on B.B.'s knowledge and that of other famous scholars.

163

who feel attracted to women as companions, as housekeepers, as wives, in the social, cultural sense, but have no idea of how to court a woman, to make her want them sexually, with the implied promise of making her happy in bed, and satisfied when out of it. "Latin" mothers see to it that their sons hasten to learn the ways of a man with a maid.

March 11th, I Tatti

A New York doctor to examine me, sent by Lawrence Berenson.* He must be well known and trusted. He did not take the slightest interest in anything about me except the bowels. He ended by making suggestions, none new or important. Clearly the intestine was his speciality, and the rest of the body did not interest him. We asked him about blood pressure and he seemed unaware of it or, perhaps, to disbelieve in attempts to raise it. The proverbial saying that after forty years a man is his own doctor or a fool is true in my experience. I diagnose my case, and ask only for remedies, and it is amazing how little doctors have to propose, and how little good they do when I try them. Yet I am not one who believes that there is a quick cure for everything, if only one got hold of the remedy.

March 13th, I Tatti

Sixty years ago Graham Wallas † said to me, "Begin with studying the wretched condition of one single denizen of the worst slums of the East End, and multiply it by thousands and by tens of thousands, and you may end by realizing what task we have before us." That was a concrete approach. Thinking of the individual human being, you cannot help identifying yourself, to some extent at least, with him. Whereas if you think of the poor in the abstract, Jew or Pole, or whatever man in the abstract, you can act toward the mass as such with no pity and no remorse. That is one of the more decisive reasons why first instinctively and then

* Second cousin of B.B.'s, and his lawyer and financial adviser for many years; drew up his will and acted as his executor.
† English political scientist and author of *Human Nature in Politics* (1858–1932). He belonged to the circle of the Pearsall Smiths in England.

more and more rationally I have got to hate abstraction—I could reduce many faults and horrors of the time to an exaggerated cult of the abstract.

March 18th, I Tatti

The garden is strewn with anemones, dazzling white, every shade of blue, violet, purple, wine-colour, scarlet, red—whence the difference? So far as the seedman was aware the seed was the same. The soil and every other condition is the same for all of those anemones. Why then do they come out not identical in colour, but in at least ten different shades? For several decades we were intoxicated with the idea of environment, climate, and every kind of material condition as advocated most effectively by Taine. Of course all these considerations were important, but negatively. They could stop or arrest the growth and development of the individual plant or animal or group or society or nation, but whether they influence essential character remains doubtful.

March 25th, I Tatti

I love the patina on old buildings, and the way cottages both as shape and colour merge into a hillside or half hide in a valley. Man's work on the way to being recovered by nature gives me satisfaction. Can all this not react on my feelings toward institutions, turning me into a so-called "conservative"? It is not that I ignore the faults of surviving societies, but apart from questioning whether they can be greatly improved, I cling to them for their patina, for their aesthetic qualities. They come high no doubt, but they were worth having. Not only for their beauty in their own time, destined to be enjoyed by the few, but as models of what it is desirable should be shared by the many—not destroyed by the crude who cannot yet appreciate them.

March 30th, I Tatti

Weeks have become days, months weeks, years months. I wonder how much longer I should have to live before the divisions of time for me were like the spokes of a rapidly turning wheel. And what of time apart from me, not in relation to human existence? Can it be without someone for whom it is? I vaguely recall reading others, the famous philosophers, and their ideas about time and space, and how much I used to think they were far-fetched. Now I am more puzzled than ever. "Billions of light years." We may as well confess we can conceive no end as no beginning, and that what lies between is a vast something that I find it harder and harder to make sure of. With age one realizes the infinite complexity of things more and more, but not more clearly.

April 2nd, I Tatti

Katherine Dunham talked with no Negroid lisp or richness of voice, on the contrary with a cultivated accent and vocabulary, and revealed an unusually subtle but rational personality, completely free of mannerisms of any kind. She complained of many things, but most of all that New York was ruining her art (and all the arts) by insisting on mere newness. To produce it creators of a ballet had to hurry and fuss, and do anything sensational, being given no time to meditate and mature. She thought the best ideas come while daydreaming, ruminating, and not when searching as for a bull's-eye in the dark. Much else that was deeply sincere.

April 4th, I Tatti

Yesterday evening Nicky went to see Jewish actors perform in Hebrew a play about the end of the Jewish kingdom, in which Hezekiah and Jeremiah were the principal personages. Even in her account of it, the play was so moving that I found it hard to keep back my tears. Had I been present I should have had hysterics. Is it or is it not great art to put one into hysterics by means of acting that stirs up all that is most emotional, no matter on how high a plane? No longer ideated purgation, but actual purgation that upsets one emotionally as the other does physiologically, and takes even more time to recover from. Is it the business of art to go so far? And where is the limit, where the boundary between actuality and art?

April 8th, I Tatti

"Sartre's nightmares are thoroughly intelligible . . . the works which it [Sartre's method] produces lack the concreteness and the *opaque* character of poetry. . . . They are like *thoughts and not like objects.* . . . In these worlds there is *ambiguity— but not mystery.*" This with my underlinings from article in *Listener* for March 23, by Iris Murdoch.* Who is she who writes so intelligently, so penetratingly, and with such a vocabulary? This kind of thinking and writing makes me gratefully, wistfully envious, while humiliating me to myself as a skimmer and a dullard. But this Iris Murdoch—and how often in the weeklies and monthlies I read in English, in "American," I come across writing as good, and marvel at the abundance of intelligence. Yet this in neither England nor America makes an *ensemble,* a church, a synagogue, as in France.

April 12th, I Tatti

What is the matter with the talker that makes him so suspect to the average officeholder, businessman, financier, bureaucrat, and their kith and kin? If I may judge by my own experience as a talker, it is because we talk and do nothing else, nothing that the other can appreciate. As if talking were not an occupation, an art of its own, the effects of which are not easily appreciated because distant. Yet how effective it is at a distance is revealed in moments of crisis when the whole of a society is suddenly found eager for a course of action that had been almost universally opposed until talk led to it. No, the last thing to be said about talk is that it has no effect.

April 13th, I Tatti

At the end of talks with friends, talks that have gone well, I find that I have enjoyed them far beyond the value of what was discussed and concluded. I realize that the pleasure was largely animal, psychological, and not merely mental. It was the satisfac-

* Anglo-Irish novelist, author of *The Bell, The Sandcastle, A Severed Head.*

tion of physiological need and call of nature to chatter. The inter-
vention of others served to promote the flow of the chatter, and
chatter seems in all the animals to be more satisfactory in unison.
We highly educated Northerners control ourselves as we control
other bodily functions, but Latin Europeans give way to it as they
do to kissing. I have heard some of my most cultivated Italian
friends say they must "talk" or burst, and at dinner tables they
talk regardless of who listens. Even in conversation the interlocutor's talk serves only as a springboard on which they jump
as soon as possible.

April 14th, I Tatti

The older I get the more I am struck by the part chance plays
in life and events. In my own case: mere chance led to my meeting the Perrys, Isabella Gardner, Ned Warren, Professor Bôcher,
all of whom helped me financially or socially during my neediest
years.* By mere chance I met Gertrude Hitz, who introduced me
to the Costelloes in London. A flimsier chance led me, footsore I
remember, past their house where I carelessly left a visiting card.
It led soon to Mary Costelloe's falling in love with me. It became
the determining factor in the rest of my life and career, lasting
fully fifty years and more. Chance again made me meet Mrs.
Gardner at the London National Gallery, where my zest for
Italian pictures kindled her into asking me to collect for her. In-
tolerable heat, in the summer of '98 or '99, drove me to Saint-
Moritz, whence came the start of such "society" life as I have
enjoyed. There I made a chance acquaintance who casually took
me to Duveen's,† and it ended in my working with them for thirty

* Thomas S. Perry (1845–1928), American scholar and educator, and
his wife, Lilla Cabot Perry.—Isabella Stewart Gardner (1840–1924), art
collector and founder of Isabella Gardner Museum, Boston. B.B. was
largely instrumental in forming her collection.—Edward P. Warren (1860–
1928), American art amateur and collector; Classical art was his special
field.—Ferdinand Bôcher (1833–1928), Professor of French Language and
Literature at Harvard, 1870–1902.

† Joseph Duveen, later Baron Duveen of Milbank (1869–1939), English
art dealer and connoisseur. B.B. was associated with the firm of Duveen
Brothers, London and New York, as expert and adviser, from 1907 to
1937.

years. Chance again brought Nicky Mariano into my life, after Mary its most determining fact. Often I wonder what would have become of me without these two women of whom I knew nothing or next to nothing when I first met them. In neither case, moreover, was my first impression a very favourable one. And even now that I am nearly eighty-five, chance has not yet ceased its operations. It brings acquaintances never heard of before, some of whom could still play a part in my life. Then talk of "historical necessity"!

April 16th, I Tatti

Yesterday to lunch, the Notesteins,* he an almost rustically simple, elderly professor, she as great a lady, in physical aspect and carriage, and as completely natural as one could have seen in imperial or royal ranks before 1914. Yet both typical Americans of the educational or the university world. Few if any foreigners, not even English, seem to be aware of the existence of such Americans, the Americans who make up such a great part of my American world. And even in real American society there still are millions of the same kind and quality. Naturally, foreigners go to the U.S.A. not for these, and therefore cannot believe that they exist, for they have gone to see Hollywood, and sensational New York, and refuse to believe that anything else exists but what they have found as they had preconceived it.

April 21st, I Tatti

Torres Bodet, now head of Unesco, and formerly Minister of Education in Mexico, spoke of efforts to cope with illiteracy in his country. Got out of him that out of many millions who neither read nor write, four hundred thousand have learned and forgotten. This confirms as still going on what Monseigneur Montes de Oca, Bishop of Potosí, told me forty years ago, namely, that so many of his flock whom he taught reading never used it, and forgot. Conversation with Bodet continued, and touched the question of

* Wallace Notestein, Professor of English History at Yale University. His wife, Ada Comstock, was for a number of years President of Radcliffe College, and an intimate friend of B.B.'s sister, Senda Berenson Abbott (1896–1953).

what mere reading and writing did for the masses. I suggested that it exposed them to the propaganda of the agitator, whose daily paper they were obliged to buy. Bodet did not answer, but talked of the Communist hold on the masses, and of how difficult it was to discover others who would guide them better. I proposed that as lesser evil (far from a good or in itself desirable), in Catholic countries, the priest could do that more efficiently and with better purpose. "And what about China?" he broke in. In China there is Confucianism and there is Buddhism, and so in Islam the ritual if not the mullah. In short, religion is a dope if you like, but given *la condition humaine,* I doubt whether the masses (as such) will get anything better. All we can do is to improve the dope little by little, as "the people" get more humanized, if ever they do, and as I believe they will end by being—in the long run.

April 24th, I Tatti

The other day I wrote here about the part chance played in my own life. Inertia, i.e., disinclination to change, to move, indolence, apathy, have also played their part with me. Did I marry for any reason more basic than that it was so much easier to drift along than to break and flounder about in search of another woman, or to hang around till another woman came and took me? And the last supreme decision, namely, to remain here during the last war—was it not the prevision of all the effort it would be to wrench myself away from all that holds me here, my creature comforts, my library, my walks, my servants, and to take part in the hectic and marching-order thinking and talking and acting I should have found in America? I could write my own life as a study of indolence, and perhaps it would cut as deep as any other approach.

April 25th, I Tatti

Chance, pure chance, that I have attained a certain ease along with reputation. If the westward course of Empire had not involved works of art as well, and Italian pictures did not happen to be the prizes most sought for and in America there had not been floods of liquid money, and an eagerness on the part of collectors to make sure they were buying the right thing and their notion that I could give them this security, as a mere scholar I might have remained a poor man all my life. For I have no talent whatever for business, and money means only purchasing value, a desire for getting the things I want. So my having home and garden and works of art that now have become "sights" for tourists is the fruit of mere chance, of luck, and little else.

April 26th, I Tatti

I never could take up with Freud or (to talk of smaller things) with T. S. Eliot, could not tolerate the late Joyce, not to speak of Gertrude Stein, because in my own mental churning I anticipated and discarded what in me might have led to them. The stone that I threw away as not to be used, they used as cornerstone of their system. Not only a certain disapproval of their procedure, but envy of their senses, mixed with some contempt for the "highbrows," the intellectuals who made up my state of mind with regard to them. Almost impossible for me to appreciate what is good in T. S. Eliot or in Freud. Of course I realize that for good or evil Freud's influence has been real and may leave permanent traces.

April 27th, I Tatti

Interested always in distinguishing between subjective and objective in sensations. Thus when young in autumn 1888 was haunted while in Greece by a smell of incense, as now 1950 and for some time past by one of onions. For some weeks past the house when I come in from out of doors seems to be full of a light smoke and even faintly smells of it. Having remarked it to servants, they denied it. So I now begin to think it is something to do with my eyes, and that I should see an oculist at once. I shall not, because I have no time, and do not as yet feel the urgency (perhaps because I do not want to know the worst)—I seem to have time for nothing but resting from doing next to nothing. I breathe heavily like a spavined horse drawing a heavy load uphill, and this after a very short talk or any concentration of effort. I do not make a business of studying my senescence, but in sleepless hours of the night it comes over me.

171

May 6th, I Tatti

The elegant and stately public privies one finds at Timgad and elsewhere must have served the lords only of the "Roman" municipalities. ("Public privies," by the way, what a juxtaposition of words!) Were houses of public worship also confined to the patriciate? The public shows (the circuses) certainly not. And where did the ordinary people perform their daily big duty? In the streets and lands, as in Madrid in Velasquez's time, or on the staircases of noble palaces as in Rome little over a hundred years ago? I suspect life for the "proles" was always different from that of the "quality," ever since there was city living on any organized scale.

May 7th, I Tatti

Women and some men keep appearing to claim relationship. I can't imagine why. I almost never can recognize how they are related, and seldom do I discover any physical trait to unite us, and even less spiritual ones. But since my *Sketch for a Self-Portrait* has brought me into the "news" I have become one of the sights of obligation, and I suspect that some who have no other way of approaching me pretend to be distant cousins. A name becomes an *idée fixe* which makes people want to substantiate it with the object for which it is supposed to stand. Among other effects it drives people to travel, to "actuate" names, any names.

May 12th, I Tatti

Within weeks of eighty-five, what right have I to complain? Although unable to work and play as I used to even ten years ago, I still can walk and talk and write and read and enjoy nature and art. My body is weakened, but still serves me. None of my organs refuses to function. I see nearly as well as ever I did, and my hearing is tolerable. Smell is narrowed. I do not smell lilies, for instance. Or rather I do, but they smell to me more like benzine. What I regret is not sexual vigour but the inability to concentrate, and above all the tricky lack of memory for names. It makes working in my field too difficult.

May 14th, I Tatti

When I last heard of her Belle Greene * was not expected to outlive the day. I am touched, moved, but not stirred to the bottom, as I should have been when for years she was uppermost in my plans, my thoughts, my dreams. She long ago ceased to be an essential part of my daily preoccupations, and now her passing does not affect me poignantly as that of a person who shared my daily life, who was an integral and irreplaceable part of its machinery. It is the last which makes death so terrible, because it breaks up our pattern of daily life. And until we restore it somehow we are in trouble and disconsolate.

May 21st, Aix-les-Bains

First lovers and discoverers of the mountain as poetry and beauty must have admired it shining snowy white on the far horizon, while they were enjoying the meadows studded with flowers, and the well-kempt woods at hand, and the massive colour of distant forests. Close at hand as I saw it yesterday at the inn of the Mont Cenis pass, the not too distant circle of snow-covered peaks seen across the iron-greyness of the foreground, and the green surface of the dark lake just below, looked as forbidding, estranging, unfriendly, and unaware of humanity as ought I can picture. Scraggly larches as we began the descent looked as wan and wilted as a pregnant woman. Lower down still the melting snow wrote cursive Arabic on the mountain, not Kufic as we saw it on the Lebanon driving from Baalbek to Damascus. Then the squalid, huddled Alpine villages, all of doubtful beauty—too Neolithic for me—and at last sweet meadows, and the pastoral amenities which like Vergil's *suave mare magno* afford such a vantage point for enjoying mountains.

* Belle da Costa Greene (1885–1950), for many years Director of the Pierpont Morgan Library, New York. B.B.'s friendship with her dated from one of his visits to the U.S. around 1910.

May 24th, Dijon

At eighty-five, Keeping Alive is now my career, and it is a whole-time job. It scarcely allows leisure for any other occupation, and of course no vacation. Even the reduced animal delights are submitted or subordinated to its pattern. Every morsel of food, every mouthful of liquid, must submit to its purpose—the purpose of keeping alive; alive at all costs, not only of even the most innocent animal pleasures, which may bring about indigestion or colds, but of all mental ones that might lead to fatigue and exhaustion, the greatest nuisance of old age. One submits, out of good sense no doubt, but also to avoid the anguished faces of one's nearest and dearest, so easily alarmed at misconduct of the senile in matters hygienic. And is it all worth while? This career for the old and those who care for them?

May 25th, Dijon

Touching, the nostalgic longing for Italian architecture and ornament that overtook Dijon in the sixteenth century. It led them to translate Gothic into Renaissance façades for their churches, and to build palaces quaintly Italianate, encrusted and bejewelled with Classicizing stone carving. In their interiors, as in the Hôtel de Vogüé, the same effort to live as a Florentine was imagined to live. And did the elderly and traditionalistic Dijonais feel something of the same distaste over the desertion of Gothic that I feel over the miscreations of the last twenty or thirty years? But surely the revolution they witnessed was not as today a denial of all that was art previously. On the contrary, it was an attempt for better.

May 27th, Auxerre

Forgotten how beautiful in proportion, how lifted up the gates of the Cathedral here and its glass—the rose window dark enough to keep out the glare of the setting sun, of the afternoon light. And the carving on the portals! The larger figures with draperies worthy of Giotto almost, like those from the *jubé* of Bourges, and the smaller as dainty, as charming, as Tanagra figurines. All edges as exquisite as in the best ivories.

The mid-thirteenth-century Gothic in France is one of the happiest moments in the history of art.

And the quaint houses. A country whose towns, in the provinces at least, remain so conservative (even if for economic reasons) can afford to talk *toujours plus à gauche*—unless of course a Stalinian police imposes its will. Could it? The French suffer administration more gladly than we Anglo-Saxons.

May 28th, Paris

I recall Tom Lamont * saying he loved France and adored Paris, and quizzingly I asked him how much he knew France except Paris, and how much of Paris beyond the Arc de Triomphe and the Louvre. I know a little more of both, yet yesterday threading our way from the Porte d'Italie to the Seine, I went through quarters I knew so little that I could not recall having seen them before. Do we know what we mean when we say that we know a great city, let alone a great country? I have known Paris as few who do not live in it. Yet when I think of it, Paris to me stretches at the utmost from Notre Dame to the Bois, and from the Boulevard St. Germain, no, from Rue Barbet de Jouy to the Boulevard des Italiens, etc. And London, what do I really have in mind when I think of London? Trafalgar Square to Kensington, and from the Thames to the British Museum.

May 29th, Paris

Spoke yesterday of my (or anybody else's) topographical Paris. And the "spiritual" Paris? They are innumerable, but what gives the various Parises a certain unity is the almost unanimous expectation of all who approach it that everything there will be more exciting, more stimulating, more entertaining, in short more life-enhancing, than the place they came from—in all that pertains to

* Thomas W. Lamont (1870–1948), American financier and philanthropist, for many years member of J. P. Morgan & Co.

"wine and women," as well as to mind in all phases. In other respects Paris is a series of cliques, mutually exclusive and even hostile, politely insulting each other; yet in each, individuals suffering from nostalgia for what is going on in other sets. And of course there still lingers on the Ritzonian Paris, the dregs of a chic rather than a great world, but where heraldry still counts.

May 30th, Paris

My different Parises. First the Rue Cujas, and the Rue de Vaugirard (ancient Hôtel Scarron), and for years the *Rive Gauche*. The students' Paris. Then various hotels in the Rue de Rivoli and St. Honoré, and finally the Ritz and chic Paris, with the Ritz all but its centre, to which I gave the name of "Ritzonia." Then the war and the Curtis * apartment, Avenue Trocadéro, and my transfer to the "Seizième," which I have never quitted since. Each transfer had its spiritual as well as social significance. It was from one atmosphere to another, from the student to the chic, from the chic to the well-to-do bourgeois. From the point of view of the individual and his "education" these transfers correspond with his natural development and advance in career, regardless almost of outer events, wars even. For which reason it is hard for the individual to realize just what has changed in his lifetime.

May 31st, Paris

Am I and is the like of me an "escapist"? What have I escaped from? Nothing that interested me. I have not turned away from the world I grew up in, and I make no effort to escape from the world around me now. It is said to be so different from the other. It is, in many material ways, almost as different as Medieval and Rococo, almost as different as Europe and China. I am aware of the material, the visual, even the verbal differences. I do not take them too hard, nor do they greatly disturb the self in me. I make no effort to run away, to escape. If anything, I unconsciously, and certainly unpremeditatedly ignore or disapprove them

* Ralph Curtis, Europeanized Bostonian, living in Paris or at the Riviera, or Venice, where he owned the Palazzo Barbaro.

as mere passing whims, which in the course of history will have no more justification than the world I grew up in.

June 3rd, Paris

Visited Rhenish picture show—how winning and sweet the candour and magic of the transitional paintings, and how naïve the search for the actual in the fifteenth century and how grotesque are apt to be its results. Throughout, fascinating colour and splendid technique. Yet why are we less stable in our appreciation of this school than of the contemporary Italian one? Perhaps just because it appeals to what remains of the child in us, of the reader of fairy stories (which I still am), while Italian art is more intellectualized and therefore one in which the grownup feels himself more constantly at home. But how refreshing it is to return once in a while to this art so full of a child's wishful imaginings and executed with such pious skill!

June 8th, Paris

After thirty years, return to Villa Trianon, Versailles. Did not recognize the way thither, nor the place. The garden only. The house where I used to stay so often unrecognizable, added to, redecorated, furnished anew, everything more exquisite. And of the Trinity, Bessie Marbury, Anne Morgan, and Elsie de Wolfe,* the last only sur-existing, scarcely alive, a skeleton with a head fantastically dressed up, a pair of dark eyes into which all life has retreated and concentrated, as if for a last, a supreme effort. She seemed wild with excitement to embrace me. What went on in her mind? A spurt of recollection of our first meeting nearly fifty years ago when she still was unsuccessful on the stage, her expectation, hers and that of the other two as well, that I would shed reflected glory on them, our companionship in Paris, in New York, and so often there at Villa Trianon—and then!

* Villa Trianon, Versailles, was the home of Elsie de Wolfe (died 1950), noted American-born interior decorator and hostess; married to Sir Charles Mendl, English diplomat.—Bessie Marbury (1856–1933), American theatrical and literary agent, co-proprietor of Villa Trianon.—Anne Morgan, daughter of J. Pierpont Morgan, noted for her philanthropic work in France during World War I; died 1952.

June 9th, Paris

Yesterday afternoon in the Salle des Sept Maîtres of the Louvre, its high priest Georges Salles led up to me, enthroned, one after the other of the individuals who ran various sections or trustees of the institution. Each was explained to me in a brief speech, and had a few words with me. Nearly all murmured flattering phrases, and I tried to say some. To those whose writings I knew, like Aubert, Charbonneau, Parrot,* it was a pleasure to say that I appreciated what they had done. On the whole the "operation," for as such I feared it, went off easier than expected. I never felt fatuous, and hope I did not look it. I had not even put on a dark suit of clothes. Latins can be so convincingly flattering on such occasions, although one knows it is for that occasion only. Yet what anthropology!

June 10th, Paris

From permanent show of "Impressionists" I carried away Manet as a painter and Degas as a sculptor. These bronzes of nudes reveal what a gift he had for playing the nude as a great violinist his fiddle. But Manet's *Déjeuner sur l'Herbe,* his *Olympia,* his *Fifre* have the mana, the numenous, the aura that emanates from Classical masterpieces. If I was worth the name of "critic" I should be able to say of what this quality consists, and thereby be able to communicate it to others. Not at all! I remain dumb-mouthed before it, like a "savage" who first saw a steam engine.

June 12th, Paris

For the first time attended a service in an Anglican church, the American Cathedral in Paris. Contrasted with a Roman Catholic service it was more, or as much, an affair for the congregation

* Georges Salles, French art connoisseur, critic, and collector; after World War II, Director of Louvre Gallery.—Marcel Aubert, French art historian, best known for his publications on Medieval sculpture.—Jean Charbonneau, French archaeologist and scholar, with Classical art as his special field.— André Parrot, French archaeologist and scholar, special field Near Eastern antiquity.

as for the clergy. The Catholic Mass is a sacrifice in which the worshippers are nearly passive spectators; the Protestant on the contrary is a performance in which they take so active a part, singing, reciting, praying under the guidance of the clergy to be sure, but enjoying exercise of function so much, that one wonders if it is not that enjoyment they really come for, although they would be horrified to be told so, and that worship of a Deity is the pretext, as all higher human activities demand a so-called spiritual or superior pretext.

June 14th, Paris

Yesterday morning looked at Medieval sculpture in Louvre with [Marcel] Aubert. Vigour, grip, vitality, surpassing anything of same date in Italy, and when it flowers into grace and elegance at least as satisfactory. Later when it becomes more psychological, toward end of fourteenth century, it is more convincing in facial expression. Only when it turns to be Italianate does it fall down into inferiority to synchronic Italy, but recovers in seventeenth century, with its monumental funerary art (which in Italy is perhaps for economic reasons inferior), and triumphs again in eighteenth century, and again in the nineteenth till Bourdelle and Despiau. French creative superiority in all visual arts (excepting perhaps the descriptive portraits in our own day) cannot be questioned by any informed intelligence.

June 17th, Paris

A bookshop of secondhand as well as of new books. First time in years I put my foot in one. Wanted to buy and send home half the shop. That is why I do not dare to go into one. I did pick up one book after the other, and the other after the third, and sent them home. Did not need them, nor shall I have time to look at them, and many are not of the kind to have appeal to future readers, even for mere consultation. The fact is I cannot resist the so momentary and yet so trifling joy of buying. In my case it is not even an *acte de puissance,* at all events not now. Perhaps a survival from long ago when I knew every *boîte* on the *quais,* and felt so happy to pick up something for fifty centimes,

179

or at most for a franc or two. My fingers itch to pick up and con every book I see in a case, and of course when lying on a table.

June 18th, Paris

The only article of dress that still can be left to an old man's caprice or taste is the necktie, but I seldom see men as aged as I am. The ties worn by younger and mostly much younger men whom I see rouse my admiration and cupidity. But when I go to a shop and look and finger them I get confused and lost, and don't dare take them or take a lot because I can't decide there and then which two or three I really want. So I have scores of ties (even when travelling) and every morning am puzzled for a moment as to which I shall choose and nearly always end by wearing the soberest that will go with the suit I am putting on. My ties are a symbol of my indecision, and an exercise in making up my mind, something I dislike doing.

June 23rd, Paris

Woke with dream that narrow road leading up to where I was living, not a definite place, was up, and I indignant because no vehicle could reach me. I wonder how the Freudian would sexualize it. Curious I never have erotic dreams, when I do dream, which is rare. The more curious as my mind when vacuous dwells a good deal on women and always with a faint erotic tinge. What a part women and the thought of women still plays in my life. Old dogs dream of the chase. In my case, is it the remains of the lifelong chase, adventure, expectation, ideal, that women have been to me? I enjoy the company of men more than of women, but I expect my cultural equals from men, whereas I am ever so indulgent with women.

June 25th, Paris

Before getting over a preference for a given style and epoch, say Chinese, or Louis Quinze, it is difficult to discriminate between good, bad, and indifferent in the style and epoch. Yesterday forenoon looked at Egyptian *objets d'art*. Conventional, even stereotyped, yet of good workmanship always. The artisan has been trained to do his utmost, and to do it well enough to be admitted to a guild, and when he has a spark of genius he adds to his workmanship a grace and charm, as in a number of young girls swimming and pushing before them tiny dishes for face paint. Perhaps it is only within a well-known convention which as such no longer interests or attracts us that we can enjoy quality or shades of quality—when the subject matter disappears almost as much as in a work of art of a merely ornamental kind.

June 26th, Paris

I am less surprised to be alive, and looked forward to this birthday with less questioning than the one of a year ago. Why? Is it that I have stopped thinking about it, and that living on indefinitely now seems possible? A limited indefinite of course. *Encore une année, Madame la Mort.* Yet, O Lady, if the coming year is to bring on another world war, then, O Friend, let me die first. All I ask is that death be swift and painless, and that I do not leave too much confusion behind me, and that Nicky be not deprived of means for decent living, and most of all that she finds somebody to love and work for, who will not exploit and throw her over. Her future is my deepest concern, and perhaps the chief reason for wanting to live on and on.

June 29th, Château de St. Firmin, Vineuil (Oise), at Duff Cooper's *

What do I carry away from Paris? Delight in the place as a work of art, the exhibitions, the Louvre, visits to Fontainebleau, to Versailles, to Royaumont. Socially, entertaining, amusing, superficial, flattering, heartless. Would care to see again as likely friends René Huyghe, Massignon, Gabriel Marcel, Georges Salles, Charles de Noailles.† And as friends in the fullest sense of the

* Sir Alfred Duff Cooper (1890–1954), English political leader; first British Ambassador to France after World War II. After retiring, settled near Chantilly. Married (1919) to Lady Diana Manners.
† René Huyghe, French art historian and member of the Academy.—Louis Massignon, French Orientalist and historian, special field Islamic studies. —Gabriel Marcel, French philosopher, essayist, and dramatist.—Charles de Noailles, French aristocrat with wide cultural interests; passionate horticulturist.

word Philomène and Jules Divonne.* "Society" Paris with its fever-
ish occupations and gossip, this society in so far as I had access
to it, would tire me again as in 1917–19 when I ended by finding
it wearisome in its futility as well as essential frivolity. So if I
did live in Paris, I'd end as in Florence by seeing few residents,
and a certain number of passing acquaintances from everywhere.
For I am an animal of a certain calibre, with certain attractions
and repulsions, which work in the same way wherever I remain
long enough.

June 30th, Château de St. Firmin

At death's door as her friends thought for months, Sibyl
Colefax † insisted on coming over to see me, as I could not go
to London, and Diana Cooper offered to fetch her from Dieppe
and lodge us both. I wonder whether, if she reflects, Sibyl was
not disappointed. She did not realize how exhausting in her state
of health the journey would be, how tired she would find me,
how little either she or I was in physical condition to enjoy each
other's conversation. Let me hope she really cares enough to be
happy to be in the same house with me. She was brave enough
to accompany us to see the pictures at Chantilly. All the time
she would talk in such a clipped, mumbling way, that neither
Diana nor I understood half she was saying, and coughing as she
talked. Nevertheless she may recount and recall this outing with
zest and joy.

July 1st, Chartres

Chartres Cathedral, perhaps the most satisfactory of all Medieval achievements in every art, except mural or panel painting.
Every other phase, architecture, sculpture, unsurpassed, and the
completeness of its stained-glass windows is unique. And its qual-

* Philomène de la Forêt Divonne, born Lévis-Mirpoix, French writer
known by the pseudonym of Claude Silve, married to retired French
naval officer Jules de la Forêt Divonne. Her friendship with B.B. dates
from his first visit to Edith Wharton's home in Hyères in 1921.
† Lady Colefax (1872–1950), widow of Sir Arthur Colefax, prominent
English jurist; noted London hostess.

Library. *Photo Soprintendenza alle Gallerie di Firenze*

B.B.'s Study with *Madonna* by Domenico Veneziano. *Photo Bazzechi, Firenze*

Dining Room. *Photo Bazzechi, Firenze*

Corridor with Cima da Conegliano's *St. Sebastian. Photo Bazzechi, Firenze*

B.B. Writing in Bed, 1954. *Photo Emil Schulthess*

ity. Of course there was fervour in the community that paid for it, but as a compendium of the arts it is due to the mastery of the architects, sculptors, and glass painters who did it. I doubt whether any one of them was conscious of performing a religious task! I believe that each of them rejoiced in the mastery of his craft, and worked at it with zest. How else account for the exquisite carving and lyrical colouring, and elegant edges, and the convincing stability and orchestral beauty of it all! Of course the craftsmen unconsciously partook of what all were feeling.

July 5th, Grenoble

Travelling is no longer what it used to be. I never was satisfied till I had trod on foot every street, poked my nose into every alley, looked at the façade of every house in every lane in towns like Chartres or Autun or Bourges. Instead, I now have to drive to see the principal buildings, and like any tourist see them only, and at times without leaving the car. At Lyons yesterday circulation was next to impossible for strangers. So many one-way streets obliging one to confusing roundabouts. I now am transported, carried, like a mailbag. It no longer is real travelling when in towns. Only in the country do I feel, as we sweep through forests and over fields, that I still am enjoying everything in sight the way I used to, that the sky line is my own. And for that I do thank the automobile.

July 6th, Digne

Elsewhere have spoken of pens dolorous and pens gay and frivolous. Mine is easily when addressed to women caressing, coddling, even amorous. Were my letters to survive and be published—a most unlikely and certainly undesirable hypothesis— it would seem that I seriously was making love to a number of ladies, all of canonical age and at the same time. I have no doubt they are as aware of the game as I am and repay me in the same coinage. It would be awkward if otherwise. Only once did a charmer ask how much I meant, and when I answered frankly she had the sense not to resent it, and we continue.

July 9th, Alassio

Called on Matisse. Had not seen him in thirty-five or more years. An apartment in a huge pueblo at Cimiez. A number of fairly large rooms and broad corridors, all one studio. Walls and ceilings, whitewashed, covered with huge distortions in black and chalk. Sketches in water colour or black and white all over the place. Found him placidly in bed, looking very comfy and *nanti*, very different from the anxious, half-starved, apostolic peasant I first met. He recalled that I owned a painting of his, and talked of the Steins.* Was happy over what he was doing in the chapel at Vence, which he was sure would be his masterpiece. Asked him whether he had ever done portraits. He showed the reproduction of a head of Tom Whittemore.† I could see no likeness. Recalled having been at I Tatti. Looking around, I discovered two busts, one in stone and another in bronze, very bumpy. Also casts of an Helladic figure with crossed arms and another of Cleobis (c. 700 B.C.), and a large Nigerian mask.

July 11th, I Tatti

Arriving at Florence by way of Prato, or indeed any of the other approaches, one gets no idea of what the town is like as a work of art. One sees that only as one gets in sight of the bridges, the dome of the cathedral, Giotto's tower, etc., etc. But to 99 per cent of the citizens of the place, Florence as a work of art means next to nothing. It is the seat of their workaday lives, and they toil and moil and drudge, and what to them are Giotto and Brunelleschi and Sangallo, etc., with all their achievements that mean so much to cultivated foreigners? We are a tiresome nuisance, except in so far as we bring money, and—to the more

---

* Leo Stein (1872–1947), older brother of the well-known Gertrude (1874–1946), painter, psychologist, and writer, later established near Florence in the Tatti neighbourhood, became a regular frequenter of B.B.'s library.
† Thomas Whittemore (1871–1950), American archaeologist and author. Creator of Byzantine Institute in Paris and initiator of restorations of mosaics at Hagia Sophia and elsewhere in Constantinople.

conscious class—flattery. Of course this attitude is not only Florentine but the same with every town that is a work of art.

July 12th, I Tatti

In Paris one felt that the interest in painting and other graphic arts was as communal, as universal, as exciting and zestful to everybody as music in Vienna. In Vienna the waiters at the Bristol would take a keen part in any discussion about the last performance at the opera or concert hall. And so, rare is the Parisian who in the course of the week has not been to a show of pictures of some kind, whether of today, or of the recent past, or of longer ago, or exotic type. And just as performances in Vienna are perhaps finer than elsewhere in music, for a kindred reason *performances* as well as creation in painting are finer in Paris than elsewhere.

July 13th, I Tatti

It is hard for me to realize how remote the nineteenth century already seems to young people—surely as much as the eighteenth century was to me in my youth. For me the nineteenth is *the* century, and great figures like Bismarck, Disraeli, Gladstone, and their like and, of course, Tennyson, Browning, Matthew Arnold, the Goncourts who were alive to me as contemporaries, are at least as remote [to them] as Johnson and Goldsmith seemed to me. That is hardest of all, to feel, not merely to know, that authors and artists who spoke to me as contemporaries are now shadowy, historical figures, who merely squeak and whisper except to those young who pour their own hot blood into the murky Styx which separates them [from the past].

July 19th, Coltibuono *

Eager to keep up with all that is published on archaeological discovery, on ancient arts and universal art in its greatest phases,

* Formerly Vallombrosan abbey, property of Marilù Stucchi Giuntiri, close friend of B.B.'s from the early thirties, when Placci brought her to I Tatti.

on European and American history, and literature. Cannot any longer, and am in distress not to be able to do it, and undecided what to discard. Should begin with ignoring current events, and all that I now read about them, which takes much of my available time and energies. What I most would enjoy would be reading the Greek authors and about them, and Roman history. It is hard to explain the almost complete satisfaction I get out of them, and a sense of mental and moral harmony with myself. Perhaps because I am sufficiently familiar with them to follow easily every new study that is published about them. Perhaps because I cannot conquer (nor want to) the conviction acquired in boyhood that they are most worth while.

July 21st, Siena

When at twenty-three I first came to Siena, it was to see Sodoma, because so highly praised by Hawthorne, and appreciated by Symonds,* and universally accepted as one of the great if not very greatest masters of the Renaissance. On frequent returns to Siena and its coasts, it was chiefly to see whatever of his could be found. True, I cared more for his early works at Monte Oliveto Maggiore, at Santa Anna in Camprena, etc., but loved his St. Catherine Chapel at San Domenico, and was delirious over his Alexander and Roxana in the Farnesina at Rome, and indulgent to the sloppiness of his later days.

The exhibition of his works seen yesterday reminded me of this, and how I drifted away, owing to increasing interest in the real Sienese, whom I at first scarcely looked at, excepting always Duccio, Simone, and the Lorenzettis. I ceased looking at Sodoma, and seldom thought of him. I realize he does not deserve the neglect, contempt even, into which he has fallen. Despite faults, he remains one of the delightful figures of the High Renaissance.

* John Addington Symonds (1840–93), English poet, essayist, and literary historian, author of *Renaissance in Italy*.

July 23rd, Vallombrosa

I wake up at Casa al Dono, and rub my eyes with amazement at the books, the periodicals, the magazines, the material for work brought up. Not only amazed at the folly of expecting to get through so much in ten weeks, but crushed, depressed, discouraged by the thought of how little use I shall make of all I have had brought up, how little I shall have achieved, how puzzled I shall be as to what books and publications I shall take up first, what pieces of writing already begun or only projected. Another instance of difficulty in making up my mind, of deciding what to do, that has vexed me all my life, and ended in inertia and listlessness. One of the reasons for travelling is to get away from these reminders of what I want to do, but shall not.

July 24th, Vallombrosa

Sat out yesterday forenoon enjoying, while Nicky read aloud, the landscape toward Monte Morello. It has an extraordinary soothing, calming, hypnotizing effect, and leads to dreams—dreams without content—a state which would correspond to dreaming life away. In the afternoon drove up to the Secchieta. It blew a gale, and I felt as if pushed by it. The distances were more than mysterious. They were magical, mystical; one wanted wings —not aircraft—not to explore, but to soar—and again without object, without purpose, just to be there, and exist there, but as seen from here. *Dahin-ness*—how much it is at the core of music, and of poetry, the evocation of a mood, a state of being—scarcely of feeling—fleeting and changing as the clouds, shaped and wafted by a gentle wind.

July 26th, Vallombrosa

A whole day with no stimulus from the outside. My ideal would be to settle into a life of almost complete solitude *à deux*, with Nicky keeping me company, reading aloud to me. I then could get the calm and repose which would allow me to think things out and bring them to black and white. I know that is the *sine qua non* for writing, and that writing is the only self-indulgence, the only satisfaction, left me, as it always has been the greatest. Yet I hanker for visitors who draw me out easily, and make me enjoy what I hear myself saying, as unexpected as if from somebody not me.

July 29th, Vallombrosa

What is it that delights and repulses me while reading a book like Emile Mâle's * about early Christian Gaul and its art? The reality was no doubt sadly inferior to the imaginary reconstruction we make reading the verses of Fortunatus, the letters of Sidonius, and the lives of saints. Is it something like the mood I am put in by a landscape with ruins, like Paestum and the ruins of Ionia? Merely that, or the comforting sense that in times so troubled, and when according to all accounts life was so uncertain, yet civilized society went on, and was not so easily destroyed as we used to be told. Or does it merely confirm my hope that humanization in our Western world has gone too far to be brutalized completely, even by such a rule as that of the Soviets?

July 30th, Vallombrosa

Orlando in his ninety-first year as lively, as eloquent, as much of a tenor as ever. No trace of being a year older than when I last saw him. Inveighed against "Western governments" (including Italy) for their cowardice, having only fifteen divisions to offer against an enemy, whereas *he* alone at the Piave had fifty divisions. All the fault of their rulers, De Gasperi † in particular! A little later, talking of League of Nations, deplored that so many pious wishes were expressed, even legislated by its members, without counting the cost and their realizability. Contradiction escaped him, in that his wishes for a Western world facing our enemy with hundreds of divisions is as utterly unrealizable, under present

* French art historian (1862–1954), noted author of *L'Art religieux en France*.
† Alcide de Gasperi, founder of Italian Christian Democratic Party, Prime Minister, 1945–53.

conditions, as any ideal of the most fervent delegate to the League of Nations.

August 5th, Vallombrosa

While everything else physical and mental seems to diminish, the appreciation of beauty is on the increase. Landscape, animals, men, women, and children, and all man-made things, fascinate, delight, and evoke my critical sense more and ever more. Yesterday toward sunset stopped at Vallombrosa. Enraptured over the light on the brownish façade of the monastery, with the detail of capitals, columns, inside and outside church, with the incline leading from the main door to the paved courtyard. And looking through grand entrance on the right at the tunnelled road leading down to Tosi, I saw a picture that reminded me of Velasquez's Villa Medici sketches, but ever so much finer. And the young women in many-coloured garments—how lovely, how paintable, at the distance from which I saw them. And then driving down toward Reggello, the fairy light over the already darkened "badlands" of the Val d'Arno, and the distances!

August 9th, Vallombrosa

Writing is almost as necessary as eating and drinking, certainly as much as love-making was in the past. It might cheer me now for the loss of virility by being reminded of all the mistresses I had in the past. But it is no comfort to be praised for what I have written in the past, and to be counselled to find satisfaction in dwelling on that. I might as well, if wanting meat and drink and unable to get either, be comforted with the thought of all the food and all the liquids I have consumed in the past. Yes, a certain amount of *creative* writing is necessary to my physiological well-being.

August 11th, Vallombrosa

Our oldest dependent after lingering for two years in vegetative condition has died, and Nicky went down to the funeral. Found the room in which he was lying filled with garlands sent by neighbours and relations, all of them peasants or daily labourers. They were sitting or standing in ritual silence preparing to carry the corpse to the church. The whole a very expensive matter for their means. Yet it is an indispensable ritual. Wonderful that even in the poorest classes birth and death should be as it were given a memorable framework of beginning and end. Ritual is what keeps societies together, and woe to the day when our traditional rituals give way to others, for that can only happen with the destruction of our societies and their being replaced by others. But in the course of time they too will develop beauty, I hope.

August 13th, Vallombrosa

In book of letters and fragments by the late Leo Stein, writing of me nearly fifty years ago, he accuses me of "I-ism," and gives as example that Lithuania had legends that I alone knew and could translate. He ejaculates, "How is it possible that only one person was capable of transmitting a body of song and story." Well, nobody was, so far as I know. I felt fifty years ago that nobody else was situated to recall them, and to be able to communicate them to the West. To this day not only legends but words, grammatical forms, and locutions of Vilna Yiddish bubble up to my memory, which show their Westphalian origin, and curious resemblances to English. So far as I know nobody has noticed them, and they may die with me. Tradition often hangs by a thread. The last person to speak Cornish was an old illiterate woman, but had it been a person of my training in philology and folklore . . . !

August 16th, Vallombrosa

Arthur Waley's unexciting, even pleasantly dull book on Po Chü-i reveals a T'ang period full of alarms within and without, eunuchs, conspirators, massacres, disorders of every kind. Safety for individuals in insignificance only, as indeed Horace in his time recommended. The figure arts of the T'ang period had always misled me into believing that it was an age of tranquillity, of gaiety, of merriment and *joie de vivre*. This is another instance of how unsafe it is to assume that the figure arts of a period can offer a true record of its state of mind. As a matter of fact, the evolution of form, impelled by an inner necessity, decides the art of an epoch, and not social and political events.

August 17th, Vallombrosa

Pleasant, amiable look of the people who approach is almost a primary need. And I get it to a miraculous degree from the two women I see most. I have been abed with fever and other alarming symptoms. I know how anguished both these women must have been, but they always approached with a radiantly smiling face as if of course nothing serious was the matter, and I felt grateful for their masks. How mimetic we are, and how difficult *not* to yield to a smile. The Japs know it so well that they meet a rebuke with a gracious smile. On the other hand, sour-visaged people may be the salt of the earth, but they spread discomfort and numbness and drive to dumbness. "Keep smiling" as a motto was taken up by American business, because they knew it paid.

August 19th, Vallombrosa

As I look on life the only satisfactory part of it is my perfect loyalty to my job. It was to send all the fine pictures that came my way to America, and to see to it that they went there as by the painters who (to the utmost of my ability to find out) had painted them. As a matter of fact, most of them were first attributed by me, and the attribution accepted as if "traditional." As by-product it brought me money, but also the hatred and unscrupulous calumny on the part of dealers whose geese I refused to take for swans, as well dislike of collectors who had been victimized by dealers. When I recall my contacts with these bipeds I feel as if I never could wash myself clean.

August 21st, Vallombrosa

People with different occupations can draw out of me wit and wisdom that surprise me more than the interlocutor. He may suppose that I have studied his subject seriously; I know that I have not. He unlocks, or rather he acts as a magnet who pulls out of me what is consonant with his interests, and that otherwise would have remained unknown to myself. I am convinced that each of us has the universe in him, and that the most gifted, e.g., Shakespeare, can on the least demand supply illuminating, interpretative creation, but even we on the margin of genius can give out glowworm flashes that have their creative value.

August 24th, Vallombrosa

I have never got over my disgust with everything that comes out of the body, whether from nose, mouth, bladder, or bowels. Even the supremest of all physical pleasures is somewhat spoiled for me by the ejaculation it ends with. So since infancy I have been overdainty, overeager to turn away from what I could not ignore, the merely animal side of life, and to exercise to *my* utmost the cerebral, visual, and auditory faculties—the visual most of all. Yet the visual has never made me feel so ecstatic as poetry and music at their best. And when poetry, music, and the visual are all combined as in a High Mass at Chartres, Bourges, or Amiens, then my soul is full to the brim.

September 1st, Vallombrosa

The cycle of life brings one back, but with awareness and approval and joy, to the dormant and vague intuitions of early childhood. How many of my guesses and ideas of those very early days, which used to make the grownups around me laugh when I tried to talk about them, have turned out to be the themes of fruitfully creative writing and discussion in the years that I have passed. And what very little I myself have contributed was there in the bud, almost in my cradle, and needed but unfolding and verbal shaping. I am almost tempted to believe that we are born with more than aptitude, with a universe which it takes genius— like that of Shakespeare—to make explicit and convincing to others.

September 4th, Vallombrosa

First forest walk, and how I enjoyed treading soft ground with naves as of Bourges and other cathedrals facing me, and rising columns of conifers sky-high, pines, spruces, firs. Glints of ruddy golden light, on stems of trees, interlacing branches, fallen trunks, and silence. "No bird sang." No hare crossed the path. Even in the heart of the forest all *ausgestorben*—killed, frightened, driven away, by *Sonntagsjäger*. The glens, the ravines, the scarcely traceable stony, pebbly, steep-sided paths! To feel again if only for half an hour the joy of treading, of muscles stretching, of the ball of the foot touching ground!

September 5th, Vallombrosa

The end of a long life should be like a fine sunset. It should colour the sky with "huge cloudy symbols of a high romance." How many times has something like this been said and how many more times thought but left unsaid. Yet commonplace as it is, and perhaps because commonplace, it never came home to me, as if especially addressed to me, as it did yesterday. Why, how? How is it that when resting or almost dozing, things passed by hitherto suddenly reveal themselves, buttonhole you, insist on being seen and known as bearing a message! One has babbled a prayer a thousand times, and all of a sudden it becomes personal, your utterance, made to order for you, and new again, not a mass product addressed to nobody in particular.

September 8th, Vallombrosa

Kenneth Clark, forgetting my age, asked why I did not write about Antique painting. For more than fifty years, I cherished the intention. It came about this way. Eugénie Sellars, who afterwards married [Arthur] Strong, invited me more than fifty-three years ago to read Pliny with her. In the light of my acquaintance with the Impressionists and their doctrines it was easy to explain certain terms and statements that had remained opaque and obscure to philological (i.e., book-learned) archaeologists. Eugénie urged me to write about Antique painting, and again and again I felt the itch to do it, and prepared myself for the task. But *il tempo fugg'e inganna*. My private, portable Hell is paved with intentions of writing that I let myself be distracted from.

September 9th, Vallombrosa

Sunset—horizontal stretches of molten rose, with dark plum and smoky slate pierced by islets of apple-green, far away to the west a sea with islets floating on it, as one sees from the Dalmatian mainland. The whole fiery, solemn, majestic, apocalyptic, and constant, with scarcely a change for more than half an hour. Till I was thirty I could not help believing that such effects were hieroglyphic messages from on high. Then somebody explained the physics of the matter, and my wonder and hope ceased. Why did I not stop to think that any signalling must be done with means that appeal to the senses and that the effect obtained by wind and vapour could be signals still with somebody behind signalling? Only much later did I ask, "Why not?"

September 11th, Vallombrosa

No illusions about my recognition in Italy. I was not given a medal by the Italian government because of what I had written, but because I procured sixty-five thousand dollars for Rimini. Likewise I doubt whether I should have been given the freedom of the city of Florence if I had not procured a like sum for the rebuilding of the S. Trinita bridge. Nor would my "myth," let us say my reputation, be what it is, if I were a scholar who could not afford to entertain as I do. The only possible recognition I have had untainted by doubt on my part is the Serena medal for Italian Studies which the British Academy gave me in the middle of the last war. True enough, in the U.S.A. I have been made member of the Academy, and offered a Ph.D. by Yale which I could not accept because I could not go to receive it.

September 14th, Vallombrosa

I wonder what the B.B. of twenty-five would think of the
B.B. of eighty-five? Would he be awe-struck to approach him
or would he prefer not to bother about a conceited, spoilt, self-
indulgent old man? The B.B. of twenty-five was both too shy
and too proud to approach famous men. What use could they
have for him and why should he bore them and expose himself?
I thus lost many chances I had and now I regret them. I now
know how gladly oldsters receive youngsters who draw them out,
who stimulate them or merely irradiate their youth. Part of my
behaviour was due to a total lack of awareness of my being physically attractive and likely to be welcome for that reason. My conceit—and it must have been considerable—was purely intellectual and bookish and my ambitions literary.

September 24th, Vallombrosa

News yesterday of Sibyl Colefax's death. Knew her since
she was eighteen, when she looked like a young begum. Something un-European in her looks always. Strange, for both her
parents were ultra-Nordic. Became a great London hostess, and
in last thirty years or more one of the few most prominent, and
latterly the only one furnishing a meeting place for political, artistic, literary, and theatrical people. A godsend for stray visitors
like me, who in a little time wanted to see their acquaintances.
The soul of generosity, and, most generous of generosities, her
sharing of friends with friends. So many otherwise dear people
keep them in water-tight compartments.

September 26th, Vallombrosa

Yesterday toward sunset took first walk in many weeks that
I enjoyed normally, through bush and briar, not slipping, not
getting entangled, stamping the ground with the same pleasure
that I used to have crushing crusts with my teeth. Again I felt,
even if in a small measure, "the wild joy of living. The leaping
from rock to rock." It was all the more inspiring as all summer

195

long I feared I never again should walk for the sheer delight in feeling my muscles straining and relaxing, and the blood warm in my veins, and the rhythmic swing of my limbs. It was almost like a resurrection. May it continue, or at least return often.

October 5th, Assisi

Feast of St. Francis—as in Middle Ages, more of a busy, crowded, buzzing, chattering fair than a solemn celebration. Imported police misdirecting traffic, huge buses through narrow lanes with turnings at acutest angles. Lower church crowded and smelly. In appearance bedraggled, sweaty pilgrims milling around and looking listlessly at frescoes. All sorts of pilgrims, among the most noticeable to my eye starved-looking English proles, with faces the colour of dirty parchment. But crowding on parapets, fascinatingly decorative as in Paul Veronese, in a humble but not less colourful way. And suddenly from the inner spaces luxurious autos, and inside huge scarlet bundles, which I happen to know are cardinals, grand dukes of the Vatican.

October 15th, Rome

Yesterday at Tivoli, a nun opened the hospital church for us and remained in prayer while we looked at the frescoes. She was of great distinction, beautifully proportioned, and all enhanced by her costume and the immaculately white coif. But her eyes, her eyes, I never glimpsed such eyes, nor can I attempt to describe them. They were compelling, absorbing, embracing but without the faintest coquetry or tropism. I could have drowned myself in them. I tried to be discreet and not embarrass her with my admiration. But what if I had fallen on my knees in worship!

October 16th, Rome

Giorgionesque sunrise, and when I looked toward the west the whole of Rome was greenish and the cupola of St. Peter's likewise. Last night St. Peter's was lit up, and looked as if nothing else existed but its golden dome and, at its base, the rest of the building. It brought out its complete beauty of proportion, in three dimensions, as never perceived by me before. Yesterday at noon its central door was open, and one could look as far as Bernini's canopy and beyond. The foreshortening was startling, abolishing what I *knew* to be at least half the distance. St. Peter's is as inexhaustible as nature. *C'est tout dire.*

October 20th, Rome

Why do we want to meet the great, the famous, the stunters, the Churchills, the Einsteins, the Lindberghs? Is it to satisfy curiosity, to be able to boast that we have seen them, the hope of glimpsing the private person behind the public myth? That alone would lead me to seek the acquaintance of certain individuals temporarily conspicuous. But as that is nearly hopeless, I have never had the least desire to encounter them. Thus I have again refused the offer of a "private" audience with the Pope of the day. What profit would it be to him, or to me?

November 3rd, Rome

Dawn and sunrise in my bedroom, which has to left a window to east, in front a window to south, and to right three mirror doors. By half opening one of them I get mirrored what goes on in the sky without leaving my bed. Then to my bathroom, full view of Alban Hills leaping to Monte Cavo, and then gliding down in soft slopes to the sea. Another full view of dome of St. Peter's, looming out of grey-blue mist. Could spend all day looking, looking, looking. How I am rewarded by seventy years of looking. I now can see, and enjoy seeing as an artist, as a painter, as a sculptor, as an architect. It is the only reward (besides creature comforts) that I value.

November 5th, Rome

Hortense Serristori to dinner looking like a handsome old lady. In her younger years she looked charming, wistful, never handsome, while in middle years she almost could look commonplace. She said that when she grasped perfectly what I told her she never remembered that it came from me. Evidently what in the course of talk she said about her granddaughter and husband being still too much in love to know whether they loved is one example. For decades it has been a thesis of mine that being in love scarcely has a connection with loving, any more than curiosity in matters of art has to do with real appreciation. Only when "in love" is over, when novelty is over, can we begin to love and to appreciate. We talked of many things, and deplored meeting so seldom now.

November 14th, I Tatti

I do resent people who not only have nothing to give me in return for the leisure they rob me of, but are unable to carry away from my conversation and presence more than the satisfaction of mere curiosity, or the boast that they have seen and heard me in my den. If only there was a way of avoiding the wastefulness of encounters that are merely spatial with nothing truly social, let alone spiritual, about them! If only one could see the far-flung persons who really are companions, stimulating and stimulated! Perhaps if I had spent my life in America or England I might have penetrated a circle, or gathered one around me, that would have given what I crave for.

November 15th, I Tatti

If there is a fruit that could have given rise to the story of the golden apples of the Hesperides, it is the kaki, the diospyros, the persimmon. In the inner garden yesterday the trees were laden with its glimmering gold, set off by the speckled amber of the leaves, strewing the ground out of which they grew. This [morning, at] sunrise, each golden apple stood out by itself as defined as a crystal, shining in the early light. The foliage this autumn is less red and russet than usual, splashes of yellow amber on the hillsides. The sun, the sun, I revel in it, live through it, am glad with it as never before. How avoid mythicizing it, if even I do not anthropomorphize it! I feel its divinity beyond reason.

November 20th, I Tatti

Wearing a beard has become a nuisance. Travelling, one is at the mercy of hairdressers who no longer know how to trim a beard. In London seventeen years ago, there was in the most frequented and fashionable shop but one who dared to attend to me, and he was a Russian. Even here at home, I tremble should my now elderly barber fail me. As it is I send for him and send him back. I discreetly try to get out from him whether he knows of a substitute, and he answers no, he does not. All of which is an allegory of how out of date I am, how much I have lived into a world in which I am the survivor from another, and how little I fit into the new one, except as a museum piece, or as an exotic performer.

November 26th, I Tatti

As I get warmed up, and feel perfectly at home in talk, I hear myself boasting, lying, exaggerating. Oh, not deliberately, far from it, but almost, not almost, quite spontaneously. It would be unconvivial and dull to stop and arrest the flow of talk, and speak only after carefully considering whether I was telling the truth, whether I was weighing my words. But even when writing, with ample leisure to stop and think, does one ever succeed in telling what one saw, what one felt, what one thought on a specific occasion? The pen has its own ways, which are not our ways, and runs away as easily as our tongues. So everything said and written must be taken as a proximation of approximate veracity, far from actuality or truth.

December 3rd, I Tatti

Alone yesterday evening, not a visitor, not a secretary, not a dependent, and the servants out of sight and out of hearing. As Nicky and I climbed up to the first floor, we both exclaimed, "How silent, how spacious!" The startling thing was not the silence, but the equally strong sense of spaciousness. Perhaps because usually people pass up and down, and along corridors, and fill them with their bustle. Yesterday when we were going to bed emptiness greeted us everywhere, and how restful it was! No, not emptiness but room, room for one to expand. No, not that either, but a curious sense of freedom, but from what? Unanalyzable.

December 5th, I Tatti

The lot of the unmarried women I have known leads me to wonder whether chaste celibacy should not be discouraged. As they get on in years, beginning with the late forties, their eagerness for male society increases, and in my presence when accidentally close I feel them vibrating with desire, no matter how old they are, no matter how unaware they themselves may be of just what is going on within them. They cling, they make every excuse for keeping close, for lingering. If I give them out of charity a kiss, they tremble, and seem ready to throw themselves on my bosom, and to cry. Married women who have had children have these as an outlet for their sexually based feelings. Gertrude Stein used to tell me she satisfied them with embracing and hugging other women. It is the suppressed feelings of the really chaste that fester.

December 7th, I Tatti

Against a pale, delicate, apple-green sky, getting lighter as you look, the featherlike sickle of the dying moon. So lovely, so calm, so appealing that it is hard to believe what one knows, namely, that what I see and feel and am are meaningless accidents. Hard to believe the contrary, and that it is not a signal, a message to calm, to cheer, to promise, to lift one's heart. Do city dwellers, do the "hard-boiled," feel as I do, and always have felt, in the presence of nature? You would wish to think so, and the poetry they read and say they enjoy makes you hope they do. Or are they too intent on their greeds to enjoy what one cannot snatch the way a dog does, running away with a bone to consume it undisturbed? If so they do not want our pity. Quite the contrary!

December 8th, I Tatti

My barber, who began at six to learn his trade and is now about seventy, has a disordered aorta, and knows that he may fall down dead any minute. It does not frighten him, nor does he bewail it. He thinks that a mature man should face his end calmly. He went on to say how much he enjoyed life, and that life meant work. When he had worked all day he came home feeling satisfied, ready to relax, and to enjoy what work had earned for him: his family, his food, his ease. In all my acquaintance, I recall no one so philosophically ripe, so aware of what life has meant. In politics as well I have found him as rational, as dispassionate as human limitations will allow, and well informed. All this with no school, no training in rhetoric and logic, no education, but contact with people.

December 19th, I Tatti

We will or consent, and most of us assume unconsciously, a certain kind of *Weltanschauung,* with all its social, political, and "ideological" implications. We use reason and logic and dialectics to defend it, or repair it, or to change it slowly, but we *will* it irrationally, and are ready, or impelled, to defend it against attack and to impose it on others, whether they want it or not. We Americans have a religion. It is *our* standard of life, and our Christian missionaries go everywhere to impose it, although they still may believe they are preaching the gospel of Jesus Christ. Our missionaries assume as a matter of course and beyond discussion that our civilization is in every way superior to that, let us say, of the Chinese. Perhaps by the way that is one of the reasons, added to the behaviour of our businessmen, why they hate us so.

December 21st, I Tatti

It had snowed and yesterday morning skies clear and air crisp. Garden pools frozen hard. Half an hour before sunset drove up to where the snow lay some inches deep. It was crackling under foot, and I enjoyed crushing it. The spectacle was glorious. The Prato Magno was piled with snow, and the bare hills glowing with the horizontal light, golden bronze and burnished like a metal shield. It was fine watching them growing crimson-coloured, and then silenced as it were when the sun abandoned them. And I enjoyed the biting cold, and for half an hour felt ageless, and alive, and almost as I used to when young on glaciers. Not that I felt young again. Does youth feel young? It may know, but can it appreciate being young?

December 22nd, I Tatti

I cannot get myself to read about artists' lives and thoughts, nor their own writings. Their ordinary doings and their reflections upon their own art are either irrelevant or commonplace and do not help us to appreciate their products. Even a Leonardo, even a Delacroix, the most self-conscious and intelligent of painters, have little to say that a person like myself, who never handled a brush, could not say as well. And as for the lives of artists, they seldom throw any light on the creative gift and quality of the artist, or make him more intelligible, although they may account for his having painted this rather than that according to his place in the social economy of his surroundings.

December 25th, I Tatti

Yes, I have learned to see after looking for at least seventy years with the deliberate purpose of achieving vision. I know now what is before my eyes, and I enjoy it not only with ecstasy, but as a wine- or tea-taster. It would be wonderful if I could communicate my vision to others. For that I should have to be a painter or a poet. I am neither. So I am dissatisfied with myself for being a luxury article of no use to anybody. That, unhappily, is my most continuous mood. But why am I the victim of this imperative? Why should I not find satisfaction in what I have achieved, and do communicate to the few who having personal contact with me are sufficiently sensitive to be kindled by my enthusiasm, by my joy in things visible? Why am I so inexorably utilitarian in my ethics? Is it only bringing up and bad habit?

December 27th, I Tatti

I feel that I belong to another world from those whose problems are all of today, intensely practical, and definitely soluble. I on the contrary am bored by the workaday problems and, although able to face them, fight shy of them. I run after speculative problems, of ultimates occasionally, but my pet ground is of racial, linguistic, national origins. Thus I have just been reading about the Illyrians, and their penetration of the Balkan and even of the Italian peninsula; of the inhabitants they found there, of Ligurians and Etruscans and Aegeans, of their languages and religions. Have had this curiosity since boyhood, perhaps inspired by ethnic names in the Old Testament, particularly in the historical books. Who were the Jebusites, the Hurrites, the Hittites, etc., etc.?

December 31st, I Tatti

I end this diary with the worst scare I ever had. In the previous war I never for an instant lost confidence that the U.S.A. and England would win through and a better world would result. Now we are up against an enemy who accepts none of our values, has none of our scruples, misuses our hitherto common terms such as "liberty," "welfare," "democracy," and does not dream of holding faith, although insisting that we must. Moreover, we remain in the dark about his resources, as about his intentions. Can he destroy us, and does he mean to destroy us?

◁│ *1951* │▷

If I had been told fifty years ago that I should live to see 1951 I should have regarded the probability as too uncertain to take into consideration. If I had not, should I have looked forward to it? And here it is. "Parts of me are excellent" still. Much else needs more attention than perhaps I deserve. Am I worth all I cost? A question I shirk but cannot suppress. What do I want out of the coming year? First and foremost to feel creative, to be able to write, to enjoy the feeling that I was writing what should be read by those for whom it was intended. Then a modest hope that my energy will not diminish, and the wish that it may even increase. And good company, men to talk with, women to flirt with, but all in moderation. Strength to sight-see, Venice, Rome, Naples, Paris, more French cathedrals. To emancipate myself from so much reading of current events, and the leisure to read the Classics in their own languages.

As guests, a French titled lady, an Austrian of highest rank, an Englishman, and a Chinese. This Chinese betrays his race by his nostrils, and by his eyes. His face is nut-brown, but hands and wrists white as of any of us present. In the way he wears our clothes, his gestures, the use of his voice, he is Western far more than the Austrian, who, despite his completely European blood and culture, is far more exotic in his gestures, his glances, his scansions, and perhaps even in his mental processes and intellectual approach. True, this Chinaman has been ten years in Berkeley, California, but seems English rather than American in all that distinguishes the two. I can discover nothing in his talk, in the way he takes part in conversation, that is un-European, as I feel so much and so immediately in a Muslim, or even in a Syrian Christian, or in almost any Levantine.

January 6th, I Tatti

Urged to write my autobiography. My refusal is due chiefly to the fact that I could not write it without speaking of my wife, of Horne, of Fry, of Maynard Keynes,* and the whole Bloomsbury set. It would not be pleasant and sweet, and such already is the strength of legendary figures like Fry and Keynes that I should not be believed. I should be regarded as a venomous, self-absorbed, conceited egoist, who had a chip on his shoulder. Then I should have to speak of all I had done for the proper attribution of Italian painters of the fifteenth and sixteenth centuries, and that too would seem incredible. As I could not but recount what I recall, and of that so much disagreeable, or incredible, it is wiser to say nothing. *Magna est mendacitas et prevalebit.*

January 9th, I Tatti

Until Hitler made us all Jew-conscious, I knew very few Jews, and seldom suspected people of being Jews or partial Jews. Now Jewish-sounding names bombard me from every page of an American periodical of any kind, and likewise, although to a lesser degree, in England, France, and least of all in Italy. Among the visitors who come here certainly with no principle of selection, an astonishing number have Jewish blood in their veins. And they now dominate in the U.S.A. in many fields of art and literature, and monopolize so-called "art criticism" and art history. An amazing proportion of Jews rise to eminence, as if really owing to oppression they had been held down for centuries, and now rebounded with violence. Yet Hitler has driven them back to the

---

* Roger Fry (1866–1934), English painter, art connoisseur, and critic.— John Maynard Keynes (1883–1956), English economist, author, and editor.

fold, and many Jews who used to ignore their affiliation with Jewry are now active Jewish nationalists, and practising Mosaists.

January 10th, I Tatti

Our acquaintance with the art of the past is overwhelmingly funerary, and taken as *Geistesgeschichte* gives us a very one-sided picture of any given period. Not so bad in the case of Egypt, where the tombs of "the Great" were to resemble to the utmost the palaces they lived in, reproducing everything that went on there. Ever so much less for Greece and Rome, although nothing like so merely funerary as in the early Middle Ages, and even the later ones, and down to the sixteenth century. So much has vanished, as furniture, ornaments, mobile works of art. So much wall painting of gay or naughty subjects has gone with change or use, and so much deliberately destroyed as in the bonfires of vanities inspired by Savonarola. So visual art gives a lopsided view of the past.

January 12th, I Tatti

Nothing rests and calms me so much as reading very learned stuff, about historical or linguistic subjects that have no relation to my own activities. I can read about Central Asian peoples moving hither and thither, pushing eastward toward China and the Pacific, westward toward Central Europe and its seas. Or about the pre-Columbian civilizations of Central and South America. Equally about Medieval Latin learning and Byzantine scholarship. And India has interested me ever since boyhood, and now I am fascinated by Mohenjo-Daro and Harappa, and the light they throw on the pre-Aryan civilization there, and its connection with Mesopotamia. But I am fed up with the Italian Renaissance, and the cult thereof. I know it too well, and what is now written about it is romance or pedantry for the most part.

January 19th, I Tatti

[Emma Melani], the woman that now devotes most of her-self to serving me, is over sixty. She left school at nine, because she was needed at home. Nothing connected with farming (including silkworms) that she did not excel in. At the same time she observed nature and people and their ways, their trades and their talk. A lacemaker who would not teach her a peculiar stitch had it filched from her while engaged deliberately in conversation while she, Emma, was following her needle. Then as a young widow she took to domestic service, and there is nothing connected with homekeeping, sewing, mending, cleaning, dressmaking, tailoring even, she is not expert in. And always a high standard of efficiency. She has enjoyed working. Had she had schooling, with her intelligence and gifts she might have gone far, but would she have been so happy having attained a position where she watched others working instead of doing it all herself?

January 20th, I Tatti

Besides every other advantage that nature—I mean landscape nature, of course—has over art, there is the all-important and most valuable one, that it excludes any and all idea of possession. A work of art may suggest to the spectator, according to his station and means, the idea of somehow acquiring it for himself, whether it be an *objet d'art* that he can carry in his pocket, a statue or a painting, or a palace. Nobody nowadays at least can aspire to mark off for himself and friends the landscape of a mountain range, or even the one stretching toward Siena and Pisa that I can see as I walk up above my own house. There is something purifying, deanimalizing in the contemplation of what is absolutely disassociated from one's workaday greedy, possessive, grasping, snatching self.

January 23rd, I Tatti

Heard yesterday that Alys Russell was dead. The last of my near contemporaries and intimates. One other survivor, older even than I am, George Santayana, is no longer an intimate, has not been for thirty years, although I do not yet know why. Robert Trevelyan, my junior by seven years, comes nearest in intimacy of the human crop. There is Bertie Russell, but he disappeared when he deserted the same Alys who just has died, and with

Ralph Perry I never felt intimate although we were brothers-in-law, and good friends. Here in Italy Salvemini, but there is little we can share now, as, despite living in the U.S.A. for fifteen years or more, he has never taken the remotest interest in our literature. He is now confined to justifying Italy's diplomacy, not as being good, but as no worse than that of France, against which he instinctively has always measured it.* Happily, I have younger friends with whom I feel on easy terms; and with one or two women really intimate.

January 29th, I Tatti

This morning at 7:15 a greyish, bluish, cloudy sky, or rather with bluish, greyish clouds, reminding me vividly of skies in Moretto at his best, and enhanced by that reminder. Strange how morning skies before the sun has completely possessed them remind me of Bassano, of Paris Bordone, of Moretto. Perhaps it is the preference those painters had for them, that taught me to enjoy them as I do. And Bellini's *Berlin Resurrection* justified my love of the first flush of direct morning sun on a scene. Titian at his most romantic in late afternoon or twilight, and most of the Giorgioneschi likewise. All wake one to a feeling that was dormant in oneself toward landscape. Indeed, I return to my conclusion of old that the greatest achievement of art is to teach us to enjoy nature—even human nature.

January 30th, I Tatti

In my time I have read all of Benjamin Constant's writing, even a cursory reading of his history of religions, and have read

* Alys Russell (1867–1951), sister of Mary Berenson; first wife of the philosopher Bertrand Russell.—Ralph Barton Perry (1876–1957), philosopher, pupil of William James; married to B.B.'s youngest sister, Rachel (1872–1933).—Robert C. Trevelyan (1872–1955), English poet and humanist, brother of the historian George Trevelyan; close friend of B.B.'s since his youth.—Gaetano Salvemini (1873–1957), Italian historian, in exile during Fascism, lectured at Harvard; author of *La Revoluzione francese, Mazzini,* etc.; founder of *L'Unità*; intimate friend of both Berensons from 1908, when Carlo Placci introduced him to them.

the most telling and most important books and essays about him. Yet how blurred, how dim, how vague has grown with the years my acquaintance with him. I now can call up a silhouette with no connected detail, only a vivid bit here and there, like the restorations they now make of war-ruined frescoes by Mantegna, with the more preserved petty fragments, stuck in the place they originally had. If one had time before one, it might be an advantage to retrace after many years to a subject that had absorbed one, and zestfully to re-examine it all. But there are too many solicitors for such attention, and the sands of my time are running fast, and who knows how soon they will run out.

January 31st, I Tatti

Plants and animals no matter how much we improve them seem to fulfill their entelechy by merely continuing to reproduce themselves. Is that the human lot also? Of the individual perhaps, but of the race as a whole? Then has all that now distinguishes us from Neanderthalers, all the material progress, and surely to a certain considerable extent spiritual as well, served only to secure continuity of reproduction? If so the human brain has overshot the mark in a thousand ways, not only by turning on itself and becoming introspective, but by enjoying functioning regardless of result, as now is the case with the atomic bomb. Indifference to result will lead scientists to produce more and more destructive processes, and lead to the annihilation of all but the most rudimentary life on this planet. Is that, then, man's entelechy? "How odd of God" if that be so. But what if He works through man, as hitherto so often has been hoped, to a further and let us say higher purpose, to realize Himself through man? Bergson said man was a machine for creating gods. What if he were one for making Deity aware of itself, becoming conscious of purpose, not subject to the mere activities of cosmic mechanics? Then the dream of Incarnation might turn out to be true, not in Jesus alone, but in all individuals of supreme gifts.

February 11th, I Tatti

Perhaps the chief difference between me and primitive-minded people is that for what happens to us they unquestioningly look for a cause outside themselves, and I—and the like of me—in myself. Thus if I see something odd, I ask at once whether my eyes have actually seen or only interpreted it, and the same with hearing. If anything goes wrong between me and another person, or a group of persons, I ask what I have done to produce it, if a party is boring whether it is I who failed to enliven it. If I fail to appreciate, it is because I am either insensitive or not properly prepared, if I fail to understand it is likewise because I either lack the brains or the training required for the problem. And this has been characteristic of me ever since I can remember, and is not due to what experience has taught me.

February 14th, I Tatti

After dinner I sat in my usual place in the corner of the sofa, and in the other corner a youngish yet already mature woman. On my right on a chair a youngish man, good-looking, very much alive. As the evening advanced, she sidled up closer, and I felt her glowing and furtively caressing. For a moment I was touched and flattered, but quickly a passage in one of Edith Wharton's novels came to my mind. It was of a youngster who sings of his love to the grandma of the beloved, and as he does so seizes the hand of the old woman and kisses it fervently. She looks at him, and exclaims, "Young man, whose hand do you think you are kissing?" I recalled this, or rather it recalled itself to put me in my place as the recipient of caresses and a glow that had to be exteriorized on a neutral like myself where it could pass for filial affection, but inspired by and intended for the young man on my right.

February 16th, I Tatti

Absurd though I know it to be, I cannot help worrying over the way things in and out of the Tatti will look after me. Gardens neglected, indoors necessarily institutionalized. All the odds and ends, the flowers, the trinkets that gave intimacy to a room, will have disappeared. I scarcely can imagine how it all will look, how the different rooms now lived in by Nicky and me and those occupied by guests will be used. A dreary abstraction will reign everywhere, except perhaps in the library. Even there strict economy and technology will reign. And who will preside, what kind of biped will replace me and mine? Perhaps at first a kind not too different from mine, but in the long run? Unimaginable! How little one owns, how quietly it goes over to others who make other use of it and so soon have forgotten Joseph.

February 18th, I Tatti

I cannot help dwelling on the miracle of man. In a multiverse of literally endless varieties of energy dashing seemingly hither, thither, nowhere, everywhere, without rhyme or reason, that life should appear on a planet, and that life produce a being like man capable of achieving what he has and attaining what he is. What a cosmos he has produced despite all that worked against him, and the amount of order he has built up, the comfort, the ease, even the leisure to contemplate, to meditate, to brood, to investigate, and to sing, to sing for the joy of creating, and not merely as the birds for pairing purposes. The wonder I feel is so joyful despite my own feeling of decline, that I lament the pessimism and the cynicism that are magniloquent today, and alone get applause from the so-called intellectuals.

February 19th, I Tatti

At the present rate of being gradually taxed out of existence, we all shall be reduced to a proletarian condition within a half century, perhaps earlier. What then? The aristocratic virus will work, and engender occupants of the cadres of leaders, creators, organizers in all fields, who may begin as a new feudalism. My question is whether the present bourgeoisie, even entirely proletarianized, will not furnish the individuals who eventually will constitute and shape the new governing class, as I have no doubt the submerged "Roman" aristocracy did in the dawn of the Middle Ages.

Aristocracy is a permanent cadre of the human herd, but its individuals have to be renewed once in so many centuries because the occupants have ceased to play their part and have degenerated into mere exploiters of their advantage. These are soon used up, and go they must.

February 23rd, I Tatti

I know enough of history, literature, politics, the arts, to ask of people who come to see me the questions that start them talking on their favourite subject, their own pursuit. They leave me recalling not that they did most of the talking, but that I cranked them up to start them running (when and if they do) as a brilliant talker. I seldom am that in the sense that Bertie Russell is, but perhaps I am a good conversationalist in the sense that I really do my best to draw out other people, and that I talk chiefly for that purpose, although I dare say I forget that purpose often enough. But women —that is another story, and there the animal and emotional appeal seems to play the chief part. Strange to me that I seem more attractive than ever to women past forty. Is it because it can lead to nothing serious and satisfies their play instincts?

February 24th, I Tatti

Nearly sixty years ago, at high table, New College, Oxford, a missionary just returned from the Far East was talking of the Chinese and their easy acceptance of death. He had been present at the decapitation of numerous criminals. All were kneeling in a row, and the headsman decapitated one after another as quickly as he could. The victims seemed perfectly indifferent to their fate, only looking to see when their time was coming. I feel somewhat the same way about my turn for the scythe of time to touch me. It makes me unwilling to get new clothes for myself, or to go to any other expense that would turn useless with my own end. And this end I accept calmly, unsentimentally, unheroically, unromantically, not even stoically. I accept it simply as a fact.

215

February 28th, I Tatti

The Numenal is followed by the Mythological as the Mythological by the Theological and that by the Nihilistical.

Out of a vague dread of what was beyond his control, beyond what he could subdue to his will with his club to begin with, then with lance or spear, followed by arrows, man came to feel a Beyond reaching far beyond his ken, and ever more alarming, that somehow he must reconcile, make terms with. So he started trying out what would make these particulars of the Beyond favourable to himself. It led him to every kind of bartering, of giving away, of sacrificing ultimately what to him was most precious, e.g., his children for immolation. In Central America man seems not to have gone much further. In the Mediterranean world, our *oecumene,* favourable conditions ultimately led to more kindly relations with the Beyond, and to various personifications of its powers. Human imagination ended according to its gifts with turning them into Myths, and in the case of the Greeks into intelligibly aggrandized human and even humanized beings, with whom in most cases one could come to terms. This was the Mythological universe which lasted till Socrates and his precursors put an end to it, through too much love of reasoning. They greatly enjoyed the free, disinterested use of faculties, which humans hitherto had been unaware of, but it led to that disintegration of the Mythological cosmos which roused Nietzsche to denounce Socrates as a Decadent—*Du hast sie zerstört, die schöne Welt;* *
and Plato was ready with a substitute, but far too sublime to be taken up by common humanity, except centuries later in the fateful distortions of Neoplatonism. Inquiry into Ultimates and Finalities—what Aristotle called "First Philosophy or Religion" —led in ways hidden as well as clear after several centuries to the celebrated theology of the Christian Church Fathers. Interrupted by a thousand years of subtilized and acute elaboration of problems that had no basis in reality, when Europeans began to criticize premises again, Christian theology crumbled and withered, and ended in reducing to Nihilism all serious thought about ultimates.

* Goethe, *Faust,* Part I, iv.

216

March 3rd, I Tatti

Life of Florence Nightingale—a perfect illustration of the nature of a "call." She herself took it for that when at last it became clear to herself what had been troubling her. And while she was being balked of answering it she sickened, grew hysterical, longed for death. All because she was born to function in a certain way and that way was at first shut to her and she found every difficulty in opening it up. When it did, her energy rushed out like a pent-up flood. Similar must have been the story of many an active mystic organizing Medieval abbeys. But whence this *entelechy,* this predestination, this kind of *sport,* for sport it is?

March 7th, I Tatti

Universally enjoyed, the discovery in a person or in print, that somebody else has had an experience like ours, reacted to it just as we do, etc. Why? It may be that we do not feel sure of our own sensations, our own reflections, our own utterances, and feel confirmed, assured, and fortified when we find them in others. I recall as a very small boy, who knew Hebrew history only through the Bible, the exultation I felt in seeing a Russian *histoire sainte,* and finding there not only the same subject matter, but illustrated with pictures. I remember feeling happy, enlarged, that the lore I was familiar with was universal and not confined to Jewry, and therein found a satisfying confirmation of its veracity. Naturally, I could not have put it into words, but the feeling of security and enlargement was certainly there.

March 11th, I Tatti

What offended prestige does to complicate life! For instance, a friend proposed coming for a couple of days, and it cost me dear to wire we could not have her. The facts are, if she came I should be far too taken up with others to give her the attention she demands, she would feel slighted and get the dumps. And when women get moody, I am apt to get moodier, and we end in sulks that may lead to a serious if momentary breach. Yet

217

such is human nature, I confess, that when I am put off, my first (luckily very passing) reaction is to suspect that "they" have postponed me to somebody more amusing, more desirable, more advantageous than myself. This even when I know it can't be so. If only one could feel without fatuity sure enough of one's position in the world, and in oneself.

March 12th, I Tatti

A young Rhenish nobleman studying for the priesthood at Freiburg. Candour, sweetness, unstudied elegance, race. I enjoyed him as a work of art, and yet a GERMAN. After all that has happened in the last forty and particularly fifteen years, the word arouses in most of us who are not German a feeling of horror, of outrage, of disgust, but with me, at least, it is not so. Not only does the word have no bad connotation, but even if it had, I never encounter an individual as anything but himself, nakedly himself, and not as of a race, a nation, a class, a sect. In the case of this young man, I was happy that English friends present almost instantaneously shed their prejudices when they saw and heard him. If only the right people knew the right people everywhere!

March 21st, I Tatti

I do not mind what race, religion, nation, or age people are, provided they allow me to forget all that while I am with them. I recall discussing intellectual problems with my stepdaugher Karen Costelloe (now Stephen) when she was not more than ten or at the utmost twelve. And now there are two kinds of young people who come to see me: the historians of events or of movements, and the practising artists, painters, poets, and their propagandists, the so-called critics. The first never let me feel any difference in age, in method, in approach to the problems that engage us. The second write me down as an old fogy, who has no understanding for the creators of today, and even less for their advertisers and interpreters. I wonder why they insist on seeing me, and sampling my talk. It is hard not to turn it into invective.

April 4th, I Tatti

What am I really, who am I? Ever since I can remember I
have striven to be somebody, something, vaguely, remotely what
I am now. It has been a constant awareness of trying to live up
to something, and a continuous self-reproach when I slipped, or
lapsed into animality, or any kind of conduct that was not up to
sample. So what I really am—is there such an animal? What
should I have been, left to myself—but what self was mine? The
infant prince of a neolithic Lithuanian ghetto, and now! How
unthinkable it all is, how impossible to go back to any phase of
our past and say that, that is I. The utmost I can believe is that I
always had a tendency to react toward things in the same way,
or rather at the same place.

April 7th, I Tatti

People are now so engaged in discovering the way a work of
art or literature or music came to be, the physiology and erotic
life of the artist before and during the gestation, that they either
ignore the product, the work, the creation itself, or interpret it
in accordance with their conclusions as to how it came into being.
They scarcely leave themselves leisure and energy to discuss the
quality of the creation, and why it is worth all the trouble
they have taken to inquire into its formation. So Carlyle's and
Ruskin's impotency would count enormously, if those authors
interested critics of today. But they are sleuthing Henry James'
sexual condition and Edith Wharton's possible illegitimacy as if
those questions would solve the mystery of their careers as novelists.

April 21st, I Tatti

Enemies could become the best of companions. Companionship is based on a common interest, and the greater the interest,
the closer the companionship. What makes enemies of people, if
not the eagerness, the passion, for the same thing? It is true each
wants to exclude the other, and to possess it entirely himself. Yet

219

what endless discussions, what approaches, what retreats, what revelation of motives, what penetrations into the soul, if only one's glands did not secrete verbo-toxic matter, which turns discussion into combat, and infuriates instead of reconciling. I could name a number of acquaintances who did all they could to ruin me, yet I felt much more excited over them, enjoyed seeing them more, than faithful friends. I gave them the name of enemy-friends.

May 1st, I Tatti

I like elderly, or rather still youngish women of the "best society," of "smart society," and am shocked when one of them is dressed badly, makes no effort to look her best. Of course it must be done with taste, tact, and discretion. I discover that my ideated sexuality (all that remains to me) goes out toward women over forty, and almost never toward younger ones. Dream sexuality, I mean ideated sexuality, preoccupies me as much as physiological sexuality ever did. Happily, it is never urgent, and ends in a desire to be as charming and as attractive as possible with women above forty who in their turn attract me. I enjoy flirting with them, stirring the remains of sex in them, *pourvu que tout se passe en douceur,* and with a touch of nostalgia.

May 5th, I Tatti

Hortense Serristori cannot understand my submitting everything to social values, why I have a sense of sin, or at least of futility if what I do does not help to humanize our species. Perhaps her inability to understand or even approve this strong need of my being is that she was brought up in a festive world, and so conditioned to it that she never questions the right to gaiety, to festivity, to luxury, to pleasure, to the "high life," in short. On the contrary, I was conditioned to a puritan society, i.e., a world where, although no longer living and acting for the glory of God, everyone was expected to work for the good of the community as a whole. Perhaps Anglo-Saxon and Prussian puritans for that reason have retained a creativeness, based on a faith in their values, that the "Latins" have lost, or never had, or not for many generations. And hence their degeneration.

May 15th, I Tatti

Bowled over by youngish Greek woman married to British diplomat. The only Greek woman I have ever seen who looked as my long acquaintance with Greek art in all phases has led me to expect a Greek woman to look. I have seen and known many Greek women. They either were good-looking like other Europeans, or peculiarly plain, with duck-bills. This woman on the contrary had the build, the breasts wide apart, the articulated profile, the face with shining dark brown eyes, well-rounded chin, and amber-brown hair. With it a fascinating vivacity of movement, of expression, of gesture. One day she accidentally took clay in her hand, and this clay said to her, "Model me, play with me, we are sisters." I wonder what her sculpture is like. I should not be surprised if it was anything but Classical Greek. And yet, the same miracle that made her body Greek may have given her a Greek talent for plastic creation.

May 17th, I Tatti

Curious freaks of memory. For instance, insurmountable difficulty in recalling who was here to lunch. I rack memory, but in vain. I consult Nicky, but my blackout obliterates her memory as well. And names, the most familiar—even Nicky's, even hers, I cannot always call up spontaneously and immediately without effort. I have to leave blanks in writing till I have recaptured a name. It almost disables me for the kind of work I was doing all my life. It depended on my knowing the names of artists, of collectors, of other writers, so that I instantly could lay hands on the items I was in need of. Better still, I knew where to lay hands on a book, on an article in the book, and often just where on the page I should look for what I wanted. All this would now require hours of a kind of blindman's buff seek-and-hide. Is one of the main reasons for my getting so little done.

May 20th, I Tatti

Countess Serristori reminds me that well before the First World War she and I had been seeing at the Grand Palais a show

221

of *"Art Nègre"* and its kin. As we were leaving I remarked that it was the beginning of a renaissance of savagery, of primitive infantilism, as the Italian Renaissance had been one of Antiquity. I had no idea, however, how soon it would happen, how far it would go, and how it would carry almost all practising artists and positively all writers with it. Nothing done today that rouses admiration, and the lust for possession, but might have been done by any artificer of backward cultures of recent years, e.g., Central Africa, and ours of several thousand years ago, e.g., the famous neolithic "Venuses" and the more accomplished "Helladic" figures. Logically, contemporary interest in the past, except among professional archaeologists, skips our Egypto-Greco-Roman world of art.

June 4th, Casamicciola

Am reading Lucien Leuwen's love story* with the same zest, same heightening of vitality, and almost same palpitating excitement with which as a small boy I used to read about Robin Hood, about Ali Baba and the forty thieves, about Aladdin and his lamp, about Ragged Dick, etc. The only difference is that nowadays the *Via Crucis* of love-making interests me more than it used to do. Any narrative can still hold me as no other form of disinterested literature can. The suspense, the transitions, the switchback of the story keep me eager to go on and on indefinitely. Indeed, it may be that the only species of writing that still is completely alive for me is the good narrative.

June 8th, Casamicciola

I maligned Ischia after my first drive around the island. I was too tired, and besides the south side that we began with is by far the most sombre, the least attractive. Since then drives and walks have convinced me that it is a real Phaeacia not only because of its headlands, beaches, flora, foliage, clustering villages, but also because its population looks so interesting and is so unpredatory. It neither begs nor tries to overcharge one. At least that

* Stendhal's novel, whose hero is impotent.

is our experience of eleven days. It has various strains, but a pre-Aryan, pre-Greek or Phoenician seems to be the dominant one. I must not forget the views, and the sunsets. I have never seen anything more Turneresque in their extravagant glory and refulgence. All in all the most unspoiled spot I have yet found this side of the Adriatic.

June 11th, Naples

How can one like me at my age be jealous when I am so aware that I and she are never the same with any other I and she? The "she" who turns to another man is not possibly my "she." Mine can fade or disappear from my life, but as long as she is vividly with me nobody else can touch her. Yet why am I so jealous when I feel that she is veering toward another male? Is it fear of losing her? Seldom that. Perhaps it is due to deep-rooted feeling that she is her sex, and the fear that intimacy with another male would inevitably lead to his participation in that treasure. Perhaps all jealousy is based on sex, for competition leads to envy as distinct from jealousy. The sexual conclusion remains so much more the same than the so varying entity created by the communion of two personalities, particularly of male and female. Unhappily, *eodem tendemus* toward physical satisfaction.

June 18th, Milan

Caravaggio exhibition crowded. Why? What does the person of average culture get out of it for his own private heart? I can think of but a dozen of Caravaggio's paintings that can have a real appeal. I fear the fact is that people will stream to any art show that is sufficiently advertised. They expect something, they do not want to be left out in the cold, if there is anything to be gained they want to be in on it—and they leave not daring to say to themselves that they have got no pleasure, nor profit—nothing but the chance to boast that they too have seen the show. And this boasting leads to their lying to themselves and to others that they enjoyed and knew why. Art is truly the happy hunting ground in the vast empire of humanity.

June 22nd, Milan

At Lentate, a smallish church filled from top to bottom with murals as at Salamis in Greece or in any of the Yugoslav churches. Key lost. While waiting for a locksmith to open it, we watched a funeral procession. Began with little tots of not more than six, shepherded by nuns. Followed old, old men with one foot in the grave, and old, old women with lighted candles. Then the archpriest in gorgeous black, priests, church menials, then the pallbearers carrying the coffin loaded down with flowers. Huge garlands preceded the procession, and all were chanting cacophonically, yet fervently. There were few inhabitants left to look on, as nearly all took part. Ecclesiastics seemed sure of themselves. All this in Italy, where the "lower orders" are overwhelmingly Communist. I wonder how many who so piously took part in this funeral vote for Stalin.

June 26th, Venice

At 6:30 Emma bringing my tea reminded me with her congratulations that this is my birthday. Yes, I am eighty-six today, and I wonder how long this adventure will go on. It is an adventure keeping alive against all the invading powers of destruction that beset me. I get dead-tired after every exertion. I sweat hot and cold when I sneeze and cough, and literally expectorate, I doze every couple of hours all the waking hours and invariably after three or four hours of sleep. I ooze sleep and tend to doze continually. And yet between attacks I still have pleasure in my body, I still dream of fair women—*il lupo sogna agnello*—I still enjoy conversation. I still take pleasure in good-looking people old and young I pass in the street, and above all I get ecstatic over the beauty of nature and the splendours of art. While I have these I want to hold the fort till the last moment. What I pray to avoid is to go on existing when I am no longer alive.

June 30th, Venice

No religion but wants to act like a theocracy, whose missionary purpose is to impose its will on as much of the human
race as it can approach. The Roman Catholic Church now in
China and Africa uses humanitarian ways. It did not even in
Europe when it had the power, nor in Spanish America. It would
not hesitate to use force in the U.S.A. now, if it dared. The Soviets
are such a theocracy, and a characteristic of a theocracy is that, as
all it does is for the glory of its god, it is without scruple, without
pity, without honour, with no inhibitions about what it does to
attain catholicism, i.e., universal dominion. Soviets so dangerous
because they are priest-police up-to-date, with every modern
(chiefly American) invention to help them impose their will. Nothing but force will stop them as in history again and again has
been the case with all conquerors, and doubly so with religious
ones, like the Mohammedans, or the Crusaders. Hence the difficulty of treating with the Soviets, and the futility of any hope of
coming to lasting terms with them.

July 5th, Venice

Afternoon at Villa Malcontenta.* Chimney [of the factory]
across the Brenta gone, but houses creeping up, so far not too
offensive. The degree of the fabric's decay is at the right point
for giving a picturesque varnish to a severe architecture. How
beautifully and sweetly reasonable it is as a composition of facets
without and as space within. What a noble life could be lived
there if outside pressures permitted—how uplifting and calming.
The frescoes, ghosts returned from the limbo of whitewash, interpret and enhance the structure and the space-feeling—perhaps
better now than when they drew more attention to themselves.
And all this, long before there was such a humanized and noble
way of country living elsewhere in Europe, even in France. Palladio's villas are not castles, nor even châteaux. They really are
country houses, meant to be retreats for people who lived in a

* Villa on the Brenta built by Palladio for the Foscari family. Property
of Mr. B. Landsberg.

great, crowded, and too bustling city, as English country houses in the last century.

July 14th, I Tatti

It is *dulce et decorum* to keep on the same servants forever, and let them become an integral part of the family. Yet it has its drawbacks. Not only in the financial drain, considerable in attending to all their legitimate wants, but the sympathy one has to give them in all their peculiar troubles, and for all their ailments. Then there is the serious danger of the body servant becoming so possessive, so tyrannical, as to reduce the master to a slave. My nonagenarian friend Guido Cagnola has a woman attending him who for fear of endangering his health not only prevents him from leaving his home, his apartment even, but discourages him seriously from seeing his friends, and plots to prevent them from coming to stay in his great empty house. "Ten years a perfect servant, ten years a faithful friend, ten years a dreadful tyrant."

July 21st, Vallombrosa

What others think about works of art, particularly European art, no longer interests me. My remaining energies are concerned with trying to find out what I myself think about them, feel about them, sum up, conclude about them. I do my best with all my equipment, all my experience of so many years, with all my training, to delve into myself, to see clearly what is there, and to try to bring it to the surface, and to make it visible and intelligible to others as truthfully as my literary handicaps will allow. I do that because it is my life, my exercise of function, the only activity which gives me satisfaction. I enjoy it, but I justify it by the conviction that what I feel and think and seriously try to communicate to others must help them to feel and understand immediately what it has taken me so many decades to reach. If I can achieve that to even a small degree, I am justified.

July 25th, Vallombrosa

Used to fling windows and shutters open wide in wintriest weather to have a good look at the moon or starlit landscape stretching outward from I Tatti. Had to give it up because it started me coughing and sneezing. Now when Nicky comes to read me to sleep, once in a while she tells me how marvellous it looks out of doors, and I picture it but have almost no regret at not seeing it with my eyes. Is this not halfway toward total blindness and the resignation to it that we are told the blind feel? At the same time, the ease with which I call up the landscape under all possible lights leads me back to a notion I entertained more than fifty years ago, namely, that the future life might be one of endless ideation based on recollected sensations, clearly or vaguely remembered, combined and recombined into composite images. Something of that way of thinking about Eternity may have been in the minds of Christian theologians of the more thoughtful kind, finding expression in various ways, various ecstasies, as in the last cantos of the *Paradise,* and in more mystical writers.

July 26th, Vallombrosa

Curious that this countryside calls up my wife more than I Tatti does. I here am reminded of the long walks I used to drag her on, not understanding how much less fit for them her tall, lank body was than my compact one. Spurts of tender feeling toward her that I almost never have at I Tatti. Here I instinctively forget her all-absorbing preoccupation with her offspring and earlier with her lover of the moment. Her last days—her daughters and their children far away, the most beloved and absorbing dead, and the others indifferent, lying in bed, not reading, nor writing. I could not find what to say to her as I looked in several times a day. She did not seem to care. I wondered how she felt and how she passed the time. I understand it better now that I too am reduced to dozing half the waking day, and find that it passes quickly enough with only wisps of recollection or thought passing through my head.

July 29th, Vallombrosa

It is being brought home to me more and more that I no longer am a contemporary, and this more by caressing admirers than by the hostile and indifferent. I don't like it, and dislike myself for not liking it. Where I differ from the contemporaries of today I am sure that I am right, that my views of life and art are the ones to which humanity will keep recurring, and although I am convinced *que c'est l'avenir qui me rendra justice,* I suffer from being treated as a dodo, a surviving specimen of a curious animal, or even as a monument of the past. All of which proves how little one is self-subsisting, and how much merely a cell of a community. My values are not valuable enough to satisfy me if no longer valued by my fellow bipeds. I am made to feel as if my prolonged existence was tolerated, but no longer required as useful or wanted.

July 31st, Vallombrosa

Reading Gide's journal of the war years makes both Nicky and myself aware of how much he and I had in common. Yet why did we not take to each other? Was it merely subconscious rivalry, the unwillingness on his part to recognize me as an equal, and on my part to submit to him as to a master? Of course he was ever so much more creative as an artist and a stylist. There could be no question of his superiority, but intellectually he may have suspected I was no inferior, and that I was not the stuff out of which adherents are made. Perhaps the fundamental difference between us was that he always was dead in earnest, took himself solemnly, and was totally lacking in humour about himself. (One of the reasons for the absence of inhibition regarding his buggery.) I am serious enough about my profession as a student of visual art, but in other respects I tend to frivolity, to jocular scepticism, and to irresponsible chatter.

August 6th, Vallombrosa

A flashy Jewess in middle years, wife of New York businessman, quiet, decent, interesting in his own field. She overdressed,

228

i.e., in a way to catch the male eye, loud, emphatic, arrogant, making great claims to culture. They collect recent and contemporary paintings, and she talks of critics and writers on art as if she were one of them. Yet she told me that she was reading in a book about Florence by an author whose name she had not noticed that the art movement here lasted no more than three generations. In short, she was as *nouveau riche* as possible, pretending to be "in it" in a way that gets on one's nerves. But why? Not that I as a Jew am ashamed of misbehaviour of another Jew. It must be due to a distaste for manifest pretense, bluff, arrogant assumption in any class, or race, or nation, but there seems to be a peculiar tendency of Jewesses recently enriched. I have known several.

August 11th, Vallombrosa

Three youngish high-caste Hindus to tea, two sisters and the husband of one of them. The young women wore saris, the man ordinary European clothes. Him I never would have taken for a Hindu if I passed him in the street of an Italian town—nor the women either. Looking closer, helped by my acquaintance with Indian art, I could have descried their ethnic origin. They talked English, and gestured and responded in every way like Europeans, and Anglo-Saxons, because they were from earliest childhood brought up like the rest of us. Yet there could not be more pure-blooded Brahmins, who, if brought up within the conditioning to which their caste members are submitted, would perhaps have been un-European and exotic. Nor had they the least touch of the baboo about them. Perhaps the Indian who becomes baboo did not start being English early enough in life—just as we who have not learned French in infancy never speak it properly.

August 12th, Vallombrosa

What am I? Not a scholar, i.e., one who knows everything that has been written on his subject. I am not an archaeologist, nor an antiquarian, nor even an art historian or art critic. If anything definable, I am only a picture-taster, the way others are wine- or tea-tasters. I happened to pass my active years when people were buying Italian painters, and it got around that I was the least unreliable taster, and the least fallible in telling whether a picture tasted like a Botticelli, a Leonardo, a Titian, a Veronese, etc., or did not. My collaboration was found indispensable by an art broker like Duveen, and it was to his interest to help build up my reputation.

August 15th, Vallombrosa

Without a word said, without a gesture or a look, I tyrannize my household by my helplessness, my manifest fragility. No breath of air must chill me, no matter how hot and stuffy others may feel, and suffer. There must be no talk in the room except what I am engaged in. There must be no strumming on the radio. No walking about. My bodily functions are of deep concern, my sleep, and needless to add my big (luckily few) and small illnesses. Why do they put up with it? They no doubt do it out of regard, out of affection they think, but "subconsciously" perhaps because of the confusion, the void, the fear of being left without occupation, not only in the gross financial sense, but as creative occupation. On the other hand, when my loves (not my domestics) have recovered from the break and the ensuing difficulties on my death, what a relief, what a sense of freedom, to stretch their own limbs, to breathe as they like, to talk, to listen, to walk about without the ever present fear of how it may disturb an over-old man.

August 19th, Vallombrosa

A man I was seeing for the first time, our Cultural Attaché in Rome, after my telling him I was too old to worry over money, said, "But you never have worried, and that is why you have lived to be eighty-six." So he must have heard of me as a sort of *Sonntagskind* "born with a golden spoon in his mouth," having lived a merry, carefree life. Such certainly I am in legend. In reality I have suffered from anxiety on the least provocation all my life long, and I have had weeks and months when I felt so blue, so worried, so palpitatingly neurasthenical that but for a miracle I could have made away with myself. Whence this myth of the jolly life I have always lived, and of the sybarite I am now?

August 30th, Vallombrosa

I am the worst of negotiators, and with no gift for business so called. Anybody can persuade me to any transaction that does not convince me. I yield the whole ground, feel uneasy all the time, and resent ever after, not the astute negotiator but my own idiocy. And yet part of the Berenson myth is that B. is a marvellous man of business who has known how to achieve a position of ease after starting from zero. I have achieved that position but through the happy accident that my judgments about Italian painters happened to inspire confidence at a time when Renaissance art was the rage and dealers were ready to pay me large fees for my advice and guidance in the dark jungle of attributions. But for that I should have had to make a hard livelihood by writing and teaching. I never could have been a popular author.

September 8th, Vallombrosa

I have been aware of what went on inside my body first, and then in my mind, from my fifth or at latest sixth year. This internal awareness is still widening and deepening. External awareness led me from the moment I could read to ever increasing curiosity about man's chances and possibilities and realizations, as well as about all knowledge that was accessible to my unmathematical intelligence. That type of my awareness is getting more and more restricted owing to enfeebled energy, and all the waking hours I have to spend in taking care of my body, and as many other hours in resting.

In my creative writing—if indeed I can call it such—I instinctively and then deliberately have aimed at becoming more and more aware of what was happening to me when reading or looking or hearing. It still is what preoccupies and torments me now.

September 10th, Vallombrosa

In extreme old age I begin to realize how recalcitrant I always have been to values that found no echo in my own realm of sensations, ideations, reflections, and imaginations. I always asked how much things, events, human creations, and most of all works of art meant to me; what psychophysical satisfaction and aggrandizement they gave. I never could stomach talk about proportions, golden sections, perspective as in themselves being criterions of visual art, instead of being at most mere descriptions of the satisfaction they give us. And the same with attempts to justify literature and music with reference to external standards. These too are based on postulation of our make-up, and nothing "objective."

September 16th, Vallombrosa

There are now a number of American citizens who went to the States not as proletarian immigrants, but as professional men, already well known in their native lands. People like Auden and Huxley from England, most German Jews who got there since the triumph of Hitler, Italians like Ascoli, etc. I call them "passport Americans," as indeed per contra I would call T. S. Eliot a passport Englishman. They who neither were born to nor grew up to the folkways, the tradition, the moral and even physical climate of a country can never react automatically to its élan and to its absurdities and follies as a native. They can only think of it either as a firm to which they have attached their interests, or a material to shape according to ideas and ideals they have brought with them. They cannot sing "My country, 'tis of thee," and fervently believe every word of it.

September 29th, Naples

Certosa di San Martino, overwhelmed by the beauty of its architecture, church and cloisters, and by the decoration, almost Cambodian in its opulence, but yet held in place by a severe architectonic framework. Sumptuous to a degree seldom attained elsewhere. The contents are fascinating to one like me with his delight in every artistic manifestation of the past, so long as it is genuine. High place due to presepi [crèches] which in the naïvest way use the acquisition of Classical art of the Renaissance to give presentation of every phase in three dimensions, with figures admirably carved and that have nothing merely doll-like about them.

232

They are alive, gay, a representation of life and familiar activities such as unspoiled eyes love to look at.

October 9th, Casamicciola

I burst with the call to get out of me what I feel about what I see, landscape, people, everything visible and thinkable. It is like the tropism toward the woman one loves when one would give anything to embrace her. And as I cannot, it is almost worse than sexual impotence. In both cases, it is not so much the possession as the identification with the object. If only I could paint it or write it as I see it and feel it and think it, the torment would end, and I should enjoy the peace of satisfaction that we call "happiness." *"Plaisir d'amour ne dure qu'un instant,"* and then the hunger, the urge, the torment begins again. A woman once told me she could find no joy in a lover's arms unless she felt sure it would produce a child. So with me, and what I have been trying to say just now. Only the child in my case is the written page. To my recollection I have never yet written a page that when just written gave me satisfaction. At most an epigram, a *bon mot,* never the complete expression of what was in me at the time, nothing like a full representation of it.

October 12th, Casamicciola

Is not my perpetual fidgeting to get rid of my petty egoism, my instinctive referring all that comes to my attention to my own infinitesimal self—is not that the worst symptom of my self-absorption, my difficulty in getting the better of my spontaneous self-regard? Yet would I want to be as un-self-aware as the Englishman who is as unconscious of following his instincts as any animal, but yet goes on believing that he is acting up to the highest standards of his set? Even as Continentalized an Englishman as Roger [Fry] did the most disloyal and outrageous as well as dishonourable things, to me for instance, and I doubt whether it ever occurred to him that he was doing wrong. He died in the odour of Bloomsbury sanctity. When I do what I should not, I know it, and let others know it, and shall therefore count as a shady character.

233

October 22nd, I Tatti

Judge Learned Hand after three years heavier, slower, more Mausoluslike, more like Trevy, and in talk, redolent of America— of the old colonies. What puts him apart from all my other acquaintance is that he never lets himself be run away with by his own zest and pleasure, but seems all the time to ask himself whether what he is going to say is what he really thinks. That makes him, although not one of the most brilliant conversationalists of my circle of friends, the most stimulating just because he is all the time ploughing and throwing up sod, and starting new furrows, so to speak. He never puts one off as Santayana and Bertie Russell so often used to, making one feel they took no real interest in what their interlocutors could say.

October 27th, I Tatti

William James used to say to us as youngsters that we did not know whether we were worth ten dollars only or ten thousand. I feel today as uncertain, and when I read about myself, more often than not I feel like crying out "Stop, stop." Almost it hurts. Why? Is it a dread of being weighed and found wanting, not by others, but by myself? Others can feed or offend my vanity, but can only call my own attention to what I, I myself, think I am worth. At rare moments, goaded by attacks, I may think a good deal of myself, particularly as against those who attack me, but as a rule and comparing myself with my own ideals, I am more inclined and instinctively disposed to feel that, to return to W. James' phrase, I am worth a bare ten, and not a thousand.

November 6th, I Tatti

If Israel becomes a going concern with an army to inspire fear in its neighbours, and influence the calculations of the Great Powers, it will redound to the comfort and happiness of world Jewry, including America. What the Jews lack is self-respect. The want of it drove sensitive Viennese to suicide. On the present horizon nothing inspires self-respect like military efficiency and confidence. Look at the Greeks. *"Un Grec"* was a phrase that enjoyed no sweet odour. How different now that they have stood up against Mussolini and even Hitler. Already Israel's army is regarded with fear by its neighbours. The only Jews who can afford to help out Israel, the Americans, will do well to pay for Israel's army, and keep it up to utmost efficiency, for the change of feeling it will bring them in their own country. They would be making a good investment.

November 23rd, I Tatti

People who stay at I Tatti keep speaking of its atmosphere of calm, of order, of living above the clouds. I wonder how much of it would remain if the material conditions were wholly absent, and even if they remained as they were and Nicky's heart and mind were not here to guide and arrange and soothe. Indeed, my reputation as a host is largely her doing, and the good will toward me of the neighbourhood is wholly her creation. I am not hardhearted, but I do not instinctively think of the wants and wishes of the people in need, and do not enjoy contacts with them, and my imagination stops short of them. I do not know how to deal with them or what to say to them. She is my almoner and deals with the "poor" in my name. But to return to the house, and its visitors, but for Nicky I should not even attempt to carry on. It takes her organizing tact, and her genuine cordiality to make friends feel the welcome they receive here.

November 24th, I Tatti

I recall writing not much more than a year ago that every part of me was in tolerable condition. I fear I must write the opposite now. Memory for names gone entirely, and vocabulary in English even diminished. Absent-minded, and restricted horizon, although brain still active but in ever narrowing circles. Aches wherever I touch my body, from skull to toe; shooting pain in my insides. Hernia, threatening hemorrhoids, feeling of repletion, accompanied with slight nausea. Nose dripping or sneezing. Throat, coughing and spitting. Wake after four hours and for better part of an hour sneeze, cough, and spit till I fall back exhausted and doze. Get

235

tired after a half hour's walk or concentrated work. All that remains intact is talk (on a light, anecdotic level) and seeing. I see deeper and clearer than ever before, and see beauty where I did not see it before, and enjoy it in actuality and in artifacts as never before. May this remain and increase!

November 30th, I Tatti

The average English man of letters knows his Latin and Greek, and more rarely his French, but scarcely ever reads German, and knows German authors only in translation or by hearsay, and German lands and people only as a tourist in search of the picturesque, or as a summer boarder on the cheap. Of German literature, German history, German intellectual and spiritual life, he knows next to nothing, or worse than nothing, a caricature of something. Yet I doubt whether any approach to thought is more remote from the Anglo-Saxon one than the German. His real affinity, I mean the German's, is not with us Westerners, is not so much with Greece as ours, and with Judea not at all, but overwhelmingly with India. Of course he is far nearer to us than the Hindu, and can communicate the mystically nihilistic, the fermenting, the ever questioning, the never resting, much better than the Brahmin or Buddhist, and therefore can supplement and correct our traditional way of thought (and of feeling too). The Russian despite such different subject matter, and even the Chinese with their still more different subject matter, are essentially nearer to us than the Germans, and therefore of less use to us. The Germans can help us to probe and penetrate, and even widen and enlarge our cosmos, as no French thinkers and writers can. That is why the English man of letters, brought up on the Classics and the Bible, but without German, is to me incomplete in his culture. There are regions of thought and feeling where consequently he cannot follow me, and his mind for the same reason lacks a maturity which I find only in those Anglo-Saxons whose universe includes Germany.

December 8th, I Tatti

We can speak of a European civilization, but scarcely of a European culture. If culture is the mental and above all spiritual atmosphere in which we live and breathe, which penetrates our thought and feeling and conditions our reactions and actions, then that culture is above all Christian. I tried to convince a very liberal Jewess that what I meant did not refer to theology or dogma, did not necessitate our acceptance of its rites even. Nor did it matter that this culture owes so much to Judaism, so much to Hellenism, and somewhat to Rome. Nowadays one cannot go back and be a Greek, a Jew, or an ancient Roman. One cannot get away from Christian ways of feeling no matter how much Judaism went to make it. This feeling is no longer Jewish because it is also Greek and Roman. Nor can we get away from the Christian calendar, its holidays, its saints' days, nor Christian nomenclature, Christian references, Christian phrases in our speech.

December 11th, I Tatti

Except that for many it is an exercise of function, as necessary or agreeable as our physiological functioning, I can find no justification for philosophy. Nor even as functioning can I give it the admiration, the veneration, the awe it inspires in its practitioners. I accept neither its premises, nor its preoccupations, nor conclusions—I no longer believe in a reality other than the one I am living. I no longer can conceive of an explanation of the universe or our destiny or mission that would satisfy me, comfort me, bring "the troubled spirit" to rest. And in fact not only do explanations of ultimates no longer interest me, but few questions of why and wherefore about anything. I want to know and attain a restful sense of "what," and that quest leaves me little energy for troubling about "why." I spin like a top and ask no questions, too absorbed in spinning. Not that I have lost the feeling of mystery, but that I accept it as a permanently insoluble one.

December 13th, I Tatti

Nicky's birthday sixty-four years ago. I was then hovering about the Luxembourg and adjacent streets of the *Quartier*. A year later I passed many a time under the windows of the house where she was an infant, when I was on the way to the Madonna del Parto and further on to Posilipo. Little did I know that she was to be the necessity, the solace, the happiness of my life thirty years

237

later. If I had not been so *farouche* in the late autumn of '88 I could have known her Baltic mother and her Neapolitan father. I might have understood her better if I had. To love her more would be impossible with my very limited capacity for loving. Nor can I measure my thankfulness for all she has been and more than ever is to me now. She takes every load off my shoulders, helps me in what little writing I do, researches for me, runs the house and all my social activities, reads to me in English, German, and French, as well as in Italian. Walks with me. Soothes and calms me when I am irascible or nervous. All that a middle-aged woman can do for an old man she does as none could better.

December 27th, I Tatti

How I enjoy, as I lie in bed, the view offered by my window. It is at a certain distance away from my bed, and the out of doors is reproduced on it as on stained glass of the sixteenth century in France, at Troyes for instance. Just now it is a mother-of-pearl, blotched with very pale flesh colour, and the branches and twigs of the big stone pine are stencilled over it. Early before sunrise the sickle of the declining moon. How the look of things out of doors affects me physically, my bowels, my respiration, and morally as well, for I quickly get depressed, even when a cloud passes swiftly over my sunshine. I remember being like that already when I was six or seven. Sunlight and temperature that suit me give wings, and I still feel like "making pilgrimages" and understanding books, and planning adventures. A beautiful sunset is *herrlich wie am ersten Tag,* but not followed by melancholy as when the sky gets clouded over in the course of the day.

December 28th, I Tatti

The tower of Babel still accounts for some of my petty but tiresome troubles. My old pupil Yukio Yashiro * arrived yesterday to stay a week. Had not seen him in twenty years, most of which he has spent in Japan, where during the last war he was en-

* Japanese scholar and Professor of Fine Arts at the University of Tokyo. Frequented I Tatti and its library early in his career, and wrote his major work on Botticelli partly under B.B.'s influence.

tirely cut off from English-speaking and indeed other European contacts. His English has become rusty, he has forgotten much of his Italian, and never knew much French. Staying in the house, a French friend who understands no English, the one language Yashiro still can use. Tomorrow comes another friend who talks Venetian and understands no word of English. I get very tired, and at times upset trying to keep conversation going between these uncommunicating individuals, and it nearly always ends by the Italophones talking among themselves, but yet in my hearing (which worries me), leaving me to flounder with the person who can express himself but incompetently in any language that I can follow.

December 29th, I Tatti

Yashiro tells us that there is no religion in Japan, neither Buddhist, Shinto, nor Zen. It is all a matter of doing certain things in a certain way. He admits there used to be a cult of the emperor, but no longer among his generation. Was Roman *re-ligio* so very different, particularly under the Empire? Did throwing a few grains of incense imply more than a tribute to authority with power? As an outlet for mass affection is not the King of England today as much a god as any head of the state ever was? But religion in Italy at least remains as in ancient Rome a matter of doing things at a certain time in a certain way. That is why Communists here resent their being excluded from the Church and cannot understand why, and feel no opposition between their *re-ligio* and that of the Soviets. Take away custom, habitual rites, and ceremonies, and what remains of religion for the mass of people in Italy, and even in France, yes and even in America where so much religion is merely good form?

December 31st, I Tatti

My earthly tabernacle is too uncomfortable to live in. It leaks, it crumbles, it breaks away, now part of the roof and now a bit of the wall. The air blows through and yet it smokes and smells. It is no longer habitable. But where to go if I leave this wreck of a body of mine? And do I exist at all outside of this miserable carcass?

. . . How has it come about that I take it as a matter of course that I am a tenant only of this shack of a body, and not merely and wholly a function of this body? And how that I cannot conceive of my *itness* having another material body, little as I can believe that I must end with this one. "Enveloped in mystery," a problem that cannot so much as be stated, let alone solved. It is not a dialectical matter, what survival after the death of the body would be like, and where and for how long—no end!

Another year whirled away, leaving little but a blur in memory. Curious how dim and even veiled my remembrance of the past, no matter how recent. I seem to consume life as I live it, without much to recollect. Or is it that I have a poor memory? Or is my memory like a clouded night sky with a star here and there piercing the duskiness? What has happened to me in the year? I have been to Ischia and Naples, to Turin, Milan, and Venice, I have summered at Vallombrosa, returned to Ischia, settled down here, never quite unpacked after various moves, "hay fever" getting worse and worse, nose cauterized. My sisters paid us a long visit and parted on board the *Bianca Mano* at Naples. All like spokes of a wheel moving fast enough to seem one whirl. And now I face another year, 1952, my eighty-seventh. I scarcely ask what it will bring; I expect so little except creature comforts.

1952

January 4th, I Tatti

I speculate often as to what I could have become if I had yielded to whims, to indolence, to amorous temptations, instead of letting myself be controlled by fear of consequences, by a sense of what was due to others, by my having a pattern of myself that must not be tampered with, by taboos of many kinds. A censor always present, watching not only over what I was doing, and in most cases commanding me not to, but even directing my train of thinking. Then my wife would not let me find my own personal way of writing, but kept trying to keep me up to her mark. So as I look back on my life, I find it lacking in spontaneity, and I wonder whether if I had let myself go I might not have been more creative, achieved more. Perhaps. But I was incapable of losing self-conscious awareness, and this did not take long to overtake the runaway every time I showed the least tendency to stray from the path of duty, i.e., to desert the guiding pattern.

January 5th, I Tatti

I may seem opinionated because I hold obstinately to conclusions of my own about things human and divine, without the ability or the desire to discuss them. I lack the ability because, having read and thought so much that I have forgotten, I cannot give chapter and verse for any statement I make and others dispute, yet I feel sure of my facts. I have no desire because I am keenly aware how much my ideas, ideals, and opinions are the precipitate of endless observation and reading and reflection, and that I cannot expect others to partake of what they have not experienced, and what (if they had the same experiences) could lead them to agree with me. So as I get older, I tend more to listen to what others say, and to remain myself silent. It seems so useless to dispute with one's juniors—one of Oscar Wilde's wisecracks—and I no longer feel the animal urge to rebound with words from what has struck my ear.

January 7th, I Tatti

Contrary to what seems general belief I have not been enterprising with women. For one thing I never put them first, unless I was desperately in love, and that happened but three or four times. I was more interested in looking, in reading, in writing. Then the feeling I had since boyhood and never quite outgrew that a woman's body was taboo, sacred, and to be approached with awe. (I should add that by "woman" in this instance I meant not women in general, but the lady, the woman I recognized as belonging entirely to my world.) My sex relations with this woman never were completely satisfactory, because I remained too aware and too eager to make sure that I was giving the woman the pleasure she bargained for. So I never have known complete obliteration of awareness, and entire satisfaction, save with "pickups" of the not-lady class before I was twenty-five. I recall a girl in Milan who had me at her mercy, and a sweet child in Ferrara whose caresses I cannot forget, and an innocent little cow in Rome who enjoyed me rapturously and made me enjoy nearly as much. Since twenty-five it has always been the lady, and my curious respect for her body, and sex especially.

January 9th, I Tatti

When young I used to be thought conceited. Now I seem to inspire—I scarcely can bring out the words—shyness, timidity, fear even of approaching me. Some on introduction remain stammering, almost speechless. Why? Because I have lived to eighty-six, because I have written books they have not read, because I am known as a sort of magician in attributing Italian pictures, because of my possessions, my hospitality, and because of the legend that now hides me from all but the few who know me intimately. My crown and glory is that it is these who appreciate me most. In my case it is not true that I am no hero to my valet. The woman of canonical age who attends to me as if I were an infant, and knows all the miseries and disturbances of my aging body, "makes a noise" as if it was sheer happiness to serve me, and the great lady who runs my house seems equally contented to give me all her energies and nearly all her thoughts, and seems scarcely to want any life apart from what she lives with and for me.

January 10th, I Tatti

Except in the very small and narrow acre of Italian painting of the fifteenth and sixteenth centuries, where I have a wider knowledge than anybody now living, I feel anything but self-satisfied. I deplore my skimpy acquaintance with languages, the fact that I can speak none grammatically, except English, that I read Latin and Greek and Hebrew with a crib only, that I have no technical competence of any kind in any field, and worst of all that I cannot write an English that pleases me. I scarcely read a page of other writers that I do not envy for their rhythm, their precision, their aerated, nimble, supple style. I feel sincerely humble before the accomplishments and achievements of others, and when I meet them, I eagerly try to get them to talk about themselves and their work, forgetting myself entirely while doing so, and identifying myself with them in their adventures of mind and body. Within me I am truly humble, appreciative of others, and delighted to express it. How is it, then, that I have the reputation of being so frightening to approach?

January 12th, I Tatti

A nose and throat specialist tells me that he has no memory for faces, but that he readily recalls a person he has treated if he can look at his nose or throat. That is because on these organs alone his attention is concentrated. So in an Indian tale I read a long time ago the god of the bow and arrow is teaching his little boy how to hit the mark. He takes him to a forest and asks what he sees. The boy says, "I see a tree." "Look again." "I see a bird." "Look again." "I see its head." "Again." "I see its eye." "Then shoot." And he hits the mark. So in all the things I recall and recognize

245

it is either a matter of pure chance that I cannot attempt to explain, or the consequence of my having concentrated completely on them, if only for an instant. An instant suffices, provided the concentration is absolute. Thus a chance recollection may be due to a chance surprise that possesses the whole of one for an instant.

January 25th, I Tatti

More and more indiscreet about people's hands, and have got to the point where with or without permission I take up the hand of a new acquaintance and scrutinize it for shape, for wrists, for nails. That gives me more information than any other source about people, their origin, and what I may expect from them. Yet how much is conventional notion that a well-shaped hand with long fingernails and tapering fingers, and a white back not too finely veined, is indication of gentility not only of birth and breeding but of character as well? Which leads me to say that I often wonder how deep are the roots on which our standards rest. Do they reach down to what is as permanent as our metabolism, or are they only the creations of custom or superstition or even of snobbery? I tend to believe that our values and standards are as much part of us as the rest of our make-up—those, I mean, that are not the mere fashion of the day.

February 1st, I Tatti

Ever since childhood I have been having glimpses, visions, penetrations, Pisgah sights that like meteors plunged through my dark mind, before I could capture them. Then as a boy I used to say that they could only be silly, seeing that they were mine and not general. Yet some of the silly notions turned out to be anticipations of moods, of attitudes, of approaches, that constituted the capital of artists like Proust. I do not say this to boast, but to point to the uselessness, and worse still the unsatisfactoriness to oneself, indeed humiliation to oneself, to have anticipated so much and to realize so little. If only I had the instruments and the industry to jot down all that went through my head the last eighty years. No doubt it is the same with every sensitive, thoughtful head. What counts is shaping it, and making it intelligible to others. That I have failed in, and can't get over my self-disappointment. Not success but getting the utmost out of myself is what I meant to live for.

February 2nd, I Tatti

Individuals as different as George Santayana and Freya Stark read and think so as to write. In Freya's case that is literally true. Santayana will not read but perhaps think more than is necessitated by his writing. Both are typical born writers. I, on the contrary, do not spontaneously put writing first and last and read seldom for writing but out of sheer self-indulgence. And when I do write it is nearly always to clear up my own thoughts, to help me find out what I think. In other words, quite the opposite of born writers I write only to think. The case of Goethe is interesting in this connection. He surely read more widely than any other person of whom we have record. Yet he at the same time wrote as much, able to transport thought to writing as easily as breathing. Salomon Reinach * had the same facility but of course more superficially and in a more limited though wide enough field.

February 6th, I Tatti

I feel tied down to my body as a hen or a donkey to a stake stuck in the ground. I scarcely can imagine getting free again from its hold on my spirits, which are low indeed. Nothing seems to work, neither my bronchial tubes, nor nose, nor bladder, nor intestine. I ooze sleep. I feel paralyzed, cannot believe I shall ever be my ever so diminished self again, have zest about anything. I say, "Come, come, you have been through this kind of thing before again and again, and got over and forgot it." Yes, but I was not approaching eighty-seven with every part of my body enfeebled, having lost its tone and elasticity. So much that one could take lightly, or at least hopefully, even seven years ago, when I had the last attack of flu! Now, it seems the day of reckoning must be near, when the body falls down like an overloaded beast of burden, and no force on earth can make it stir again.

* French archaeologist (1858–1932), close friend of both Berensons from their early days in Paris.

247

February 8th, I Tatti

I instinctively divide myself up into a negative and a positive self. The positive self is what from earliest awareness to this day I have tried to make of myself, that I have aspired to be with a *vis a tergo* far more consistent and persistent than will in the ordinary sense of individual will. It has been more like an unconscious, un-willed force that turned me into a kind of dynamo performing certain functions. That positive side of me always excites my curiosity and my mind. On the other hand, I am not interested in what is mean, cheap, dirty, squalid, sordid, lying, cheating, envious, jeal-ous, vindictive, flashy, showy in myself. Not that I am anxious to hide anything, but that I try not to let these vermin absorb my attention, the way it now is fashionable for the advanced writers to do, and to keep me from my main purpose, which is to be as free of all these vermin as is possible given one's invincible animality, and to attain complete humanity.

February 11th, I Tatti

Instinctive disinclination combined with taboo keeps one from talking about one's achievements, one's own contributions, one's own payment for passage and keep on the ship of life. On the other hand it is falsifying history to let it be written as if oneself had not helped to make it. In my own case, and particularly in the field of attribution, not only through my lists have I made more change than others, but through my connection with the dealers, Duveen and Wildenstein foremost, I have fixed the authorship of hundreds of pictures which have passed through their hands and gone to public and private collections under names that I gave them. No doubt colleagues knew or could know that that was the case, but it was only human nature on their level that they ignored their indebtedness to me.

February 16th, I Tatti

I am disgusted at the automatic way in which my mind re-acts when I hear of a death, no matter how much I may have en-

248

joyed or even loved him or her when alive. The spontaneously immediate reaction is to ask how it will affect me. I overcome it quickly, but all the same it remains a blot on my selfhood. How impossible to get away from animality, not less but more impossible when one has reached my age, and one is tempted to be self-indulgent, indeed encouraged to be by the lovingly self-sacrificing women who in various ways on various levels attend on me. I do not aspire to saintliness (the which is always based on selflessness), but I know from a long struggle with my self-awareness that the more I think of non-self, the happier I am. That is one reason why I love to read on subjects that have no possible relation to myself, my career, or even my daily dabbling with politics.

February 20th, I Tatti

Often I wonder whether we Americans are doing well to keep Western Europe as a mistress whom we pamper to the utmost of our means in order to prevent her from whoring with North Asia in the shape of the Soviets. Or to take a more respectable metaphor, we are injecting money into the veins of the West European economy, and goods for immediate consumption, to strengthen and arm her against the temptation to abandon the struggle. And at bottom West Europeans resent what we are doing, urging them to live at a pace and to work and play in ways that demand more energy than they possess. They are exhausted and feel it. Their efforts tend to be galvanic like the various "Youth Movements." They seem to want nothing so much as to be let alone, perhaps even at the cost of being without all the material (or even spiritual) things that we are trying to do for them. I wonder whether it would not be better in the very long run to leave them severely to themselves to find their own level, and if that leads to their being overwhelmed by Siberia, i.e., the Soviets, let them try or suffer the experiment. My own feeling is that they would end (after how many years!) in recovering. They could then start from the bottom, rise to push back the Siberian Soviets, resurge in the confidence of their own strength, and rejoice in the effort. It could be argued that our American attitude toward Western Europe is to treat it as an invalid that can be cured quickly with all the latest products of our pharmacopoeia, and that it would be as ineffective as most such attempts to keep an old and exhausted body alive and kicking with youthful vigour. Perhaps, changing the metaphor again, Europe must lie fallow till it recovers from the abuses of the last forty years.

February 23rd, I Tatti

Yesterday as fine a day as one could have ordered. Bright sunshine, air with a touch of ice in it—a bare *soupçon*—daffodils waving gracefully, shy snowdrops, golden-yellow crocuses. Toward five drove up some one thousand feet to see whether an almond tree we knew and loved was already in flower. It was just bursting out, petals white with a faint touch of rose that one sees in certain shells. Beyond the cinnamon-coloured slopes leading up to the meagre trees of San Clemente, and way beyond to the right the Prato Magno capped with snow, and stretching surprisingly westward. Altogether sight and sound and feeling on skin could scarcely be more happy. *Un jour entre les jours* to be recalled in moments when one needs comforting. But followed this morning by a blanket of mist that makes everything look spectral, ghostlike. No more reason for change than what goes on in my own body.

February 25th, I Tatti

Hanna Kiel * has been reading aloud more and more of her German translation of my *Sketch for a Self-Portrait*. My surprise kept increasing as she read. I seldom recalled that it was I who had written it, and that it was about myself. Surprise was rather that I had not hitherto appreciated an author I was supposed to have read. Had I read it? I wrote it and so must have read it, yet never before *d'un trait* and not for proofreading or errors in translation. Hanna Kiel's version is so good that I never looked out for mistranslations, nor indeed did my ear catch any. So I listened as though to pure literature written by anybody else.

* German writer established in Florence. Translated B.B.'s *Italian Painters of the Renaissance, Lorenzo Lotto, Aesthetics and History* into German. Editor of the *Berenson Treasury*. A frequent and welcome guest at I Tatti.

250

February 28th, I Tatti

Many years ago when the *Academy*—a London weekly—was still appearing, I read in it a sonnet by Samuel Butler which I have never forgotten. It was about our meeting again after death —"meeting on the lips of men." And while still alive where do we meet so much as on the lips of men and women? They chat and talk and discuss us continually, and woe if they don't. How much the quality of our lives depends on what they say about us and how interested and excited we get to find out what they do say. It is what they say, what we guess or think they say, that makes us feel what we count for, what we are worth, almost what we are to ourselves. If we could believe that nobody ever heard about us should we feel that we are living and not merely vegetating? What we think is being said about us is, according to Dante, what individuals crave for, even after death and out of the depths of Hell. Dante sees no one in the Inferno who does not ask him to talk about him when he returns to the land of the living.

February 29th, I Tatti

Once in a while I enjoy clowning, back-slapping, poking in the ribs. Why? Because it rests me to relax on my own natural level? Has all my life been an endeavour to rise above this level and now that I am old I find the effort exhausting? Yet I cannot forgo the task of "climbing the ever climbing way," feeble as I now am. So occasionally when I can sink to rest, relax on my natural level, I like it. But is it my natural level? Have I ever had one, or many? Clowning is my private carnival, or what is carnival but communal clowning, and enjoyed for the selfsame reason that I enjoy it? Yet the spectacle of communal clowning bores and tires me, and I have no doubt that those who see me but do not clown with me are as disgusted with me as I with the crowd.

I woke with my body numb and my mind muzzy, feeling altogether more tired than when I went to bed. I have to doze off and rest to recover. Nor do I feel as if I had come to the end of fatigue. Of course it is much worse now, old as I am, but it has been so for many years. I have to crank myself up to get going, and then, wonder of wonders, somehow the machine has been charged and can make an effort, and still works, even if with creaking and clanking. I cannot recall feeling completely relaxed, ironed out with a sense of rest like the ichor of the gods coursing through my veins—not since my thirtieth year. That used to be the reward of work, or play, or love-making. That was happiness positive and I remember recognizing it as bliss. Perhaps that was youth feeling young, as distinct from later years, no matter how fruitful and pleasant.

March 1st, I Tatti

The young are marrying earlier and earlier. One result may be that they will take, as their eighteenth-century forebears did, a more matter-of-fact attitude toward love. Festering sex will not have time to mount to their heads as romantic love. Sex relief, early sexual satisfaction, will tend to bring male-female intimacy down to the level of other animal needs and fulfillments. Ultimately even the taboos about sex may disappear, those taboos which I felt so awe-inspiringly when a youngster, and that I have not quite conquered yet. Cynicism and pornography may disappear. Who is cynical about food, and no one dreams of turning feeding into a shameful pursuit—not even gluttony, not quite. Yet man will be lost when the gingerbread of sex has lost all the gilt that romanticism embellished it with!

March 5th, I Tatti

Hullabaloo about George Moore on centenary of his birth. A godsend to pound-a-liners at their wits' end for subjects to write about. I wish I had the leisure to write about my experience of him. With me, in my presence, he was emphatically assertive of crude, uneducated notions, and would not be laughed or argued out of them. Perhaps it was an unconscious way of getting the information he wanted and clearing his mind. He was full of *malice* about his colleagues, but once or twice with a gleam in his eyes he clawed at me suddenly like a nervous cat. In a sense, his ignorance was an asset because it enabled him to approach subjects with the zest of discovery, as in the cases of the *Brook Kerith* and the *Abélard.* His *Ave, Salve,* and *Vale* greatly surprised me and will perhaps be read longest. He achieved a babbling, rippling style of narration which at last made him able to write any story with a leisurely charm seldom achieved in my time, not in English at least.

March 6th, I Tatti

Yesterday to tea, three Bostonians old enough to be of my world, two women and a man. He finished his studies at Oxford and there was acquainted with my brother-in-law, Pearsall Smith. Had in consequence perhaps a roundness, a smoothness beyond what Boston alone could have given him, a polish and even an elegance, the more acceptable as it exhaled a faint perfume not of provincialism but of colonialism. The wife still kept a fine, a trifle Amazonian figure, but spoke a charming English and seemed as cultivated if not as learned as her husband. The other woman, of humbler economic condition perhaps but as agreeable in speech and manners, had been a teacher at Smith College. All three had an ease, a promise of intimacy which I in the course of my days have often found among Bostonians (or other heirs of good New England stock and tradition) and seldom elsewhere, not even among my British acquaintances. The touch of colonialism makes the difference perhaps.

March 7th, I Tatti

Colonialism is not provincialism. Provincialism ignores or resents what goes on in the more advanced parts of one's own country and dreads what comes from abroad. Colonialism on the other hand feels for the homeland of its race or equally of its culture with yearning to partake of what is going on there in all fields. There is thus an element of adolescence, that is to say of wonder, of aspiration, of affectionate reverence, that gives a charm to individuals and societies who possess it. New Englanders of my kind had it toward England and some of us toward France and Germany and more of us toward ancient Greece and Rome. It is a quality that the grown-up countries lack almost entirely, except perhaps

253

toward the ancient Mediterranean, but more on the side of Anglo-Saxons and Germans than of the Latin countries.

March 8th, I Tatti

I suffer as much from "hay fever" after having tried painful cauterization as before, if not more. Yesterday for instance I did not dare to go out at all because the sun was dazzling, the air icy, and the wind pitiless for me now. (How I used to enjoy its buffet!) And the worst is my growing fear that it is this climate, this place and garden in particular that do not suit me now. Yet I cannot and will not leave them. I am now too entwined with this landscape not to bleed to death perhaps if I try to disentangle myself. Nor can I leave my library. Not only is increasing it one of my real interests and satisfactions, but what work could I do without it? Only purely lyrical, and that I am not fitted for by gift or training. I should feel adrift with no anchor, no direction, tossed or at least cradled by events and encounters that pushed me like a billiard ball without giving me the stimulus I get from my library and surroundings here.

March 16th, I Tatti

Nearly eighty years of reading have left in memory so many questions that I am eager to have answered or at least discussed that I pounce on anyone who can offer help. Thus the present Prince Clary * turns out to be a repository of information on almost any event or partaker in events of the ex-Hapsburg Empire of the last hundred and fifty years. No problem, no personality, he cannot illuminate and penetrate with an intimacy and precision of almost personal experience. He has it not so much from reading as from living traditions of individuals he has known, and from unprinted material in his own archives, and those of his friends and relations. And so with others who are living repositories of information more alive (as it were) than one finds or one feels in books. There is, too, something in personal communication that

* Prince Alphonse Clary Aldringen, Austrian aristocrat, formerly owner of Schloss Teplitz in Bohemia; established in Venice since 1948.

no printed page can offer. It has the warmth and glow of things lived, and convinces and brings home.

March 25th, I Tatti

In 1514, the year of his death, and then in his eighty-fourth year or so, Giovanni Bellini signed and dated and I believe painted as well as designed a portrait meant to look in attitude, in line, in shape, as 1514 as his own up-to-date followers, say Palma or Titian, would have done it. I know few instances of senility more distressing, indeed to me almost more so than the many representations of the old man trying to seduce a young woman. To go back on one's self, to despair so much of one's own vision, to try without conviction to adopt a world not his! To prove that he had not outlived himself, that he was as young as his children and even grandchildren in art!

A law of psychological gravity keeps us down to the date of our birth just as much as material gravity down to earth. Some, like Goethe, were lucky in that the whole cultured world followed them closely as leader, and none conspicuously broke away and galloped forth and far.

March 28th, I Tatti

When finishing my *Drawings of the Florentine Painters* I suddenly became aware how it should be done, and so differently from what I had done. I began to realize that any work I did or could do was only exploratory, no matter how many years I had been at it; only as I was approaching the end did the full sense of how it should be done come to me. But I could not turn back and begin it all over again. So everything I published is only the exploration of a subject, and never what I, at my best, could say about it. Exploration, however, used up what energy I had available for that subject, and other subjects were enticing, or even clamouring for treatment.

I am now recasting what I was working on sixty years ago nearly, and see how it should be done. I see the structure and all its parts before my eyes, but lack the staying power, the concen-

255

tration required, and even the time, for I have to waste so much of it resting.

March 30th, I Tatti

Robert Witt * gone—the last of the disinterested dilettanti, disinterested in so far as they had no intention to write or to speculate but of course wanted a bit of kudos, who constituted the recently defunct Burlington Fine Arts Club. They used to congregate there almost daily to chat and gossip about collecting and the new works of art that turned up, promoting interest in the exotic (or what then was exotic) fields. It was easy and genial, and enemy-friendly. Now this has been taken over by the state, by the Arts Council, with all the results of state or quasi-state interference; a wholesale appeal, dictated by the most persistently vociferous human loud-speakers, lusting for cheap sensationalism and shoddy glory. The real dilettante has disappeared, and the English ideal of the gentleman will not long survive.

March 31st, I Tatti

Robert Witt happened to read in a daily that I had been dining at Downing Street. This impressed him far more than what I had done as an art historian, although he had been one of my warmest supporters. But dining with the Asquiths—it was before the First World War—that appealed to his British values as something far beyond any scholar's achievements. And with an affectionate smile he pointed out that I now could aspire to Parliament, forgetting, as most then did, that I was not a British subject.

Much as I felt at one with my English world I never shared all its values, and least of all their hopes of reward. I regarded knighthood as comic and almost insulting, and was rebuked for it by Eric Maclagan,† who took it seriously as a recognition of merit. And of course the precedences that then were still maintained

* Sir Robert Witt (1872–1952), English art connoisseur, founder of the Witt reference library.
† Sir Eric Maclagan (1879–1951), English art historian and author, special field Italian Renaissance sculpture; for a number of years Director of Victoria and Albert Museum.

touched me not at all. All I cared for at table was to be placed between conversationally inclined women. In short, the whole British *tarif* and social values meant nothing or next to nothing to me. I cared for and respected French decorations even less than British. Nothing used to seem to me more puerile than to aim at getting ever mounting ribbons and bibbons of the Légion d'Honneur. In Italy the same and worse. It filled me with disgust to be addressed as "Commendatore." I should add I am equally put out when called "Professore."

What all this tends to prove is what an outsider I have been. An insider accepts all the values of his group and strives to attain them.

The snob aspires to rewards, as situations based on values and career and training he cannot really believe in.

April 1st, I Tatti

Can any individual feel complete in himself and have no need of others, neither of their material or spiritual help, nor of what they may think of us? The complete solitaries who retired to meditate, meditated about God and their relation to Him, and tried to abandon their will to Him, to lose themselves in Him. They communed with what was not themselves. A complete solitary nowadays would be a pathological case.

Such considerations, which have haunted me since youth, have led me to wonder whether the group we belong to has not a hold on us from which we cannot completely detach ourselves, because we are active creatures, and to act means doing something that we expect the group to need and appreciate. We can work for the joy that working gives, but we seldom would go on if the group could not use the product, or worse still if the group had no need of us, no use for us, or if we ourselves did not believe and hope that even if the group did not appreciate us now it would do so in the future.

April 11th, I Tatti

I presume that I do not escape the law of averages, and am therefore an average man—in my impulses at all events. The average man cannot help identifying himself with what he hears about whether in song or story, and with what visual representation is offered to him. So as nowadays music, *Dichtung*, painting, sculpture, nearly all visual products offer him nothing but the most deflated images of life, is it a wonder that the average man gets discouraged by the arts that used to be a *promesse de bonheur*? What do they offer him now but images of low life, of vulgarity, of animalism of the grossest and most perversely exciting kind! What can it lead to but to despair of living a human as distinct from a beast's life! How can the creators of these monstrous, obscene, depressing, yelling, screaming, agitated sights and sounds fail to see what harm they are doing? Are they so far engaged in thoughtless functioning that they know not what they do?

April 12th, I Tatti

Among the couples who come to visit me from the U.S.A. the majority of those under sixty have been divorced and have chosen a new partner. In other words their first marriages have been but trial marriages although if they had had the patience they might have become permanent ones. A moment comes in almost every marriage where it seems impossible to go on, and yet if only one has the patience to live and feel and think and work through it the real marriage can be reached which means sexual and social and spiritual understanding of each other and of satisfaction and repose in that relation. Those who have not got the steadfastness to hold on will roll into divorce. If lucky they may profit by what they have unconsciously been learning in the first marriage. If not then they go on, women particularly, throwing up one partner after the other, panting for something they have never had and unaware that it is not in them to find it.

April 13th, I Tatti

Nature (i.e., landscape), books, the arts, and responsive, stimulating individuals and sex of course have been my life, my world. My contacts with people have never been satisfactory the moment opposed interests were concerned. I learned early to expect no more from others than I was willing disinterestedly to give myself. Active life always seemed a jungle. When young I either did not fear it, and thought I could cope with it, but less and less as I grew older, and in more recent decades I found it, or was touched by it without recoiling. I discovered that "good society" was a mask for every kind of egoism, the moment the wearers put it off to talk "business." Then I encountered no scruple, no pretense to good will, to playing fair. So I avoided the world, and the world showed me no desire to use me in any way that I could accept without more or less degradation. I have no contacts with it nor do I, or even did, understand the rules of the game it was playing.

April 20th, I Tatti

The other day a friend passing through Rome was pickpocketed. She went to the next police station and lectured them on not being sharp enough to jail the thieves. "And if we did," was the answer, "who would feed their children?" That is typically Italian. Before taking action Italians spontaneously think of how it will affect an individual's livelihood, while we think only of punishing, revenging, reforming in the abstract. I remember my indignation against an art critic who was writing up pictures he was out to sell. When I spoke about it I was asked how I expected him to feed and clothe himself and his wife and children. A great deal of what strikes us in Italy as too easygoing on the part of the law or as actual condoning or favouritism is really humanity. Our law takes only abstract thought of what may happen to the punished and those who depend on him.

April 23rd, I Tatti

To lunch yesterday, a Jewish couple, intellectuals, he as scholarly-Germanic as possible, with no un-Aryan touch anywhere, while she on the contrary could have been a bedouin squaw darting out from her black tent in the desert. That he should have been so Teutonic is not surprising, but that she should have preserved all the physical traits of the Hebrews of the Exodus in the desert seems like a startling instance of the persistence of one original stock. Curious that in the same Jewish family there will appear

259

both Aryan and Semite, each in most pronounced form, scarcely there to start with. Must be due to mixing of the two races in course of millennial contacts, and on a considerable scale. One does not find the like in the truly Semitic lands, except of course where European crusaders and tourists have left their seed. But after all, how purely Semite was the Biblical Jew? Hittite, Jebusite, Calebite, did they not all help to make him, and who were they?

April 28th, I Tatti

Hipkiss * of Boston M.F.A. told yesterday of an old spinster who appeared at his office with a parcel of photos. They contained a series of the finest English silver from mid-sixteenth century to nineteenth that he had ever seen. He expressed admiration and the hope she would lend them to the Museum. She snapped back she would not, she would give them. After all, what else could she do? Obviously she had nobody else to leave them to. Her life's hobby had been enjoyed, and now what better than to see them placed in a museum where they would be properly cared for and enjoyed? Lucky old woman! When I think of my dwelling, my pictures, my knickknacks, going to an institution that will economize or abandon what is not severely useful, pack the works of art into a gallery, and all the odds and ends in glass cases, it makes me wish to put off dying! If one has no heirs, who will continue to live as one has lived in the nest one has created? There is nothing to be done except in despair to leave them to institutions.

April 30th, I Tatti

"Ich bin ein Fremdling überall." In the first place I was brought up not to think of my birthplace as the soil I sprang from, but as a station on the way to Jerusalem. Every Atonement Day ended with the shout of "Next year in Jerusalem." Then I was wrenched away from all my childhood's experiences and loves and transplanted to Boston. The twelve years I spent there inoculated me with all the explicit tradition of that culture-centre, and I left

* Edwin G. Hipkiss, American student of art, on the staff of the Museum of Fine Arts, Boston, 1919–54.

260

it at twenty-two a complete Bostonian patriot. Perhaps had I stayed and made a career there, I might have forgotten my origins or let the rare recollection of them not interfere with my integral assimilation. But I did not stay there. I went away never to return except as a visitor. I still consider Boston my home, but Boston would no more claim me than the so-called "Arabs" claim the Israelis. Abroad in Europe I was far too Bostonian and American to be taken for out-and-out English, and on the Continent languages betrayed me everywhere as a foreigner. Nor did any class in any country want me. Instinctively they felt that I was not one of them. They were right. The chief reason is that I never wholeheartedly could share their values, their standards, their aspirations, and least of all their follies, their patridiocy, their cannibalism. So even if they were ready to accept me, I seldom if ever could have felt that I was an entire member of any society, any group, any nationality. I am a devoted citizen of the U.S.A. but I never speak of myself as an "American" without mental reservation. I am an adherent of Anglo-Saxon culture and institutions, and at the bottom have always brushed aside merely political differences between the various Anglo-Saxon communities. I feel American or Jew only when I am attracted to either for stupid or adolescent reasons. Otherwise I am neither Jew nor American, nor wholeheartedly an adherent of any group, social or political.

May 2nd, I Tatti

Strange how ordinary but well-to-do people nowadays try to make their homes look like ultra-chic hotels, while the chic-est of these hotels do their best to make one feel as if one were at home in one's own private apartment. There is something icy, forbidding about a completely prefabricated house with everything in it up to date and looking not only as if never lived in before, but as if one could never live here and make it feel like home. No, a home grows out of one's tropisms, one's whims, one's caprices. The ideal would be to be born in one made by one's forebears, to be raised in it and to live oneself into it while it belonged to one's parents, and then to accommodate it to one's needs and tasks when one inherits it. No longer likely in the present historical horizon. Then at least one should make one for oneself. That means staying put for a lifetime and to live in it leisurely. But leisure, leisure, where art thou!

May 11th, I Tatti

The unreconcilable difference between me and the Christian and other ascetics is not so much in our ways of life—although these are abysmally different—as in our purpose. They submit to the severest discipline to attain a magical result, the Christian, Mohammedan, or Hindu Heaven, while I aspire to become a work of art as a human being. My aspiration is more self-aware, but in other respects no different from the ideal of the *kalos k'agathos* of the Greeks, the knight of the Middle Ages, the French *honnête homme* of the seventeenth century, and later on the English gentleman and above all the Goethean *gebildeter Mensch*. I need no other myth—if myth it be—of becoming educated, i.e., of getting out of myself all that goes to turn an animal into a humanized being, a work of art.

May 13th, I Tatti

I cannot understand why people want to say that they have been to I Tatti, and want to see me. I never wanted to see people except with the hope of getting on to real relations with them. I was far too busy as a young man to bother about private collections unless they had some work of art I had to know. So I am really bored, annoyed, vexed to have become a showpiece as it were under a glass case, and my house a museum. All because *Life* and similar papers have written about me. Not very laudatory. That does not seem to matter. The mere fact that such papers have written about one makes one and one's house goals of pilgrimage. Nor is it as if I were a popular writer, or a striking, flashy personality. Just because I have been written about. Oh, yes, autographs—my name in my own hand on one of my books they will never read.

May 19th, Casamicciola, Ischia

As late as last October I sat out coming here from Naples, and paid for it by several days in bed. This time I did not dare to stay in the open, but huddled in the saloon with fellow passengers who did not reconcile me to the average man. The wind used to be my passion. The harder and colder the more I used to enjoy it. Now it has become such an enemy that I do not dare to accept its caresses. Not the wind alone. New-mown hay that from early childhood intoxicated me has turned so hostile that the least approach fells me, or rather irritates all my so irascible mucous membrane. Then I know not what and how many other flowers do nearly the same. Strange to discover malignancy where for so many, many years one used to find delight and joy! In the abstract I always knew that from our conception on, everything in existence was out to destroy us. As until so few years ago I was sturdy enough to resist (almost unconsciously), I knew but did not realize how active they were, and how victorious!

May 27th, Casamicciola

I never wanted friends for the material, social, etc., help they could give me. On the contrary, I avoided asking favours from those I considered friends. A friend is somebody who stimulates me and I can stimulate to talk. I mean to express ourselves more creatively (at least along certain lines) than when by ourselves. When the stimulation no longer occurs, it is a spent, an exhausted friendship, and continues as a burthen and a bore, except for brief moments of reviving the past or when the intimacy is so perfect that words no longer count and it is happiness just to be together.

Unfortunately, in a long life one gets barnacled over with the mere shells of friendship, and it is difficult without hurting one's self to scrape them off. I now waste a serious part of my time and energies in receiving and having long or short visits from such unstimulating and devitalizing former friendships. Out of a sort of *pietas* for my own past, as well as not to hurt them, I keep up with them. A case of a thing coming high which I do not want to have.

May 29th, Casamicciola

When I began to collect for Mrs. Gardner there was not in America a score of pictures worth looking at. I regarded it as my mission to send as many Italian works of art (and incidentally others too) as I could persuade collectors to acquire. The idea of private gain scarcely entered my head at first and for a long time. Only when I realized what gain dealers were making out of my authority and reputation did I begin to ask for my share. Indeed, if Duveen abetted by his lawyer had played fair by me I should have at least double the capital I now have. I should be able to endow I Tatti as I hoped to do instead of leaving it perhaps a mere library and not the lay monastery for leisurely culture that I dreamt of. And what has become of the Duveen fortune divided between his wife and daughter and possibly two or three assistants? I cannot help regretting all I could have done with money to do what I pleased with, according to my own ideas and judgment.

June 3rd, Casamicciola

I scarcely know anywhere in the countries I have visited a spot of more varied and unspoilt beauty than this Ischia offers. Two days ago the Waltons * took us to a *rond point* not far from their cottage whence the sea and the distance were as heart-pulling as any I have felt, and the boulders and rocks and jagged masses piling up to the top of the Epomeo closed one in as in a cup. Below everywhere bottoms, pits, holes, filled with myrtle, with tamarisk, and wild olive. It was numenal as I felt it at the top of Capo Circeo or on the road from Alabanda to Halicarnassus, or at Phigalia, and at a few other sacred spots.

June 11th, Salerno

The landscape between Sorrento and Salerno, the Amalfitano especially, one would not believe in a picture. Indeed, it recalls

* Sir William Walton, English composer; spends most of the year at his villa at San Francesco, near Forio, on the island of Ischia.

264

Mantegna to such a degree that one could almost believe that he had studied it and reproduced it in some of his pictures. The vast toppling crags, cliffs, rocks, promontories, full of vast orifices, niches, cavities, and human habitations filling most of them, clinging to the sides, every bit of cultivable ground shored up into terraces and pergola horticulture. Endless stairs leading everywhere, as paths do elsewhere. One wonders whether these habitations were not suggested by Byzantine Meteora, and like them to get away from danger of attack, and to be safe against gales and tidal waves sweeping over the dry land. You have to see it to believe it.

June 12th, Salerno

When an undergraduate I published some verses in the *Harvard Monthly* which began with "Ringing silence hisses around the numbing thought"—I forget the rest—and went on in starkest pessimism. Did I mean it? A bit perhaps, but chiefly because it was easy to do. Pessimism like calumny is easy to do, and attracts immediate attention. The gossiper and the writer may find this out soon enough, and a little encouragement from the current mood will procure them successes that bring endless imitators in their trail. On the other hand saying good things about life in general and individuals in particular and making it interesting is a serious task which few can achieve with credit. *Ergo* do not take too hard the pessimism of writers. Mostly rhetoric.

June 13th, Salerno

Yesterday Salerno all agog with Corpus Domini procession. In the cathedral square—all the palaces, windows, balconies, terraces, like flower beds but of human beings, hangings everywhere, and a continuous stream of clergy, novices, penitents issuing from the cathedral, ending with old Archbishop under baldachin carrying the Host in both upheld hands. Poor man, I could not understand how he would manage processioning for an hour through the town. Ground everywhere strewn with every kind of flower. Brass bands, jubilation, festive happiness. The Church can furnish that kind of *sfogo*, several times a year. What can the Kremlin offer? Military parades, speeches! Can these compete with chants, with

265

spectacles, with rituals that are the outcome of thousands of years of effort to exteriorize man's imperative need of rejoicing, as again of mourning? I cannot believe it. Wherefore I prefer Catholicism.

June 21st, Brindisi

In every town, townlet, and village processions or preparations. In Gallipoli scores, a hundred perhaps, of virgins in dazzling white raiment and heads crowned with gilt circlets, slim, elegant, nubile creatures, lovely to behold against the wide, open sea. Two thousand years ago a similar procession composed in the same way could not have looked different. The further south one goes in Italy, the closer one comes to customs and usages, and above all communal rites, that unsophisticated humanity has tried and experienced and for thousands of years found satisfactory, comforting, life-enhancing. The myths have changed, although not so much as the names, theologies have gnawed at them, but essentially they remain the same whether prehistoric, Hellenic, Medieval, or Tridentine—eternally pagan, and suited to human nature. How much else that stupid rationalism has made away with, as stupid archaeologists have made away with features in old buildings.

June 26th, Naples

My eighty-eighth year. Looked out a few minutes after four. Sun not up yet. Sky a rose colour as if painted with water colours on marble. Did not realize before yesterday what grand mountain scenery lies between Foggia and Benevento. Fascinated by twelfth-century capitals in cloister of Santa Sofia at Benevento. They riot with animal activities and hunters, all of the most energy-communicating kind. Halfway to Naples the highroad became an endless suburb too narrow for the traffic and in bad repair. Truly, the approach to great cities is a disaster. Venice was the exception, and Ruskin's description of what it was to arrive in Venice fills one with regret for the loss of a paradise. *Les jeunes* do not know and do not miss what a world we had, but theirs is to me all but unimaginable.

266

July 2nd, Naples

I hesitated to call on Croce. Asked Alberto Albertini *
whether my call would be welcome and was assured it would be.
It was and could not have been more cordial on the part of his
wife and two daughters present. He was perusing an eighteenth-
century pamphlet on burials at Naples. Looked rather less puffy
than last year, but his speech has got so mumbly and slurred that
I could scarcely follow, although Nicky could to some extent,
and his womenfolk perfectly. A well-dressed young man came in
and stood in attitude of devout attention as if at a religious ceremony. A bottle of vermouth was brought with no tray, and was
offered. It was nasty stuff. Curious that the Croces never invited
us to a meal although they so often have lunched with me. I am
sure it is not meanness—shyness perhaps, owing to our different
standards of life.

July 6th, I Tatti

The heat gilds the landscape. It is golden-yellow at noon,
yellow as ripe corn. It feels relaxed, maternal, not yet matriarchal,
but maternal, like a woman who has had enough children but is
still far from old. A relaxing, comfortable, silent peacefulness possesses me in this great heat, and could I strip naked and remain
in the shade I should enjoy it positively, and not merely put up
with it. I wish I could describe better the kind of happiness midsummer always has given me, ever since my infancy almost when
the wide extents of ripe corn stretched away endlessly and gave
me even then a feeling of security, of peace, of happiness. The
harvest songs of all peoples have given vent to it, but not in words.

July 9th, I Tatti

In the library I am preparing for students of art history and
human culture, any book is worth while (no matter how rubbishy
in other respects) if it has even one illustration not to be found
elsewhere, one text not easily to be had in other books. When such

* See note, p. 5.

a reproduction of a work of art or text becomes accessible in serious books, the rubbishy, the mediocre ones should be got rid of. I have not the heart to do it. I feel an almost tender sympathy for any book, and want to treat it as if it were conscious, and could suffer. I pity the dead book—and how many even in my library already are dead. Like Joan the Mad with her dead husband I cannot get myself to bury them, or even to throw them out to sellers of old books. I sometimes wonder how I came to have such feelings toward books, as if they had some life or were fetishes. Can it be because I was taught as a very little boy that everything in Hebrew was to be treated with regard?

July 18th, Vallombrosa

Accustomed to talk freely, and say whatever happens to occur to me at the moment, I find it difficult when journalists come to see me, to interview me, to be cautious, to hold back, to be on my guard. Then suddenly panic seizes me and I implore them not to make public what I have said, to treat it as "off the record," and even to forget it. It is asking more than they can fulfill, even if they promise, for journalists must function as journalists. They not only cannot afford to forget a *bon mot,* a biting characterization, a good story, but cannot help distorting it by their professional need of bringing all they know to the understanding of the meanest intelligence—among those who read at all. I already have had some distressing experiences, and yet I talked yesterday to a professional interviewer as if he were a bosom friend to whom I could entrust secrets.

July 22nd, Vallombrosa

I am "fed up" with the Renaissance, with the Medicis, Benozzo Gozzoli, Marsilio Ficino, Machiavelli, and needless to say Savonarola. I feel about it as Max Beerbohm must have felt when he wrote *Savonarola Brown.* Politically it was for Italy a time of decline and fall. Intellectually the Quattrocento can scarcely compare with previous and following centuries. Only in the visual arts did the Renaissance really create, or ordain for the future. Perhaps our way of housing and *streeting* and even educating would have come about without it, but certainly the Italian Renaissance started it. I must take back what I said, in favour of the first fifty or sixty years of the same Renaissance as described in Voigt's *Wiedererweckung des klassischen Altertums,* when humanism was a pioneering adventure, a voyage of discovery into realms of wonder and prospective delight.

July 26th, Vallombrosa

Just read Bertie Russell's reminiscences of Keynes and Lytton Strachey. Word for word what I would have said about them. Everything I read of Russell's (excepting mathematics and pure logic) comes as near to what I think and could say as is possible in the case of two persons separated for forty years. Why? Because of his abandoning Alys. That perhaps was the base, on which Roger Fry built up the myth of a disreputable, dishonourable Prussian-minded ghoul, lusting for power and riches, with unscrupulous but ever so subtle ways of getting what he wanted. Perhaps? Or did Russell from the beginning feel that I did not belong to his world, glad to get rid of me? Then why did he frequent me with apparent delight for so many years, so that in his writings again and again I discover a story I told him, or a turn of phrase that was mine?

July 31st, Vallombrosa

I have two acquaintances within easy reach and yet we do not meet. One is Max Beerbohm, whom I never frequented and only came across once or twice in other people's houses. The other is Santayana, an intimate for many years, who then all of a sudden told me to my face that he did not want to see me any more. When we bumped into each other since, by accident, he was condescending and sneering. Yet we three have much in common even if it is only that we belong to the nineteenth century and to its men of arts and letters. What prevents our meeting again? On the part of Beerbohm not so much distaste as indifference. As for Santayana, it may be indifference too or that he is too proud to make the first move. How often I have come across in the world I have known and

269

in history the impossibility of making the first move on the part of the person who ought to do it.

August 7th, Vallombrosa

All through my career I have suffered from so-called friends or mere acquaintances who came to ask me favours that they must have known I hated to do, and yet could not refuse. A decent person should never ask for what it is difficult to refuse. Yet it ever so frequently happens to me and not always from people who cynically were aware of having put me in a corner. Strange they have not been taught it was not "cricket." I deliberately use the word so dear to the English because despite their cult of "cricket" English people can be just as insistent on getting what they want out of me as others. I could for instance match every Italian transgressor with an Englishman—to speak of the only nations I have dealt with.

August 11th, Vallombrosa

Yesterday annual procession from the church to an altar erected for that purpose at the bottom of our garden. The garments, the canopy, the monstrance, the chant of the priests and communal bawling of the congregation, the fervour—all reminded me of that Minoan low relief of a similar procession thirty-five hundred years ago. There too priests shaking sistrums, the worshippers open-mouthed carrying palm branches, etc. I doubt whether in feeling and fervour there was much difference between the Minoan function and that of yesterday, whether one could have answered better than the other why and what they were celebrating, nor whether the answer was more than something learnt by rote that meant little to the individual. To the one of yesterday as to the Minoan it meant a rite, and as a rite to be performed in a certain way and no other, and to enjoy doing it, and feel safer for having done it. So certain ritual performances outlast mythologies, outlast dogmas, and may go on for thousands of years more.

August 17th, Vallombrosa

A couple from Albany, N.Y., to stay. He a sort of pontifex, or *accoucheur* of bridges, and she organizer of canteens, both wherever our armies went during last war. They met in Constantine and married a couple of years later. He hale and hearty at sixty-four with the face of an angel; and she a few years younger, keeping a beautiful figure. She a Kentuckian and he from Albany, now their home. Most striking about them their goodness, their innocence, so refreshing to encounter. I know that many millions of such Americans exist, meaning harm to nobody, believing or more than believing, taking it as a matter of course that everybody means well by everybody else, therefore bamboozleable and hard to de-bamboozle.

August 22nd, Vallombrosa

Spat blood yesterday forenoon, and again in the afternoon, and knowing next to nothing of physiology got frightened—cancer of stomach, lungs?! A gloom came over us. At my age one must be prepared for the end, every kind of end. Unfortunately, it may be a very lingering one, inspiring sulks, gloomy withdrawals, inability to get the better of them, to rise above them. I cannot help recalling in what a state of stony sulks I found Salomon Reinach a few days before his death. I do dread that sort of end. I wish mine would come as a lightning stroke, or instantaneous stopping of the heart. Which reminds me that when I was an undergraduate at Harvard the rather odd boy of Royce * spoke of the death of a companion as having "stopped" like a watch. Why not, if the heart is a mechanism like the spring of a watch, a bit more complicated.

August 25th, Vallombrosa

If only I could find *l'épithète juste* to evoke the guests at dinner yesterday. There was a distant relation of mine, a young woman of thirty or so, a blonde, slight, very elegant Florentine, about

* Josiah Royce (1855–1916), American philosopher and teacher; professor at Harvard, 1882–1916.

forty, with a dash of English blood, married to a completely Ang-
licized Scot, voluble, no inhibitions. Her husband, sporting, a
great reader, a publisher, peruses everything he prints, very typical British gentry. An American in the forties, slender, dark, perhaps a remote touch of Jewish blood, stimulating, a contagious
laugh, a universal favourite, adored by women. Each of these so
different from all the others, and playing together like a well-
trained quartette. That harmony of togetherness at a table is an
achievement of civilization, one of those achievements that it has
taken thousands of years to bring about. May it go on improving.

August 28th, Vallombrosa

A friend or a domestic makes a dash to fetch something, and
I wait for it and it seems an eternity, although they return in a
minute. But that minute spent in marching time, in living and
feeling and suffering mere time with no events that engage and
absorb one, is the quintessence of ennui, of boredom. I would de-
fine or rather describe boredom as the awareness of time dragging
on with no engaging, absorbing events to fill it. That happens to
me either when I am too indisposed to read or work or talk. Or
when I have to wait. A dislike for waiting can be increased to in-
tolerable boredom and the "hurry up and wait" of almost all working for others has prevented my taking up any career of a sub-
ordinate, and even to employ others who might be tardy when I
needed them.

August 29th, Vallombrosa

Two dreams: first, stole two small but important pictures
from the Louvre. Then tried to explain why, and wanted to return
them. That dream due perhaps to talking so much about pictures
with John Walker. How account for the second? I was placed
in a dining room next to Cocteau, who embraced me, radiant with
joy to see me, and began to recall aloud all he remembered about
our early meetings. If it should turn out that he died in the night,
there would be matter for the occultists.

August 31st, Vallombrosa

The most important event in the history of Europe is the change-over from the ancient Judeo-Greco-Roman attitude toward religion to the Christian one. The absurdest enemy of Christianity cannot deny the fact, even if he still persists in questioning the existence of Jesus of Nazareth. But how it came about, by what means, through what individual, is as disputed as any or perhaps more than any other question in history. To Christian writers the "why it came about" is answered by "that it was the will of God, and by the working of the Holy Ghost, through consecrated individuals like the Apostles, the Church Fathers, and their successors to this day." If they had absolute faith, they would not dread history because even the Holy Spirit has to work through human beings and human beings are weak and gross and envious —animals, in short, that even the Holy Spirit cannot control. As for the rest of us, we argue and discuss and dispute, cast our nets wider (as Eduard Meyer has done), and now Freudians and Jungians and students of South Sea anthropology will offer their explanations. I for one cannot abstain from reading all I find time for. Now it is Klausner's * *From Jesus to Paul* translated from the Hebrew. Thus far the author has given the *bouillon de culture* in which Christianity developed. He is well informed and shows little, indeed no, anti-Christian bias. On the other hand no fact and scarcely a consideration with which I am not already familiar. Why do I go on? No doubt, in hopes of some ray of enlightenment.

September 8th, Vallombrosa

In the autumn of 1888 when I first came to Rome, the Borghese Collection was exhibited on the ground floor of the palace. One of the most admired pictures was the one believed to be the authentic portrait of Cesare Borgia painted by Raphael. Nobody believes that any longer and the picture is entirely forgotten. A change of taste? If you like, but having nothing to do with anything specifically artistic. A change entirely due to the fact that it is no

* Joseph Klausner, Israeli scholar and historian.

longer believed to represent Cesare Borgia and to be painted by
Raphael; not to the recognition that the picture is of mediocre quality, but simply to considerations as external to the work of art as
the interpretation of the subject and who painted it. In fact changes
of taste hitherto have had nothing to do with its quality but only
with the subject matter, which seemed to please the fashions and
whims of the moment. Does it explain the change of the last decades, the greatest to have happened so swiftly in history?

September 11th, Vallombrosa

I am still ready to plunge into any subject suitable to my
competence and pursue it into its minutest details. These particularly because I far more desire to know how the author I am reading gets his results than in his conclusions. So I can foresee no
weakening of my lust for reading, no matter how many more years
I have before me. There scarcely (for instance) exists an historical
subject that could not absorb me, nor an anthropological, nor folk-
loristic, nor religious. Perhaps the history of Christianity excites
me most of all. That history almost makes a believing Christian
of me, for the same reason that the Florentine Jew whom no fellow
citizen could convert, but returned from Rome a convert because
the Lord must be behind the Church if anything so wicked, so
corrupt, could go on flourishing. Yet scarcely more so than lay
powers.

September 14th, Vallombrosa

The Joe Grews * here yesterday. Alice tried to praise a book
she was reading, *Isabelle,* by a French author named Gide. Did I
know him? She thought he must be worth while, because a friend
of Claudel's. This from the daughter of the most up-to-date
Bostonians of my youth, the Tom Perrys. Married young and has
been in diplomatic circles ever since. Perhaps mostly American
where perhaps the chief classics are the Social Registers and the
romans à clef. I wonder whether Diana Cooper, who lunched yes-

* Joseph Grew, American diplomat, author of *Ten Years in Japan.*

terday, brought up in an equivalent *milieu* but in London and living a similar life among Englishmen and Frenchmen, would have proved us wrong! But think of Mme Greffulhe,* who in 1914 heard of Degas for the first time and asked me whether I had! Truly the culture of "high society" ladies is incalculably spotty!

September 18th, Vallombrosa

Have been hearing about Conant, the President of Harvard, and about his contempt for the arts. How he keeps cutting down expenditures for art teaching with the result that this has fallen lower than in any of the other great American universities. That is no comforting news for me, who leave my collections, my house and fields, my library to Harvard. Indeed, Conant's indifference is proved by the fact that he was in Rome some few months ago and never took the trouble to come to see the legacy I am making to Harvard. Friends clearly felt this is a disgrace, and carefully hid from me that he had been to Rome. Only yesterday eve did I have the definite assurance that Conant had passed some days there, and was even taken by Mason Hammond † to Hadrian's Villa.

September 20th, Vallombrosa

When the nearest as well as dearest, and dearest because nearest, are out of my sight, I suffer agonies of anxiety lest something happen to them. For fear they should suffer if hurt, or sweet life be cut short? No. My first and overwhelming thought is of the inconvenience, or worse still the revolution, it could cause in my life. Am I then utterly heartless, or am I simply the average man? Are there individuals who love others for the others' sake without reference to themselves? I want to penetrate, but do not hope to conclude. The human heart is a quicksand, and one sinks into it, deeper and deeper, and never comes out to *light*. Meanwhile I suffer for what seems to me heartlessness and the feeling that I

* Madame de Greffulhe, French aristocrat, supposed to have served as a model for one of Proust's characters.
† Professor of History at Harvard University.

275

never can get over selfishness and self-interest—in short, of being a cannibal.

September 28th, Vallombrosa

A newspaper agency called me up yesterday evening to ask me to give them a few words about Santayana, who died the previous day. After leaving Harvard because they would not make him full professor, he abandoned America with bitter feelings, and transferred himself to England, to Cambridge, where again he found no rest, concluding that Englishmen were not made for philosophy. Drifted about Paris, was frequently the guest of Charles Strong * at Fiesole, and lived finally in the convent of the blue nuns in Rome. Always grave, the hidalgo already when he headed the regiment of Latin School in Boston. Believed himself to be Spanish to the core, and kept frequenting his sisters at Avila, one married to an estate agent and the other a nun. As a philosopher I cannot judge him, although I enjoyed his *Life of Reason,* as the five volumes appeared one after the other. I read *Animal Faith* and then stopped reading his philosophy. As a thinker and writer, his *forma mentis* and his style always seemed to me at least as New England as my own. Unamuno asked me who was that so very American writer with such a Spanish name. As a stylist Santayana had the gravity that characterized him in life, distinguished, occasionally elegant. Little if any sense of humour. In life he was not particularly generous. He could snigger at the discomfiture of his best friends. Friends? Attachments, perhaps. Friends, I doubt. William James said of him, when he and I were still undergraduates, that Santayana kept his heart on ice. I wonder whether he died a Catholic with all the rites. Were he capable of accepting a church it would have been the Catholic, but I doubt whether he was as near to being one as I am, for he had little if any feeling for aesthetics, and Catholicism is mankind's greatest art creation, the which therefore pulls at my heartstrings with a thousand hands.

* See p. 316, note.

September 29th, Vallombrosa

What is comfort but the reduction to the condition of a ruminant chewing the cud, breathing easily, the viscera quiet, no organ rebellious, on the contrary all harmonious, warm, and inwardly cosy. And happiness is the same *plus* a pretext to explain and justify the feeling of complete satisfaction. Both states are more physiological than mental, let alone moral. Perhaps that is why they are—with rare exceptions—uncreative. "Divine" or even devilish discontent is more productive. Happy nations have no history. Like the animals, they live, they die, they are forgotten, ultimately disappear without a trace like herds of cattle or other quadrupeds. Yet we all long for happiness and we Americans identify it with comfort, which we do attain, and strive with self-satisfaction and missionary zeal to impose our happiness on the rest of mankind. If happiness is more physiological than psychological what is the exaltation one enjoys when one has laid an idea and cackles over it like a hen? According to the James-Lange theories I was brought up on, all feeling is merely physiological and yet I don't understand, or rather I do not want to admit, that the exaltation of discovery, of invention, of achievement, of victory over oneself or of others, is merely physiological. Then ecstasy too in all phases would be so, the ecstasy of the noblest mystics and saints, the exultation of the martyrs, the sacrifice of patriots all due to physiological processes without which they would not occur. On the other hand why balk at the process, when it attains the happiness we crave for?

October 3rd, I Tatti

I suppose that if the present King of Sweden were only Gustave Bernadotte, and his wife not a Battenberg, I should not perhaps be so enthusiastic about his being, as he is, so utterly free from societyish and political nonsense, and so keen an archaeologist. As it now is, his titles and his situation scarcely come between us, or he would not condescend to stay with me, nor I aspire to have him as a guest. But who will believe that my horn is not the least exalted by his visit, and that the publicity it

277

gives me annoys and even alarms me. I shrink from being talked and written about as a private person, although up to a point I do want to be known and appreciated as a writer on art. And believe it or not, I want my writing known for the good it may do!

October 10th, I Tatti

The King of Sweden is the most completely humanized person of my acquaintance. He seems to be absolutely without any feeling of class or rank, of anybody being below him. Also in politics he is the most complete liberal, opposing no measure that promises improvement of conditions for "working" classes, is even a believer in universal suffrage—at all costs. Speaks of his kingship in the most impersonal way as a job he at present has to do, without the faintest perceptible trace of pride—left to himself, he would prefer to be an archaeologist, an excavator, a traveller and studious sight-seer. His real passion is Chinese art, particularly the bronzes. It is said that his wife once said: I thought I was marrying a Crown Prince. It turned out that I married a professor.

October 12th, I Tatti

Among my friends Salvemini is one of the brightest, sunniest, as well as best-intentioned to be fair and just. He now at eighty has a finer head than anybody else of my acquaintance, I mean cranium nobler, more distinguished. Yet such is human nature in its competitive aspects, that talking yesterday of the time when Sforza and Pacciardi were in exile in the U.S.A. he implied that their relations with the State Department were somehow not disinterested. His judgment may have been based on the fact that as practical politicians they were ready to compromise, while he the idealist never would. Behind that, however, I smelt the smoke and stench of animal competitiveness. The same that makes it so difficult to do justice to anyone in one's own profession —whatever that be, even of a spiv.

Likewise with nations. Salvemini as Italian can criticize Eng-

B.B. Looking at Guatemalan Sculpture, 1957. *Photo David Lees, Life*

Nicky Mariano Reading to B.B., 1948. *Photo Dimitri Kessel, Life*

B.B. with Nicky Mariano in Santa Chiara, Naples, 1955.
Photo David Seymour/Magnum

B.B., 1954. *Photo Emil Schulthess*

land and America, keenly and bitingly, but never with the heart
and rage that possess him when Italy's rival France is concerned.

October 13th, Rome

Recent article on Homeric question in *Revue de Paris*. All
such studies, interesting and even fascinating in themselves, lead
one astray and far away from the one important thing, which
should be to enjoy Homer as a timeless work of art, as literature
of universal appeal. Indeed, one almost would think that but for
the "Homeric question" Homer already would be forgotten. If
that is so, forgotten he very soon will be. What a world in prospect,
a world without Homer and Vergil for all the Western nations
and the Bible in the King James version for the Anglo-Saxons.
What will our English speech be like when it no longer echoes
the rhythm and the phraseology of The Book? I cannot imagine
a culture as distinct from a civilization without the Bible, the
Greek and Latin and the later Classics. It will come, of course, but
what will it be like?

October 20th, Rome

Performance of Katherine Dunham. All based on Negro
beliefs, rites, and holiday extravagances. From our point of view,
it is a call of the wild, and a very successful one. It wakes up and
brings to life in one even like myself the sleeping dogs of almost
prehuman dreads, aversions, aberrations, appeals. The shrieks so
staccato, the metal of the instruments, the dry crack of castanets,
the shimmy-shakes, the stampeding, all go to one's marrow. How
all this would have horrified most of us fifty years ago. Should
have found it squalid, vulgar, shaking, and now babes and suck-
lings come with their parents to see and hear and be entranced,
hypnotized, overwhelmed. We feel at last free to return to the
primitive, the infantile, the barbarous, the savage in us, even the
way Greeks of the best period did to Bacchic rites, so wild, so
cruel, so filthy!

October 25th, Rome

James Rorimer * yesterday to tea. Congratulated him on three and a half million given to the Cloisters by Rockefeller. He corrected me. It was ten million. What could I have done fifty or better still sixty years ago with ten million. All of Mrs. Gardner's collection did not cost three million. Those were the days when for the little St. John stripping for the desert by Domenico Veneziano I paid ten or at most fifteen pounds. It cost the National Gallery half a million and more. Nowadays a tiny Christ on the Cross by Sassetta is priced at thirty thousand dollars. Fifty years ago one could have had it for a couple of hundred francs. And highest prices due more to my own writing than to any other reason. If I had a proper percentage on the rise of prices, I now would be able to realize the foundation I had in mind when I first thought of leaving I Tatti, its contents, and the rest of my estate to Harvard. History will never know what part I have played.

October 30th, Rome

Tea at the Quirinal. Cuirassiers at doors, and well-groomed servants. Reception room in surprising good taste, although sumptuous. Ushered in and discovered Einaudi on one sofa, and his wife opposite. Emilio Cecchi † and two other men with him, and two women, one of them Leonetta Cecchi, with her. Introduced to those I did not know, and of course could not catch the names. One seemed to keep a certain distance toward me, and he turned out to be the editor of *Il Mondo,* and the other a musical critic on same paper. Very affable and flattering, Einaudi himself asked me what works of art used to be in the Quirinal, and when I answered, he seemed to have nothing more to say to me. I went

* Director of the Cloisters, New York, 1949–55; Director of the Metropolitan Museum of Art, New York, since 1955.
† Well-known Italian writer, stylist, literary and art critic; married to the painter Leonetta Pieraccini. For many years on friendly terms with B.B., of whose *Italian Painters of the Renaissance* he made a masterly Italian translation.

and sat by his wife, who from the timid professor's wife I used to know has become a very distinguished-looking and behaving great lady, playing her part to perfection. He, poor dear, looked anything but at home in the Quirinal. On the whole a satisfactory affair.

October 31st, Rome

It is next to impossible (for me at least) to talk about myself, particularly about my more distant past, of (as George Moore used to say) "the days of my potency," without fabulating, exaggerating, idealizing, and outright lying. In a way it is parallel to the trills and sequences of sopranos and choristers in the singing of the part, with no more deliberate intention of boasting or showing off. Next to impossible to be prosaically accurate, to be unlyrical in talking about one's own past, and that is the reason why it is considered bad manners to talk about oneself. Only that women whom one excites draw one out, lead one on—to make a fool of oneself. I have no resistance when an attractive female calls me.

November 4th, Rome

High ecclesiastic *parloir,* as attractive as "cold shape." Enters a gorgeously vigorous, vital, portly, you can't say old man, with magnificent white beard reaching down almost to his pectoral. No such beard since Tagore's, the which his son told me it took hours to keep in its splendour. With a rose-purple cap on his head and ample robes advances Cardinal Tisserant,* greets me, asks me whether I prefer to talk French, Italian, English, and goes on in English. Tells me about his numerous occupations, including a bishopric, and then expands on his various tours to America. Without self-consciousness and too happy for vanity, he manifestly could not be more contented with his life. Considering all his occupations, I did not dare to keep him, and got up to go at

* Eugène, Cardinal Tisserant, Dean of the College of Cardinals. First met B.B. in 1932 through Jacques Truelle, then Attaché at the French Embassy to the Vatican.

281

the end of twenty minutes. He did not detain me. Nor did he ask me anything about myself, my work, my life. . . .

November 8th, Rome

Curious how even intelligent women abuse familiarity by neglecting to remain works of art with their bedfellows. They will lie with their faces smeared, their hair in curl-papers, in jackets to keep them warm, and then are outraged because the male sidesteps with females who understand their business as females, who know how to keep men. And the female in turn is attracted to the male who, he too, remains a work of art, and knows his "way of a man with a maid." Familiarity may breed contempt. I have in mind a case of a woman who lost a husband, largely because "unbeknownst to himself" he was piling up distaste for the way she got herself up in bed, distaste which ended in disgust, so that he jumped out of bed shouting that he would never see her again.

In all relations let not familiarity kill intimacy. Approach your bedfellow as if you had loved him for years, and were going to lie with him for the first time.

November 10th, Rome

Often grudges and resentments steam up from the depths as vapours from a dunghill. Not only against others, but against myself. Recollections of deliberate naughtiness against Mother, when I was not five, and all the meannesses, sneakiness, cowardice, and disreputable and dishonourable things I used to do—partly when I knew no better. Those gnaw at me, and more than the treacheries, disloyalties, and calumnies of people like Herbert Horne, Roger Fry, or Geoffrey Scott, who owed me so much and whom I loved and trusted so much, not to speak of all I stood for fifty years from my own wife. I try to suppress these evil thoughts, but they will rise up and befoul me when I am feeling low and vacant. I do not dwell on them, and as soon as I can rouse myself I shout *Retro me Satana*, but it is not always easy to shake them off, to dispel the clouds and be serene.

November 11th, Rome

Have been good friends with Margherita Sarfatti * for years, but only yesterday could I get her to talk about Mussolini and Fascism. We agreed about events, occurrences, all that happened. She denied none, but when we came to discuss how and why, we seldom agreed about the how, and never about the why. We saw things in different if not always opposed perspectives, and intentions and notions in each case took on entirely different aspects and bore different interpretations. Again another nail in the coffin of History as she is written. More and more do I understand that the Chinese finally eschewed History altogether, and confined themselves to Annals. In such and such a year such and such a thing happened, with no attempt to account for it, to justify it, or to condemn it. All the same, the philosophical, or psychological, or economical, or sociological romances we regard as history make fascinating reading—as do all well-written novels.

November 13th, Rome

Kenneth Clark is in every way a *homo novus,* but his father was rich so his career is not regarded as a success story, while mine is, because my father was poor. Yet he has had every possible success, held high positions and continues to fill them, frequents highest official society, and is considered the best art lecturer in English language, the best art writer and critic ditto, has a brilliant wife in foremost ranks of fashion, promising children. Yet his is not a success story, and mine is—not because I have done this or that, but only because I have succeeded in attaining to enough money to live decently. K.C. not only inherited his fortune, but increases it. He buys and sells works of art, and that counts only as a gentleman "exchanging" a good thing for a better one. If I sold any picture I should at once be put down as a "dealer," because I started poor. So success is really a question of mere money, and nothing else. Much else I have done counts for little, beside the

* Member of wealthy Italian Jewish family; very close to Mussolini until the racial laws obliged her to seek refuge in South America; author of the biography of Mussolini entitled *Dux* and of many essays and articles.

283

fact that I have achieved what to the *grosse Publikum* can be procured by MONEY only.

November 18th, Rome

My primary desire in sight-seeing is to enjoy what I am seeing, but with colleagues and often even when alone what we enjoy is not seeing but discussing what we are seeing and passing on to discuss another work of art and seldom if ever stopping to enjoy it, to meditate without words, to lose oneself in it. Indeed, I get the impression that with most art historians the question of enjoyment of quality no longer comes up at all and that our only object, only purpose, is to attribute and date, having done which or failed to do it, our interest in the work of art is exhausted. But placing the object in its time and naming its author is amusing and enjoyable enough to be its own reward, and I dare say for most of us it is all we get.

November 21st, Rome

Croce is dead. Despite everything between us, our almost opposed approaches to all arts and to some historical subjects, I have always esteemed him as the greatest influence on intellectual life in Italy. He was much more the *Duce* in matters of the mind than Mussolini ever was in politics. His influence was not always one that I approved. He was a narrow conceptualist and anti-psychologist and anti-empiricist to such a degree that to my recollection he never mentioned Bergson and when I sent him Ralph Perry's two volumes on the life and thought of William James he did not even acknowledge them. He may have resented my standing out against his *Aesthetics* and his art theories in general. On my part I had a certain feeling against his assumption of sovereignty in all matters of thought and politics. Yet for all that and under all that I have had a deep affection and respect for him, and perhaps few will sincerely and lastingly regret his departure more than I do.

284

November 28th, I Tatti

Percy Lubbock after a year we had not met looked more hulky, was blander, and somewhat Johnsonish. But a Victorian Cambridge ultra-radical in thought, while conventional *au fond,* in the respect for the accepted ritual of his class. Characteristic that in the *New Statesman* he likes the politics and dislikes the reviews, while I abhor its politics and take it only for its reviews, even as I am more of a mind about art (if only it were free) with Stalinist than with Western up-to-daters. Percy is angelic in putting up with his immobility and his all but total blindness. He no longer can see objects before him. He lights his pipe, and I fear lest he drop it lit on something inflammable. He reaches for his glass. Yesterday he cried for whisky that was not drowned in water. An oddity of his literary taste is his contempt for Trollope, and all readers of Trollope. Thackeray remains his king of novelists. All in all a most lovable oldster.

December 7th, I Tatti

At last I seem to have found the epithet that best describes my attitude toward myself. "Self-absorbed" never sounded right, because it implied something like habitual indifference to others and their interest. "Self-aware" is too passively the mere onlooker. "Self-interested" carried with it the connotation of being interested in one's own aggrandizement only, which certainly is not my case. My case is well described with the words "self-curious." I am curious about myself not first and foremost because it is *my* self, but first and last because this self can be studied by me from within, and constantly discovered in contradiction not only with its outward manifestations but within and ever more within, far more than without. I fancy the well-trained bourgeois self is completely canalized to flow cheerfully to the social purposes it serves. *My* self seems to toss and whirl and dive and dip, and ever rouses and never satisfies my curiosity about the human ego, which I can study in my inner self only.

285

December 10th, I Tatti

A young Swedish woman working for the cinema—so Botti-cellian in every possible respect, form, colour, expression, every detail, that I could tell to just what period, what picture, she belonged. Now it is as good as certain that he never saw types like this far Northern young woman. No more than the Greeks ever saw Anglo-Saxon and other Northern women who so resemble their best sculpture of the fifth and fourth centuries B.C. And remember the Greeks were smallish, and not as a race good-looking. The artists evolved these types out of their call to give the human shape tactile values, movement, and, in the case of Botticelli, to refine on his inheritance from Filippo Lippi, as he left his legacy to Filippino, etc. But in literature the same—Shake-speare never saw, never frequented, people like those he created. They came to him from his innate, intuitive connotion about human types, as well as their conduct, and his gift of telling words.

December 11th, I Tatti

Toward noon yesterday drove up to crossroads high up and walked back on the highroad. Dazzling, glowing, radiant, caress-ing sun. To my left above the cypresses on the hillside a sky of a blue I had never seen before, a blue as of stained glass, the kind that alternates with magenta in Turkish windows of today. On the opposite side the tawny, lion-coloured cliffs and terraces of Monte Ceceri. Under me, over expanses of discoloured foliage punctuated by the honey-coloured oaks, sparkled the windows of Florence shrouded in a faint mist that gave point to the compo-sition of a view dominated by the dome of the cathedral. What on earth could one see lovelier! Not even from the height over Damascus. Just back from Rome, I became aware of how much the landscape here was detailed, while the Roman one was all great sweeping curves that do not draw you to themselves but lend you wings.

286

December 12th, I Tatti

Yesterday to lunch a pleasantly nimble, readily responsive American, in fact a New York Jew of Russo-Polish origin. I enjoyed his company, as I do that of most cultivated, clever Jews. And yet there was something missing, something the Greeks lacked and envied the Romans for having, *gravitas*. It is not to be solemnly serious, overweighed with a sense of one's mission, or vulgar importance. It is an imponderable which the thoroughbred Englishman (among others) has, and which a person like myself (always coming back to myself) lacks. Is it the lack which tempts me to clown too much, and exposes me to being treated like one by journalists who come to interview me? Or is it that I cannot take myself too seriously, and when others do I begin to cut capers, as a means of getting away from what to me is stifling unreality?

December 13th, I Tatti

Sixty-five years ago Nicky was born at Naples. Twenty-two years earlier I was born near Vilna in Lithuania. But Nicky's mother was a Balt, and Nicky herself was brought up partly in Estonia, and when the first war came found herself marooned there, but all along enjoying the way of living there with her baronial relations and their standards, in preference to the rather morose existence with a severely professorial father in the suburbs of Florence. What series of accidents has brought us together, and kept us together, closer and closer! I, every day more dependent, more grateful, more devoted. The accidents would take long to enumerate from first to last, and of course they happened to individuals who could take advantage of them. Who could have foretold then, as she was in her cradle, and I passing again and again under her windows at the Mergellina in Naples, that accident after accident would bring us together in a union that (humanly speaking) could not be nearer perfection?

December 14th, I Tatti

Yesterday Horowitz,* the publisher who brought out my *Italian Painters* a few weeks ago, talked of publishing the book in the same form with four hundred illustrations not only in the *langues principales,* French, German, Italian, Spanish, but also in Dutch and in the Scandinavian languages. I asked him about Russian and he thought there might be a way of arranging it. Fifty years ago all this would have made me glow with self-satisfaction. Now I feel scarcely a ray of joy. In an abstract, aloof fashion I am glad that my art gospel is getting more of a hearing, as if it did not concern me but was for the general good. Horowitz thinks that the reading public is only catching up now with the book. I suspect it is the four hundred illustrations at a very low price rather than my doctrines that appeal to the public.

December 17th, I Tatti

Woke with a nauseating feeling of dust and ashes, and of life ending as modern towns do in *terrain vague,* tailing off into dust heaps and slag pits. There is always an abundance of material for worry, for fear of the insoluble, for a feeling of utter incapacity to cope with their multiplicity. You recall having had these dreads again and ever again, and yet having lived on and in a limited sense prospered. True, but you were not so enfeebled by extreme old age, and the one person on whom you built your house of life is herself getting older and overburthened by all she does for you, so that you may be free to enjoy reading, writing, talking, flirting even. How frail a foundation, and if anything should happen to her, where would you be, and your house of life would turn out to be a house of cards, and would tumble about your ears, leaving you no shelter but in suicide. *Absit omen,* but such black thoughts do haunt me, and are not easily driven away.

* Bela Horowitz (1898–1955), founder of Phaidon publishing house in Vienna, which he transferred to London in 1938. His daughter and son-in-law keep up the tradition of publishing lavishly illustrated art books.

December 18th, I Tatti

This house and all its contents, furniture, pictures, books, are accumulated not so much as more lately you imagined for a definite purpose, but simply because you enjoyed having objects around you that delighted whenever you looked up, books you loved to buy because it gave you pleasure to buy them, etc. Then all of a sudden that was not enough and you were seized with the lust to perpetuate what is after all only (as it were) the exudation of your body, the fruit of your particular way of functioning. Surely the Goncourts were more generous, who left their art treasures to be scattered and thus allowed others to enjoy getting and possessing them, instead of impounding and preserving them in an impersonal collection that no private person can clutch as his own.

December 19th, I Tatti

But one cannot live entirely without a pattern, without the illusion of purpose. Without them nothing seems worth while any more. One realizes how much each particular objective depended for its value not only on being part of a pattern but on the firm belief that that design, that pattern, would keep its wholeness and all its parts indefinitely. It is all illusion of course, for without the personality that spins it out of itself the pattern loses its shape like thread without the reel it was wound around. And I know it and never wholly ignore it, yet I go on longing to perpetuate what I have shaped. Could a rational being be more irrational? On the other hand what should I do, what should I be without the irrational that we remain aware of, combat and yield to? Has there ever been a completely rational human being? Certainly none ever recorded. In fact history but for the irrational would not exist.

December 21st, I Tatti

"Daisy" Chanler * is dead, the last of my contemporaries. Was a survivor of a generation prior to mine intellectually, although she could have been at most three years only my elder. Daughter of a missionary and a snobbish mother, brought up in Rome to the cult of Roman high society, she naturally ended as a Catholic. Yet being American, she took her religion too seriously, and handed it on to all her offspring to the fourth generation. There was something expansive, generous, radiant about her, and a perpetual adolescence of mind that made her eager for contact with what she could follow and try to assimilate in what was going on in the upper reaches of recent but already consecrated literature and art. A great reader, in German as well of course as in Italian and in French, she was like Edith Wharton, with whom one could discuss any book of European interest—but never on the sociopolitical plane. It will take generations before the emerging world of today will see her type.

December 25th, I Tatti

Rebecca West and Henry Andrews, her husband—between them they seem to have been everywhere and to have read everything and known everybody. He particularly speaks faultless German, excellent French, and gets on in Italian. He seems particularly to have known every Englishman intimately that I know but superficially. He knows his Classics in art as well as in literature, French cathedrals for example, and all that is in them. All that and a businessman, an *homme d'affaires,* and not the least a professional *érudit* or *homme de lettres.* England in my time produced his like. I wonder whether *les jeunes*—"the youngs," as Edith Wharton used to call them—are fostering such "Faustian" individuals. The most remarkable of that kind was Prince Alexander von Thurn und Taxis, an Austrian who not only had all the qualities and attainments of an Andrews, but was a musician

---

* Margaret Winthrop Chanler (1862–1952), American brought up in Rome; intimate friend of Edith Wharton's.

as well, a fine violinist, and President of the Viennese *Philbar-monie*. They will be replaced, but when and in what shape?

December 31st, I Tatti

Balance of 1952. Leaves me not in worse health so far as functioning of this and that organ is concerned, but feebler, less inclined to make an effort, to walk or work, drowsier, requiring more sleep, and deafer, less quick in "catching on" to what is said in my hearing.

From the outside it must seem like a very successful year. *Rumour and Reflection,* which for years no publisher would look at in U.S.A. and was kept back at Constable's in England, had fair success in the latter and great in the former. Better still, *Italian Painters of the Renaissance*—thanks be noted to the Kress subvention of fifteen thousand dollars and my forgoing of royalties, and selling at a derisory price—is enjoying great popularity. Also my booklet on the *Art of Constantine,* published only a fortnight ago, has been reviewed already in a two-column article of the *Corriere della Sera* by Cecchi. All that must stand for extravagant success to my enemy-friends, not to speak of the "Anons" who dislike one for no reason whatever.

To me these "successes" mean little or nothing, for I know that they are not the fruit of the year's functioning. It is due to garnering and "selling" the past—not to creative work. It is that which turns these successes not only into failures but to melancholy reflections on my present incompetence. That rather than the worry over the future of my idea of turning I Tatti into a home of culture, which may be wrecked by Harvard's hitherto unexpected refusal to accept the legacy, that worries me and prevents me from taking any pleasure—never would have been great —in what to envious and even sympathizing outsiders may seem crowning triumphs.

1953

January 1st, I Tatti

Some few years ago I expressed surprise on New Year's Day to be still alive. I have got used to going on living, even though I remain doubtful about seeing the next New Year's Day. I have no prophecies to make. We seem to be going through a narrow canyon with very high, steep, smooth sides. We jostle along, kept deep down by the impossibility of climbing up, and pushed forward by the impenetrable crowd behind us—the crowd of events, what Italians and others call "historical necessity." I cannot foresee any happening that would make a great, an immediate difference—not even the death of the most conspicuously important individual on the earth's surface, namely, Stalin. Nor do I expect the triumph of taste, and still less of reason. Perhaps they only have stooped to conquer, but apparently they have stooped so deep, and in such a quicksand, that recovery may be slow, and they certainly, taste and reason I mean, will not emerge triumphant over the bad taste and unreason of the masses, in the course of the year now beginning. Wherefore patience and shuffle the cards.

January 2nd, I Tatti

Amazed at Kafka's minutely detailed self-awareness as revealed in his diaries. Santayana (who by the way was the first to tell me about Bergson, placing him on a level with Zeno) sneered at Bergson for his self-awareness and gave it an intestinal origin. I wonder whether in both cases and in the case of Proust as well (not to mention my *Minderwertigkeit*) it is not due to our Jewish origin. Hunted, always insecure, our ancestors must have developed unusual gifts of inner as well as outer observation,

295

the which nowadays turns us into psychologists, scientists, novelists, critics. In the case of Kafka his outer observation surpasses almost anything I can recall, for minuteness of detail and searching penetration. Indeed, almost sordid and even stercoral. His diaries smell strong of the ghetto. One would think Kafka had no gentile friends or even acquaintances.

January 4th, I Tatti

A typical day! Chat with Luisa Vertova. Walk in garden with Kiki Ritter. See Nicky in her room. To lunch, Fräulein Kiel, who tells me I am an inspiration. Nap. See Nicky again. Read letters. Tea pandemonium. I come down, find a crowd, shake hands with people I do not know, recognize Mattioli, sit down beside him, and talk for two hours, he talking back, interrupted by incursion of Molly Berkeley with her small protégé Vittorio, aged ten. I ask him something and his little body becomes a most expressive arabesque, needing no words. Further invasion by Nannina Fossi.* Note how very much her face is like her husband's. Young son with her, her facial expression, but his father's way of walking. After an hour and a half Dario Neri and Paolo Moroni to dine, and we discuss publication of *Lorenzo Lotto*, and I try to damp their eagerness to include colour reproductions. They tell me that my *Estetica e Storia* has sold best of all my books, and that they are bringing out a new edition.

January 15th, I Tatti

Faces in all illustrated weeklies, and worst of all in *Life* and other U.S.A. weeklies, are so depressingly, discouragingly dull! And most are faces of important individuals, who have played

* Luisa Vertova, graduate of Florence University, attached to the Tatti household, 1945–55; translated B.B.'s publications during those years into Italian; 1955–61, married to Benedict Nicolson, editor of *Burlington Magazine*.—Molly Berkeley, born Lowell of Boston, widow of Lord Berkeley, owner of several attractive houses in Italy. It was in her Assisi house that B.B. spent his ninetieth birthday.—Marchesa Nannina Fossi, daughter of American-born Countess Edith Rucellai, whose mother, Mrs. Bronson, had been a friend of Robert Browning and Henry James.—Nicky Mariano was recovering from an attack of pneumonia.

or are playing a part in public life in all occupations, as pioneers or men of letters. Most of them would go into one of a half-dozen baskets, so much are they alike. With such faces to deal with, one is amazed to reflect on how much they do achieve and, with society as unintelligibly complicated as ours has become, that they can carry on at all. I suppose it is that each contributes his mite, and the machine knows how to use them.

January 16th, I Tatti

Reading what I wrote yesterday about faces—Tuesday's *London Times* reproduced the face of President Conant of Harvard, bringing the news that he will be High Commissioner and presently Ambassador to Bonn. Not a gleam of sensuality, of sensitiveness, a contracted, tight-lipped look, as if far away from common humanity, and absorbed in abstractions, and incapable of coming down to the individual, the human personality, the private X, Y, or Z, and not the mass of which this person is a part. What a fate for an institution like Harvard that began in order to educate Congregational ministers, then little by little became famous for its humanities, till President Eliot began, and this impersonal scientist completed, its transformation into a series of technological schools, in which the humanities are barely tolerated, so long as they submit to existing, scarcely living, on what will just keep them flickering without wholly going out like ill-fed flares. Faces, faces, yet I never see one I don't want to classify and study.

January 17th, I Tatti

More often women's faces look human, pathetic, worn, *restes de beauté,* appealing, or hard to classify. A great help when I can assimilate them to faces in the art of the past, to faces in sculpture and painting. My wife and I used to make a game of it, to see whether a given face could have been done by this or that artist, or in this or that time or place. Leaving costume, hair, kerchiefs, etc., aside, faces in all epochs of the last twenty-five centuries have much in common with our own, and in Egypt twenty-five centuries earlier. Not so in centuries between 500 and 1400, when with rarest exceptions art was incapable of seeing and reproducing what we (my contemporaries, I mean) see in objects before them. I return to faces; there are those that haunt me although I have seen them for a second passing me in the street, about whom I know nothing, women's faces only, that keep bobbing up in memory through the years.

January 24th, I Tatti

Day before yesterday, radiant, scintillating, drove high up with Freya, walked till within easy distance of Bagazzano, and turned toward Gamberaia. Always on ridge there used to be three secular stone pines, elegant although patriarchal. No longer there. Why cut down? For lucre? Ranges of Prato Magno and Falterona shining, dazzling, white-hooded with driven snow. Gamberaia in noonday shimmer, a ghostly ruin, looking like stage scenery for a highly romantic play. Then Settignano. An hour and three quarters' walk without ache, without feeling tired. A *Kraftprobe*? Unaccountable. How could I do this, I who seldom can walk more than half an hour? And all the time Freya and I were talking. I noticed that she scarcely looked, although I am sure she enjoyed. I looked and looked, but when it comes to describing, it is she who would describe what I had seen and not I. For the gifted artist a glance is a sufficient springboard. He requires little observation.

February 2nd, I Tatti

What is America and particularly the U.S.A. but a Magna Europa! In the early days, down to Goethe, it was still a dreamland so that he could say, "America is within us." It was Brasiland, California, names for regions of faërie. But now what is the U.S.A. but an anthology of all the peoples of Europe? Every nation in Europe, Europe in the widest sense, including the Near East, is represented there. And though competing and not loving each other, they live there peaceably. How? Because they have left frontiers behind them, and languages. Because they all aspire to become and as soon as possible to be regarded as full-fledged

298

Americans. Because they willingly (on the whole) submit to the ideals and ideas and folkways of the British pioneers who first settled the country and gave it a pattern that could be enlarged and multiplied as on a cloth, so that New York City became New York State, and the Thirteen Colonies became the Forty-eight States which now make the U.S.A.

February 6th, I Tatti

It is not accepted, still less understood, that chatter, communal chatter refined into talk, is as physical a necessity as a call of nature. Suppressing it does not lead immediately to bad results, wherefore it is not recognized. In the long run the results are bad enough, and account in part for revulsions in so-called thought, in the attitude and approach to questions, in the revulsions to the suppressed subjects of talk. Thus for generations sex was ignored as subject for discussion. Could be sniggered over by naughty small boys of all ages. Then the dykes broke down and the floods began to inundate dinner tables in the most respectably fashionable houses, and to absorb most novels, fiction in general, and public interest. Publication of Kinsey Report, and its fabulous popularity, would have been inconceivable forty years ago. Not only was sex taboo, but all references to the excretory functions of our bodies. Now one talks of them as of course.

February 9th, I Tatti

I read less and ever less for anything but the confirmation of convictions and prejudices. That is why I peruse so many periodicals. They strengthen my own beliefs by more statements, or by information deliberately or unconsciously sifted to confirm my way of thinking. Reading matter of the day that does neither for me, I reject, and with scorn. So each of us reads himself into an hypnotic condition as effective as the faith of past ages. The past ages believed in Heaven and built churches, and monasteries, as a sure way of getting there. We believe in what? In the kind of society, human society, that the machine will bring about. It is an aesthetic ideal no matter how little we may think so. For what could such a society be if realized, except a work of art existing for its own sake and for no ulterior purposes—not even the greatest happiness of the greatest number. Endurance of suffering, ascetism, heroism, self-sacrifice all for an aesthetic ideal.

February 10th, I Tatti

"Berenson Canonized" is the title of an article that appeared in yesterday's *Corriere della Sera*. Emilio Cecchi there talks of my *Italian Painters* in a way that could not be more satisfactory. And a very brief moment of satisfaction it did give me. It was followed immediately by the feeling that nothing like it will appear in my own country or in England, the language group to which I belong. That lasted a second only, and was succeeded by the better thought that "the Berenson" who has been canonized was not the Berenson of today but the Berenson of sixty years ago. Could I believe that I then was so far in advance of my age that only now have I come into my own, *that* might be some comfort. Again but a minute or more. All as almost nothing in the face of the fact that I did my best so long ago, little in sixty intervening years, and that now I am as dried up as a waterless rivulet. Oh for an hour of feeling creative!

February 11th, I Tatti

How I hate the thought of money, yet with the years I have become ever more aware that the question of cost in terms of money was behind everything. The perpetual omnipresent consideration is one of how much money it will take, from a drink at a café to instrumenting the greatest, most effective material projects, to the most ideal, most impersonal, most humanizing purposes. *Pas d'argent, pas de Suisse* used to be said sneeringly by the Parisians of the eighteenth century. Now we all may sing in chorus, *Pas d'argent*—RIEN. How I shrink from the idea of cost in all shapes, but most of all in the shape of money. I go so far as to dislike having it on my person. One of "the blessings" that ease has brought me is that I can afford to let others conduct my finances, and even to pay big and little for me, so that I never need pay a hotel bill, pay a cab, give a tip. One of the things I feel most grateful for to Nicky is that she does it for me.

February 15th, I Tatti

Staying here, Renato Guttuso * exhales candour, good will, geniality, kindness—nevertheless not only a Communist but a Sovietist. How account for it!? Perhaps there is no accounting for it, any more than for equally humane and in other respects highly rational Christians who accept the theory of Redemption and, if Catholic, deliberately ignore or gloss over the many crooked and shady doings of the Church Militant. I ask Guttuso what he would do if the Soviets ordered him to kill me. His only answer is that they never would. Yet I hear that on the platform he can be a stout defender of Stalin, "Father almighty," and all his ways —many of which Guttuso can scarcely believe to be human. The fact seems to be that we live in water-tight compartments with no communication between them, not even *par osmose*. Few of us are completely integrated, thank Heaven. What a monster a completely integrated pattern of a man would be!

February 18th, I Tatti

For many weeks it was touch and go whether Harvard would accept the legacy of I Tatti, and I kept waking at nights with a cold sweat, worrying as to what I should do if it, Harvard I mean, refused. Even in the daytime I had fits of *angoisse* over it. Yesterday we were merrymaking after dinner and a wire was handed in to say that Harvard did accept the legacy. I looked at it, went on talking and listening, and forgot all about this telegram with its glad tidings, bringing such relief from what would have been an ocean of worry. How different if the wire had announced refusal! I almost certainly would have been unable to go on conversing. My bowels would have burst, my chest been unable to breathe, my face flushed, my head too heavy not to droop on my shoulders.

Such is the contrast between the effect of good news and bad

* Italian painter.

news. It would seem as if we took the Good as a matter of course and the Bad as exceptional.

February 19th, I Tatti

I often wonder at my being so ready to make new acquaintances, and at how eager I am for new friends, new loves. Mere animal need of novelty plays a great part, of course. Yet there may be something else, the possibility that a new friend, a new love may reveal a new facet, a new side, a new angle of ourselves to ourselves, thereby not only enlarging our knowledge of ourselves but actually increasing the area of ourselves. The people who can do that to us, and for so long as they can do that, remain our nearest and dearest. When they cease producing that effect they get superfluous, and if they continue claiming intimacy may become a burden and finally a nuisance.

February 26th, I Tatti

At times I seem to myself to be a typical "Talmud Jew." "Talmud" means "learning" *überhaupt,* and that has been my chief pursuit, that and brooding, dreaming, yearning, longing, but except for travel disliking activity and dreading events. I can pore over books, or reproductions of works of art, and enjoy reading about happenings, provided they already have happened. I do not enjoy pregnancies as a spectacle—pregnancies in events no more than in women. Perhaps absorbing interest in what is going on is dictated largely by one's instinctive desire to get out of the way of trouble. That gives them a palpitating dramatic interest. But I am sure that there is no real escaping troubles even if one escapes them maimed and with scarcely a shirt to one's back. So I am fortified in my passivity, in poring over my Talmud. Only my Talmud now ignores Jewish learning and is concerned with everything that is human.

February 27th, I Tatti

The other day Queen Helen * of Rumania came to tea, and we chatted. She seemed to enjoy it, and was pleasantly natural, and came out with nursery lore and rhymes as if she were English and not royally international. All in all she was not nicer nor more companionable than hundreds of English or American women I have known in my day. Yet what made me enjoy her more than I should have the Anglo-American youngish women, as intelligent, as communicative, and as attractive? Is it snobbery, feeling flattered to be treated as an equal by royalty (even if royalty *ausser Dienst*)? No doubt there is that, but there is besides (as in most snobbery) a tribute to our instinctive sense of what any person symbolizes, and in the case of king or queen to the highest degree. I for one cannot rid myself of that feeling in their presence, and when they treat me so as to make me feel their equal, I cannot help enjoying them as I should not if they were my equals, and as devoid of symbolism.

February 28th, I Tatti

Unless one is reading for mere pass-time, and because one has got enamoured with the style of a writer (and the same holds true of all other artists), it is wasteful to want to know all his output. After a while you know his approach, his manner, his atmosphere, you have nothing more to learn from him, he can procure no new sensations, no new reactions. Wherefore I never had the desire to read the whole of Scott or Meredith, Henry James or Conrad, or any foreign author. Is it pass-time, self-indulgence, that leads me to read the whole output of Russian writers like Aksakov, Leskov, Turgenev, Gogol, Goncharov,†

* Helen, Queen-Mother of Rumania, in exile. Sister of the present King Paul of Greece, owner of Villa Sparta at San Domenico di Fiesole.
† Sergei Aksakov (1791–1859), Russian author; known mainly for his three volumes of reminiscences, *A Russian Gentleman, A Russian Childhood, A Russian Schoolboy.*—Nikolai Leskov (1831–95), Russian novelist, author of *The Blind Alley,* etc.—Ivan Goncharov (1812–91), Russian novelist, best remembered for his *Oblomov.*

Chekhov, all of Tolstoi over and over again, and nearly all of Dostoevski? Why do they excite and hold me, why can I even now return to any of them and enjoy them as if I had never heard of them or read them before? Is it the mere fact that I spent the first ten years of my life as a Russian subject, although a Jew in Lithuania, or is there something deeper, an affinity of nervous and cerebral make-up, of instinctive outlook and consequent reaction?

March 3rd, I Tatti

The faintest of shimmering silver hazes as toward noon yesterday we trod the slopes of the ravines along the flanks of Monte Ceceri. No glimpses of a town, or suburbs, or even of farmsteads. Nothing to indicate where we were. Under foot, crocuses, anemones, reviving grasses and large-leaved plants. Above, a crystal sky. The air invigorating and fragrant. I enjoyed my legs, my arms, my lungs, the coolness on my cheek. Glimpses of unrecognizable distances, romantic and magical. To right the vertical walls of the so perforated hills, shining like mica, and streaked with greyish violet, caves and quarries, with stonecutters' huts as in many a Bellini landscape, and a rivulet at the very bottom which we crossed and crossed again. For an hour I felt young again, master of my body, instead of being as so often "a bit of a soul carrying a corpse," or rather the prisoner of my body.

March 5th, I Tatti

I wake and feel as if I were as stiff, as unarticulated, as monolithic as a marble slab. It takes me half an hour or more to begin to feel warmth and life in my viscera, and muscles unbound and beginning to relax. At last, after some time, restfulness begins to possess me, and I enjoy a moment of physiological happiness, bien-être. So I call this condition of extreme numbness, dullness, and fatigue with which I wake, as the effort to rest from resting, from sleep. Even if I have slept sound and well, and shall profit by it later in the day, the recovery from what should be the repose following sleep is dull and at times dreary. It is as if every bit of me had slept independently of every other and died or nearly died in the effort, and that on waking these different bits had to be gathered together and reintegrated, put together like smashed crockery. I do not ask for "scientific" explanations. I have ceased believing in their answers.

March 6th, I Tatti

How bored and tired I get of my own face seen in the glass, dull, inexpressive, anybody's. I could envy women, young ones in particular, young up to sixty nowadays, whose coiffeur, hatter, and dressmaker can change their aspect from day to day, and even from morning till afternoon till evening. The same women in morning and evening dress or ball dress! We males now are condemned to the same face, and its changes are slow. Beards are out of fashion, and if you have the courage to give it a shape you want you must carry your own barber with you, for you seldom will find one even in the greatest cities who won't spoil it. How I envy the males prior to the nineteenth century and particularly those of the twelfth, who had almost as much freedom to frame their faces and adorn their bodies as women now have. "Give me new faces, new faces, I have seen the old ones a fortnight or more." And I have seen mine for generations of men.

March 12th, I Tatti

When a Dalai Lama dies his spirit enters that of an infant, and the wise men of Lhasa go in search of this infant to install him as the reincarnate Buddha, or whatever divinity it is (memory fails me). Is there not a parallel between this and the accepted Christian legend of the Adoration of the Magi, who came out of the *Morgenland* (how much more poetic than East) in search of the newborn God? (How well Milton has caught the spirit of their quest, in his ode on Christ's Nativity.)

Again a case of parallelism arising out of the human psyche, and not of diffusion, although if diffusion then from East westward, the East where incarnation and reincarnation seem universally believed, incomparably more and in a different spirit from how (if at all) it prevailed in the West, our Near East. And the

305

entire story of the Incarnation—could it have arisen in Palestine and the Aegean without more Eastern influence?

March 13th, I Tatti

My body often seems like a citadel undergoing a siege. The enemy is at the gates, battering away, but at the same time tapping here and there all around the walls on the chance of finding spots undefended, and of easier penetration than the massive gates built to withstand attack. So when I suddenly feel an unusual fatigue, a new needle sticking in, I ask whether that may admit the enemy to the last refuge. I am not frightened, I am scarcely concerned, rather I am interested in a contemplative way, as sheer curiosity. If I were in the condemned cell awaiting execution, but not sure of the exact date, I wonder what my feelings would be. Would I be so agitated, my bowels so burning and twisted that I should long to have done with it, or with Mme Du Barry cry, *"Encore un instant, M. le bourreau"*? How little I can foretell what I should feel in moments of life and death, how brave, how cowardly; I do not trust myself.

March 16th, I Tatti

Stencilled against my window the more delicate branches, the twigs, the needles of the stone pine change patterns kaleido-scopically without ceasing. Or it is like a dense cloud of swarming bees against a sunless, almost white sky. The cypresses like plumes bend forward and backward. The chimney roars, the wind penetrates through the windows and doors, which never quite close the openings. How I still love the sight and sound, and how I wish I still could enjoy the buffeting and the boisterous onset of the wind the way I used to until not so very long ago. It was from boyhood on one of my realest pleasures. Now it literally takes my breath away, and I do not dare to encounter it. This is the third day that I have not been out of doors for fear of the wind and its ravaging effects on throat and nose.

March 20th, I Tatti

In the good old days the *homo novus* could hope, and as he looked around him was inspired to hope, that the house he built or rearranged, the contents he so excitedly gathered and arranged in this and that room, would remain indefinitely as he left them, on his demise. It gave him the feeling that he would not wholly die, but much of him would survive, his taste, his will, the realization of his desires. There always was change, but houses and their contents could remain scarcely disturbed for generations, for centuries even. Nowadays change is so rapid owing to economic causes chiefly, but also to the fact that the U.S.A. gives the lead in all things, and that so few Americans feel attachment to what is left them by their forebears, or even to what they themselves have built up—no more in fact than to their clothes. If they can afford it, they do not hesitate to move altogether every little while, or to rebuild and refurnish.

March 25th, I Tatti

Except as spectator, avoid groups no matter how alluring, how authoritative, how powerful, who have different values, different standards, different premises from your own. They never will understand you, nor value you except as it suits their (not your) purposes, and they never will regard you without (perhaps unconscious) reservation as one of themselves. On the other hand as a spectator, as an outsider, you can enjoy any spectacle of life as you enjoy the theatre. Woe to him who wants to live the life that on the stage the actor seems to be living. Frequent "society" of all kinds from court to café but only as onlooker, and cuddle up to people who have had your schooling, share your premises, and have your values. With them you can discuss to a purpose and clarify and enlarge your ideas. From others you can acquire facts, and points of view, but in essence they are as foreign as if they were Tibetan, or worse still Soviet-minded products.

April 13th, I Tatti

Only in the very few last years have I gradually become more and more aware of how sex dominates us, of how it is always there, no matter how tucked away, and told to behave and be good while we are at our business, or the world's business. We humans, so polished, so clean, so sober, so ready to soar into the realm of the spirit—how easily we are deviated by a passing glance that betrays interest and how readily we respond. Do we ever meet a person for the first time without asking ourselves whether we would want to go to bed with them? Is this universal, are we all like that, or am I oversexed? Certainly not I, if I may judge by the most admired "highbrow" novels of the day. Which by the way leads me to ask whether these novels do not help to make us far more sex-conscious than we need be, giving shape and colour and words, words, words to what is a vague animal urge? If so then the puritans of all sects are right in their disapproval of so much literature and art we admire and enjoy.

April 15th, I Tatti

Why do I feel more at home, more at ease, more easily and pleasantly stimulated, with the Englishmen and better still Americans of my own world, more at one with them than with Italians, or French, or even Germans, although in some Germans I feel a depth deeper than any I can touch with others. Is it because I have so many points to which I can refer with Anglo-Saxons, assured I shall be stimulatingly understood, *à demi-mots,* and never need to explain, never meet with disappointment? Perhaps that is it, and also no doubt that Boston found me in the twelve years I spent there between ten and twenty-two in such a receptive, such an absorbing state, when I picked up all that could be picked of the educated New Englander's *Weltanschauung* to the obliteration of nearly all that had gone before, the fantastically concentrated ghetto world; this last so obliterated that it took Hitler and perhaps old age to revive it, bring it back to my daily divagations. But I do not yet feel at home at all with Jews as Jews, unless like

Isaiah Berlin * they have absorbed as I have the English-speaking world on top of their Jewish one.

April 21st, I Tatti

To tea, a Bishop and his wife, two of the most utter inno-cents of my acquaintance, and such as found only in U.S.A. and among people of oldest stock. To keep going they must have somewhere a touch of David Harum, but it never appears. Every-thing is good and true and making for righteousness and goodness. Life, contact with people, events, nothing seems to teach them that their rosy view, their trustful approach, are perhaps not ex-actly correlated to the jungle that society is for most of us. They seem "unbamboozleable." This Episcopal Bishop of America on the Continent must have had plenty of encounters that Conti-nental Europeans would have found odious, disheartening, despair-ing. Not he. He was conditioned to see things *en bonté,* and cannot see them otherwise. Should he not be envied, instead of being taken for a mug? How much does it profit one to know so much that is not good, to be suspicious of motives, to expect little from others? Why be so eager at all costs to eat of the tree of knowl-edge?

April 24th, I Tatti

Within a year I have got to know through accidental en-counter in a hotel Paul Getty,† who had with him a young woman as collaborator on a book about his collection. I took a mild interest that pleased him, and it led to his sending me photos of Greek fragments I approved of, and then to his coming to spend a few days here. I got to know more and more about him, chiefly through his collaborator, but not him. Then a few days ago came an architect, from Chicago, who turned out to have worked for Getty and known him, and told me that his, Getty's, ambition was to be the richest man on earth, and that he nearly was. Yes-

* Sir Isaiah Berlin, M.A., Russian-born English philosopher, essayist, historian; Fellow of All Souls College, Oxford.
† American oil magnate, founder of Getty Museum in Santa Monica, California.

terday there appeared another couple, also of Chicago and friends of the architect as well as of Dan Rich, who introduced both couples as trustees of his museum. All know Getty, of whom I knew nothing a year ago, and who is now a prominent figure, and nucleus for others to gather round.

April 29th, I Tatti

The Countess Serristori stimulates, draws me out as no other acquaintance of the last fifty years. Surpassed only by the way Edith Cooper (younger half of the Michael Field * couple) did in the early 1890s. She helps me plumb the depths and soar to heights, fancy-free, uninhibited, about ourselves in ourselves, and about our relations to others of our own species, about man's instinctive cosmos, about the immeasurable light-years of the universe revealed by mathematics and astronomy, about acquaintances and their ways, about historical figures of the not too distant past, and in short about anything that flashes through the mind or surges up from the depths of memory. No results, nothing to record, but life has offered few greater pleasures than unobserved, unpremeditated, unguided, wholly free talk with this most inquiring spirit of my acquaintance.

May 3rd, I Tatti

To tea at Windisch-Graetz's,† mother eighty-eight, daughter and blind son, who live in a small house with tiny *podere*, at the end of a long, sandy lane, almost inaccessible, on the way to Grassina. Modest living can scarcely go further. Indeed they are isolated, for having no vehicle they only can totter to the tram, the which they tell me is not only overcrowded but hard to climb into. So they stay put on the bit of land, and it would seem not

* "Michael Field," pseudonym of two English literary women, aunt and niece: Catherine Harris Bradley (1846–1914) and Edith Cooper (1862–1913), who wrote and published their poems and plays together. Both very close to B.B. and Mary during their early years.
† Princess Christiane von Windisch-Graetz (1866–1962) and her son, Prince Hugo (1887–1959), Austrian aristocrats; formerly owned estates in what is now Yugoslavia.

unhappily, accepting and not kicking and raging against their lot. Is that because they are thoroughbreds? I rather think so. Despite manifest poverty, everything about them is in the best taste. The living room serves as dining room. Not an objectionable article of furniture or knickknack, lampshade in best taste. Every object suitable to real comfort—comfort as understood by folk who long ago have learned to distinguish it from show and splash. In short, an exquisite Biedermeier atmosphere prevailed, and good humour that did not seem put on for our visit. The old lady, only a few months my junior, with a delicate profile, Roman rather than Germanic, wrinkled, still gay, playful, nimble, and the blind son uncomplaining, read to by the hour and writing history. Has documents read out and dictates. Like Clary, like Franz Liechtenstein * and other Austrians, he is, owing to interest in the part played by his family, a real historian. Told me what I did not know, that Windisch was Wendish Graetz (i.e., Slavic Graetz), and that it formed part of the Patriarchate of Aquilea. That [his ancestor] the Marshal, who was blamed for inviting Nicholas I to invade Hungary to help Austria in 1849, had never done so, but, although he could have proved that Schwarzenberg was responsible, kept silent so as to avoid troubling the new reign of Franz Josef.

Am I a snob for having enjoyed and admired?!

May 6th, I Tatti

I study Walter Lippmann's face and head. Rather German type, scarcely anything Jewish. When he listens his eyes take on a curious look as of a perfectly smooth deep lake. Features of hard wood. The face is of a labourer, and thinker and worrier. Dresses neatly and in good taste. Talks with a somewhat raucous voice. Scarcely any gestures. Smiles convincingly and genially. Can be good company, joking, but never *ausgelassen*. Gives clear answers to questions, and his estimates of people are decisive, never leaving you in doubt as to what he thinks about them. Vast acquaintance

* Prince Franz von Liechtenstein (1853–1938), Austrian diplomat with widespread cultural interests who frequently stayed in Florence before World War I. From 1929 to 1938, reigning Prince of Liechtenstein.

with *dramatis personae* of American politics, and sincerely tries to be fair in discussing them within the issues in which they are involved.

May 12th, I Tatti

Prince Paul of Yugoslavia * came out with the idea, entirely new to me, that the unstability, the extravagance, megalomania, of Kaiser Wilhelm II was not at all Hohenzollern as exemplified by his father and grandfather, but Coburg, through his mother. He cited the examples of Queen Victoria's mother, the Duchess of Kent, of Leopold of Belgium, of Ferdinand of Bulgaria, of Marie of Rumania (the showy Queen), and finally of the present Duke of Windsor. Why not include Queen Victoria the Queen-Empress herself, and her son Edward the Caresser! It is an interesting train of thought, biological rather than historical, and a case in the study of heredity rather than of politics. How are these characteristics acquired which are so persistent that they still seem to play havoc in the Belgian court? Nothing puzzles me more than the contemporary science about heredity. I find it difficult to accept.

May 16th, Naples

Patricia Luce tells me that her husband's family (the Henry R. Luces) have no private life at all. Know nobody, see nobody, who does not collaborate on their undertakings. Reporters, reporters, and nothing but reporters, their sole company. She and Henry live modestly, she and a cook doing the housework, and she attending to two babies. No time for reading, very rare visits to concerts, to theatre. All interest concentrated on "writing up" public affairs, writing for the masses. *Aber ist das ein Leben!* All that wealth as useless by-product of activity, serving no human purpose, certainly not for the creators of this wealth. An ant or bee existence. No doubt there is a certain momentum in it which carries along and may even produce a minimum of zest.

* Member of the Karageorgevitch family, Regent of Yugoslavia, 1934–41. B.B. met him as a boy in Saint-Moritz, and a solid, lifelong friendship developed later on.

June 16th, Naples

Yesterday forenoon with Iana and Fabrizio Alliata and Fosco Maraini to the very top of the Monte Pellegrino. Matchless view over the circle of ragged mountains to the sea on every side.

To lunch, the Lampedusas, she deep-voiced, arrogant, but well-bred, he charming, cultivated, gentle.*

Sailing away from Palermo, heart bursting because it was all *"zu schön, zu schön."* Infinite beauty, "and the pain of finite hearts that yearn." If only one could possess it all, and keep it, one would be a god.

June 20th, Naples

Afternoon with Maiuri and De Francisci † to look at the "Via Appia," in the sense of a stretch of tombs leading from amphitheatre of Pozzuoli toward Capua, and still in condition of Roman Appian Way about one hundred years ago. Then all around Baiae and the remains Maiuri is digging up of a great watering place of the time of Nero. Finally to view beyond Capo Miseno. Both at nearly every step deplored the utterly unsuitable buildings going up, and their inability to stop the ruination of the past nostalgic beauty of this region, now victim of industrialization and overpopulation. There is a law to protect the landscape, but nobody knows of a serious important case where it was applied. The whole of Italian legislation with regard to art and town building and landscape, a piece of silly hypocrisy, and effective only as it gives journalists something to write about when every important subject fails them.

* Princess Iana and Prince Fabrizio Alliata, daughter and Sicilian son-in-law of art collector and industrialist Count Vittorio Cini.—Fosco Maraini, son of sculptor Antonio Maraini and an English mother; explorer, author, and photographer, known for his books on Japan and Tibet.—Prince Giuseppe Tomasi di Lampedusa (1896–1957), Sicilian aristocrat, author of *The Leopard*; married to Italo-Baltic Baroness Wolff-Stomersee, a psychiatrist.
† Alfonso de Francisci, Neapolitan archaeologist, Superintendent of Antiquities in Naples, successor of Maiuri.

June 26th, Rome

My eighty-eighth birthday—shall I have another? I want
another and another, although every year, every month even, my
body gets more unfit for habitation as a dwelling, and rebellious
as slave of my mind. There is so much I still want to and could
write, so much in nature and art and people I still could enjoy.

The gains of the past year are that I have revised my
Lorenzo Lotto of sixty years ago, and sent it to the press. *Rumour
and Reflection* is the only book that cost me no effort, has had
considerable success, and the fully illustrated edition of my *Italian
Painters,* a great one, for that kind of book.

The loss is in elasticity of body and mind. My blood
pressure a couple of months ago rose alarmingly. Limbs stiff, hands
tingling, heats, memory of names gone, and for faces greatly
diminished. Tire quickly and more and more time wasted resting
with eyes closed, harder of hearing, drowsy.

June 30th, Rome

The Picasso exhibition here leads me to question whether
Picasso would have taken to crisscross patterns of violet paint,
wholly or partially unrepresentational, or enigmatic with no
enigma, if he had discovered his talent for sculpture and his genius
as a ceramist earlier, at the moment when he must have felt
that his gifts as a Classical draughtsman did not avail him. He
might have spared us the plunge into deeper and deeper infantilism that his intervening painting has committed and encouraged, and attempts at chopping up the human head and limbs
into segments which he then superposes. Part of his even more
than Joyce's or Eliot's popularity is due no doubt to the facility
with which he can be imitated. Anybody can take paints and
produce something that looks very like a Picasso, and indeed the
Galleria di Arte Moderna has hundreds of them, to an eye like
mine not easily distinguishable from Picasso himself. I wonder
what the Philistines of a world fifty years hence will say to all
this pathology of the arts.

July 1st, Rome

Good-bye to Rome. Shall I ever see it again? Life so precarious at eighty-eight, and even more than previously. In the last weeks I have looked back nostalgically at every place I left, like Lot's wife when she left house and home. I have not turned to salt, nor yet to stone. On the contrary, looking back, nostalgia, is the source, no matter how hidden underground, of much of the *Dichtung* of all times. Parting, ever parting. *Verweile doch, du bist so schön.* Palermo, Naples, Rome, how one longs for them, despite the depredations and the monstrosities committed for the sake of the *esigenze della vita moderna.* Longing and nostalgia (in moderation) have been my condition through life. As a boy of ten in Boston, I slept every night dreaming with radiant vividness that I still was living the day in Lithuania. Now I dream little by night, but more than I should by day, and nearly always of this and that place, this and that person that I so gladly would see, would embrace again, yet without expecting it to come true.

July 2nd, I Tatti

After hot train journey home again at 5 P.M. Tea, chat with Alda [Anrep] and Luisa [Vertova]. Then walk in the garden, fresh and lush, pure air, a paradise. House cool, windows shaded, shabbiness hidden by dimness, and all satisfactory. Strange to find one's own home of fifty years so unexpectedly delightful after being away for a few weeks. In those weeks I thought only of how interesting and admirable was what I was seeing, and never thought of home. When about to return I rather dreaded to find it flat and dull. Instead, sparkling, inviting, yet cosy. I wish I had the leisure to delve deep and bring back an understanding of my true relation to this place and all that therein is that I have brought together in the last sixty years and more. To my knowledge, such an investigation has never been made.

July 4th, I Tatti

Lewis Mumford: have been reading him in *New Republic* and elsewhere these last thirty years, and reviews of his books both in U.S.A. and in England on sociological, urbanistic, as well as literary subjects. Expected to see an older, and more intellectual type of "intellectual." Instead, a rather lively, bright-eyed, still middle-aged person, looking, talking, and behaving like a doctor. Discreet, modest, not embittered although all his writing has brought him no great ease of life, and travels with wife, daughter, and niece in distinctly skimpy fashion. Wife still handsome in Giorgionesque fashion. In every way a "jollier" person than his publications led me to expect. I cannot read a writer no matter how abstract without evoking an image of his looks, his bearing, his speech. I seldom find myself so far out when I meet an author in the flesh as I am this time.

July 10th, I Tatti

As a matter of history: Herbert Horne came about 1895 to spend a few weeks in Florence, to do a [book on] Botticelli ordered by Bell to be ready in a few months. I convinced him it would take years to do one. It led to his spending the rest of his life here, and to the "Museo Horne." * Charles Loeser I brought here, and here he remained to enrich the Palazzo Vecchio with part of his collection. Another I brought here was Charles Strong. It may have led (but I am not sure) to his daughter's marrying Cuevas and to the [creation of the Cuevas] Ballet. Then I was responsible for Cecil Pinsent, arrived as a gifted but raw youth, whom I employed to rebuild I Tatti.† Its style was repeated

---

* See p. 128, note.

† Charles Alexander Loeser (1864–1928), contemporary of B.B.'s at Harvard; American art collector and connoisseur; for many years established at Villa Gattaia in Florence. Left part of his collection to the city of Florence.—Charles Augustus Strong (1862–1940), American psychologist; married daughter of John D. Rockefeller; owner of Villa delle Balze in Fiesole.—Cecil Pinsent, English architect, who started his career by planning the first enlargement of I Tatti in 1907. Later on he built the library, and twice enlarged it; he also laid out the gardens.

with variations for Strong's house at Fiesole, for the Origo Villa at La Foce, and for work as far-flung as Yugoslavia and Greece. So my presence in Florence and the individuals I attracted or shaped or influenced were of some benefit to the town of Florence. I am not the only foreigner who has done so, and as much. Who recalls us, except on tablets!

July 21st, I Tatti

Yesterday as fresh and crisp and rare as Russell Lowell's "day in June." After tea with John Coolidge,* to Bagazzano. Visibility perfect, and sky line subtle. Bagazzano an ideal abode for rustic living. Talked of my dreams for future of I Tatti; how I should like students, past their Ph.D. or not striving for it, to enjoy four years of leisure in which they could mature, find themselves, and be prepared to write, to lecture, to teach. Four to come and four to go each year, sixteen always present. Coolidge said little but looked concerned, and finally said where could we find such scholars. I confessed that at present even eight might be hard to discover, but that eventually we could, by going further afield, not only to England but to other English-speaking lands. Coolidge rightly saw there the greatest initial difficulty. I encouraged him to take long views, to hope that a better crop of young people might come up among whom there would be enough, able to profit by what I Tatti could offer. Our talks will continue.

July 23rd, I Tatti

History as writ. With regard to Harvard's accepting I Tatti and my estate. Various versions all tending to make out as chief opponent President Conant. From John Coolidge I get a confused account, and yet he was at the centre of the storm. He could not tell exactly what happened, what caused the flare-up, and who was responsible for its happy ending. It does seem that the Corporation had done something behind Conant's back, and that I Tatti might have fallen victim only because the question of my gift came up during his wrath. Out of reticence people have not

* Since 1948, Director of Fogg Museum of Art, Cambridge, Mass.

told me who were the chief opponents, but I have had differing accounts of who favoured it. Nor was the meeting at New York of the visiting committee so decisive (although it ended in my favour) as Francis Taylor * made out. In short, the question did come up and was settled in my favour. Chinese Annals would report no more, nor can I find out either why the question came up or how it was settled. And this such a petty, simple affair!

August 7th, Vallombrosa

How limited is *Bildung*—culture! To think of all one is excluded from by not reading German! Again and again and again I want to talk to intimates about books in that language I have enjoyed, and almost never do so. It is to no purpose if they cannot read, and they are not the kind that get translated. My own culture, how limited without Russian, let alone Chinese. How few are as aware of all they miss as I am. There must be in Russian and other Slav languages poetry, memoirs, correspondence, that I am shut out from, and that might enlarge my horizon and deepen my feeling.

August 15th, Vallombrosa

I resent friends' having friends I would not have for friends. Why would I not have them? I disapprove of friends' having curiosities, beliefs, superstitions, extravagances that I do not share. Why? Surely a rational being should be happy when his friends call to his attention, bring into his life, interests and persons that his situation, conditioning, and instincts have not given him. Is it jealousy, is it envy, is it the lust for dominion? I fancy it is all of these, envy that friends can acquire and enjoy and feel enriched by people and things and thoughts foreign to us, jealousy of friendships from which we feel excluded, of intimacies we cannot penetrate, fear of losing hold of friends because of their too great absorption in others. I have been fighting against these

* Francis Henry Taylor (1903–57), American art historian and critic; Director of Worcester Museum of Fine Arts, 1931–40; Director of Metropolitan Museum of Art in New York, 1940–55, and then again until his death Director of Worcester Museum.

meannesses ever since childhood, but with no success, only I have learned to control my first positions, and to oppose them.

August 21st, Vallombrosa

Shopping is an exercise of power which we all enjoy, from the infant who spends his very first pence, the poor woman who markets, to the billionaire who pays half a million or even a million dollars for a certified and historical work of art, or double or triple or quadruple that amount for a yacht. The art or book collector satisfies this shopping instinct and urge in various ways. He will not only enjoy the exercise of spending, but his skill in buying cheaper than others, in discovering rarities that escaped others, and in getting the better of the seller. The element of speculation plays an important part nowadays particularly when people are fed up with stories of how works of art that went for nothing in the relatively recent past now sell for fortunes. In my experience with collectors, few are those who really cared for what they had as works of art, who got joy out of them. For most they are comforting symbols of power, or objects of hopeful speculation. Indeed, I forgot to speak of collecting as a pass-time, like all shopping, to those who enjoy it.

September 2nd, Vallombrosa

"Freedom from contempt" is what the Jews need. Surely no other "people"—I mean a group held together by habits, manners, customs, traditions, rituals—no other people that has come down to our day with an uninterrupted history of a good three thousand years has served mankind so well. It has given Christians and Mohammedans their religion, it has never ceased contributing to thought and literature, and in the last hundred and fifty years no other people has been so creatively, so fruitfully active in every phase of human activity, even military when permitted. Yet the fact that contempt is felt for them by the majority of non-Jews makes them not only resentfully unhappy or cringingly eager to be good bourgeois, toeing the mediocre line in every land, but also to feel this contempt for themselves, to the

319

extent of suicide as in the case of Weininger.* The remedy may
be found in statehood plus—very much plus—military glory, the
only value we all recognize as supreme. Should the Jews establish
a powerful military state, contempt for them would disappear.

September 7th, Vallombrosa

In yesterday's *Corriere della Sera* appeared notes from Ojetti's
diaries. One reported what I said about Proust, and was fairly
accurate. Another was about my last meeting with Oscar Wilde.
Ojetti ends with Oscar's last words as being "I am a Christian,
and like Christ will speak evil of no one," or words to that effect.
Now what Wilde really said was "Bernard, you forget that in
every way I want to imitate my Maker, and like him I want
nothing but praise." Ojetti noted within hours what he made
me say. He had no reason to change it, yet after such a brief
interval, he distorted what Oscar had said. Then you want me to
believe in the *ipsissima verba* reported of talks—even stenographi-
cally! And these reports, where historians weigh every syllable,
are the material that builds history.

September 27th, Maser

Only four days since leaving Casa al Dono, and it already
seems ever so far, far under the temporal and spatial horizon.
Why? There I lived last summer a monotonous, restricted life of
small compass. Since then days crowded with events. Change of
place is an event, and every town one stops at, and even if one
only passes through, and supremely what one sees and does. In
Bologna, the picture gallery, and at Monselice the fabulous castle
so full of a number of things, the Giorgione of Castelfranco, and
finally Maser with its numerous and varied guests, each a character, each an event. I suspect it is the number and complete otherness of events that leave in memory a sense of ever so much that
has happened, and compared with it, the little that went on at
Vallombrosa ends by taking on the quality of something long

---

* Otto Weininger (1880–1903), Austrian psychologist and philosopher,
author of *Geschlecht und Charakter.*

past. In a sense changes of scene, one quickly following the other, may give the illusion of prolonging life, and crowding it with memories.

September 28th, Maser

Yesterday with Freya Stark at Asolo, charmed by the amenity, the humanity, the graciousness of the landscape. Giorgione and Bonifazio did not have to imagine. All they had to do was to transport their visual recollection into paint. Freya's home on a promontory with gnarled, almost Jerome Bosch trees, shrubs, flowers, lawns, and the remains of a Roman theatre. Inside, a work of art in its kind, and far from being a mere *machine à vivre*, every room with its own character and purpose. An enviable bedroom study at the very top of the house. Everywhere interesting books. Freya never reads a paper, seems totally deaf and blind to what is going on in the world, in our world at least. But I wonder how much faith she still has in the Arab one. She used to try to de-Arabize them out of sheer love, and to turn bedouins into effendis. Would she still? She seems to have abandoned them for Turkish Asia Minor and its Greek past. She will write about them with the communicativeness she has learned so well, but no longer as an agent of the British Foreign Office.

October 14th, Venice

William James used to say that the business of philosophy was to make distant things seem near and near things distant. Is it not true of all the arts, and indeed of all thinking? What does any explanation do but make a distant because unfamiliar problem seem close, and near? In the visual arts, genre reveals what is unfamiliar, hence in a way distant, the attractiveness, the hitherto unfelt charm and distinction of familiar, that is to say nearest, things. On the other hand, overfamiliar things can be transfigured by giving them place in noble surroundings, and in an appealing and evocative landscape. The present rage for painting bottles, and particularly almost opaque, greenish ones, does not produce genre, for its interest is not in revealing a new quality in these

321

bottles, but in the "scientific" treatment of light and shade. A Chardin, a Crabbe (in his verse), a Wordsworth (in his) can make us see beauty in a loaf of bread, in a rustic cottage, in a daffodil. Their interest is in what things mean to man and not to mere science.

October 16th, Venice

Koestler and others of his kind observe, or rejoice, or despair because the Jewish youths born and bred in Israel cease to look, or act, or behave like the traditional Jew, and become peasants, hulking, blond, even dull. Maybe, but the Israelites and Judeans of old were overwhelmingly peasants, and nearly all their rituals (of course most of their feasts) were in connection with sowing and reaping, dew and rain, and crops in general. Yet *terre-à-terre* as they must have seemed, who produced a nobler literature than this tiny nation of peasants? From Amos down, with the possible exception of the Isaiahs and Ezra, who were the prophets and historiographers, but peasants and the grandsons of peasants? And why should it not happen again?

October 21st, Milan

Spent yesterday forenoon being shown what the restorer Pel-liccioli * is doing to Leonardo's *Last Supper*. He explained that he worked with the simplest means, with a penknife or even a razor. The point was to know where to scrape. Looking close with strong magnifying glasses, and under powerful reflectors, what came out was something like the *tessere* of a mosaic, some of gemlike quality. Yet as a whole the figures loom out of a mist, and when we climbed down from the platform where we had been looking microscopically and touching with the hand, and stood at a not too great distance, the composition as a whole made the impression of a faded chromo. When fresh it must have impressed with the bulk of the figures, perhaps the earliest to take up space to all but the exclusion of surroundings, and with

* Mauro Pelliccioli, considered one of the ablest Italian restorers of paintings and murals.

figures in themselves of impressive proportions. But why such villainous types! The grouping in triplets one behind the other in depth altogether admirable, and for seated figures especially. Below the tablecloth *terrain vague.*

October 26th, I Tatti

The pedant is a person too stupid to feel and to go for the heart of the subject he is treating, and therefore gathers all the irrelevant information, and merely tangential, and elaborates it as if it were the really significant matter in connection with the theme. His plodding goes under the sound name of research, and the more insignificant facts he brings to light, the bulkier his public. Then in his subject the more is he appreciated and rewarded by the pedantocrats who rule most institutions, universities, academies, art galleries. How rare a scholar who has a sense of significance and its by-product, a sense of proportion.

October 29th, I Tatti

How easy and warm the atmosphere between born Jews like Isaiah Berlin, Lewis Namier,* myself, Bela Horowitz, when we drop the mask of being goyim and return to Yiddish reminiscences, and Yiddish stories and witticisms! After all, it has been an effort (no matter how unaware) to act as if one were a mere Englishman or Frenchman or American, and it is something like home-coming and reposing to return to "Mother's cooking." The great majority of us who can enjoy this return are of Russian origin, and to some small extent descendants of the first generation. I doubt whether Sephardim enjoy it or many of German extraction, and probably no Anglo-Saxons of third generation. For them their Jewishness counts as little as Catholicism to Catholics in matters political, indeed even less, and yet a Catholic can count as wholly, unquestionably English or American, while I doubt whether in either community a Jew ever ceases being a stranger.

* Sir Lewis Namier (1888–1961), Russian-born English historian.

October 30th, I Tatti

I used to be anti-Zionist. I was and am an assimilationist and saw no reason for establishing a Jewish ghetto anywhere, and least of all in a hornet's nest like the Holy Land. Moreover, I wanted the Arab peasant and bedouin left to live his exceedingly uncomfortable but far from unhappy life undisturbed by Westernism.

Hitler's organized attempts to destroy the Jew made a place of security for the remainder imperative, while it revived sentimental feeling among Jews for the land from which they regarded themselves not separated but only exiled (as I can guarantee from my own experience). On the other hand the Arab peasant and bedouin were being missionarized by British philanthropists (who of course were not aware that they were greatly enjoying exercise of function) into becoming a town proletariat of effendis. To a person like me to whom culture and even civilization, even "law and order," are above race and patriotism, there remained nothing in the Arab world worth saving, and certainly not to the extent of keeping out a people who would, if allowed, improve the situation of the Arabs themselves. This would have happened if, when the war between Israel and the Arabs began, the Mufti and his followers had not obliged the Arabs to desert their homes, to run into the wilderness with the expectation of setting up a grievance against the Jews that would keep Islam boiling with hatred of the Jew, and fill the sentimental Briton full of pious resentment against Israel.

November 7th, I Tatti

I shake and tremble as I rise from sitting down, I walk unsteadily till I get into my stride, I hunch and my head hangs forward, in short my body behaves like everyone else's who has grown old. Yet I never expected it would come to that. That I should submit to the average—never, never! And is my mind as doddering as my body? I cannot believe it, although I know how shrunk my horizon is, how restricted my present range of impersonal interests, how disinclined it is to making an effort. All the same I have the feeling that as an instrument it is as good as ever. And if not, then are the youngs—*les jeunes*—right in ignoring me altogether, or taking my pronouncements as symptoms of advanced senility? That I should come to that—I, son of the morning who had the animal conviction that he could never get senile no matter how old he got. One does not escape the law of averages.

November 12th, Rome

Cannot get over the poor impression made on me the other forenoon by the frescoes in Sistine Chapel; let alone the herds of tourists bellowed to by their guides, the actual paintings as mere pictures are at present anything but enjoyable. Apart from the great Perugino on the interior wall, the other great compositions, the best Botticellis, are on the outer wall where the sun prevents one from seeing them. The ceiling stark, gloomy, and the *Last Judgment* darker and gloomier by far. What would a dilettante unacquainted with the subject of these designs, with their iconography, get out of them, in their present condition, what would he think of them? He would be bewildered, and if Muslim or Hindu or Far Easterner conclude that admiration of these frescoes was part of the Christian cult and had little to do with art as he understood it. How much traditional admiration still influences us, how difficult to make up one's mind that these Sistine frescoes are scarcely enjoyable any more in the original but only in photographs!

November 13th, Rome

Until ten years ago distance scarcely existed for me. I felt free to walk as long as I pleased, and seldom got tired enough to become aware that I still was far from my goal. Now I am painfully distance-conscious. From this Hotel Eden, where I live, it seems far to the Porta Pinciana, or Trinità dei Monti, distances that used to seem a mere step. I used to walk over the Appian Way all the way to Albano, and feel only a pleasant fatigue, and when I began to rest a delicious ichor coursing through my veins.

Do we always get aware of things through privation, and re-

325

main unaware when we abound in them? Is that why Italians un-spoiled by the recent importation of culture-snobbery are so un-aware of art and beauty, while we Americans are so painfully aware seeing that we have little or none of our own, and we talk and write and discuss, and make messes with paints, and discuss techniques, all because hitherto we have been so sterile artistically? But the British? They are almost as art-conscious as we are, are they aware of their inferiority as artists to the French, and perhaps suspect that much of their art of the past was produced by for-eigners?

November 14th, Rome

First encounter with Mr. Luce, husband of our Ambassador, and founder of *Life, Time,* and other influential periodicals. Was put off by his pronunciation of English, but soon got over it. Asked me about Alexander the Great. I told him what I knew, and thought; again and again he pulled me up, accusing me of having changed the subject. Probably he had just read it up, and therefore like royalty made me feel as if he knew all about it. Even if just acquired, he handled the matter intelligently, and asked probing questions, and seemed to understand my answers. Would have made a much better Ambassador than his wife. I had always thought it was her lifelong wish to be Ambassador in Rome. Now I hear the Embassy was offered to him, and that he refused it for himself but asked to have it passed on to his wife. She has plenty of gifts, but I question whether they fit her for the job, whereas he could have carried it easily.

November 24th, Rome

I recall how I felt when I finished my *Drawings of the Floren-tine Painters*. I had worked on the book night and day, and broke down directly. I could not go on, but I felt as if I ought to do it all over again, entirely re-sort the material, approach it differently. In short, I was convinced that what I had achieved was only prepara-tory to what should be done, and I was unhappy and had no mo-ment of satisfaction when it appeared in print and overawed by its mere bulk. Nor since then, more than fifty years ago, have I sent any writing to press with the feeling that I had done all that I could with it, that it said all I had to say, and said it in the way most communicative and persuasive. What a rapture if one could obtain a complete evacuation of one's mind. When I have dealt a certain time with a subject I get tired, too tired to go on or to turn back. In short, I learn how to begin when I have finished.

November 25th, Rome

As I stepped out of the car yesterday I congratulated my chauffeur [Hugh Parry] on his skill in threading the moving, coiling, ever changing maze, labyrinth of traffic in the streets of Rome. It takes a sure eye, quick decision, and an obedient hand. No wonder an acquaintance of mine broken down with intellectual work was urged by his doctor to drive his own car to St. Paul's through London traffic. The concentration demanded would take his mind away from his worries.

Auto drivers, cutters, the rare barbers who still can trim a beard, require the precision of eye and surety of hands that could turn them into fine draughtsmen. Indeed, tailoring is drawing destined for a quasi-spherical body. Being so utterly without skill, I tend to admire them inordinately, and technicians, painters who really know all about their craft, or bronze casters like Bearzi of Florence. When he speaks of his trade now and through the ages, I feel like a charlatan to pretend to myself that I know anything, and dare talk about it.

December 27th, I Tatti

Went to see Michelangelo's *Bruges Madonna* [exhibited at the Bargello]. Head and face anticipate many of his later works, even of such an advanced type as the warriors in the niches of the New Sacristy of San Lorenzo. At the same time recalls early figures in Bologna and in Siena. The draperies do not cling, but billow and envelop, yet model the body they cover. Arms and hands relaxed, completely at rest, but seem to indent what they rest on. Head of Child too big, too important, almost pushing His Mother into the background. The back summary but grandly sweeping, and the stone the Madonna sits on conventionalized as in earlier

327

Greek sculptors. Composition of the whole crystalline in its completeness, exists for contemplation and worship, but for no transitive activity. I could look at it minutely, almost hypnotized for hours together—if only I had the group to myself. There was a crowd, and I kept wondering what they really saw and felt, what it meant to them, what they were aware of while looking. Of course far more than they could put into words.

December 31st, I Tatti

Chief events of 1953. McCarthy's reign of terror, and its effect on European attitude toward America. Growing contempt of Europeans for Americans and their ways. We already are hated as much as the English were, but they never were despised as we are. Death of Stalin in his bed. I always hoped he would end on the scaffold after confessing that all his life he had spied and worked for the Western Powers so as to get pious, humane Russia hated as no people has ever been before. More hysteria deliberately pumped up by some Italians about Trieste, but really in favour of recapturing the Roman Empire in its widest extent, say c. 100 A.D. French shrill impotence, and determination to sulk and kick and sabotage every effort to yield to the inevitable, namely, to surrender the world over what she cannot hold, and to make friends with Germany, while Germany still asks for it.

1954

January 1st, I Tatti

The formidable James Conant, until last September the nu-
clear-minded President of Harvard, a sort of American Molotov
by reputation, came with his wife, and turned out to be slight,
youngish-looking, affable, ready to talk, human, and friendly. Wife
rather elegant in a New England puritanic way, daughter of a
lady with whom I flirted when young. From all accounts he was
the strongest opponent of Harvard's accepting I Tatti, on the
ground that he did not think it wise for that institution to get involved in commitments at such a distance, and under such different political conditions. Not a word said about this till he got up
to go, when he whispered how glad he was that the Corporation
had accepted I Tatti and that I was freed from worry about its
future. All so different from what I expected. It is so hard to judge
as human beings people one knows only by hearsay.

January 11th, I Tatti

"Je ne pense que quand je parle" is not as bad as Daudet
intended when he invented the phrase. For instance, I think a good
deal, and at times seriously, without talking—or writing. But it is
wispy, like cloudlets changing shape and melting away. Rarely
does one think things out unless talking or writing. Talk is apt to
be more stimulating than writing, and often I hear myself saying
what I could not have concluded in silence. The pen can do the
same and perhaps more, but more rarely and after greater effort.
Wherefore I need stimulating company to help me to function at
my easiest, and (on the whole) best. It must be company that
shares my interests, and is ready to discuss them, not merely eager

for information, although they too, if they ask leading questions, can start one off. If they ask question after question, then I am at my best.

January 22nd, I Tatti

Persecuted by editor of book telling what prominent persons the world over believe. To be put in five hundred words. I have glanced at many of the testimonials, and find no juice in them. As for me, what do I really believe? I scarcely know. I believe one thing one moment, and another another. I have few certainties, none of metaphysical, theological kind, in the nature of a creed. I believe that by the structure of my mind I am incapable of grappling with ultimates. I have convictions, and aspirations, and hopes all with regard to man and his place in the universe, a universe which knows him not. Man may be an entirely fortuitous by-product of blind energies. Yet once here, it is his best to build a world of his own where his mind and heart work together to produce individuals who will enjoy exercising functions that are good for the community.

January 25th, I Tatti

A vagrant held up before a judge says, "Yes, Your Honour is right, I am a thief, a cutpurse, a pickpocket, yes, but that I am a contemporary cannot be taken away from me." From me it can, and I am treated either as a daft old man who has outlived himself or as a revered sage of the past. And I recall so readily when I was "in the foremost ranks of time." Perhaps the clearest proof of my senility is my insisting that I am right, this perverse generation wrong, and that *l'avenir me rendra justice,* to speak with Anatole France's Pontius Pilate. No, *l'avenir* will be too busy to bother about the like of me, and besides will have no need of me, will have individuals who will stand for what I do now, but express and communicate it more convincingly, more persuasively. So there is no balm in Gilead to salve the vanity and loneliness of the old left high and dry by the retreating tide of life.

February 4th, I Tatti

Nicky and I see the same figures in clouds, same faces and profiles in carpets, rugs, tree stumps, and other nonhuman shapes. The moment I attempt to tell some happening at which we have been together, she automatically either contradicts or modifies what I have just said. So it is always with people who live together. Yet we expect to know of any event of the past not only what happened, but how it happened, and above all—what interests us most—why it happened. Nobody denies Magna Carta, but the liberalist accounts current in my youth about the farsighted, nineteenth-century attitude toward the public weal of its signatories is anything but accepted nowadays. Yet popular history is still written to recount not what, but how and why, as if it were the ideal of what should be happening today. Should history then be only chronicles of "wasted time"?

February 5th, I Tatti

Cyril Connolly. We parted more than twenty years ago when he was going to join the Nicolsons,* then members of British Embassy in Berlin. Had been staying with us as protégé of Logan's, and for me to inspect. I encouraged Logan to go on modestly financing Cyril. Since then heard of his marrying, of living fancifully, of his bibulousness, of his getting enormously fat. Read him and greatly admired *Palinurus,* and parts about Eaton in *Enemies of Promise.* All in all had no great desire to see him again, and none to have him as a guest.

He arrived yesterday evening, ever so much better-looking than as a youth, with a jolly, florid Irish (but not Kalmuck) face, and head disproportionately big, broad-shouldered, and not so corpulent as I had been led to expect. Drank at table only. Would have no whisky before going to bed. We agreed about most topics, and enjoyed sharing dislikes. On the whole discovered we had the same values. Came from Naples, where in four days he had seen

* Sir Harold Nicolson, English diplomat, critic, and man of letters; married to Victoria Sackville-West (1892–1962), poet, novelist, and famous horticulturist.

333

all the recent discoveries to write up for *Sunday Times*. Wife slim, blonde, perhaps too shy, too young to make an impression. Seems (I fear) interested in art history and archaeology.

February 7th, I Tatti

Et haec meminisse juvabit; since Homer at least, man has enjoyed recalling the past with people who themselves partook of the same past or were near enough to it to be interested. "Do you remember"—a question asked by Cyril Connolly again and again, yesterday, and "Did you know?" It was a pleasure to fabulate, I say deliberately "fabulate," because recollection as recounted tends to be fable, and to discuss events, heroes, personages of the past who will be forgotten when we are no more except when some young pedant digs them up and dusts them and puts them away in a thesis. Who will read Gide, for instance, except for a year or two after his demise! Who reads Villiers, Barbey, or even Laforgue, not to speak of the excellent novelists still admired in my youth. Cyril was eager for recollections of those remote days, and gave pleasure. Probably nobody else ever will—too absorbed in the admirations of today.

February 12th, I Tatti

The Allen Tates * staying with us. She bulky and opulent, novelist and critic in her own right, but do not know under what name, nor what she writes. He slender, alert, with a head recalling those supposed to be Plotinus or Chrysostom, and with dazzling expressive eyes. Both Southerners, knowing all the American writers of today. She kept butting in, but he managed to tell me a good deal about most of them. Penn Warren had been a friend of their youth, married a rather difficult wife and, persisting in covering her conduct from others, ended by stiffening and getting opaque. Edmund Wilson on the whole a jolly giant. Mary McCarthy better critic than novelist. Capote of small account, etc. One gets from them the impression of a very busy, buzzing,

* Allen Tate, American critic and poet; married first to the writer Caroline Gordon, then to Isabella Gardner.

bustling literary life, whatever its values may be. Had had close contact with Robert Lowell in his youth, and with his first wife, Jean Stafford, author of *Boston Adventure*. All in all, a most interesting couple, a good investment.

February 14th, I Tatti

Like other Americans, I used to jeer at Irish peasants, and Calabrian simple folk who at a funeral would spend the savings of years in display and feasting. For years I have known better. It is an expression of their eagerness to spend, for "conspicuous waste," the which are among the most enhancing activities of the ego that exist. It puts them for a day and a night on a level with the wealthy and the princes of the earth. After this outburst they feel more contented with themselves in the humble station to which the Lord has called them. Now I envy them this capacity for Bacchic extravagance and momentary exultation. I have never been able to forget myself and my condition, to partake wholeheartedly in any communal extravagance.

February 19th, I Tatti

Until the First World War all of us who did not live in slums, and even they, enjoyed spacious dwellings, large square rooms with high ceilings. One could walk about in them, breathe, expand chest and shoulders, feel no matter how unconsciously that man had made dwellings for himself suitable to his aspirations. Then the cellular system, started for hotels, giving the inmate just enough room to dress and undress, with the quantity of air he should breathe overnight carefully allotted. This won all dwellings. Now in great cities we live in small low rooms, to me depressing, crushing. Indeed, I feel like a crushed hat, as if I had to peak my shoulders, to breathe with economy so as not to use up the air. No useless space giving a sense of freedom; only enough to find shelter in—in short, a return to the most primitive conditions of being "indoors," only mechanized, cellularized, pigeonholed. *A nous la liberté* to live like prisoners, but Kafka-like not to know why, yet too stupid to be discontented.

335

February 24th, I Tatti

I go back in memory to my youth when I went to see an art museum, a building, a famous landscape, with reverence, with happy awe as to a cathedral service to which I gave myself entirely. There was little mere curiosity, mere desire for information. It was more like a religious experience. Something of that still remains with me after nearly seventy years of ever growing familiarity with the work of art. That is why in writing I instinctively begin by trying to communicate to the reader my own feeling toward the object I am going to discuss. Other students plunge immediately into polemicizing, into tearing to pieces, into disembowelling the work of art, in the effort to find out how it was done. The mechanical interests them exclusively. Because we live in a mechanical age must we treat everything as a mechanism?

March 7th, I Tatti

In the last thirty years I have been in love seriously once, and lightly a number of times, but have loved one woman only, and that woman is Nicky Mariano. Not only, but I love her more and more and more every hour that so miraculously I remain alive. My love is not only one of deep affection, glowing affection, but of joyful gratitude, freed from any touch of grudge, any reserve that gratitude is often tainted with. She works with me, she thinks with me, she feels as I do, she is the complete companion, entirely responsive. Then she takes every material burden off my shoulders, business, finances, all the sordid side of life, and yet has the energy and makes the time to read to me, to edit what I write, to housekeep, to be a busy social secretary, to play the gracious hostess, to tolerate my flirtations, to comfort my lady-loves when I begin to be bored with them.

March 8th, I Tatti

De Sade—the lubricious imagination of a feebly masculine or wholly impotent male, with the pitiless logic of a Frenchman, combined with the total absence of pity, of consideration, of the

336

capacity for putting self in the place of others. If the ego is free, owes nothing to anybody, cares for sexual pleasures only, then he logically can push his satisfaction to any excess that physiology permits. No reason why he should stop at anything, and a sexual satisfaction as indeed all physical love tends to enjoy giving pain as well as caresses. Sade enjoys his satisfaction the more, the more he tortures the object of his lust. His "logic" is never broken down by human contradictions. It is as impersonal and pitiless as a mathematical problem. I doubt whether a De Sade would have been conceived out of France.

March 9th, I Tatti

One's old acquaintances seldom get old beautifully. C. M., fifty years ago a dashing cavalry officer, now puffed out, bulky, immobile. Klemperer * such a handsome male, mistaken while kneeling in prayer in Cologne Cathedral for a romantic hidalgo, now hobbles, conducts seated, dares to eat nothing, looks wretched and *hurt*. Almost every day I could report the like of other acquaintances who have grown "old along with me." Are they responsible for it, is it the lives they have led or had to lead, or the predestination of inheritance? Yet nothing appeals more than elderly and old people who not only have kept their looks but improved upon them with calm distinction and natural dignity that youth cannot have. The ideal life should improve looks as much as mind and heart.

March 10th, I Tatti

My idea for what is to become of I Tatti could be stated in a few words, although to be made official it would take many. I want it to be a hostel for a number of students between twenty-five and thirty to enjoy the leisure to mature their talents, their gifts as talkers and writers, the leisure to sip works of art in all phases and kinds, verbal, visual, musical, to express them so vividly that they will want to communicate their experience to others, after finding the words to do so. At the same time I want them to live in the present as the continuation of the past, to study the

* Otto Klemperer, German-born orchestra conductor.

337

past that is still alive or deserves to be resuscitated, and to live in and study the present as the matrix of the future, and of this future not as remote, removed, but as beginning today and going on quietly with no jerks, still less leaps. In short, a preparation for *im Ganzen, Guten, Schönen resolut zu leben.*

March 13th, I Tatti

Why do I wriggle and toss at the idea of being biographied? It makes me uncomfortable, and unhappy. Is it only because there are so many big and little episodes I wish forgotten? Of course, I have much behind me that I hate to recall, and hope will not be remembered against me. Every kind of *lâcheté*, meanness, pettiness, cowardice, equivocal business conduct (due more to ignorance and the ethics of art dealers than to my own nature), humiliations, furtiveness, ostrichism, etc. Yes, all these and more and worse that rise and denounce me in the hours of the night when I am not quite awake, and defenceless against all the nastiness that an uncontrolled mind churns up from the foul depths of memory. How passionately one wants to forget! No—not these only or chiefly. I dread having my life written as the "success story," as it is bound to be, seeing that economically and socially I had to make my way from nothing at all. Yes, economically and socially, but I never from earliest dawn of consciousness felt proletarian or inferior to the highest class anywhere. I never felt that I was climbing, being promoted from an inferior to a higher standard of life, to a higher social class. I felt only that I was coming to my own, what I had always regarded as belonging to me, of which, for no fault of mine, I had been deprived. So the notion of being written about as an Horatio Alger hero—"Ragged Dick"—is in the highest degree repugnant. Why care, seeing I shall not be alive to suffer!

March 15th, I Tatti

The figure of Alcinoüs keeps coming up as the symbol of a serious grown-up view and attitude toward the future. He knew that his kingdom would perish, not as always in the Old Testament because of the wickedness of his ways, on the contrary because he had befriended and sent to his home a fugitive from the wrath of Poseidon. No matter what noble lives we live, die we must, and perhaps worse than that, nothing may remain of our efforts to humanize the animal in us, and to create a more than merely animal house of life. We go on creating, improving, dreaming of ever nobler conduct, and realizing it to some extent, regardless of their and our caducity, because the better of us are born to function creatively. There is no happiness except in functioning according to one's own nature, and for me Alcinoüs symbolized that attitude toward life, and is therefore my patron saint. What a sweet saint, father of the exquisite Nausicaä, and benefactor of Odysseus.

March 25th, I Tatti

Ernest Hemingway is impending, and I look forward with a certain dread to seeing and knowing him in the flesh. Hitherto we have only corresponded. His letters seemed written when he was not quite sober, rambling and affectionate. I fear he may turn out too animal, too overwhelmingly masculine, too Bohemian. He may expect me to drink and guzzle with him, and write me down as a muff. I know him only through his writing, the which I admire greatly here and again, but seldom a whole book. What can he know of the real me? Has he seriously read anything I have written? Has he been taken by my myth? Has his present wife, whom I led through my garden some years ago, given him ideas about me? What, I wonder, does he expect? I dread arranged meetings, I prefer to meet people unexpectedly, casually, with no responsible feeling that I must see them again, or encounter resentment.*

March 27th, I Tatti

Old friends, old loves even, who have lost their sexual and mental power to stimulate me—what can one do to get rid of them? The advantage of the inanimate work of art is that one does not feel called upon to commune with it except when one feels like it. You can't do that with humans. They want to be talked

---

* Hemingway fell ill in Venice and never came.

339

to, made much of, caressed, particularly when it is women one sees seldom. And one drifts apart and abysses of difference open out, and one has to ignore them for politeness' sake, to avoid hurt and cruel endings to friendship. The strain is there, and boredom, the greater when the friend is dying to talk about what either you entirely disagree with, or that has no interest for you. In a long life like mine, I have accumulated too many as good as dead friendships, and worse than dead, for the dead make no further demands unless it be through our own bad conscience with regard to them.

Would I really like to be ignored, dropped by old friends who now bore me?!

March 28th, I Tatti

Fiat experimentum, ruat coelum. Nothing will stop scientists from carrying on research and experiment, and damn the consequences, even the smashing of the earth in pieces. Even if they were treated as dangerous criminals and eliminated accordingly, new ones would be born who against all prohibition, all threats, all executions, would go on functioning to the utmost of their gifts. Most humans are satisfied with mere existence, like all other animals. If they can grow and feed and enjoy creature comforts, and reproduce themselves, they realize themselves completely, expect no more, ask no more. If gifted, they cannot bear the mere animal round, and at all costs will insist on functioning according to the inspiration of their gifts. If stopped, or rather if one attempts to prevent their functioning, they become legal criminals. The born criminal is a human who can function only against the good of society as a whole. In the rare cases of the born murderer, the only thing to do is to eliminate him. The ingenious safebreaker, the born forger, not only the financial one but the artist who can only function *à la manière* of some admired artist of the past, the drug seller, the white-slave trafficker, the drunkard, the slugger—the greater majority is composed not so much of criminally abnormal as of genuinely gifted people who cannot live except by exercising the antisocial functions with which they were born. Nor can they be made to function normally. I recall having tried my

340

best to get Federigo Joni* to stop forging Quattrocento pictures. He could not. The paintings he tried on his own were so jejune that nobody would buy them, and he was bored doing them. What to do with these gifted antisocial offenders is a problem that must be dealt with in relation to their gifts.

March 31st, I Tatti

"J'ai lu tous les livres"—far from it, but I no longer can stomach generalizations. I feel as if I know them all—all those in realms that are in my ken, and in my possibilities of understanding. I still enjoy illuminating or suggestive facts. In the visual world, on the contrary, where generalizations are absent, I am more receptive than ever, abler to enjoy every kind of art that (in my feeling) is art, and more even than in art is my capacity for enjoying nature, macroscopic and microscopic—landscape of every kind, and the flowers and grasses and weeds of the fields, and animals of every kind, including humans. I could look forever at faces, and the passing show in the street would delight me if I had the time to give to it. My sense of—no, I mean my eyes procure me more happiness than ever since childhood.

April 5th, I Tatti

Strolled by myself in garden. Anemones of all colours on slopes. "Solomon in all his glory was not like unto them." Wisteria ready to burst through. Watched the shoots and saw that the tips of most were budding. Missed the beautiful exotic irises that Mary used to procure for the small ponds she made, and that still are there. Walked up the stairs to the *parterre,* and revelled in the order and beauty of what was before me, the lawns, the terraces, the clipped hedges, the ponds, the cypresses fronting the *limonaia.* Turning around, I enjoyed the still young ilex wood, and its light and shadows, and the vaulted arch ending up in a niche. In the *parterre* itself the ruined statue of a Phidian Hermes, and then the two huge walls of cypresses making a grand avenue with its waving

* Sienese painter, restorer, and clever imitator of antiques.

grass. Further and around to the pine grove, past the spreading fig tree to the violet bed, to the kaki tree, to the medlar tree, to the view of Corbignano.

April 9th, I Tatti

I ought to be cured of instinctive resentment against my nearest and dearest when they do anything for themselves or for others, particularly for others, unless I too come first. For fifty years I lived with a woman who, except in the first years when in love with me, thought first of her offspring, then of her lover, and then and if then of me. Yet instinctively I still react with grumpiness to any interest, any occupation, that Nicky or Luisa, or indeed anybody near me has apart from me. *Alle denken an sich. Ich nur denke an mich. Me first* is the instinctive cry of little ones, and I for one at eighty-nine am still there. The Francis II of Napoleon's time was hearing someone praise another, and impatiently interrupted with "Yes, yes, but what does he say and think about *me, what does he do for me?*" Perhaps we could not live if we got rid entirely of instinctive preoccupations with self.

April 11th, I Tatti

No leisure. That is what I miss most at my age. I have collected the books that I looked forward to reading at ease when I was old. I planted a garden where I could stroll with a book of verse open in my hands, and occasionally looking at the trees and flowers. Now that I am old I have no time for either, least of all for browsing among my books. This diary is full of these complaints. Perhaps the greatest disappointment of all is the lack of spacious days with nothing to accomplish but the freedom to enjoy the harvest of one's years. Quite the contrary! Attention to health takes up most of the time that is not absorbed by long rests, sleeps, dozings. The hours when I can read are so reduced that I scarcely dare embark on a serious book, and I waste myself on periodicals, snippets, and light "literature." Woe is me!

April 13th, I Tatti

For a male who feels, without admitting it to himself consciously, weaker sexually, and feebler mentally and as a character, the female's devotion will end by being oppressive, and lead to his breaking away. The female will bewail his betrayal till she finds another "rag baby" to build up into the most desirable object in the world. With the female in that case, the male is not at all so much a *machine à plaisir* as an activity, a career. When he leaves her, she is out of a job, does not know what to do with herself, cannot shake off preoccupation with him, goes over their past and misinterprets everything in their present in the effort to get rid of her yearning for him. Should he die while she is in this state, she transfigures him into a hero, into a god.

April 15th, I Tatti

Yesterday afternoon some thirty people of all nations gathered here to visit the library, eat and drink, and shake hands with me. I am sceptical about the usefulness of societies like this of a European cultural union. What do they achieve, except facilities for travel and sojourn in divers places? I shook hands with all, exchanging conventional greetings. Only one had something to tell me. He was Jean Wahl * of the Sorbonne, who told me Bergson used to speak of me. I am always surprised when individuals of eminent fame remember me. To be sure, I saw Bergson a number of times, yet that he should speak of me to another philosopher surprises me. Even more when Einaudi—now the President of Italy—recalled that I saw him once, as long ago as 1922. So Walter Pater when I met him remembered that I, utterly unknown and only twenty-one, had once written to him. Would I could receive young people who write or come.

April 16th, I Tatti

Yesterday starting down from Montebeni to Settignano I met on the road two young women. One was dark and of no interest,

* French philosopher, pupil of Henri Bergson.

343

the other carried the dark one's newborn babe tenderly wrapped in her arms. She was so beautifully proportioned, had such an exquisite oval face, eyes of deep amber, and a general look of such loveliness, that I could have embraced her rapturously there and then. With no erotic or even animal intent, but out of sheer joy in meeting on a country road such an apparition. How often one encounters young women, and young men too, whom one wants to stop and worship for their completeness as works of art! How seldom one sees among the field workers in Italy what in the rest of Europe is a peasant type.

April 18th, I Tatti

The Jews and the Greeks based their history on a liberation, the first from Egypt, and the second from Persia. The Christians, a combination of Jew and Greek, founded their history, their myths, on the Resurrection, with the promise of life eternal for every individual. What happened before? Did early Hebrews and Greeks think less of the future, live more in the present than the later ones? Were they still emerging but not yet emerged from the purely animal condition which may be altogether unaware of death? And is not the awareness of death the chief distinction between animals and ourselves? Has not the awareness of death and *timor mortis* been the chief preoccupation of fully self-conscious mankind, and the fountain spring of most of its thinking and planning, from the first endeavours to preserve the corpse, to Christian Scientists who deny death? How few face it even now!

April 26th, I Tatti

Since boyhood I have cared only for companionship, for stimulation of mind, for conversation, in females as well as males. During adolescence and maturity even, the last thing I aimed at with girls and women was to sleep with them. Never did I then or ever since regard friendship as an association for mutual benefit. I never have appealed to a friend for material help, nor even to use his influence in my favour. I never could take business relations for friendship, despite the "shoulder slapping" often entailed. Only in my middle years did some women attract me sexually, and

344

more and more as I grew older—not the rare women I really could love with no thought of sexual pleasure, although it might follow as fruition. Always loved women for the adolescent quality of their minds, in gifted ones lasting into old age.

May 9th, I Tatti

Ray Bradbury,* the writer of "science fiction," and his wife. He only thirty-three, simple, easygoing, no inferiority complex, not shy nor on the defensive. No "education" after fourteen. Began to write at fifteen. Seems to have escaped being stuffed with pseudo-problems that worry young writers, and make them howl to the moon. Tried to persuade him to drop the framework of science and to write without that cast-iron skeleton, assuring him he had enough psychological creative power and gift of words to become a novelist of the Classical tradition. Extraordinary in many ways. For instance, he came out with a statement of what he expected from art that almost word for word was identical with what I had thought of writing, or had written a few hours before. Nothing "self-made" or culturally *nouveau-riche* about him. *Floreat!*

May 10th, I Tatti

I enjoy Yvonne Hamilton † for her physical and verbal nimbleness, her radiant laugh, and her ability to liberate my need of salivating chatter. Her talk is stimulating, vivifying, although it never gets beyond gossip about common acquaintances, about new books, new plays, new theatre and music performances. What helps to make it all alive is that she speaks not with authority, but with experience—what things and people meant to her. I must confess that my senility, with its disinclination for using mind, delights in Yvonne's bubbling vitality. At the same

* American writer. B.B. had written him a fan letter after reading one of his volumes of science fiction, and had been disappointed not to receive a reply, when Bradbury himself suddenly appeared.
† Daughter of Conte Ansaldo Vicino di Pallavicino and of Beatrice Haskard; married to the publisher Hamish Hamilton. B.B. met the Hamiltons through Lady Colefax in 1947.

time, it does tell me of what is going on in London Town, and helps to keep me in touch with events (pleasant or unpleasant) that count at the moment, and that even I must not ignore.

May 11th, I Tatti

I fear a change for the worse is taking place in my body. Cough continuous, instead of as hitherto in crises after several hours. Moments of extreme and sudden collapse, as yesterday P.M. starting to toddle with Serristori, and had to sit down almost at once, and did not recover until after we had had tea, and she had left. Each time as we say good-bye, we ask each other with looks if not with words whether we shall meet again, and each time I say to myself, "Now as never before" the question is imminent. Perhaps I am the last surviving person to whom she can say, "Do you remember," the last who understands nearly all her references; for I have known (after my fashion) all the people she still gossips about, or discusses.

May 13th, Venice

Except the mere masonry, nearly all the external ornament and interior furnishing of San Marco are gross loot from Constantinople. So are most of the objects in the Treasury. Incomparable things in their way, glass, crystal, every kind of precious and semi-precious stone, enamels, mountings—enough to give one a fever. Unhappily, all behind glass, objects that crave to be handled. The hurry to see everything before I got too tired to see. One should return for an hour seven times at least. Invited by Patriarch * to call. A paunchy, good-humoured prelate, put one at ease by his greeting, took us up to his study, cosy, free from *bondieuserie,* and filled with books. Turned out to be a lustful bibliophile, and enjoyed showing us books he had acquired in Constantinople, while special Papal Envoy—chiefly folio works, marvellously bound, about Constantinople and the Near East. I forgot the

* Angelo, Cardinal Roncalli (1881–1963), at that time Patriarch of Venice, was elected Pope, taking the name of John XXIII, in 1958.

Cardinal and Patriarch, successor to St. Mark, and behaved as with a fellow bookman. Not only did he not resent it, but wanted to see me again.

May 14th, Venice

Vittorio Cini,* the only Faustian Italian of my acquaintance. He enjoys nothing so much as constructing, building, creating. I refer not only to all he and his two partners have done to create interest. Nor do I refer to his collections. These he makes partly because he enjoys shopping, and partly perhaps as a speculation. But San Giorgio is the apple of his eye. He has nearly finished the construction, furnished with all the elegance of the past and comforts of the present, scouring the world for suitable rugs, tables, chairs, monumental library cupboards; besides a naval school on the English model, theatres, lecture halls, etc. He lives for this creation, and nothing makes him so happy as to show it—as happy as an infant with his mud pies. He remains a child, and that is the source of his captivating charm.

May 21st, Venice

Told Riccardo Bacchelli † I could wish for two things—either to have everything or to need nothing, preferably the second. Never reconciled to the weak flesh preventing the spirit's flight. But for physical limitation I could enjoy everything that lives, everything that is, every thought, every work of art, to the point of identifying myself with what I was experiencing. Bacchelli broke in with "Then you would be a god." And why not? What can human, as different from animal, destiny be, if not to become gods, or at least to be on the way to godhood? As it is, I am inclined to being a Quietist, a Manichaean, weary of my prison of flesh, weary of being a little soul burdened with a corpse. How

* Count Vittorio Cini, wealthy Italian industrialist and art collector. In memory of his son, killed in an airplane accident in 1949, he created the Fondazione Giorgio Cini, a cultural centre on the island of San Giorgio Maggiore, Venice.
† Italian humanist, novelist, and literary critic, author of the epic novel *The Mill on the Po.*

to get rid of it, without dying altogether? Can the spirit manifest itself only through the flesh, and is it only a function, an exhalation of the flesh?

June 2nd, Venice

If Nicky did not attend to all business correspondence, financial, publishers, and with some friends, if she was not housekeeper, reception clerk, travel agent for visitors, telephone girl, etc., etc., she would be (and at times is) the ideal help in my work. She knows all I know, and now her memory is much better than my own. She has read aloud to me in four languages for thirty years at least, looked at art and nature, travelled with me in antique as well as lands of today, she sees in objects just what I see, phantasms in tree stumps and dried branches, images in clouds, shapes in landscape. She understands me *à demi-mot*. We differ about ethical, political, and religious matters just enough to stimulate discussion in the rare moments of leisure. In brief, I can't imagine life without her. My world would crumble, and leave me alive perhaps, as an animal, or even a vegetable, but not as myself, if she should die before me. *Absit omen!*

June 5th, Venice

I learn that Kenneth Clark is preparing to write about me as a product of my American "contacts," as well as of contacts with Vernon Lee, Janet Ross,* Edith Wharton, and the like, abroad, i.e., in Europe. What will come out I shall not see, nor do I greatly care. He proposed to write about me as the "New Winckelmann." † That might have proved interesting. As a matter of fact, apart from what one owes impersonally to one's education, the influences on my formation have been William James personally and as professor, Matthew Arnold and Pater as writers, Burckhardt and Morelli in my profession as attributor and critic.

* Janet A. Duff-Gordon Ross (1842–1927), described her life in Egypt in *Reminiscences*; correspondent of the *Times,* 1863–67; traveller and author, owner of the estate adjacent to I Tatti, Poggio Gherardo.
† Johann Joachim Winckelmann (1717–68), German art critic, rediscoverer and expositor of Classic art; had a great influence on Goethe.

348

My career has followed from my being regarded (even by my worst enemies) as the safest attributor of Italian paintings. Social "contacts" have had little or nothing to do with either my formation or my career, no matter what (and not so much as believed) they may have done with my life. At all events they have had next to no influence on my work, on my thought, my writing.

June 13th, Venice

To the Greek Church to see its treasure. Of course it was not visible. Tolerable architecture, interior filled with ever-the-same icons and *bondieuseries,* nauseatingly stereotyped. Synagogically stuffy atmosphere. Boring to extinction. Felt as if my veins were cut and my blood dripping out, leaving me all but lifeless. The only pleasant feature was the priest, who looked as handsome as the warriors on the stele of Persepolis. He came only months ago from Mt. Athos, yet was clean and beautifully costumed. Greek Consul, who tried to interest me in the way he had been induced to buy a great lot of what I call prenatal Grecos, and discovered they were no good. By the way, a couple of days ago I saw in a side chapel of Santa Maria Formosa a Birth of the Virgin or of the Baptist, obviously by a follower of Bonifazio's, assigned to Greco.

June 15th, Venice

Francis Biddle * would not hear my diatribe against universal suffrage, accused me of oratory, and solemnly affirmed his belief in democracy. I do not blame him, for Americans are brought up to believe in the sacred word "democracy," and few learn to question its meaning. He of course puts me down as a rank Tory, yet I wonder whether he or I would be ready to take a man on his merit no matter what his society status was. When it comes to the individual, I have scarcely a touch of class feeling. If he loves his job, I am ready to treat any workman as my social equal, and if I don't frequent him, it is for the same reason that I do not frequent official and smart society, because we have no common sub-

---

* American jurist, writer; attorney general of U.S., 1941–45; American judge at the Nuremberg trials.

349

jects for gossip. Americans of Francis Biddle's class make a greater distinction between political and social equality than do most Europeans. In Paris and Vienna one used to see people in salons that you never would encounter in the salons of New York or Philadelphia, or even Boston.

June 22nd, Venice

An Englishman here on a visit. Has read more novels than I have, and much else that I read. Wants to see all the famous works of art, and I suppose to hear all the good music. Yet he repels me as a *Kulturphilister*. Why? Perhaps he takes all these things as relaxation, as change from quotidian business and chores, as enjoyment not so very different from sensual pleasures like food, drink, and sex. To the cultured man "all those things" permeate the whole life as a truly religious Christian, Mohammedan, Jew, Hindu, etc., is permeated by his faith and precepts. As the Christian was in Medieval Europe, without a creed, dogmas, and theology, *Bildung*, culture, is a religion, and since early boyhood I have always felt it and taken it and acted as if it was one. People of the Oscar Wilde kind are *Kulturphilister* because they take culture as outside ordinary life.

June 26th, Venice

I enter my ninetieth year. It was something of a wager with myself, rather like Werfel's *Tod des Kleinbürgers*. What did I do, what happened in the eighty-ninth year? Did little, wrote a few articles for the *Corriere della Sera* of Milan, prepared *Lotto* for the press, and likewise the short notes on Sicily, began work on the catalogue of Venetian painters. What happened was becoming aware of myself as an historical personage, as somebody whose life had something exemplary about it that could and should interest others. Difficult, because recalling life as I lived it, it never occurred to me there was anything that escaped the laws of average in what I was living and how I lived it. Perhaps that is why I dread biographies of myself being mere masses of anecdotes with a *bénisseur* intention or a malicious one, but inevitably off the mark.

350

June 27th, Venice

Ritual performances for birthday. Cables from friends in U.S.A., telegrams from England and Italy, congratulations from obsequious clients. Then after dinner members of Institute for Study of Venetian Art gathered to drink my health. Smothered with flowers. Presents of sweets and of ponderous volumes. I wish I could enjoy such matters, or wholeheartedly partake in any ceremonial. I never can. Even at my wedding I remained a spectator. Why can I not partake of anything communal, feel wholeheartedly at one with a community big or little? Why can I never feel that I belong? Was it the accident of my career and all it attracted and repelled, or was I born to be a spectator, impulsively, passionately interested, yet never taking part, nor feeling that I partook—a sympathetic stranger? Not an "outsider," for he craves to be an insider. I never did.

July 1st, I Tatti

My real religion is the desire for a society in which the whole man will flourish, while exercising multiple high functions. Races, nations, peoples, societies are evaluated by what they contribute to that end. I question whether for the last thirty centuries any people have contributed more than the Jews. They have inspired and started the great religion of the White Race. They have contributed since they have been allowed to do so to every effort at philosophy, at theoretical and practical science, to every branch of literature, to history. In the arts they are, it is true, less creative. Little or nothing in the visual ones, and in music and the theatre more as executants than as creators. All in all, they have been surpassed only by the French, Germans, Anglo-Saxons, and perhaps Italians. Put against their achievement what other ancient peoples, e.g. Greeks and Armenians, have done since their reacquired contact with the West, and their superiority is great. Compared with the Arab-speaking world, their output of work promoting civilization, culture, high living is overwhelming. In comparison, the Arab world has nothing for centuries, not since ibn-Khaldun has a Muslim written anything, or done anything else of a creative and con-

351

structive contribution to the City of Man. Nor have I heard of their writing anything for themselves, as in a measure Poles claim to have an appealing and beautiful but unexportable poetry of their own.

In comparison with what Jews for three thousand years have contributed that is still operative, still fermenting, still creative, "the Arab" is nowhere. As a bedouin he is picturesque and romantically appealing for seeming to need and want nothing, and being free to do what he wants (it is little enough). As a townsman he has scarcely put foot on the lowest rung of civilization. Yet such is still the force of anti-Jewishness, that the majority of the Christian world is outraged by the Jew who returns to the Land of Israel, where he regards the Arab as intruder and usurper, in which, the survivor of torture and massacre, he wants to ensure for himself a city of refuge. Cramped, confined, always on the *qui vive* against the Arab marauder supported by all the Oil Interests, yet the Israeli Jew not only makes the desert smile like the rose, but pursues every kind of intellectual work, including good history, on as high an average as is being written anywhere in the European world. But pious anti-Jew pity for the Arab will have none of this.

July 6th, I Tatti

A fortnight of trouble with my teeth, and dreaded visit to the dentist. Came off yesterday. Capecchi, my doctor, and Emma, my valet-maid, present to feel my pulse and to bathe head and hands with spirit. Injection in gums to deaden pain. Dentist's brutal assault. Splutter of blood, and bleeding on and on. Horrid night. Swollen lips, gums, aching in a dull but persistent way and still bleeding. Yet the incubus is removed—for the present. The few still alive teeth may outlive me. What cowards we are, or rather I am, about physical pain, how I dreaded this dental torture! Yet what kept me awake for an hour at least was not my mouth but my chest. Gases were trying to break it open in their effort to escape. It is now a frequent recurrence, almost any night, and often enough in the daytime. Have I ever been free from aches and pains? They have made me self-aware.

July 10th, I Tatti

Toward noon yesterday drove up to above Vincigliata and through a blaze of golden broom reached the pine grove from which I can walk either over stony, steep paths and precipices down to highroad above I Tatti, or through the grove itself to a side road that eventually leads down to Settignano. Took the last, and every step was ecstasy. Sight, sound, smell, the nobler senses, happy. I could not help stretching my arms as if in gratitude to the Maker of it all. Only ten minutes from my house, and this beauty of tree and shrub and rock and fell, with one's eyes soaring over the amethystine town to the distant high horizon, or to the Falterona. Past cottages, neat and trim, situated to catch in the summer all the coolness wafted from that distant mountain range. But for wanderlust, no need of going elsewhere. What are the views from the heights above Damascus compared with those I was enjoying of Florence and its beyonds in every direction!

July 12th, I Tatti

It has taken me a long life to begin to realize how little literature, art, ideas count with the governing classes of all countries, and how little they are respected. Education is mere training for jobs. Beyond that goal, reading, travelling, enjoying the arts, is pass-time, or subject for chatter as a momentary substitute for gossip. Perhaps the governing classes are right in not taking seriously anything that does not obviously and quickly contribute to the material welfare of their own class, and in more enlightened conditions to the community as a whole. "Intellectuals," by which I mean people interested in things beyond momentary ideals of welfare, are apt to toss about in a welter of notions that have no foreseeable value to the workaday life of society. The able, not the intellectuals, "turtle eat."

July 22nd, I Tatti

Yesterday morning in a state of exasperation because I could not find, search as I would, some few pages of mss. I needed.

My nerves were jangled. We drove up and got out and walked. Golden broom at our feet, a crystal sky above, views stretching to pure rhythmic horizon, the roofs of Florence a shimmer of grape-purple far below, dome and tower veiled in harmony with the rest. It did not take long before I was smoothed out and felt like lifting up my hands in gratitude for being able to appreciate these gifts that the summer day was so generously showering upon me. How I enjoyed the moment, how happy it made me; I was at one with the world and with myself. I needed nothing, I asked for nothing, I was comforted for the rest of the day, its chores and its bores.

July 27th, I Tatti

The trouble with most Americans is that they are puritans. A puritan can be as inclined to vice as any other son or daughter to the Fall, but instead of enjoying his lechery, or his drink, and in rare cases his food even like Gargantua, the Frenchman Gide, the Irishman Oscar Wilde, he dreads, hates, and is at war with his pet vice. As this vice is always getting the better of him, he is humiliated, hangdog with himself, tragically unhappy. I have known cases where they tried to get the better of their vice by trying to outdo it, to obey Luther's recommendation, *Pecca fortiter*, but only to plunge deeper into self-contempt. This will go on till the American will learn to take things easy with himself as well as others, to let well alone, to let things take their course, not react violently and demand immediate remedies.

August 3rd, Vallombrosa

I read history of commerce, trade, with avidity. Partly because all exchanges between region and region, big or little, interest me, all sorts of exchanges, above all in thought, in religion, in learning, and in all the arts. And in part because these "humble" exchanges are part of the actuality that disposes while kings and courts, and parliaments, and saviours of society propose. I get a better sense of history when I read that while at war merchants of Tunisia write to their Genoese correspondents to carry on with them as usual. Just now read of Jewish traders coming and going

354

between India and Tunis. What gossip, what tales, what actualities they must have carried as well as merchandise. Also read about the aid of Continental traders to Scotland's resistance to English aggression, helping to defeat the Edwards and contributing to the victory of Wallace and Bruce.

August 9th, Vallombrosa

Where do certain women get the authority to assert their opinions, impose their standards, their preferences, their conclusions? Surely not from intellectual superiority, nor from manifest exercise of sound sense. They impose it by sheer force of obstinacy and loud assertion. One realizes the uselessness of arguing with them, because they cannot listen, nor indeed understand if listen they did. One yields to their conceit, their shameless conceit, as one does to the weather, or to an "act of God." At best these women are absurd and comic. At worst they are nuisances to avoid. Yet such is the power of obstinate wrongheadedness that it gets the admiration of character—and a bad character is still better (so we instinctively think) than no character. God save us from the unavoidable association of these women. A counsel of perfection is to turn a deaf ear and smile. They take it for consent.

September 1st, Vallombrosa

I easily fall into blaming Italians for this and that. They are blameworthy of course. Who is not? Should I find people more satisfactory as administrators, as responsible citizens, as businessmen, as friends, as loves, elsewhere? I doubt it. So what I blame is human nature, its limitations, its tricks, its subterfuges, its tropisms toward ease and advantage, its vanities. More of one and less of another in different lands. The sense is probably the same. My worst experiences have been with English people, not with Italians. There is no predatory trick the British government failed to use when as after the First World War it was increasingly in straits. The French ever so much more difficult to live with than Italians, and the Germans in the bulk. Austrians better, but unreliable in my experience. On the whole I must conclude that Italy is not only

355

the most inhabitable part of our world, but that its people are easiest to live with *quand même.*

September 7th, Vallombrosa

Yesterday Nicky led me down below Casa al Dono, from terrace to terrace, and finally to a glen more romantic than I could recall seeing in unfaked-up nature. There were the rocks, the overhanging trees, the waterfall, the pool, as scenic as if arranged by a *metteur en scène,* as thought out as a Ruysdael or Courbet, yet, I repeat, man's brain or hand had nothing to do with it. Had never seen it before. Would have gone far, on foot, even now in my ninetieth year to see the like, and here it was under my feet. Had I known of it even four or five years ago, I should have gone there often to enjoy its freshness, its sounds and smells, and glints. Now *retrahere pedem* takes it out of me. Of all the *Entbehrungen,* the one I mind most is not being able to take the walks I used to enjoy so much. Climbing takes it out of me, even if it lasts only a quarter of an hour. Not so many years ago I still could not resist dashing up a hill.

September 8th, Vallombrosa

A bad night, scarcely an hour's continuous sleep. Mouth as of vinegar, and chest oppressed by gases that would not come out. Yet I ate very little at meals yesterday. Hard even to guess why my body behaves as it does. Perhaps I indulged too much (for my poor stomach) in mushrooms at luncheon. I like their smooth texture and earthy taste, and I eat them (ever so rarely) because they recall soups made with mushrooms that as a very little boy I used to enjoy so much in Lithuania. For we do eat with memory, as in what does not memory play its part! Would "Mother's cooking" still taste so wonderful if we ate it for the first time and not as it were commemoratively? Surely as almost everything experienced in the years when senses were fresh, and exercising them was joy. To recapture them, what happiness!

356

September 15th, Vallombrosa

Besides all the housekeeping, arranging arrival and departure of guests, attending to most of my correspondence and affairs, Nicky now insists on helping me with my present task of cataloguing the Venetian painters. It is sheer delight to be helped by her. She knows highways and byways as no other secretary I ever have had. I scarcely need tell her anything. She knows exactly what to do, what are the problems, what the snags, where to turn for information, and how reliable it is when found. Most of all to me is her joy in doing it, her happiness in working with me and for me. It seems impossible when working for me that she should not feel tired, seeing it is all on top of what as hired labour it would take at least two well-trained persons to do. Her interest in my welfare, her selfless delight in my achievement, her self-effacement, self-forgetfulness in my task, are traits I have never found in others. It seems as if in all activities, the better one does them, the less one thinks of reward.

September 19th, Vallombrosa

Here I am nearly ninety, prepared as few to enjoy delicately with or rather through my eyes, my ears, my touch. I should give myself up to looking and seeing, to listening to sweet voices and beautiful sounds. I should cherish and reread all the Classics with my present understanding. I should help to form the young for the pure pleasure of it. I should live disinterestedly, as a kindly spectator. Not at all. I am possessed by the demon of productive work. I spend my ever diminishing moments when I still am really alive on study of photographs, with a view to compiling a new catalogue of Italian paintings, with a view to perpetuating my own attributions, my own errors. I bother and worry about publishing. I read for information and seldom for pleasure. I get cross over the ways of the world, particularly over the art productions and art appreciation of today. This last is so absurd, seeing that if they do what I do not care for, they do me no personal harm.

September 29th, Vallombrosa

Leaving this *angulus,* which smiles on me as much as Sirmio did on Catullus. Each time I come here, I enjoy and appreciate it more, although I no longer can take the exploring forest strolls that I used to take so very few years ago. I miss them nostalgically, but there is a certain compensation in giving more attention to detail of earth shapes, of tree trunks, of foliage, of wild flowers, and in connecting these with the passing seasons almost as if they were the pointers on a dial. Have been here just two months; and, but for the fact that Casa al Dono faces due north to escape the heat so that it already receives no sun and is too chilly for my old body, I would gladly linger here, to enjoy the autumn changes, the distance from "the madding crowd," the uninterrupted leisure for regular hours, and freedom from petty interruptions. I leave with regret the more poignant as I may never come here again, alive. I should like being buried in the pathetically rustic cemetery here.

September 30th, Bologna

A committee has been set up to study the problem of "art" at Harvard. My recommendation (if I were consulted, which is not likely to happen) would be to get away from the Fogg, and its museological and collector's interest, and to universalize the study of art history, to get away from painting (and its shadows, drawing, engraving, etc.), and to launch out into a program that would include all the visual arts of all times and places. Beginning with pre-reflective, pre-self-conscious arts, to Mesopotamian and Egyptian, and Greek and Hellenistic, and post-Hellenistic, Romanesque, Gothic, Byzantine, of course, then Renaissance, and post-Renaissance in Italy, France, Spain, with side steps to Holland, to Germany, to England, not to speak of Flanders *à travers les âges,* etc., to our own year and day. This would imply a faculty of its own, with its own separate interests, represented by competent teachers, who would regard themselves as part of one unit, whose business it was to teach and inculcate a rational and acceptable knowledge of all the visual arts in all fields, including not only

358

painting chiefly, but sculpture, architecture, and all contributory ornamental arts. All studied first in themselves, and then as contributing with literature and music and philosophy and ritual to the humanization of man. I wonder what the committee now set up by Harvard would make of this suggestion of mine!

October 1st, Bologna

My barber, nearly seventy-six, spoke yesterday of how he used to go on foot to Bologna, to Milan even, and of course to Siena and Perugia. In ecstasy over sunrises and sunsets. A suburban Florentine lad who began his trade at seven. Likewise my own body servant Emma loves effects of sunset and all beauties of sky and ground. Surely they were born with this capacity, as indeed I was. All that education, reading, discussing has done is to make me more aware, to make me recall more and more that from earliest consciousness of the existence of nature, I was responsive to its visual and every other sensual appeal. In me, owing to favouring circumstances, this sensitivity has reached fruition, as I am sure it would in them if they had had my opportunities. For in both I discover not only aesthetic sensitiveness, but going with it a very high degree of intelligence in all fields, and a capacity for thinking clearly. How discover such gifts in lowest as well as highest classes, and concentrate on giving them every opportunity, should be the major problem not only of education but of government.

October 7th, I Tatti

It is a pity that owing to my age and perhaps worse still to my manners younger men are seldom natural with me. Afraid of giving themselves away, of my ferule, of reprimand, particularly if they, like Kenneth Clark, have been as it were pupils. So like royalty I seldom get to hear what people really think. They want to avoid discussion, to spare me and themselves. So no matter what one does to put younger people at their ease, they are overburthened by my presence, and more than they would like to admit by my existence. Nearest and dearest may breathe more freely when I am well out of the way, shoot out like a plant that

359

has not had all the direct sunlight it needed. A parallel is my elder sister, who so overwhelmed the younger one that she, while the first was alive, never dared to be herself. Now that the elder one is gone, she comes out with the full expression of her hitherto half-suppressed real self, and is twice the person she used to be.

October 27th, I Tatti

What have I learnt in the course of the years that I did not know when young? First and foremost, the never diminishing hold that sex has on us—sex, its derivations and disguises. Then that each of us is the centre of his universe. Furthermore, the alarming power of catchwords, of mass intoxication and hypnotization, and the feebleness of the individual when part of the mass. Finally, that many enjoy mischief-making, and many others are positively sadic, that envy and jealousy play an important part in life, and yet that no one person is altogether evil, or any one person altogether good. That even the most revolting human being has to love somebody, if only a cat or dog. That you can't count on others, any more than they on you. When all is said and done, life has been wondrous canoeing down an unexplored river, full of reefs, snags, rapids, Niagaras, but such fascinatingly interesting and at times beautiful scenery, and people on the banks.

November 2nd, I Tatti

Are women who are self-aware more anxious about their desirability as females than males are about their virility? B. H. told me she nearly lost her mind, did lose it for months together, because her husband had ceased to want her, and years later her lover abandoned her. Life became senseless. One of the most cultivated and intellectual women of my acquaintance always used to speak of "I as a woman" and kept running after males to make sure they still desired her. It has been her ruin, and now, a wreck, she has nothing real to live for.

In my long life it never occurred to me to think of myself as a male. Looking back, I recall what I now recognize in girls and women as looks and gestures that surely were of desire. I was unaware of them, except when the woman made unmistakable advances. Not that I was not aware of sex when young, but it took the form of enjoying females who drew me out and were good company; not as bedfellows merely.

November 7th, I Tatti

Eight at luncheon yesterday, all eating, but only one manifestly enjoying every morsel, and not merely stoking with his heart in other things, and that was Vittorio Cini. Except the French, we Northerners seem incapable of concentration upon food—let alone other carnal pleasures—with sheer animal intensity. I have seen Frenchmen enjoy food, French women enjoy love-making with a completeness of sheer animal satisfaction that yet had no touch of vulgarity about it. Descendants of puritans, we take our animal pleasures almost as if they were mere calls of nature, to which we had to submit and get through with as quickly and decently (and furtively) as possible. Even at the table we talk and forget we are eating, whereas rich Flemings will munch and smack their lips, and not say a word to distract attention from their delight in the process of eating.

November 11th, I Tatti

One of the joys that have taken flight is that, undressed and ready to get into bed, I used to fling window and blinds wide open, and smell the odours of the garden, and gaze at the stars, and try to distinguish the landscape in the dark. The stars in their courses used to fascinate me, the way they were carried up and down, right and left, by the movement of the entire firmament. Then one night I breathed in too much icy air, and since then I have not dared to expose myself at the open window. In warm weather I could, but laziness has got the better of me.

November 15th, I Tatti

My very little vocabulary, my lack of vivifying phrases, my indolence besides, prevent me from portraying the variety of people who come to I Tatti. They are of all Western nations, excluding none, and even Hindus and Japanese—rarely a Chinese.

361

Anti-Soviet Russians not altogether absent. If only I had the gift of verbal portraiture, what a gallery of individualities I could gather! As it is, I scarcely attempt to characterize my guests, convinced that I shall produce nothing better than a blur, at best a vague silhouette. Yet I feel their individual traits keenly, their naturalness, their pretentiousness, their taking themselves as a matter of course, or trying to seem other than they are, or their whimsicality or absurdity. But the word or phrase that will call them up, as a visual portrait would, I cannot conjure up. Could I have if, instead of passing my life looking, I had spent it learning to express myself? That is a problem I cannot get rid of.

November 23rd, I Tatti

The moon counts for the "lower orders" and agriculturalists especially in a way that we American city dwellers cannot imagine. Nor indeed have we ever heard of the moon as of any consequence except with the tides. Here in Tuscany, the moon's course determines nearly everything. Weather of course, births, number of moons after conception. Neither hair nor nails cut except with waxing moon. Harvesting likewise. Gathering of grapes, pressing, barrelling, bottling. Moon in everyday life. And indeed the earliest, the Mesopotamian calendar, which still fixes our Easter, is entirely of moons, and the orthodox Jews' and Mohammedans' still measure time by the moon. In France some years ago I wanted to order a barrel of natural champagne. I was warned that when it came to bottling it I must be careful to have it done with the waxing moon. The sun was too long in its visible waxings and wanings for early man to find in it a measurer for his times of occupations. So while worshipped almost metaphysically and remotely, the moon was a presence of every week and every day.

December 1st, I Tatti

Marc Chagall comes from Vitebsk but has nothing Jewish about him in looks, in manner, in any peculiarities. Yet he paints almost nothing but ghetto life—and in a semi-naïf, rather childish fashion, does it with enough feeling to "put it over." His wife looks as little Jewish as he, only she is dark, slight, and with a sari and a wart on her forehead would pass muster as a high-class Hindu. Whence these curious types appearing in Jewry? The Hindu I cannot trace at all. The Egyptian-like Doro Levi or Anna Maria Cicogna,* with their skulls so overdeveloped behind the ears, must go back to the far, faraway days, when Israel was in Egypt. In my own face and features I trace a Germanic something, not infrequent among Central and Eastern European Jews. To go back to Chagall, I enjoyed his simplicity, his candour. He, though a famous painter, seemed in no way inclined to talk about himself, no touch of the average painter's self-adulation and fathomless conceit.

December 11th, I Tatti

Artistic, not private, personalities of artists have absorbed me through life. Artistic personalities are built up on the works still existing that can be ascribed to them. Hence the justification of searching for correct attributions. Not only of the great masters, but of the small fry who imitate them so much that their paintings have been attributed to their masters. If we learn the tricks of these imitators, we can establish their petty personalities, and thereby are enabled to demonstrate that this or that painting was done by them, and not by the genius they were copying. That is my reason, my excuse, for spending my last years in trying to arrive at the most probable attributions for all the Italian pictures from c. 1300 to 1600. The difference between my present and former attitude is that now I am more interested than I used to be in the idea of the artist, and less inclined to exclude what was not his actual handiwork.

* Doro Levi, Italian archaeologist, now Director of the Italian School of Archaeology in Athens; met B.B. in Athens in 1923 during his student days.—Countess Anna Maria Cicogna, younger daughter of the Italian financier Count Giuseppe Volpi; established in Venice and, for part of the year, in Tripoli, at the Saniet Volpi, a Turkish villa inherited from her father.

363

December 13th, I Tatti

Toes ache and smart. Soles of feet hard, unbendy. Legs stony. Left arm heavy. Entire left from top of head to tip of foot more troublesome than right. So head and left ear—occasionally a shot of pain darts there. Chest sore with coughing, and nose red with wiping. Cannot get rid of phlegm which oppresses me. Eyes watery. *Eppur si vive.* When I get absorbed in my work, or enjoy conversation, I revive, forget my aches and pains, and *expectorations*. All return the moment I stop working or being with stimulating guests, and are doubly distressing—almost drive me to despair. Yet I do not want to die, although I do not cling madly to life and am ready to go, and expect to be summoned suddenly, with no previous notice. What keeps one going at my age? Is it so-called clinging to life? Not in my case. More likely sheer inertia, the inertia that has played such an important part in my career, and now keeps me going, although with no promise of continuing.

December 14th, I Tatti

Got out of jeep at ruined chapel beyond Castel del Poggio, and told chauffeur, Parry, to go on to almond tree. As he was just starting, Nicky wrenched the heavy door open to take out a scarf I might need. The door flung out, and threw me down, and down I rolled over a steep declivity of rocks and boulders. I rolled two or three times, and banged against a boulder that stopped me, but nearly broke my spine. They came to pick me up, and with their help I walked to get into the jeep. While rolling I did not think of getting killed, but of breaking my hip, and I was anguished by Nicky's cries. I got home shaken, doctor came three times, happily discovered no serious damage, but back ached furiously, and only less more than thirty hours later, now that I am writing. It was Nicky's birthday, and my life is the present I make her. She refuses to see it that way, but feels guilty, and cannot forgive herself, dear loving soul! What a genius for pure, true love she has!

364

December 18th, I Tatti

History as she is writ is still overwhelmingly political, i.e., at bottom, personal, mythical, epical. Political history disappears before the history of inventions. As a child of five, now eighty-four years ago, steam was still in its infancy. Crawling railways, and steamships, were all that distinguished that time from Antiquity, from remote Antiquity, from the invention of the wheel, for instance. Now after eighty-five years everything except our own unchanging bodies is changed. How much has politics had to do with this change? Next to nothing. But politics and wars are subject to myths, whereas great inventions are largely anonymous. It is only the person who like Marconi has pulled a trigger who is remembered for a while, and not all who worked to make his act possible. After all, the greatest achievements remain anonymous even in art, as is the case with Medieval architecture, because they are a difficult subject for myth.

December 19th to 27th, no entry.

December 28th, I Tatti

Since last entry unable to write, because when I tried to my ribs ached too much. This result of a tumble down a steep, scrubby, rocky slope. No bones broken, but entire "cage," spine and ribs, shaken up so that I can scarcely draw breath without pain. Ever since, dreadful nights, tossing about to get rid of pain in back.

Guests, Anna Maria Cicogna, Derek Hill, Jean Rouvier, Umberto Morra.* Till two days ago saw them a few minutes at a time by my bedside. Yesterday and day before, got up for lunch and dinner, and took a toddle in inner garden.

* Derek Hill, English painter who lived in the Tatti Villino, 1948–52, and remained a close friend and frequent guest at I Tatti; introduced to B.B. by Ben Nicolson.—Jean Rouvier, son of French diplomat, at present French Cultural Attaché in Munich; met B.B. through Mrs. Kahn in 1936.—Count Umberto Morra di Lavriano, anti-Fascist Italian man of letters, Director of Italian Institute in London, 1954–57; close friend of both Berensons from 1925, when Carlo Placci introduced him to them.

All sorts of thoughts arose in me, the which, put down in proper fashion on paper, might be interesting.

Nicky sleeping very light in my *anticamera,* getting up when she hears me cough, and reading aloud till I doze off. No deep, no real sleep.

My escape so miraculous I could believe I was spared to give me time to repent—of what sins? Theological, chiefly.

December 31st, I Tatti

1954—a year in which Old Age has increasingly got hold of me, making me timid about going downstairs, increasing every natural deficiency, restricting more and more the time I can walk, or talk, or work. On the other hand, I have never enjoyed work more than now. Indeed, it is almost the "only carnal pleasure" left me. In spite of everything, I have done this year most of the catalogue of Venetian paintings, finished and even put through the press the new edition of the *Lotto,* written a monthly article for the *Corriere,* and kept up a continuous correspondence with women chiefly. A new woman has swum into my ken and although we met for an hour or two only, we have been writing every few days. I wonder how this friendship would stand the test of being together.

366

1 9 5 5

January 1st, I Tatti

The New Year begins with a rosy, dewy dawn, one star still shining Christmassy bright. I am recovering from the fall that could have killed me. Preserved miraculously, but suffering great pain in back and ribs, and after so many days in bed, discomfort of bedsores. But energy is returning, and soon I hope zest for work. Meanwhile I answer letters piled up during the days when I was too ill to attend to them. I read the usual dailies, weeklies, and periodicals. The last three days I have been getting up in time to walk on Nicky's arm in the garden, and to lunch and dine with her and whatever guests or rare outsiders. Jean Rouvier still here. Yesterday to lunch, ex-Queen of Rumania, singularly devoid of nonsense, a good sense of humour, and beautiful eyes. Told me my old enemy Beppino Gherardesca presented my *Lotto* to her sister the Duchess of Aosta,* boasting of his objectivity.

January 4th, I Tatti

There is scarcely a trace of aristocracy left in Europe. What remains is a new heraldocracy. This no longer dreams of governing, but of getting rich, in rare cases by work, but more often by selling its quarterings for a mess of bank notes, paid out for marrying heiresses. The effective rulers now are the plutocrats, and plutocrats at all times have longed to be aristocrats. If they

* Count Giuseppe della Gherardesca, member of Florentine aristocracy, Mayor of Florence under the Fascist regime; nourished a particular animosity against B.B. for political, and perhaps also for personal, reasons.— Duchess Irene d'Aosta, sister of King Paul of Greece, widow of the Duke of Spoleto (1909–48), who, after his brother's death, had become Duke d'Aosta.

could not be so themselves, their daughers could be titular ones, and their grandchildren semi-aristocrats. The real aristocrats now want nothing but money, while the plutos are eager for quarter-ings. So one now sees heirs to emperors, good-for-nothings with princely titles, selling themselves to Americans, or to successful *brasseurs d'affaires* of their own nationality, for the money it brings them. If ever we have aristocracy again, they will come from the people who really have run the show, the show in all its phases.

January 7th, I Tatti

Few so-called art lovers go beyond adopting a certain moment, say the Renaissance or Louis Quinze, or certain regions, China, Africa, Byzantium, or getting everything attributed to the great names like Raphael, Giorgione, Rembrandt. Few get to feel the difference between good and bad and indifferent in the field of their predilections. All or none. Whereas what means real feel-ing and appreciation and judgment in art is not the genre but the individual case. That is what the abstract thinker about art misses just as much as the vulgar enthusiast, and where we count, we who learn to feel and distinguish and to make up our minds about what a given artistic personality could or could not do, and whether a work of art under discussion could or could not belong to it. The student who can do that will soon be able to appreciate good, better, and worse, in any field of art.

January 9th, I Tatti

I recall from school days Velleius Paterculus* asking how it was that important men tend to come in constellations. I can-not recall his answer, and whether indeed he had one. My answer is that as in the vegetable kingdom there are good years and bad years, so as well in the animal kingdom including man. Man has good crops and bad crops. When the harvest promises to be good, we have crops of remarkable individuals making history, writing literature, architecting, sculpting, painting, etc. A good tradition

* Roman historian born about 19 B.C., author of a sketch of Roman history in two books—*Historiae Romanae libri duo*.

370

may help to bridge over a poor or poorish crop. Today, when all tradition is ignored, the poverty of the crop manifests itself as seldom in the past. Then we must recall that almost continuous wars since 1914 have burnt or frozen many a promise by killing off the most likely young men before they could achieve more themselves or beget offspring. It may take decades before a good human crop occurs.

January 15th, I Tatti

I am getting better, really excruciating pains rarer, am able to take part in conversation and to enjoy it so much that I forget my aches. I take more and more interest in my job, and return to it every morning. But faith, confidence in my body, has not yet begun to return. I feel unsure, timid, hesitant, and when I hear around me talk of travel, I doubt whether I ever shall do any again. That is still my present state of mind, but I have not given up hope that with returning bodily energy, I may be able to resume my life as it was before my accident. I hope Nicky too will succeed in getting over the shock she received when she saw me flying through the air. I saw it as I was falling, her face quivering like jelly, and transfigured by horror. I may recover sooner than she will, seeing she thinks she was the cause of my accident.

January 24th, I Tatti

Fosco Maraini showed us his coloured pictures of life and scenery in Japan. What struck me was the presence of a fair percentage of males who could be taken for Mediterranean. Less so the women. And as here in Tuscany, peasant girls good-, even distinguished-looking. Geishas smart but not whorish. Priests looking as priestly as they do here. Crowd folds hands and takes attitude of adoration as we do. Surely we have not copied one another. So it must be something instinctive common to all men—to all in a somewhat similar state of civilization. Scenery except for Fujiyama not very different from Italian. Fosco says the Samurai class has almost entirely disappeared. The ordinary crowds seem at least as jolly as ours when merrymaking, but brighter, gaier, more inventive. All in all, "the Jap" seems to be very much like

371

ourselves. Of course in these pictures we were shown no specimens of high aristocracy.

January 30th, I Tatti

My first reaction toward cold and affected hostility, toward calumny, is of savage vindictiveness. Then sense gets the better of me, and I have never defended myself, and never revenged myself. I have never wasted my spare energies, although on the other hand I have never boasted *Mehr Feind', mehr Ehr'*. I should be ready to have fewer *Feinde,* even at the cost of less *Ehre.* Yesterday I heard of a number of hostile acts, and after a second all I felt was fortified determination to leave behind me work enough to establish my authority, my way of seeing things, my conclusions, as well as my methods for years to come, to serve as real steppingstones for advance, as stimulus, as springboards, and not as inscribed tombstones of ideas. On the whole that is what I have had in mind ever since maturity.

January 31st, I Tatti

I love the words "human," "humanization," "humanized," and "humanist" and "humanities." What do I mean? With regard to the last two, nothing to do with grammar or study of Latin and Greek. I mean any activities of a literary kind that tend to "humanize." And now I come to what I mean by "humanize." I mean (on the whole) the faculty of putting oneself instantly and on every occasion under the skin, in the heart, in the muscles even of another, and in ideation to react as that other would. Unless one were "sadic," would one deliberately be unkind, cruel, massmurderish like Hitler or "Herod," the inspirer of pogroms, the persecutor for religious, I mean theological, reasons like so many Christian great men and even saints? And what is imagination but the same vivid and spontaneous putting oneself in another's place completely? It is the lack of this imagination that leads to cruelties and atrocities, particularly where it is a matter of mass murders. Hard to avoid some no matter how feeble feeling for individuals, but when it is a mass, it is easy to forget individual suffering.

"Imagination" in the arts (under other names, e.g., *Einfühlung*) is nothing but making one feel as the object imper-

372

sonated is supposed to be feeling not only consciously but unconsciously, physiologically, how he breathes, how he presses the ground when he stands, how he weighs when he sits, how his arms and hands and feet are relaxed. Even with landscape and buildings, imagination humanizes them by calling up possibilities of living in them, or with them, or conjuring up memories of happy moments, or evoking yearning, longing, dreaming of states of happiness. All comes back to "Put yourself in his place," in all circumstances, and in all encounters and experiences.

February 5th, I Tatti

My wife used to fear my seeing people I had prejudices against. She was sure I would lose the prejudice and embrace them as bosom friends. That happened yesterday with the Santillanas.* I was unfavourably impressed by him many years ago before he left for America. Has been there all the time since, and now I discover in the first place that unlike other immigrants, he has not adopted the commonest ways of Americans, but has remained wholly a European. Then cultivated, ready to talk on general matters in all fields, and not merely to pontificate in his own. Furthermore a glowingly human wife with radiant smile and caressing eyes. Now it seems a pity that we have lost so many months of their company. Here only for a term to lecture on his subject, the history of science. Says only a few female students attend.

February 8th, I Tatti

Last few weeks have given an hour or more every morning to looking at photos of Tintoretto and Veronese. The pleasure they give me is different in kind from what I receive from looking at photos of earlier works, even when by Titian. They give me a fullness of satisfaction, as if the whole of me was engaged, sensually as well as sentimentally and intellectually. Tintoretto with his penetrating and persuasively convincing portraiture, as well as interpretation of sacred and profane story, and Veronese with his fullness of life as one would live it. Tintoretto's only rival as inter-

* Giorgio de Santillana, Italian-born American scholar and Professor of History of Science at M.I.T., Boston; his wife, Dorothy, at present senior editor in the publishing house of Houghton Mifflin & Co., Boston.

preter is Rembrandt, and Veronese is scarcely paralleled by any till we come to Tiepolo and the French eighteenth-century painters. But they all are on a less vital level, at times bluffing.

February 9th, I Tatti

Paolo Guicciardini dead. Was ailing with heart trouble for some time past, but here a few weeks ago and seemed well. Elegant, distinguished, both quietly and without show, of a dry humour capable of irony and *malice,* not a deep thinker, but for a Florentine patrician of today and a former courtier, keenly aware of other than grovelling family interests. Not concerned with politics, the which like other Florentines of his class he endured rather than tried to direct; devoted like Alba to the history of his family's past, and in particular to the memory of the historian Francesco. Of him and regarding him, Paolo kept publishing new material, on beautiful paper and in attractive print. We met to talk of archives, of books, and questions of history. His once handsome wife (whose gossip I enjoyed) died a couple of years ago, and left him with no home life. Nobody of his kind to succeed him.

February 11th, I Tatti

I insist that art has two chief tasks. To interpret, to exalt life, to teach us spectators to see the beauty of things as if works of art already. For the practising artist, to find ways and means of making him more and more able to perform this task. Visual artists of today deliberately do none of these things. Then what is their place in the community? Only *qu'il faut vivre,* and that they can live in no other way, and being sufficiently able—like "sturdy beggars" of Elizabethan days—to impose themselves on the public, find so-called critics to sing their praises and sell their products. Someday the world will discover it has been fed on air, at best on foam and not beer, and will discard the masterpieces of today, and perhaps regard its supporting it as an aberration, as a shady episode. Meanwhile I shout to a public that is a desert of understanding, with no sounds but yelps of jackals.

B.B. and Nicky Mariano, 1956. *Photo Derek Hill*

B.B. and Nicky Mariano Walking in the Tatti Garden. *Photo Emil Schulthess*

Rosamond Lehmann, 1952. *Photo Derek Hill*

Countess Hortense Serristori, 1954. *Photo Bazzechi, Firenze*

H.R.H. the Queen Mother of Rumania, at Villa Sparta, Florence

Sir Kenneth Clark, at Saltwood Castle, Kent

February 16th, I Tatti

The paradox is that I have a very low opinion of my abilities when I think of myself in the absolute as it were, without comparing myself with others. And even when I do, many people have skills and capacities which I lack entirely. My utter unfitness for mechanics reaches up and down to my lack of interest in continuous thought. My thinking is saltatory, inspired, not logical. For which reason I am short of breath intellectually, and have little to develop and argue on any subject. The paradox is that yet I seem to have made the impact that I have not only by my writings but by my presence with people who meet me. It must be what is called personality, but a something that oneself cannot estimate or even feel as others may. Perhaps the magic works only when I am present, or while I am being read, and then only.

February 18th, I Tatti

I wonder how many lives, not in literature or as printed in history, are lived from beginning to end on a pre-established program. Of course there is "character" parrying or profiting by events, but as I look back on my own life, what program did it have? To make the best I could of myself. Then the conviction that I could say and do something that would pay my passage on the ship of life. Nothing more definite. Everything else subject to accident. No attempt to integrate and make as it were a logical Palladian structure out of the House of Life. If I built it at all, and did not let it be built for me, it was piecemeal, and only its ruins may pile up into a vague utility. Surely the same is true of all lives, even of heroes and saints, and of all figures in song and story.

February 23rd, I Tatti

Bertie Anrep died yesterday in the early hours. Since then dependents take turns in keeping him company, like a "wake" although without the drink and rowdiness to which a wake can turn in Ireland. (What can happen in Italy one may learn from one of D'Annunzio's early short stories.) What may be the origin of this practice, and of accompanying the dead to the grave? It is a practice carried on, as I remember, in Paris where old men, bareheaded, nearly or as famous as the dead, trudge miles, all the way to the Père Lachaise. Whatever it was, it is lost in the night of time, and for us of recent generations difficult to trace, because difficult probably to imagine. Was it affection, tender pity (most unlikely), or fear of the ghost and his resentment against the living, the envied survivors? Was it to reconcile him, to calm his vindictive indignation at being deprived of sun and air and motion —in short, of life? All explained no doubt in Frazer.

February 24th, I Tatti

What was through life my own feeling about death? The death of animals did not concern me, but instinctively the death of humans did. Why? Could I at five or six feel that the genus to which I belonged should not die, and that it was something unthinkable? I certainly was overawed by death when I first encountered it at the deathbed of my grandmother. I always have avoided seeing a corpse, and although I received my wife's last breath, I ran away the very instant. There is something numenal about death, which goes over to the feeling that producing it deliberately, that is to say killing a person, is the greatest of all crimes, and to many people an event of highest and even sexual excitement. I cannot reconcile myself to taking away life for any reason whatever. Seldom have I been so horrified as at the cold-blooded judges who sat through the serial hangings of war criminals at Nuremberg.

March 10th, I Tatti

Freya Stark asked how I liked her book on Ionia, and I told her that it displayed too much recently discovered, undigested learning. She did not deny or take offence, but confessed that it delighted her to write about what she had just "got up." The infantile eagerness to talk of just discovered facts stays by us through life. I may already in this diary have mentioned Mrs. Frances Burnett as an aging and famous novelist discovering the earth was round like an orange, and her eagerness to communicate it to others. A few days ago Cyril Connolly came back from a short stay in Egypt bursting and dripping with information about its art and archaeology, and history, expecting me to wonder and rejoice as if I did not know it all. And how often I have urged people to read a book or to see a place, only to be chided for not having been sufficiently enthusiastic about it—with a bubbling enthusiasm that would soon cool off.

March 11th, I Tatti

Excitement is what we crave for, whether we are aware of it or not. (We are less the victims of this kind of "call of nature" when we are aware of it.) Possibly as strong as sex—perhaps stronger. In the perfected welfare state, where everything will be done for one's comfort, and adventure entirely excluded, what will remain to excite and give zest to life? I recall the schoolmaster who expressed his amazement that we as a class were so excited over an object so unexciting as a new arithmetic book. Small boys and girls will still enjoy such excitements, but grownups, what besides *circenses* will they have—if indeed they will be allowed to exist with their bad example of competition and the demoralizing excitement it evokes? The perfected welfare state either may end as an ant community with human semblances, or be reduced to boredom and sigh with *ennui* like pious pre-Christians in Limbo.

March 13th, I Tatti

In one of her books Mabel Dodge * says that by passing through her bedroom, D. H. Lawrence turned it into a brothel. Sex did absorb him far too much, it haunted him. In the same way some, indeed many, people today have the Midas touch by turning most matters into questions of money. I recall how shocked I was when Harry White, Ambassador of U.S.A. and a gentleman by birth, breeding, and reputation, asked about a fellow countryman what his income was, and whether it was around a hundred

* Mabel Dodge Luhan (1879–1962), friend of D. H. Lawrence, author of *Lorenzo in Taos,* etc.

thousand dollars. One of the most odious hours I ever spent was at Cannes with Gulbenkian.* On a long and tiring walk he insisted on asking what I thought was the money value of every picture he could think of. In vain I tried to say that I did not know, that I seldom thought about venal values in connection with works of art. I know of course that to most Americans money is only an orientation, but not so to the new type of Mithridates, for whom there are no other values.

March 14th, I Tatti

Jules Romains wrote *La Mort de Quelqu'un*. His ghost (shall we say) gets more alive and dies down according to what the living say about him, and the number who talk about him. Assuming that I do not escape the law of averages, and that what happens to me happens to most people, my own self flares up or dies down, or trembles or fluctuates as others deal with me, are kind or unkind, polite or rude, appreciative or denigratory. I seldom if ever burn with a flame unaffected by the breath of others, by what I feel or read or hear that they think of me, how much they want me, how eager to get away from me, how many heartily love me or hate me. In short, I feel as others make me feel, and scarcely ever like a self that has shape and substance of its own, regardless of what it is to others, and what they make of it.

March 17th, I Tatti

St. Patrick's Day—how well I remember its celebration in Boston and New York, with proletarian crowds, green ribbons in the lapels of their coats, marching, strutting in procession through the principal streets. They too have grown up with the country, and East End Boston and Chelsea have produced an ambassador to London, whose son is senator, ousting Cabot Lodge. They influence our foreign relations to a considerable degree. Without their sympathy for ultra-Romish Spain and its Franco, our brass hats scarcely would have succeeded in doing all we have under-

* C. S. Gulbenkian (1869–1955), Armenian banker, oil magnate, and art collector.

taken for that revolting polity. They favour every reaction toward Rome, papal Rome, the Vatican I mean, every move against England. Yet in a sense they are not Roman Catholics at all, but Irish ones, and their religion is not Christian, but a *jihad* against England. Only after that does American-Irish Catholicism think of the Vatican and the Pope. A dangerous element in American foreign relations.

March 18th, I Tatti

A woman of say forty-five, still handsome, still full of sex appeal, herself amorous and enterprising, writes well and publishes, has had every kind of life-enhancing experience as news correspondent and in encounters with events, confesses that now the centre of her life is not a new husband, nor her career, nor adventure, but a little boy she has adopted. The maternal instinct, and to exercise it to the full, is what the average woman is after, and that alone procures complete satisfaction, happiness even. No matter how depraved, no matter how exalted. What would Elizabeth of England have become if she had had a child? But did not Catherine of Russia dote on her grandchildren, hating her son? She may have been the "exception to the rule." Not women only. Males likewise cannot live without loving.

March 20th, I Tatti

From an early age children should be taught to appreciate and value the beauty of things in themselves, and not only as painted or otherwise reproduced. (The psychology of our preference for the picture to the object reproduced deserves serious study.) Sunset, sunrise, sky effects, all natural effects, the beauty of buildings, houses, street scenes, the charm of everyday objects in their places, the loveliness of human beings, not only of the young but of all ages, and of all animals of course, etc. That sort of education might lead people to value, appreciate, enjoy what costs them nothing, and at the same time turn them into potential super-painters. Then make them appreciate all the beauties, man-made, that cost them nothing or next to nothing, like the works of art in public museums.

March 27th, I Tatti

Certain individuals invite letter writers, induce them to correspond, as others are good hosts. The best hostess I have known, Rosa Fitz-James,* was far from intellectual, or even clever, or stimulating in herself. She had the art of knowing, of feeling rather, how twenty individuals would go together, stimulating each other, and go away feeling they had functioned satisfactorily, in good company. So with letter writing. Mme de Sévigné's daughter was probably anything but adequately responsive. In our own day, Princess Radziwill † wrote to di Robilant, who when a military attaché impressed one as rather dull. Now Hamish Hamilton tells me that Ottoline Morrell ‡ was the recipient of brilliant letters from all sorts of correspondents. She was mentally a "flibbertigibbet." What it is that makes people stimulating recipients of letters remains a mystery. Perhaps a parallel to the ear of Midas.

March 30th, I Tatti

I still go on asking what I carry away from seeing and meeting people. I might as well ask what I carry away from eating and drinking. A certain amount of gregariousness, chattering oneself and pretending to listen to the chatter of the others, seems almost as necessary as meat and drink. No visible result, nothing added to our mental capital. Once in a blue moon, a dog's life, one hears or overhears some word, some phrase, that draws the cork of the bottle that we are, and out comes the imprisoned genie, who carries our entire bulk high into the empyrean. How seldom does this occur! Yet I still go on expecting from every person who comes to see me some contribution to knowledge, some

* Rosa de Fitz-James, born Gutmann of Vienna, noted Paris hostess before World War I.
† French-born wife of Polish-Prussian magnate Prince Antoine Radziwill, noted for her political salon in Berlin and for her letters to the Italian diplomat Count Robilant. Died in 1915.
‡ Lady Ottoline Morrell (died in 1938), wife of Philip Morrell, well-known hostess, who entertained, in her beautiful house near Oxford, Garsington, the most famous writers of her time, including Virginia Woolf, D. H. Lawrence, David Garnett, James Stephens, etc.

widening of vision, and I still can feel as disappointed as when an undergraduate at Harvard. Life should have taught me that conviviality, conversation even, are mere tonics, and rarely enriching.

April 2nd, I Tatti

What a day yesterday. To lunch, a Russian from Paris, an arithmetician, proud of his last book. To avoid talking about such a boring subject, I jumped from pillar to post of gossip. Then while still resting from my siesta came a young woman with appealing ways and soft eyes to get me to say a few words about some of my pictures that *Time* is going to reproduce. Downstairs meanwhile the Costers were waiting for me with their guests, my colleague Alazard of Algiers and his wife.* With them I gladly would have chatted, but there were others I had to be polite to, and so got deadly tired with the effort of being all things to all men. Finally in the evening Francis Taylor and his wife, whom I was meeting for the first time, a slender almost elegant silver-headed woman, reminding one of, rather than resembling, a Louis Quinze *marquise*. Francis broad-faced, with pointed nose, looking like one of the apostles in Leonardo's *Last Supper,* talked of his retirement to Worcester. I wonder whether after seventeen years of the Metropolitan and New York, he won't be bored in the small town.

April 8th, I Tatti

Sam Behrman,† famous as entertainer and wit, as stimulatory. In this house he is entertaining enough, but not more than many others. I dare say we do not know how to draw him out— perhaps we have too few acquaintances in common, and these too bourgeois to draw out his most brilliant shafts of wit. With me

* Charles Henry Coster, descendant of Dutch New York family; historian; married since 1926 to Byba Giuliani, one of Nicky Mariano's close Italian friends.—Jean Alazard (1886–1960), French art historian, for a number of years Professor of Fine Arts at the University of Algiers, translator of B.B.'s *Aesthetics and History* into French.
† S. N. Behrman, American playwright and author.

381

alone he is stimulating and gets me to say, because of our common ghetto origin, what I seldom say to others. He is too responsive, although I suspect that it is his pose to be *bénisseur* while he is with one—so enthusiastic in applauding all that comes out of my mouth, that I almost wonder whether he really has been listening, and if so, whether he grasped what I was babbling about. Like other *bénisseurs* I have known, he may be at bottom severely, even harshly, critical, and like them seldom allows others to know or even guess what he thinks.

April 9th, I Tatti

I could fill the page that I fill every morning with my aches, pains, heats, coughs, sneezes, etc.—in short, with the physiological events of the previous day and night. They seem to be without rhyme or reason, depending on neither what I take in and give out, nor on what I am doing. A good night's sleep for instance is apt to be followed by a day when I feel dead-tired and bad-tempered. In consequence, the older I get, the more do I feel that my body goes its own way, and that I can do very little to control it, and indeed to understand it. Nor have I ever met a doctor who seemed to know more about my own body than I do. I am inclined to believe that already we know more of what goes on in a celestial body a million light-years away than we do about our own, about the human, let us say about the animal body.

April 14th, I Tatti

We cannot help being affected by what others think of us. New arrivals like Irish in New England and New York, Jews in Germany and Austria—those among them who tried to get out of their ghettos met with rebuffs that diminished them, and worse, read and were influenced by what they read, and at times went as far as to become, chiefly in the case of clever and aspiring young Jews, anti-Semitic, and to an extent that made them bitter over the sad lot of being born Jews, and in some cases, as in Weininger for instance, led to suicide. So with our work. We do it because it is our way of living, of functioning, yet if what we do is not appreciated by others, we soon cease to believe in ourselves, lose the zest for work, and end by doing it listlessly, and poorly. We cannot live normally satisfactory lives apart from the group in which we were brought up, or to which we give our adherence.

April 23rd, I Tatti

Reading the *Iliad,* I feel that the Trojans were more civilized, more humanized than their Greek invaders. Yet Homer himself was a Greek, and how shall we account for (to say the least) his impartiality? Possibly he looked on the Trojans as beings in no way different from his own people, only that he may have admired their being more urbanized than European Hellenes. More probably "Homer" had the genius of impartiality even as Shakespeare had, and felt equally tender to one side as to the other. If so, "Homer," i.e., the Greek spirit as early as the eighth century B.C., was civilized enough to admire the enemy and feel tender toward him. No parallel with it in Hebrew literature of the same date, or indeed anywhere else until nearly our own time. Certainly not in the Germanic Nibelungen or Gudrun. A faint glimpse in Icelandic sagas. If I am right about Homer, it puts the Greek "Bible" above ours.

April 26th, I Tatti

Various ways a biography of B.B. could be written. The most fetching would be of the Horatio Alger kind, the immigrant Jew boy from "Poland" who rises to affluence and eminence. Fabulously exciting could be one recounting the transition he witnessed from a neolithic civilization in Lithuania to the modern one of today. He recalls seeing the first electric light as a globe in a circus. In his youth in Boston steam, gas, and electric telegraph were the last inventions. All, all, all the wonders of material advance have occurred since then. The best, the most revealing account of him would be first of his library, when each item was acquired, and what signs are found of his having read or perused it. Supplemented by the date when he acquired each work of art. Completed by the story of his travels, of his house and garden and land. More psychological of his marriage, his friends, his enemy-friends, his enemies.

April 29th, I Tatti

The most sympathizing of publishers refused to bring out an English edition of my notes on Sicily. A trifling event, yet it momentarily life-diminished, shrunk me, made me feel smaller and—colder. The English-reading public seems to want to read about what they should be looking at. They travel, so to speak, with their ears, not with their eyes. Or is it the same with all "cultured" travellers? They feel what they see to be a page of cuneiform, or Sanskrit, and can get an inkling of what it is all about not from an interpretation of what they should see, but from the messes of anecdotage they are fed with in the presence of what they are supposed to be looking at. I know all that, and yet I lust for their admiration, and am sorry that I cannot "sell" myself to them. Perhaps my regret is not that they do not want me, but that I suspect that I cannot appeal to them.

April 30th, I Tatti

The older I get the more convinced I am, as I concluded and preached already in my twenties, that the proper exercise of function meant life, meant liberty, meant happiness—no matter what the consequences—hanging for the murderer, prison for the bank breaker, thief, forger, *vogue la galère* for the spendthrift and for the social agitator.

Some are born to exercise the profession of painters, and no matter what starvation they may incur, what rebuffs, what failures, paint they must, and many and nearly all French painters are predestined. But their output depends on the spiritual climate of the day, which they cannot help being affected by. They have my sympathy, little though I may enjoy or admire their output. Picasso is the supreme case of our time. Paint he must—no matter what. With us in England and the U.S.A., the call to paint is rare and feeble. Painting is taken up by young men who leave our great universities and, not knowing what to do with themselves, choose an occupation which like painting seems and is treacherously easy at the start. Soon they come across snags, and having had no training as artisans, they are led by their college education to use their intellectual attainments and learning, and begin to theorize, and search for Eldorado, the Brasiland of the "Old Masters' secret." They end by being theorizers, and art critics, like Roger Fry, or even Ricketts, or Denman Ross.* The youngest of today logically have thrown over all that made painting an art, and daub and slash and dab, with no pattern, no representation of course, and call it proudly "abstract," nonrepresentational art. Picasso does it with his tongue in his cheek.

May 1st, Siracusa

Train straight to Siracusa. Crowded to utmost. Long journey to dining car. Meal excellent, and well served. Acrobatics of waiters as with plates full they kept balance running up and down. But in all three classes as we passed, the same more or less proletarian aspect, and slovenly habits. Corridors crowded, almost impassable, and little politeness. Dirty paper, cigarette stumps, strewing ground in and out of compartments. Interesting faces rare. Following morning, May 1st, glimpses of grand scenery, and fine alluvial plain, and Straits of Messina. Could not help looking professionally to discover resemblances with Antonello's backgrounds, so often representing straits. Ferryboat, crowded with more proletarians than ever. Good restaurant but too late for *my* breakfast, and far too early for lunch. No dining car from Messina to Siracusa, and no food provided. At Catania tried a *cestino*. Contained nothing any one of us could eat. Cloven foot of Italian ideas of being up to American standards.

May 2nd, Siracusa

Morning in museum. Struck by likeness of archaic sculptures with those in Athens. Therefore a Panhellenic style must already have existed as early as 600 B.C. Famous Venus better than I remembered, back admirable. Great Paleochristian sarcophagus has distinct traces of painting. Afternoon, theatre, wonderful geometrically, but view spoiled by factory chimneys, and the whole

* Charles Ricketts (1866–1931), English painter, art critic, and stage-set designer.—Denman Waldo Ross (1853–1935), American educator and collector of Far Eastern art.

ambience so suburbanized. Fort of Euryalus happily unspoiled, and in parts almost as fascinating as Kom Ombo on the Nile. No sordid touch anywhere to be seen, and silence of a world in utter ruin. All in all, and increasingly so on every return, one of the most impressive sights left us by Antiquity. Departure delayed, more than an hour standing around for passport officials to come around. Very rude and surly and vexatious when finally they deigned to appear. Horrid experience I'd rather not repeat.

May 3rd, Malta

Steamer *Argentina,* a bit old-fashioned, but perfectly comfy, with courteous personnel and punctilious service. On board, Caputo, Director of Antiques at Florence. Gave him a piece of my mind about the hypocrisy of the cult of *Patrimonio Artistico.* Several hours at Malta, taken in charge by Sciclunas,* father and son, both Oxonians, the younger one completely so and employed as reporter on labour conditions in Italy. Were shown cathedral, where I greatly admired Caravaggio's *Decapitation of Baptist,* his finest work after the *Calling of Matthew,* indeed in some respects finer. Lunched at *the* Club, over-gorgeous, and not impressed by its frequenters. Malta made a wonderful impression, honey-coloured cubes rising over each other in irregular tiers, and the town itself elegant in palaces and churches, streets alive and all breathing an air of free vitality. No obvious signs of war damage, despite over a thousand bombardments. British!!

May 5th, Tripoli

A gentlemanly and most respectable Californian, who the previous evening had been to see the female dancers in Cairo, when asked what he thought of it said, "Pleasant or unpleasant, it is an experience." I may say as much for the whole of life, including extreme old age. Weakening of every physiological or-

* Giacomo Caputo, Italian archaeologist on the staff of the Fine Arts Service; at present Superintendent of Classical Art in Florence.—Sir Hannibal Scicluna, Anglo-Maltese civil servant and scholar; author of book on Church of St. John in La Valletta, Malta.—Edward Scicluna, son of Sir Hannibal, expert on international labour questions.

gan, digestion, intestines, waterworks, difficulty of making it, and dripping, tired all the time, and sudden all but collapses. Urticaria, bedsores, increasing deafness—and *toute la lyre* of symptoms of decline! "Pleasant or unpleasant"? Decidedly unpleasant! Yet would I not go through with it, even if it leads to a second infancy, provided awareness, unknown to infancy, remains? All experience that does not cost others too much is worth having for its own sake, pain if not *ultra vires,* and pleasure even if dulled, dimmed, and muted. So I live on, surprised each morning to be still on the ground, still an animal, still suffering and enjoying, and at moments enjoying aesthetically.

May 6th, Tripoli

Every day something happens to remind me that the continent of Memory is crumbling into the ocean of Forgetting. The other morning in reading I came across the name Knossos. For a few seconds I had a vague teasing feeling that I ought to know what it was, but could not place it. Then it came back, all my years of reading about it, and my having stayed there for a full week at least. Even one's inner self gets dimmer and more blurred, and I end by retaining nothing but a feeling of mere existence, little more perhaps than a baby feels soon after birth. I wake up when at work, or engaged in conversation, or enjoying the world, as I do for minutes often, and the caresses of women. Alive as well as feeling sick, with disturbed intestines, smarting bladder. Of such is the Kingdom of Eld!

May 12th, Tripoli

Invitation from Oxford to attend the Encomia, and to receive the degree of Doctor in Letters. If I had received it some years ago, it might have given me great satisfaction, and I should have hastened to accept. Now I can only think of in what words to couch my refusal. Partly indifference to honours of that, or indeed of any other, kind. Chiefly the fear of the ceremonial, the being one of the *dii minori,* and that once in England I could not avoid revisiting all the principal museums, and seeing all the people I wanted to see. Besides, to go back, it is an honour bestowed too

387

late, and given to all sorts of individuals I think little of, and given through wirepulling and individual interest, not really as a considered estimate of one's merits. Yet had it come years ago, how I should have rejoiced, and how friends would have congratulated!

May 20th, Tripoli

For the first time in weeks enjoyed the freshness of the early morning of a warm day. I often recall how it tasted when I was a child of five or six in Lithuania. The lime blossom scented the air, there was refreshingly penetrating coolness, there was the Russian mounted cavalry band leading the troops past the garden. And for most of my life, the enjoyment of this golden hour has been the measure of feeling well and full of zest for what may come the rest of the day. Seldom do I feel it now. I remain not quite awake, although I drink tea and begin to read. Only the morning coffee brings me to myself. What a hemmed-in, diminished self, invalidish, tottering, doddering, forgetting the ideas that flash through the mind, almost before the flashing itself is over. And yet, and yet, I would regard my present state as an interesting adventure, if only it led on as adventures should. Despite the lack of illusion about the end, one somehow manages to live as if life would never end!

May 22nd, Tripoli

Urged to write my ideas for the future of I Tatti, I have done so. I doubt whether it will have any effect. What follows will be in accordance with the current tendencies of the moment. For instance in the field of art history, I cannot induce young or old to leave the Mannerists, and study real artists like Andrea del Sarto and Paul Veronese (I even seem to feel a growing indifference to Velasquez). So I Tatti will serve the idols of the day, and its students will ignore, because they cannot bring themselves to take an interest in, the serene worlds of Classical art and literature, what is of all times, and not of the present moment, when "men sit and hear each other groan," and groaning is the only utterance that interests. So I steel myself to the philosophy of the turtle in the *Panchatantra*—

388

"yad abhāvi na tad bhāvi
bhāvi cen na tad abtatgā."

["What is not to be will not be.
If it is to be, it will not be otherwise."] *

May 31st, Taormina

In Roman theatre a middle-aged American woman with a human face and expression sitting in ecstatic meditation. I could infer from her shoes and dress that she was a person of small means, a schoolteacher perhaps who had worked years and years to save up enough to make the pilgrimage to the Past. My heart goes out to that class of American female. I know her yearnings, her longing, her dreams, her hopes of seeing the lands, the ruins, the remains, the works of art that inspired the poets and novelists she has lived on. She travels in the least expensive way, braving hardships, sordid boardinghouses, deadly fatigue. She will return home, to a drab home and monotonous life, and recall and magnify and embellish her so brief experience of "abroad"—of that vast continent which contains such countries as Italy and Greece and England, and France and Germany. The nostalgic American is my companion, and I could wish to embrace them all.

June 11th, Naples

Cumae. Struck by resemblance of the *Antrum Immane* described by Vergil, and rediscovered in recent decades, with underground temple in Malta. If pre-Hellenic, how is it that the natives could not defend it against Aegean invaders? May have been an island close to the shore, like Castel dell'Ovo in Naples, and many other Semitic and Greek first settlements in the Mediterranean, easy to defend against natives, yet close enough to be in touch with them! How many times I have been to Cumae,

---

* For the translation thanks are due to Professor Daniel H. H. Ingalls, of the Department of Sanskrit and Indian Studies at Harvard. According to him, the verse quoted by B.B. in this form is not from the *Panchatantra* but from the *Hitopadesa (Book of Good Council)*, a reworking of stories from the *Panchatantra* together with other stories.

from my first visit in December '88 till now, and how I got there, and with whom. I recall with *Wehmut* repeated visits with my wife, when we still were young and strong, and wandered about and around the wooded shore as well as the Acropolis. Always suggestive, nostalgia for one's own past as well as for the historical. The sea always carrying on its "listless chime, time's self made audible." Today again, roaring, moaning, murmuring, purple in distance and cruel green near at hand. What views of Ischia, of Procida, of more distant cameo-like Capri! *Die alte Weise,* how it grips me still, but it is the grip now that counts, and not the message. Indeed, there is no more message. It is IT. IT is its own and only purpose, IT is intransitive.

June 15th, Naples

An hour at the museum with the Antique *objets d'art,* gold, silver, glass, cameo, crystal, ivory, and could not have been happier. Pure delight, especially in all those arts, the treatment of foliage. Their appreciation is a real test of sensitive and intelligent feeling for art. No illustrative element, no story, nothing to lead one astray to fancy enjoying art when one is only interested in an anecdote. Me these little masterpieces delight as only the works of the greatest painters, sculptors, and architects. I am ready to grant a scale of value, provided each attains the supreme. I enjoy architecture more than sculpture, and sculpture than painting, and all three can attain a sublimity that perhaps is not found in the "minor arts." Yet for sheer pleasure on a more workaday level, give me some of these exquisite toys of genius, and I shall be happy and grateful.

June 18th, Rome

Whoever made the new arrangement of Vigna di Papa Giulio Museum has taken a lesson from jewellers and art dealers who have studied and perfected the art of displaying their wares. I see no harm in museums' learning from them. *"Fas est ab hoste docere."* But most archaeologists, including my ultra-Soviet-minded friend Bianchi Bandinelli, are indignant because outraged. What do they want? That the work of art should remain unenjoyed, and serve only as a *cadavre* for anatomizing, or as subject matter for meta-fussics, Freudian interpretations, or stimuli for Re-search? The work of art surely was meant to be enjoyed, and all occupation with the work of art should serve to make us enjoy it more penetratingly, more appreciatively, in short more completely. "Me all the erudition of the pundits tires." I could wish their activities interrupted for half a century. Then they might start again and afresh, and look without preconceptions begot by footnotes, and footnotes upon footnotes.

June 19th, Rome

Short look round at Borghese. Enjoyed Canova and Bernini, yet both sin by lack of grip. Hence being more illustrative than plastic. No merit in Caravaggio now so prominently, almost provocatively, displayed. Bored by most of the paintings, including even the Titian and Raphael. The only picture to give me complete satisfaction was Correggio's *Danaë*—seemed by far greatest and most important picture in the collection. How much fault-finding, when one is not in a state of grace toward works or art. So much allowance has to be made even in the presence of the greatest feats of the painters and sculptors. Easy to see the faults and carp on them. On the other hand I never see Caravaggios without having (as it were) to lift myself up by my bootstraps to give him anything like the admiration that is now tributed to him. The case too with some of far more recent date, as for instance certain Cézannes. At the back of my mind there always lingers a doubt about even my admiration, and as few ever I try to be genuine.

June 22nd, Rome

An hour in the Capitoline Museum. I keep asking myself how many of the objects there I should care for, could enjoy now on purely artistic grounds. But for attribution, dating, *sauce historique,* there might be but few. Among paintings the early Titian *Baptism,* among bronzes the so-called *Brutus,* among marbles a few more perhaps, four or five. *C'est la sauce qui fait manger le poisson.* I have tried to get at the object pure, itself, enhanced by nothing external to itself, have tried to attain a quasi-mystical union between the work of art and myself. Have I succeeded? How rarely do I look at an Italian picture without enjoying it more if I can attribute and date it. Or may I say I enjoy it most when these adventitious problems are settled and well behind me, in presence of the work of art, and I can abandon myself to un-adulterated enjoyment to the point of ecstasy!

June 28th, Assisi

F. Mason Perkins,* now past eighty, fine features, shock of white hair, artist's hands. Brought up in China, and consequently apt to treat everybody the way Anglo-Saxons treated Chinese. Said yesterday he spent several years in Japan. Became a pianist of some praise in Vienna. I first found him in Siena in the nineties of last century. Nearly starved. Started him writing. If memory does not fail me, Mary wrote the article on Andrea published under his name in *Burlington Magazine,* and wrote most of his *Giotto.* Set up in Siena as prime authority on Sienese art, and encouraged by anti-Berensoners to assume role of rival. Then his matrimonial affairs engaged my wife's sympathy for his wife, lead-ing to his insolent conduct to my wife. After that, growing cool-ness. Finally left Siena for Assisi, converted to Catholicism with intense fervour. Gave up writing. His collection of paintings in a squalid state, and scarcely an enjoyable picture in the whole lot. One, nay the only survivor of the pioneering days of connoisseur-ship, when we worked out the artistic personalities, which the youngs of today handle so deftly with no idea of what it meant to us.

July 1st, I Tatti

Do not know where to turn, what bundle of hay to munch. Mountain-high accumulation of books sent as presents [for nineti-eth birthday]. Others filling the corridors, and every available table, ledge, and chair in my study. Scores upon scores of letters, and

* American art connoisseur and collector (1874–1955), lived for years in Assisi, and left his collection to the Franciscan Convent of San Fran-cesco.

ever so many telegrams to answer. The thought of it makes me sweat and feel dizzy and despairing. Guests arriving to stay, and others to meals. Withal I am eager to write articles on Calabria, anxious to get on with proofreading of books in the press. "Faster, faster, Circe, Goddess." Who will free me from hurry, flurry, the feeling of a crowd pushing behind me, of being hustled and crushed? How can I regain even for a minute the feeling of ample leisure I had during my early, my creative years? Then I seldom felt fussed, or hurried. There was time for work, for play, for love, the confidence that if a task was not done at the appointed time, I easily could fit it into another hour. I used to take leisure for granted, as I did time itself.

July 15th, I Tatti

Tea with Duchess Anna d'Aosta,* in her villa just under bumptious Torre del Gallo. A view of utmost charm and romance with not a minimal speck of ugliness—a sheer miracle. It would never occur to one to suspect the existence of a sprawling mixed pickle of a town below. Delightfully laid-out garden in steep decline, exquisitely kept. Indoors the acme of comfort and cosiness, no pretence, no display. The Duchess a bulky woman with a Valois profile, and delicate young daughter. A friendly, familiar atmosphere, an ease of chat, all result of high breeding. And that is why I enjoy seeing people of that "category" once in a while. I do not aspire to be one of them, and still less to be on familiar terms with them. Contact with them is "otherness," and at the same time stimulates historical and even zoological interest. We can know from what "animal farm" they descend, as for few of the rest of us.

July 16th, I Tatti

I recall writing about the Spartans who ceased to be of the leading class when they could not contribute to the "black broth" of the gentry eaten in common. I pointed the parallel to the same today virtually. Since then I have discovered that equal spending

* Born Anne de Guise, widow of Duke Amedeo d'Aosta (1898–1942).

power unites people into a society of plutocrats over our Western world at least. American billionaires, the very few remaining ones in England and France, Greek and Armenian money-makers, Mexican grandees, Jewish adventurers, all unite in a world based on fabulous spending. They attract all kinds of parasites, young men particularly as *cicisbei* for their women, helping them to spend, and thus getting pickings for themselves. Extinct royalties frequent them as well, e.g., the Windsors. It is a society that would be worth studying before its disappearance, as surely it will disappear in a generation or two—for good? I wonder.

July 19th, I Tatti

A review of last volume of Sismondi's * correspondence. With a change of names, and allowing for my inferiority of gifts, position, and opportunities, this volume could have been written by myself. Same distance, despair over the way things were going, same dread of the future and what would become of humanity, same feeling of isolation and immolation. Yet I myself born into this painful world he foresees. I passed on the whole a happy childhood and youth, and until well into my forties felt I was in perfect harmony with my world as I lived it. I wonder whether any thinking person goes on long after forty finding the world to his taste, and to his wishes. One's private world is a suit of clothes that wears thinner and thinner after forty, and ends by leaving one naked and ashamed not for oneself, but for the later generations whose clothing (so to speak) we deplore so much.

July 22nd, Vallombrosa

A pleasant youngish man to interview me about Bertie Russell, whose life he is writing with his consent. He wanted to know what I recall of Bertie. It is not much. Bertie acted as if his divorce from Alys, my wife's sister, necessarily made us enemies. Nothing of the sort. Mary as well as I understood, and I, at least, sympathized with him. Perhaps the misunderstanding was formed by Ottoline Morrell for reasons of her own, perhaps by Roger Fry, who I keep discovering made enemies for me where he could. So

* Jean Charles Sismondi (1773–1842), French historian of Italian descent.

394

we never saw Russell again, till 1936 when he came to lunch, and behaved (or so it seemed to me) condescendingly toward Mary and arrogantly toward me. Since then he has been in Italy again and again (as I discovered later) but never approached me. The pity is that he has no greater admirer of his qualities as a writer and thinker. He might have found me as stimulating as I certainly should have found him.

July 25th, Vallombrosa

If Milton were here now he would not go home and write "Thick as autumnal leaves . . . in Vallombrosa." No more leaves at Vallombrosa. Higher up the great cathedrals of beeches are being cut down. Lower in the deep ravines grand old chestnuts are fast disappearing. Nearby a lovely ladylike birch starved for a trickle of water and was allowed to die. A bit higher up a grove of Norway pines, all cut down. To make room for the sombre dark bottle-green firs, which now make the whole of Vallombrosa look almost dismal even in full sunshine. Nearby, a glorious walnut tree, very faintly in the way of the Forestry camions, pitilessly hacked down. A clump like Rembrandt's etching of *Three Trees* made away with for some petty convenience of the Forestry administration. The least feeling for landscape could have instigated mercy of these depredations. No protest on the part of Italians, and I being a foreigner have no right to raise my voice. One of the handicaps of being a *Fremdling überall*.

July 28th, Vallombrosa

I no longer read metaphysical or theological books and essays and articles, nor psychology since it has become overwhelmingly Freudian. Excepting subjects based on mathematics and mechanics, I am still brimming over with curiosity about everything, but for information rather than interpretation. Generalizations bore me. I have encountered most of the ideas that can be discussed about every type of literature. They are so limited and originality about them more often than not consists in a slightly varied phraseology, and occasional epigram, often cribbed from forgotten writers of the past. But anything concerning peoples, climates, life in all possible places, still keeps my attention. So does gossip about the

395

expanding universe. Archaeological finds of every sort on every part of the earth still excite me, and the history of languages, their connections, their vocabularies, their etymologies. I still enjoy a good novel or short story, and can read the Classics with delight. If I had the leisure I would read them every day, and all from Homer and the Old Testament down to the end of the nineteenth century.

July 29th, Vallombrosa

Forty-eight hours of bronchial fever, in a state of coma. Could not think or read, or be read to. I just existed, and was aware of existing. Not too uncomfortable, except when trying to cough up the mucus in the bronchial tubes. Nicky hovering over me with face beaming with love to give me courage. Confessed just now that last night she came four times to my door on the chance of seeing a light or hearing me stir, and coming in to help me, or just to hold my hand. Emma helpful as nobody has a right to expect, ready for any self-sacrifice to alleviate, to remedy, to heal. The love I get from the women who help and serve me comforts me. I cannot be the greedy, grasping, selfish being that I so often hear I am supposed to be, if my entire household from Nicky to scullery maid are so devoted to me, vie for the honour and privilege of serving me. I often conclude that Nicky is my greatest achievement. To have won the love and devotion of such a woman is more to my credit than all my publications, collections, and even library. *"La gloria di Don Bernardo."* I have loved and have been loved.

August 4th, Vallombrosa

Despite probable lapses so very long ago that I do not recall them, I have rather avoided than tried to insert myself, to frequent societies where I might not be wanted. Yet I recall barbarous rudeness on the part of men—seldom women—with whom accidentally I happened to find myself, and how determined they were to make me feel that I was not one of them, that only as it were an unhappy accident brought us together. Especially so in my earlier years in Italy, polite, over-polite Italy. I recall com-

396

plaining to Placci, who sighed and groaned, and confessed that he then at the height of his society popularity had encountered rudeness, even brutal rudeness, not only from Italians of so-called nobility, but from French as well. To this day I am amazed at the lapses of good taste in manners on the part of people of all nations supposed to be the most highly civilized.

August 8th, Vallombrosa

Harold Nicolson now looks the rubicund, condensed Anglo-Irishman. I am delighted to discover how much he and I agree, about individuals we both have known or known of, about events, e.g. Munich, and about the peacemaking organizations of UNO, etc., so busy bustling and buzzing today. One always retains a shadow of doubt, about one's deepest convictions, about one's most persistent judgments, and is relieved to find another person who independently and with far better advantages by way of contact with people and events comes to the same conclusions. It confirms them and strengthens confidence in one's own mental processes and judgments. One of the most life-enhancing experiences. Harold seems physically and mentally to have nothing in common with wife and son—at least not on the surface.

August 11th, Vallombrosa

No great institution has been so eager for talent from whatever rank as the Church. A swineherd's son (so it was believed at the time) could become Gregory the Great. Yesterday to tea, a young priest, son of a village carpenter from Tosi. He first came here a few years ago, and I recognized at once that he would go far. He already is secretary to the Papal Nuncio, now in Bern, and has been in Belgian Congo. I should not wonder if he ended as Cardinal Secretary of State—at least. Spoke with simplicity and complete objectivity about colleagues at other legations and embassies, and about various missionary groups in Belgian Congo, with particular approval and even admiration of the Swedes. Of various American groups he said that they took things easily, wanting first to live their own lives, and then only as missionaries.

397

Made extraordinary impression of physical health and mental clarity.

August 13th, Vallombrosa

Yesterday a long fit of reminiscing in the ear of John Coolidge, partly in answer to questions. It must have sounded like senile boasting, but I was not aware of exaggerating or leaving things out that could satisfy curiosity. It never occurred to me before as yesterday what a miracle it was for a boy of twenty-two, and who had scarcely ever seen Old Masters, to go to the Louvre and pick out all the pictures of all schools and epochs and at a glance feel that they were the worthwhile ones. They remained so to me, ever since. I rarely had occasion to discard or to add to those then on view. And memory! After a few visits, I could have gone through the galleries, naming each picture and its subject by memory. At the time it did not occur to me that there was anything exceptional in what I felt and retained. Only now do I realize how gifted I was for seeing and feeling. No wonder I was eager to find out why I felt works of art, why they meant so much to me, why I lived them!

August 17th, Vallombrosa

I am unhappy that I no longer can read all the interesting books that appear, nor give time to enjoy the Classics. I still would like to caress all the young women who attract me. I never cared much for food, drink, or tobacco, and now regard nourishment as mere stoking. What I miss more than books and young women is roaming on foot and travel in Antic lands. One has before one, spread out, all the walks, swift mile upon mile, that one so joyously used to take, and now can only be saddened to recall them. I have less longing to revisit great cities, except for their art treasures. My dread of their noise, their bustle, their confusion, my fear of not resisting society enticements, all get the better of any wish to visit them again. The Near East, "landskip with ruins," I still long to see again.

August 20th, Vallombrosa

Hitchcock,* whom I recall as a rather rotund and unattractive young man, appeared yesterday, transformed into a breezy, middle-aged, full- but not loud-voiced, Viking type of American. It is the kind I fall for regardless of attainments and achievements, because I find them life-enhancing.

"Twelve Poems" of Walt Whitman, selected from the first edition of *Leaves of Grass,* and obviously with the purpose of showing one phase. This phase of a frank, joyous sensuality, free from pruriency, from irony, from cynicism not only new in the still so puritanical, so sexually furtive and hypocritical New England of nearly one hundred years ago, but anywhere in the Western world. I never took it in before, how Giorgionesque, almost Titianesque—using my *immer Fachmann* comparisons—Walt was. Never before because I somehow missed those lovely passages in the welter of deliberate ill-bred self-advertisement, the yawping, shoddy rhetoric of so much of Walt's writing. He aged beautifully, as my wife, then a young girl, who saw a good deal of him, assured me, telling me in detail of his way of life.

August 25th, Vallombrosa

Memory, so forgetful of most pleasant, happy, joyful moments, of which as a rule only a vague recollection remains, this same memory is full of grudges. Old age does not dim or obliterate them. On the contrary, the old are full of grudges. Why is this? Perhaps memory like most in us is intended to warn, to provide against, to prevent, to protect. None of this is required for the good, the happy moments. On the contrary. The cry of *Nessun dolor* is wasteful of energy. The grudges, the recollections of evil may have served, and may serve again. Or it, whatever it be, like so much in the animal world, and in man in particular, is the product of an excess of a good thing, a wasteful excess. How I wish I could get rid of grudges, of all offences to my happiness,

* Henry Russell Hitchcock, American, Professor of History of Architecture at Smith College.

399

to my vanity, to my self-esteem, to my self-importance, to my place in society, to my abundant life, in short.

August 27th, Vallombrosa

Finished reading the Old Testament. The "historical books" are fascinating as residues of millennial tradition, but far more for sticking so close to human nature, unadulterated and unembellished. Lovely, an idyll like Ruth. Glowing lyrical elements in Song of Songs. Delicious story of adventures in Tobit. Esther a fascinating narrative spoiled by the ferocious end. In the Psalms an appeal to all hearts. Shrewd reflections in the canonical wisdom books. Very disappointing all the prophets, with of course marvellous moments of ecstasy, or gorgeous evocations. Most of them turn propagandists of Jahve. For them no racial, no national, no tribal distinction counts. Only whether they will go on worshipping Baalim and Ashtoroth, or Jahve. Israel first and then Judah chosen to convert their neighbours. In no other sense a "chosen people." No goyim, no *barbari* in the Old Testament.

August 30th, Vallombrosa

A letter congratulating me on the success I had in life. It hurt me because I now realize how much I could have done and said. A day scarcely passes without my feeling deeply penitential about my life, without my thinking of this and that subject I might have written about, and that would have been really worth while writing about, instead of devoting my best energies to the solution of such absurdly insignificant problems. Almost from infancy I have had a feeling about self, about life, and later on and for the last seventy years about art, which I have not remotely communicated to others, desiring everything from within, from the entelechy of each of us, and all of us combined, and not from conceptual and abstract rules as if revealed from Sinai, or Athens, or Rome.

August 31st, Vallombrosa

Boswell's *Journey in Italy and Corsica*. The ribald young man imagines he is in love with the high-placed lady it is his ambition to have. His desire gets so insistent that he believes he is going mad with being in love—like Majun, of whom of course he never has heard. He is in lust, and has not the faintest idea of what it is to be in love. To be in love is a state of mind which by hidden and devious ways may end physiologically, whereas being in lust is merely physiological. Being in love may lead to a permanent relation, and a happy one. Being in lust more frequently to a revulsion, as of Ammon for Tamar, or sheer satiety, separation, and divorce. The difference should be made clear to the young people who in America are still too puritanical to indulge lust illegally, and rush to marry the object of their lust. Whence the now all but universal divorces!

September 14th, Vallombrosa

To tea yesterday, one of the great ladies, "art lovers," and collectors of an aristocratic New England town. Probably pretty when young. Now bewigged, fluffy, yellowish, an old pussy. Her mind as fluffy as her face. No sign of a mental root anywhere. All superficial, and even trivial, saved (if?) by a certain almost too clinging eagerness to approach what she probably considers the fountainheads of culture. What a contrast to Englishwomen of parallel station. If interested in culture, they have had proper preparation, and are aware of what it is all about. They can hold their own in a discussion. They can ask stimulating questions. Seldom the case with the wealthy American art patroness. She has no preparation, no sense of anterior probability; only what she has been told by dealers and other exploiters of her wealth and situation.

September 25th, Venice

Even now with so much to spoil it, all the way from Maser here an almost uninterrupted "garden city," with fine stately

houses visible behind trees. Civilized and prosperous, as few regions elsewhere. To the very end of the Republic, the Venetian
gentry must have been rich enough to live with distinction, with
comfort even, as well as beauty. They had space and leisure,
and nowadays there is less and less of either. Even well-to-do
people live in relatively cramped apartments, and as for leisure,
it has abandoned our world. One never enjoys feasting one's soul,
with no urge to be "up and doing." If I did not dislike slogans,
mine would be "Space and leisure." In my own case, I am ever
so much more creative when I have both. After enjoying them,
Einfälle come abundantly, and find words easily. So space and
leisure (for me at least) are the antecedent conditions for work,
although not yet work themselves.

September 28th, Venice

Chinese Ballet at the crowded Fenice. Little talk, and that
sounded like any European speech. Music as if plucking on the
wires of a zither; impression as of mewing kittens. But supreme
the training of the body, of which participants had a control utterly beyond anything I ever conceived. Rolling about, leaping,
jumping, in short acrobatics perfect but nothing new. What took
my breath away was to see two scarves waving over the head of
one of the actors, and remaining erect and parallel. But that was
nothing compared to what all the actors did with long, broad
strips of tissue, which they waved about producing intricate inter-
lacings and arabesques and wheel patterns at will. Skill such as
these imply a patient training, a command of muscles, a supple-
ness of action utterly beyond anything attempted in our times,
although probably the late Greek world knew them.

September 30th, Venice

At Giorgione show accosted by an American painter who
wanted the honour of shaking my hand. By a young woman who
wanted my autograph. By a class of young people guided by their
priest, who begged to let me be photographed along with their
group. What satisfaction does all this give people, I wonder? It
is not in my gamut. It never occurred to me to address an author or

artist I was not properly introduced to. Certainly never to ask for an autograph, or to be photoed along with a celebrity. So I am puzzled by the vagaries of human desires. I cannot say that I am displeased to be admired so patently. On the other hand it gives me little or no pleasure, and if insisted upon I get bored. Yet I con papers to see if I am mentioned, and in what connection, although *finding* my name gives me scarcely any pleasure, and *not* finding it as little disappointment. The absurdities of our reactions surpass understanding.

October 4th, Venice

An "eye" that has learned to see needs in Venice no artist, no painter to interpret it. The meanest *calle,* apart from probably having fine façades, in satisfying perspective, offers pictures of loveliest colours, and tone, again and again recalling Vermeer's views of Delft. Fabulous variety of turns, of lanes, of *chemins qui cheminent,* of bridges, sculptured bannisters, bas-reliefs, magnificent capitals, of Byzantine as well as of later work. A perpetual feast for the eye, beggaring any painting. And yet! I look with joy more than wonder at Carpaccio's paintings of the more monumental Venetian buildings. Why? In my case it is not wonder at human skill (with a share in it of self-admiration). Is it possibly the reduction to a scale that makes it more accessible?

October 17th, Venice

The moment one begins to talk about oneself, one is apt to lose the sense of fact, although a feeble mentor remains, and without meaning to lie, one exaggerates one's past prowess in all fields, the part one played in events, and even fabulates about having been present at historic occasions. Taken by the zest of talking to receptive ears, one has no time to choose *le mot juste,* makes a dash at what one means to say, and ends with a series of quasi-musical sequences. On the principle of "What I say three times is true," one may end by believing what one has said, as in the flagrant case of the Prince of Wales, who really believed that he had been at the Battle of Waterloo. A hair divides this kind of talker from a deliberate liar, yet the difference remains,

403

and in judging of a person one should keep it in mind. I for instance never mean to lie, but often hear myself saying things that "ain't quite so."

October 20th, I Tatti

Stoppage of bowels for three days. Known to whole household of ten or more servants. Had been given as information, no order! All in suspense. When toward dinnertime I was deconstipated, I almost could hear hymns of rejoicing. Their conduct as spontaneous and uncommanded as possible. It is as if I Tatti was a Versailles, and I a Louis Quatorze, and the servants my courtiers. Those courtiers probably felt toward their King something that in actual sensation was not so different from what my servants feel about me. Awe toward superiors, whether by birth, wealth, situation, or achievements, hitherto has been instinctive, and is already manifest (to our sense) in higher quadrupeds, in horses, in cattle, in sheep. Nowadays perhaps children either may not inherit, or take by *osmose* from others such feelings, and have no awe, no more than young Siegfried for Wotan.

October 27th, I Tatti

"After eight centuries of bondage, art is free." This proclamation reaches me as coming from the new Director of the Boston Museum of Fine Arts. So all the art of Italy from Cimabue and the Pisanos has been done under restraint. I feel like giving three cheers to the chains, the manacles, the immobilizing stocks that have produced such results. But only the last eight centuries? Has art been less free in the last eight hundred years than in the preceding eight thousand? It has never been free of the effort to represent the world that we perceive with our eyes. Capricious persons may prefer crude, awkward, incompetent attempts at representation to the more successful ones, the more brutal to the more elegant, but hitherto painters and sculptors through the corridors of time have always tried to represent what they thought they saw. Now I would ask what emancipated art with its unchecked freedom means to do better than when under bondage.

404

October 30th, I Tatti

Fräulein Sarre,* handsome, distinguished; last saw her in 1927 in her father's home at Babelsberg near Berlin. Memory served me, and brought back my connections with her parents and with the art world of Berlin. Her father virtually started rational collecting and study of Islamitic art, and made the collection of that art in Berlin. Now for the most part destroyed or dispersed. Only M'shatta survives, although damaged. Turfan murals gone, so are most of the Egyptian collections—in fact much has been destroyed or disappeared. Fräulein Sarre and her mother now live in Switzerland. I asked about her grandfather, Humann,† Romantic archaeologist, *vis-à-vis* of Newton of the British Museum. What a world has disappeared, in its way so admirable as Baltic society down to 1918. If I could see Fräulein Sarre again and again how much *temps retrouvé* I could gather, about the cultural Germany I have always loved.

November 8th, I Tatti

I expect less and less from people. Far from rejoicing in iniquity, I recognize that others have their own pressing needs, their own preoccupations, their own anxieties, and have no leisure to think about me when out of my sight. I ask them, and indeed have never asked more except of a wife, to be playfellows, to be stimulating, to be life-enhancing. So far as I can recall I have never expected friends to be friends in need, and indeed the friend I have had the greater part of my life burst out once with the ejaculation, *"Est-ce que vous n'avez jamais du chagrin, vous?"* Perhaps that accounts for the legend of my having lived always above the clouds, serene and calm. Far from it. Only I never communicated to others, least of all to strangers, the storms that raged within me, and burst out (if ever) only with the women I loved, and from whom I expected a full return.

* Marie Luise Sarre, daughter of Adolf Sarre (1865–1945), outstanding connoisseur and collector of Islamic art, creator and for many years Curator of Islamic Section in Kaiser Friedrich Museum, Berlin.
† Karl Humann (1839–96), German, Professor of Classical Archaeology.

November 11th, I Tatti

Difficulty in hearing continues and increases. Most talkers are too loud and their voices have overtones that confuse one. The voices I hear best are low and clear ones. These *en tête-à-tête* I hear perfectly, unless confused by the booming or humming or ringing of other talkers in my hearing. I learn to smile and nod approval, to shake my head as if hearing. I suit my responses to the faces and not to the words of the people who talk to me. One may well ask why I go on seeing people, and the only answer I can offer is that like all higher animals I prefer the presence of my kind to solitude and silence. Then occasionally, despite drawbacks, I am stimulated to talk, and I enjoy it when I say things worth saying that I had never, or seldom, put into words before. Luckily, that happens often enough to encourage me to go on seeing people.

November 15th, I Tatti

The King of Sweden, now my guest, arouses my utmost envy. Not because he is a king on a throne, nor that he has all the advantages of his position—they would not repay me for all that an actual king has to perform nowadays, and that I could not put up with for a week. I envy him for boyishly enjoying as a "lark" everything he has to do, all the inspections, all the receptions, all the speechifying, all the listening, all the deciding, all the careful consideration, and all the ceremonial of a king on a throne. And he enjoys digging at fresh excavations, and is indefatigable at sight-seeing, and discussing works of art unsignalled, and thinking the better of them for that reason. Then there is nothing he has to do he does not enjoy, even entertaining at huge banquets. What can life offer more than that? All is pleasure, and never a chore!

November 16th, I Tatti

Catalogue of Toulouse-Lautrec exhibition at Philadelphia, contributed for greatest part by private owners in U.S.A. What do those publicly respectable *grands bourgeois* have to do with this art? Surely not the purely pictorial qualities, which despite repugnance of subject matter appeal to me. What can the subjects of Lautrec pictures give these American over-rich, over-comfortable, over-fed, over-dressed individuals? This world of disillusioned, embittered, cynical, vulgar, or Satanically elegant males, and aggressively shameless, vicious women—all rejoicing in iniquity. Do the owners of these paintings ever look at them to ask what they mean? Perhaps it is enough satisfaction that they could afford to buy them, and to be on a level with others, a trifle their social superiors, who bought them first. Something of that kind may be all they get from owning them.

November 20th, I Tatti

For the first time reread Henry Adams' letters to me. They all are ejaculations about a world where there is nothing left to attract one, about his own imbecility, and the imbecility of all in power. I suspect he enjoyed writing in this vein, and addressed his outpourings to me because I was an outsider who therefore would not be offended by what he said about insiders, like Theodore Roosevelt and Cabot Lodge for instance. That he never took me for an insider of his own set would result in his "mistering" me to the very end of his correspondence. He never addresses me as "dear Berenson," and of course not as "B.B." Yet he seemed to enjoy writing to me, as well as talking to me. I do not recall being more than a listener, one perhaps who could ask stimulating questions.

November 23rd, I Tatti

Owing to Nicky's momentary disability [a broken ankle], the house suddenly is like a reel of thread when the reel is taken away, and the thread lies limp, a tangled skein. One realizes how everything, positively everything, depends on her. Had two couples to luncheon. Could not distinguish which woman was wife to what husband, and placed them side by side instead of apart. Everything at a standstill or confused. No wonder my fear of fears is always what would become of me and I Tatti while I occupy it if Nicky left me. How much of love is in that fear? Much, yet nothing compared to the gratitude, the devotion, the mysteri-

407

ous and even mystic glow of tender, caressing, all-loving feeling toward her that possesses the whole of me, outweighing all the love I feel for all other women and men.

November 26th, I Tatti

Photos of a farm on the Merrimack at West Newbury, Massachusetts. I spent July 4th, 1880, there, sitting in water up to my neck for coolness' sake, and reading *Werther* in a Reclam edition. I recall spending Christmas holidays there, and tramping in and out of Newbury forest, on muddy, slushy roads, returning in the dark. Used to have long talks with farmers, who all turned shoemakers in winter, and gave rise to the shoe industry of Haverhill and that region. Used to have wrangles with one who had read Voltaire. *A propos* of something in politics I recall his words— so fatal in international affairs: "Till the overt act is done, no action can be taken." One youth, tramping from Newburyport to Portland, met a chum going the other way and asked where he was going. "I am going on a spree, and the Lord only knows how I dread it." That is the spirit in which most descendants of Puritans even now go on sprees.

November 27th, I Tatti

Calamandrei,* just returned from China, where his Communist son has an important post as Communist. All perfect, at least as perfect as nature (including human nature) will allow. Perfect administration. No violence. Government of law and order, government by persuasion and appeal to reason. Everybody contented. No beggars! No prostitutes! Shanghai a severely puritanical community. Yes, he went there expecting all that, and saw what he expected, like my Anglo-Saxon and French friends who came here when Fascism was still young and fresh, and they could not and would not believe that there was anything amiss in Mussolini's Italy. A French skit appeared in which are described the adventures of a French bourgeois and his daughter

---

* Piero Calamandrei (1889–1956), Florentine jurist, writer, and anti-Fascist politician. Founder of review *Il Ponte* and Rector of the University of Florence after World War II.

who come to Italy. She is raped, abused, he jailed, and yet delighted because all incident to a rule of law and order. Assuming much of what Calamandrei did see was there, surely it is a solution of great tension, an heroic effort (if you like) based on enthusiasm that cannot last long, and soon enough will return to the normalcy of the eternal Chinese. Returning to a non-Communist regime, returning to Hong Kong, he felt let down. Of course he no longer felt sustained by the tension prevailing in Communist China.

The previous evening Harold Acton * gave an account of his Chinese friends executed by the present regime, of mass murder, of misdeeds of every kind. Let us admit he was prejudiced against, as Calamandrei for. But the photos of trials, with bourgeois kneeling abjectly before people's courts, the treatment of American soldiers, the treatment of missionaries, the "brainwashing," surely cannot be American newspaper inventions!

How difficult to see what goes against our concepts, against what we have made up our minds about. Even when a glimmer of fact does reach us, we quickly forget it, and go on talking according to our preconceptions. These we accept because they chime with our prejudices, and accept them joyfully as feeding our concepts and justifying them.

November 30th, I Tatti

Bildung—when did the craving, the universal passion for it take such an absorbing hold on the Germans? I cannot recall that it triumphed before the earlier years of the nineteenth century. It occurs to me to wonder whether to a certain extent it was not due to the influence of Jews, who then were beginning to be, as converts of course, prominent in the higher public services, and as thinkers, scholars, and writers. I recall from my childhood with what respect learning was held in the ghetto, how the well-to-do would aspire to husbands for their daughters rather among the young Talmudists than among the successful young businessmen.

* Harold Acton, English poet, historian, and essayist; from 1932 to 1939 Professor of English at the University of Peking; owner of monumental villa in Florence. After his return from Peking one of the intimates of the Tatti circle.

Independently I found the same cult of learning, of the intellectual life, in New England and its Diaspora. I remember that as late as 1903 I used to try to convince Americans that it took as much brains to be a great businessman as to be a great scholar.

December 3rd, I Tatti

Have I got to the Age of Boasting? Certainly I have no desire to boast. If people draw me out, or if the occasion offers, I do talk of this or that, and no doubt involuntarily embellish, carried away by the zest of talking. (My tongue often utters what I had no intention of saying.) On the other hand what I recount, and never thought of as exceptional, may sound boastful today. After all, few are well on in their ninety-first year, and keep even a parcel of their wits. It might be said as well that my being what I am now is a *boast*. As a matter of fact, I am in my *fort intérieur* far from satisfied with myself, and far from wanting to make an impression of being other than I am. I have taken life as a matter of course, with nothing unusual about it.

December 4th, I Tatti

There are women of all ages, from fifteen to seventy, whom almost at sight I could take to my bosom and embrace, while others, beautiful and with every social quality, leave me full of admiration and affection, but whom even in bed I would not want to possess. Why, where, lies the solution of the problem? It is purely physical, I believe. Something so far from spiritual or even psychological, that it may not be even physiological but merely chemical—like the attraction between certain gases. Akin to life-enhancement, but more definite, more urgent. And life-enhancement, a phrase I make so much use of, what is it, how explain it? Is that too only physiological? No, certainly not, for an element of value intervenes that lacks entirely in the sexual relations. In women particularly, I suspect when a male attracts them there is nothing that can stand in the way of their yielding to him. If the coast is clear, no moral or aesthetic considerations count.

I enjoy more than ever my noonday walks, no matter what

410

the weather, unless it pours. Yesterday as I drove up the hills, I was delighted with the honey-yellow foliage that dominated the landscape. The sky mother-of-pearl, in horizontal layers of clouds, the light without sheen or sparkle, restful, calming. I enjoyed my legs, crunching the pebbles under my feet—the way I used to enjoy crunching a crust of bread when I had teeth. If only that half hour could have been lengthened, extended with its pleasure in mere living, to the rest of the day, the day now so shortened for me, when I am fully alive and not (as is the case) half asleep most of the twenty-four hours. The out-of-doors, particularly a thousand or more feet above I Tatti, on foot, still makes me feel young again, forgetting the aches, pains, nerves, coughing, sneezing, wheezing, due to the burthen of my ninety years. *"Je suis bien fatigué."* Not what I do now, but life, living, has used me up.

December 6th, I Tatti

If I see people again after no more than six months, no matter what their age, I perceive a definite change, maturer, riper, older, thinner, fatter, and in the more aged, elements of swift decline toward senility. I used not to perceive this. Am I more observant now, or am I awake to others' changes because I perceive them so much in myself? Be it as it may, people more than ever before seem to me now like the flowers of the field or the leafage of the trees, from bursting from the bud, to the parched and yellow state before they drop to the ground. Distressing to see the sudden and precipitous decline from vigorous middle age to senility with all its deformations of features, and shape, and bulk. Also from the freshness and charm of youth to full womanhood, and in Anglo-Saxons to full manhood. "All flow away, nothing stands still." Again I ask, why do I feel it so much now?

December 8th, I Tatti

Never motor to Florence without anticipation of possible accidents, and yesterday on top of it the fear I might collapse of heart failure and die in the dentist's chair—anticipation rather than real fear, for I scarcely can be said to fear dying. Accompanied

411

by my adoring valet-maid, aged sixty-four, and family doctor, she washing me all the time with *eau de Cologne,* and he holding my pulse. Dentist, whom I have had for some thirty or more years, frightened and nervous, sticks needle into my gums and then begins to pull out wisdom tooth. Comes out in bits, and he goes on crushing away till he reaches the jawbone. I stood it well, and he kissed me for being so *bravo.* Did he expect me to scream with pain? Curious, Italians do not seem disciplined to pain, yet their surgeons do not seem to bother about alleviating it. Got out of dentist chair, and down to the car, and home, where I remained by myself reading until dinnertime. Dined as usual with Percy Lubbock, Anna Maria Cicogna, and Willy Mostyn-Owen * as my guests.

December 11th, I Tatti

S. S. loves me dearly, but betrays me because she has no idea of what I am and what I want to be. She extorted from me a consent to write a "profile" of me. It has now become a life which she proclaims as "official," and done with my "collaboration." My collaboration consists of telling her "not to," or in never mentioning the matter. Has been here just now a whole week, and every morning we walked without referring to the "life." Instead of writing of my growth and achievement as a work of art, she wants to compose an encyclopaedia about my career. It will be statistical, "factual," irrelevant, anecdotical, always ignoring the man within, his real friends who helped to make him, his reading, his loves, his hates—in short, all that as I look back on my life, I realize counted. I wish I could stop her. To teach her is impossible.

December 12th, I Tatti

Helen Huntington, wife of her cousin Archer, divorced him to his great grief, but got from him an income of fifty thousand dollars in gold for life. She was a *femme inassouvie,* and eager for

* William Mostyn-Owen, young English art student who worked at I Tatti from 1954 to 1958 as B.B.'s assistant in preparing the new edition of the *Venetian Painters of the Renaissance.*

fame as a novelist and as woman of high society. Cold as a fish. Took [Granville] Barker when she married him off the stage, and tried to establish him as a country gentleman in England. Did not work, and moved over to Place des Etats-Unis, Paris. I knew her as Archer's wife, and as I was with one toe in Parisian society, she invited me repeatedly to meals attended by French generals, second-class society people, and a very few Anglo-Saxons. Again and again I saw them privately. On me Barker made the impression of a gifted but weak creature who had never grown up, and was afraid of the future. He died before Helen, and she went out of her mind soon after, and died.

December 15th, I Tatti

Complaining is aimless, but groaning is almost unavoidable and brings relief. Croce used to say *chi non si sfoga muore*. Nothing can stop the rush toward totalitarianism, whether of the state, or of the Managers. Nothing can stop total mechanization. Nothing can stop the disappearance of the artisan. When he has disappeared, there will be no more joy in work, and everybody will be looking for pleasure elsewhere. A world already all but here. Survivors like myself are tolerated because we are few and impotent, or even gaped at as fossils from a past epoch. Why should I mind? Why groan? I shall not be here to suffer from it! With Mark Twain I ask, "Why bother about the Future? Has the Future ever bothered about us?" The very young will always accept the *bouillon* in which they spawned, and intensive propaganda will condition them to their present. So they won't be unhappy, and long for my Past.

December 17th, I Tatti

Except for "acts of God" (as English law calls accidents), my instinct is to regard everything that happens to me as coming from myself—my *physique*, my temperament, my impulsiveness, my lack of judgment, the facility with which I yield to an urge to be agreeable to people, and to pass the moment I am with them pleasantly, and of course the facility with which I yield to women. Except in a rage, I seldom accuse others of anything worse than

413

acting according to their nature and their interests. Knowing what I am, I no longer expect others to be so different (not at least on a lower line) from myself, and I expect so little that I seldom am deeply hurt when I fail to get it. Of course this is Fatalism, but Fatalism too is not perfect, and there are chinks and leaks, and faint possibilities of freedom to change and improve. But we do not live to prove or disprove the problem of Necessity and Freedom. We live as under given circumstances we must.

December 19th, I Tatti

Since many years I have speculated on how long Christianity would last, and with it Antiquity. At the same time I realized that we still were living in what in the future world will count as the Antique world. I never expected the change to happen so precipitously as it is happening now. Some people take it as final. I do not. For one thing, Catholicism seems more powerful than for two centuries or more, and as long as that prevails, it cannot abandon close connection with its Judeo-Greco-Roman past. For another, Antiquity still has a strong hold on an *élite,* numerous and strong enough to carry the torch till more and more are relit. I always felt that Nazi hatred of the Jew was really hatred of Christianity, Christianity that had to some extent succeeded in Romanizing and humanizing, and therefore (according to the Nazi doctrine) emasculating the primitive Teuton. I believe that despite the present tyranny of the mechanistic view of things we shall continue representing Antiquity for yet a while.

December 25th, I Tatti

Yesterday soon after five I felt a call of nature and went to satisfy it. I then lay down on my study couch, to rest, but got more and more uncomfortable, and could not join guests for tea. Toward 6:30 I thought I'd better go to bed. Then toward midnight I heard the Christmas bells, but they did not cheer me— I began retching, vomiting, belching, that lasted till five or six the following morning. It was painful, felt as if I was hurling out all my insides. Would come every few minutes in wrenching spasms. After a couple of hours I felt as if I was completely emptied of whatever it was. Yet soon it began again and worse than before, and worse and worse. No touch of fever, and mind unaffected, lucid. Nicky and Emma Melani and Emma Falciani with me all night long, doing their best to comfort and ease, kept smiling. Their smiles did not take me in, for they somehow seemed rouged on their faces rather than real. Capecchi had less control of his face, and I caught him giving a desperate look at the others. I laughed out loud and said, "Why do you try to hide from me that you despair of keeping me alive? If you think I am dying, tell me so, for I have various matters to attend to before I die." In chorus he and the others swore that nothing of the kind was in their faces, that I surely would never, and so on and so on. Several hours later Nicky confirmed that Capecchi did give me up, and asked what arrangements she had made for administering me the last sacraments. The thought, the very expectation of immediate death, perhaps because I did not believe it, did not frighten me in the least. I was absorbed in the faces in the room, and the expressions flitting under and over them. The deepest of that night, and the early part of Christmas Day, surpassed my suffering.

December 30th, I Tatti

Christmas morning, although I obviously was better, Capecchi still over-alarmed called on the greatest medical authority of Florence to help him out. This authority, Lunedei, who obviously had been told he might be seeing a dying man, looked, examined, and pronounced that *it* was not the end, but only an "episode." To the others he said he had never seen such an old man with such a "golden heart," and such freedom from arteriosclerosis, arteries so elastic. By Christmas afternoon I was sufficiently out of pain to allow my guests to come in for a minute each. Both Kiki and Virginia could not have been more consciously loving and tender. But the prize goes to Nicky, who never left me all night of Christmas Eve, and to Emma Melani. To encounter such love, such devotion, such self-sacrifice, is an experience worth paying for with all I have been through during this crisis.

Up and down, but on the whole more up, I am gaining strength, and returning to "normalcy," on a lower level of utility

415

I fear. The dysentery at the end of the German occupation aged me by years, and my fall over a year ago by even more years. But for these two disasters I now might still be feeling seventy and not ninety. I fear I now shall feel near a hundred. Write no letters, three short notes in all. Read weeklies and dailies only. Nicky out loud Dawson's extracts from thirteenth- and fourteenth-century friars, on mission to Tartar Khans, and accounts of their rule—such a prophecy of Soviet imperialism!

Shall I be better for my sickness, as well as of my sickness?

The whole drama (as distinct from less and less distressing aftermath) took place in less than twelve hours. At the time I felt as if years were passing, and slowly. I could not have believed in the subjectivity of my feeling. On the contrary, I *knew* it was real DURATION. Only after days have I recovered a normal conviction that it lasted a mere twelve hours at most.

Knowing (if not believing) that probably I was dying, strange I took no interest whatever in death as death, as presumably the end of all things for me. I remained, when not in the throes of belching, a rather amused or touched or loving spectator of the people in the room.

I return to "normalcy" and see before me a basketful of letters and telegrams to attend to, and piles of periodicals, not to speak of books. Books ordered, and books sent by friends, by publishers, by aspiring writers. How to cope with it all, and the "friends" who want to come to see me? Oh, for a lodge in a vast wilderness—not too wild and remote.

December 31st, I Tatti

Serious illnesses are to the individual what wars are to the public. They are as it were landmarks, that cannot be changed or moved, and make real, not merely calendar, dates. Thus the fall I had December 13, 1954, causing an alarming illness, made a division of before and after like the First World War. The all but mortal trouble I went through this Christmas night will count for the rest of my days as the Second World War does to people as a whole.

416

1956

January 1st, I Tatti

The year starts out with a windless morning, a cerulean sky with quiet cloudlets lying peacefully shepherded over the tips of the cypresses, as from my bed in the back of the room I look through the window. The sun has not yet asserted itself, although already risen. I am fairly comfy in my bed, and ready to face yet another year.

January 5th, I Tatti

I wish friendship were not so much a *one-way street*. At my age so very few stimulate or enhance me by their presence, or amuse me in any way, that I do not feel in the least like going toward them, as they seem eager to come to me. No doubt their motives are praiseworthy, though like all human motives very mixed, but their coming makes me long for people I would like to see to satisfy my own whim, my own pleasure. Why do I go on seeing people? At my own table I rarely hear what is being said, and at teatime it is worse. If I get anything at all out of seeing others, it is perhaps a rudimentary return to mere animal gregariousness. I never quite understood why people wanted to frequent me. Or did they? Now it seems as if mere curiosity rather than real interest, let alone affection, moved them, and I fear those who do cling do so out of convenience or habit. How tired I get of seeing them, and yet, would I rather they did not come?

January 7th, I Tatti

Day before yesterday I enjoyed complete relaxation, every bit of me, inside and out, at rest. My mind did not work at all, although I was aware of how happy I was, as perhaps never before in my memory. I was not thinking. I was not questioning. I was not dozing or dreaming. I was enjoying perfect bliss. It was physiological, and perhaps due to a very mild touch of fever. It was existence pure, simple, unalloyed. Did the Fathers who developed the Christian idea of Heaven know like experiences, and erect them into the condition of the Saved? Possibly. To me it was an experience that had nothing mystical about it. I recognized it as entirely physiological. Is it possible that some individuals live long stretches of time in a perfectly balanced, completely relaxed, completely harmonious state? Can it be artificially produced by drugs—like mescaline? No matter what the origin, the convincing actuality of my experience cannot be dimmed by any explanation of how it came about. If it could be reproduced, how eagerly I should want to repeat it.

January 10th, I Tatti

I wish a Dante would arise who would write: how one day I was in a dark, damp, murky wood. Enormous great trees were pushing out smaller, more elegant, less robust ones. The tall ones were topped with crooklike growths, some ending in a mitre, and some others curved like a question mark. I stumbled about, fell and picked myself up, kept looking back, but there was no turning back, and ahead the darkness was frightening. All sorts of things were weighing me down, and scratching my feet. My ears stunned by the sound of the great trees creaking and bursting. Then I got aware that there was a desperate struggle going on for complete occupation between the question-mark and the mitre trees, and at last the mitred ones disappeared, and only the question-mark trees remained. They replaced all other growths, an infinity of question marks, nothing, nothing but question marks—questioning what and questioning whom?

January 25th, I Tatti

Citizenship—what does it mean? Not necessarily "nationality." Are Huxley and Auden less English because, fully formed and with great reputation as English writers, they transferred their residence to U.S.A.? Salvemini taught at Harvard for years and never heard of Hawthorne. Indeed, while in the U.S.A. for many years he never ceased to be absorbed by purely Italian problems. I have been in Italy for sixty years, and am not a bit of an Italian. Why have I not taken Italian citizenship? Because I still identify citizenship with nationality. Let me explain. Nationality means identifying oneself with the entire *past* of a people, its political and social history, its great men in all fields, its myths, and its present position. That did happen to me in the twelve years of my boyhood and youth that I passed in Boston, and I still feel that America is my only country, and Boston my only home. If I have a "spiritual home" it is the literature of the English language. But I could not be a British subject, nor an Italian. Indeed, I do not feel quite easy speaking of myself as belonging to any country, even the U.S.A.

January 27th, I Tatti

One's imagination at times runs away dreaming of a possibility that matter was, or could be, transmuted into pure mind, and that a kind of survival of spirit might be conceivable. All seems absurd and childish, realizing as I do at my age that my mental faculties diminish at least as fast as my physical ones. I can no longer tackle any subject that demands concentration, or even effort. Every day I discover that huge stretches of memory have sunk into oblivion, like icebergs in the warm ocean. I now am capable of forgetting the "just where" of less continuously cited countries, not to speak of towns. I forget most names. As I look at photos my own attributions begin to lack validity, because I forget how I got to make them. My mental horizon more and more restricted, shrunk, closed in. I recall fewer and fewer people among those I have met in recent years. In short, mental collapse seems to go parallel with physiological.

421

January 30th, I Tatti

"Where the soul climbing higher Sees God no nigher." "Beginnings and ends." I am not made to think about them, about how *all* began to be, and how all will end—if it ever will end. I cannot conceive what was before or what will be after, and still less of a before and an after. So I regard metaphysics as metafussics, and with Aristotle identify it with theology. Hence my hostility to Christian theology in general, and to Catholic in particular. It overshadows ritual, the which in all churches has formed in the course of ages the way for the poor human heart to cry its anguish, but also with the second Isaiah the comfort of aspiration. For aspiration is an activity in itself, and by itself a comforter, a Paraclete. Wherefore but for its theology and its institutionalism (of which later) I should be an ardent supporter, or at least approver, of the Roman and Greek Churches. Theology gives the Roman Catholic priesthood a pride, an arrogance, a conviction of being set apart as initiates into mysteries beyond the ken of the laity. It justifies the hierarchy in assuming the right to use the laity (no matter of what class or category) as lost sheep utterly helpless and unable to live or die without the Church, nor of course to get to Heaven. Therefore the Church in the eyes of its hierarchy cannot claim too much power, and behaves too much as an institution. All institutions tend to become corporations, without souls, bureaucratic, with individuals using and abusing and subduing them to the wants and appetites of the individuals composing them. So here I am in deepest sympathy with Catholic ritual, and not adverse to its discipline, but with a distaste for its theology and a dread of it as an institution. Yet I am painfully aware that institutions are as necessary to religion as the body to the spirit. That an institution cannot escape becoming a bureaucracy with all its lust for power, pelf, and ease! So I cannot in conscience rebel violently against it. On the other hand, I cannot adhere to it, and there is in my deepest self a something that prevents me from adhering to any handmade chart of the spiritual universe, and its illustrative texts. Any more than I can wholeheartedly identify myself with a people as distinct from a political, useful entity like a nation. I feel the mystery of exist-

ence, and above all of awareness, every day of my life, and am too
much in awe of it to talk glibly of a God, His intentions, purposes, and preferences.

February 1st, I Tatti

The Mozart celebrations bring me back to my conviction that
genius is an inexplicable sport in the human crop, as perfection
is in pears, other vegetables, and animals. Here he was at twelve,
all there. Not only prodigiously precocious, but with all the newness of his style, his favourite airs, his dramatic sense, his rhythm,
etc. Attempts to explain how it came about are puerile. So with
Shakespeare. It is the incapacity of the mediocre to conceive of
genius that compels them to look for a man who lived a grander,
fuller life than that of the historical Shakespeare—to Bacon, to
Derby, to Marlowe even. In other fields were not Homer and Plato
and before them perhaps the Jewish writers of the Old Testament,
as well as the later Jesus of Nazareth and Paul of Tarsus, equally
sports in the human crop? The explanation we are inclined to look
for in the Infinite may really hide in the infinitely little, and
utterly escape imagination and our capacity for conceiving.
Wherefore I accept genius as a miracle.

February 2nd, I Tatti

With very short intervals, ever since Christmas Eve I have
been living the life of an invalid, preoccupied with bladder and
intestines, doctor once and even twice a day, thermometer to take
temperature every hour or so, high fever at times, potions, pills,
tablets every half hour. All attenuated just now, but already habituated to this kind of artificial life, and less and less disposed to
make an effort to write, to think things out, to plan, to see people,
to dress for dinner, in short to submit to my life-long disciplines.
I fear settling in to this invalid existence, being kept artificially
alive, dozing most of the time, reading nothing requiring concentration, not daring to touch a novel for fear of getting excited,
avoiding friends who want to discuss seriously, and other friends
who do not amuse me, because I no longer am interested in the

423

gossip they bring. Occasionally I enjoy new faces, new voices, although I do not hanker for them.

February 10th, I Tatti

There is danger of my gliding into the blissful state of the senile invalid. I am so comfy and feel so cosy in my bed, and except in moments of misbehaviour on the part of nose and throat, belly and bladder, am contented to doze, to think not at all, to want nothing. Time passes swiftly. The difficult moments as yet are when I feel too energetic to be doing nothing, yet too feeble to want to do anything, even to write short notes. An Italian phrase has haunted me for many years, for fifty years at least. It is *sta aspettando la morte*. That could easily be my lot, if I do not pull myself up (by my bootstraps!) and get to work. I still am eager to get at the photos, to shed ink, but how long will that last, at the pace at which resigned indolence is creeping through me? I have hated the idea of existing as a vegetable, or less, but it now looks as if I could end by not minding it at all.

February 12th, I Tatti

The historical books of the Bible gave me an unquenchable curiosity about human, racial, national origins. All my life I have been reading about these questions, and have lived through various winds of doctrine, and now I feel sceptical about all theories not based on material already historical, as for instance the deciphered "Hittite" inscriptions. If we succeed in deciphering the kind of writing now being accumulated, from Pylos, from Mycenae, from Crete, etc., that will add a considerable page to real history. The Etruscan problem remains as enigmatic as ever. The theory now gaining credence is that the Etruscans were autochthons, relatively little affected by Aryans, but having affinity linguistically with Basque and Georgian. Now I do not know any Georgian, but Basques have nothing somatically in common with the present Tuscans. So I remain on the fence with regard to the origin of Etruscan speech and of the race. Perhaps all these speculations are mere pass-time, idle curiosity, getting us nowhere.

424

February 16th, I Tatti

I have nothing to say that has not been said, and besides few if any want to hear what I could say. So why do I write? Surely it is to exercise function, to be doing something, to kill time, than which nothing is harder to kill. In fact we never succeed in killing it. We try to smother it by overlaying it with any and every kind of activity, and if the activity is a productively satisfactory one, we forget all about time. If our own activities are not satisfactory, and bring us no pleasure, no contentment, time begins to drag, and to run away from it we pant after excitements, one after the other. We never try to make friends with time, to swim in it as in a friendly, sustaining stream, to bask in it. No, we must always be up and doing, no matter what—provided it is something that not only occupies us but wins the applause of others. Thus we are flattered into believing that our mere functioning has a public interest and value.

February 18th, I Tatti

Video meliora proboque, pejora sequor. I see how foolish it is to get indignant and unhappy because my insatiable ego has not got his way, but the same ego makes me miserable, despite my clearsighted vision. Not only do I suffer from offended vanity, conceit, and other types of self-regard, but am made unhappy by the way things have moved away from my world, the now seemingly so idyllic world of my youth. Not only in every phase of art, but in politics. The spectacle makes me suffer acutely, as if a personal injury were being done to me. It is all such an offense to my universe as I will it. So it is not only the physical universe that ignores me, but the human one seems to know me as little. The few who still are aware of my existence shrug their shoulders and sneer.

February 22nd, I Tatti

Washington's Birthday, a school holiday, and I recall as a boy Washington Street in Boston, free from snow but with an icy wind blowing dirt in one's face, and shreds of dirty paper in the

425

air. Yet it spelled the end of winter. So even in windy, icy Boston and its coasts, the taste of snow in the air gave place to something like the odour of violets. It was the taste of spring. And I used to enjoy every spot where spring took over winter, and took pleasure in it, as I much later found so marvellously evoked in one volume of Aksakov's trilogy about the breaking of the ice, and the advance of the spring. Yesterday, walking up and down in the very front of this house, I felt something soft, caressing in the air, and a smell and taste as of a nosegay in my nostrils and on my lips. Owing to the Northern winter we have been suffering, we may here in Italy enjoy although in haste some of the drama of the sudden coming on of spring.

February 25th, I Tatti

Material things apart, the greatest change between now and seventy years ago is in the attitude toward leisure. Now there is no such thing. If you are not materially active, you do not enjoy the delights of ruminating, dreaming, meditating, contemplating, but hasten to be doing something, no matter how useless, how vulgar, how merely gregarious. In my experience you can have ability without leisure, but ability only, and not creativeness. Real ideas come to me while relaxed, and brooding, meditative, passive. Then the unexpected happens. An illumination, a combination of words, a revelation for which I made no conscious preparation. And seventy years ago one had time for everything, for disinterested reading, for equally disinterested discussion, for activities whose only result was to strengthen, refine, and clarify our own selves as works of art, and not as now to be considered only when producing material results.

March 1st, I Tatti

Kenneth Clark writes that the installation for Louvre drawings is now complete, and perfect in arrangement, in accessibility, in service, and in comfort. How different from fifty-five or more years ago when I was working on the Florentine drawings. All drawings were then kept pell-mell with no classification except omnibus ones like Italian, and there was no proper, no comfortable way of seeing them. The room was an attic. I used to climb up to it and then wait in a long narrow corridor, defiled with the stale smoke of the rough guardian, until M. de Chennevières appeared. He was a charming man, and he alone could show the drawings. He kindly gave me appointments but generally was from half to a whole hour late. Full of apologies and courteous to a degree, but scarcely had I warmed up to work when he would get up and say that to his utmost regret he had to catch a train, and had to shut up shop. As a rule I got half an hour on an average of work for an hour of waiting. One time when M. de Ch. had more leisure, it was to receive a "client" who came to ask for his "protection." So I discovered that in France the relation of "client" to "patron" was still going on as in Rome of old.

My experience in Florence was of another sort. No difficulty of access or leisure for work. But the room for study literally was a den, which the director, Signor Ferri, rendered malodorous and foggy with the smoke of his "Toscano." Many of the drawings were framed under glass, and I had to pay him ten gold lire to have them unframed so that I could examine their backs.

March 10th, I Tatti

Happy is the man who finds pleasure and satisfaction in his job, and does not hanker and strive to get a financially and socially and politically more remunerative one, that will procure him neither pleasure nor satisfaction, because not in harmony with his specific exercise of function. Snobbery, ambition, dissatisfaction, frustration are the state of mind in any condition of life of those who do not find and exploit their capacities but work desperately to get occupations and situations for which they are not suited. They may even attain all material reward and appreciated positions, but internally the sense of failure haunts them incessantly. So the religions that advised contentment with the lot to which the Lord had called them were right, no matter how archaic their phraseology. Few obey them now, and few are happy within, no matter how showy without.

427

March 18th, I Tatti

I do not recall being taught manners, politeness, regard for others, to try to please, to avoid fruitless discussion. Either they came "naturally" to me, or I picked them up mimetically. As I picked up languages. I have never set out deliberately to learn a language, except of course the dead ones. I picked them up by ear, never learning their grammar and orthography. Wherefore I cannot write Italian or German, and even French, although there I feel more competent. (An odd break happened about thirty: I suddenly stopped being able to pick up a language, or learn to read it.) Not only speech, but I seem to have been picking up all my life and almost unconsciously one series after another of interests, pursuing them zestfully as long as they fed my curiosity. *Beatus qui potuit rerum cognoscere causas.* Now I realize there is no such knowledge.

March 19th, I Tatti

History, based surely on documents, led a recent English writer on the Dreyfus affair to conclude there was no anti-Semitism behind it, and that the army (but for Esterhazy and Henry) were Christian gentlemen who did their best. Now I lived through the *affaire,* and was in Paris off and on through most of it. Anti-Semitism was rampant. Paris was reeking and drenched and soaked with it, and most Academicians and other writers were anti. Only a handful (a full one) of thinkers and writers were for him [Dreyfus]. High society rabidly anti-Jewish. Never have I encountered such expressions of hatred, of loathing, as I used to hear against Jews from the mouths of Parisians. They went so far as to say cynically it did not matter whether Dreyfus was or was not guilty, but the army must be established as incapable of error and of course of malice. It was a horrible outburst of anti-Semitism, which Hilaire Belloc brought over to England. There he had little following, but—did not shock people.

428

March 28th, I Tatti ✓

Igor Markevich * went once in midwinter to Warsaw. He called early on a friend still in bed. This person got up, went to the tap, filled his mouth with water, warmed it thus, and then washed his face with it. That is the way popular writers and lecturers on art and literature and cultural subjects work. They read up a subject, generally one entirely new to them, and pour out what they have learned into a book. Of course that too requires a gift of the pen, and a certain degree of momentary feeling for the subject. Oddly enough, the English-speaking world takes wildly to this sort of writing. Possibly because they do not enjoy looking for looking's sake, and prefer reading to seeing, and smelling, and tasting with their own organs, and prefer the words of rhetoricians who spit out what they have just warmed up in their mouths, like the Pole at Warsaw.

April 5th, I Tatti

To tea yesterday, a Harvard man of the class of '88. Beautifully groomed, deaf, accompanied by a son of twenty-four, who told me he had a still younger brother, although father now was eighty-nine. Did most of the talking. Harvard, his own ancestors, Boston and New York, his career, his connections, his clubs, his associates—seldom met a person at once so old, so contented with his past as well as his present. Still fishes, still travels, his first visit to Italy, enjoys every moment. Cheering to see and hear somebody so aged, and yet so *content de lui-même.* I doubt whether one still would find his like in the Europe of today, where the utmost one would get from the old would be Christian or Stoic resignation. The situation of the hereditary well-to-do in the U.S.A. has not yet been so disturbed or even destroyed as in Europe, where even the super-rich are ill at ease, and inclined to extravagance, just because they no longer believe in their stability, and therefore "eat and drink, for tomorrow we die."

* Russian-born composer and conductor; B.B.'s guest at the Villino, 1941–45.

429

April 9th, I Tatti

People with no eyes in their heads, incapable of looking at a visual work of art till they are possessed by its specific, intimate, uncommunicating quality, if at the same time "philosophers" and "thinkers" will map out the realm of art in a rational universe, as Santayana did so admirably and B. Croce so (to me) incomprehensibly, but have no potency to enjoy it or even feel it. I cannot help believing there is a kinship between their attitude toward art, and the excited interest in sex of the starved lovers, who will read and even write pornographic books to assuage their burning impotence. Theologians as well. I can recall telling Frank Costelloe sixty years ago that they reminded me of the sexually impotent, because for the most part incapable of genuine, spontaneous, mystical *élan*. I have tried at various periods of my life to read "aesthetics." Interesting as they may be, I never discovered in the best of them, Hegel for example, anything to help one appreciate a specific work of art.

April 15th, I Tatti

Vocabulary constantly diminishing. I never had one adequate to my purpose, and it has been a handicap preventing me from giving even a small part of what I might have achieved as a writer. Names of birds and flowers (for instance) I could not retain, nor even of trees. So I could not be the verbal landscapist that my feeling for "nature" could have made me. It is much worse now that verbal memory of every kind has abandoned me—or (at least) is unwilling to obey me. Less and less can I find words for feelings and thoughts that arise in me, for observations I still can make. For my power of enjoying and suffering from things visible has increased and refined, so that my heart leaps up at the sight of flowers on the table, or those I see in the fields, and still more looking to the horizon, and its line of demarcation, and all I can see between it and my own eyes. If only I could convey it to others! Baffled, a feeling of impotence invades and possesses me.

April 16th, I Tatti

So many American young and youngish women make an impression of integral innocence, as if no longer animals with needs, wants, appetites, and passions. They look as if no material feeling could prevail, no unseemly, no evil thought approach them. No other females are like that, not even Englishwomen, not quite. Oddly enough, the nearest to Americans I have found is among Italian high middle class, not anywhere in the world of fashion. A Greek young woman might have conveyed the same sense of innocence, the young wife for instance in Xenophon's *Oeconomicus*, and no doubt youthful Roman ladies as well. It is not a look void of experience only, but as of a veil of gentle goodness over the features and face. In that phase they have a beauty of works of art, as have little children when happy. After thirty all of us, male and female, have to work hard to retain or acquire qualities as works of art.

April 18th, I Tatti

If parallel lives were still being written, it would be worth while to write about Isaiah Berlin and myself. We come from the same kind of ghetto, came under similar Anglo-Saxon conditioning, and have both been readers, writers, thinkers. Yet the differences are striking. He in moments of crisis like the last war played a very considerable part, while I played none in the First World War, when of an age to have done so. He lectures on philosophy not only at Oxford but at Harvard and Chicago. He is Fellow of All Souls, and I have never belonged anywhere. He is idolized in official society, and I have no place in it. Whence the difference? Temperament, endowment, happier and better endowed than I, better technical preparation, less censorious—more genial, in short, perhaps also more brilliant, more entertaining, more good-natured, although with no less *malice* in his talk. Why then a Berenson myth, and almost no Berlin one!

April 20th, I Tatti

Cannot get over my surprise that ability can go with so little intellect, such a lack of interest outside the training and conditioning it has received. Perhaps its success depends on its lack of vision, of interest not concerned with its task, of the subservience of all energies to this purpose. *"In der Beschränkung zeigt sich erst der Meister."* It is so effective and in a sense so mechanical. After all it is vision, it is imagination, it is dreams that start not only newness, that enlarge horizons, but stir the embers, feed the flames, and through trial and error end by the inventions that the merely able use and live by. Yet ability alone is rewarded with emoluments, with honour, with fame even—although very temporary. *La gloire* for those who make successful use of what is already there.

April 29th, I Tatti

As I work over the photos of Florentine painting, I feel more and more inclined to disagree with my former attributions and combinations, and to understand objections of adversaries. It occurs to me to question whether that is not due to my loss of visual memory. When I had it, I could distinguish subtil resemblances and differences that escaped others, and now escape me. Shall I now yield to my present condition of what may be sheer senile incompetence or stick to conclusions arrived at when I still had an eye of my own? That is the problem before me, as I work on the Florentine masters, and I do not yet know what course I shall take. Whatever I do, *les chers collègues* will exult and boo. "Why has he disturbed our sleep to go back on all he amazed us with, when it was only to end by agreeing with us?"

May 3rd, I Tatti

How unaware I was till extreme old age of the animal, the female in women I considered of my own world. There were others of course who provided sex relief, but did not count otherwise. The women who did count were in a realm apart, where animality, sex, did not exist. They all were Beatrices, and I a worshipping Dante. Now I scarcely approach a woman of "my world" without feeling the moment she gives her hand how cold or how warm she is. And the majority are women glowingly hot even. Were I still potent, I could bed with many, and think the better of them, and feel affection toward them. Not only with women, in men as well, I am more and more aware of how much we are animals living between eagerness for satisfaction of all kinds, and the constant palpitating fear of deprivation, of damnation and attack. How little reason runs me, I realize more and more as the days pass.

May 7th, I Tatti

Krishnamurti to tea: affable, responsive, conceding all my objections, and indeed our discussion was scarcely controversial. He insisted nevertheless on a Beyond, and that this was a state of immobile, uneventful existence, no thought, no questioning, no—what? He rejected my contention that such a state was something beyond my Western cast of mind. I went as far as to ask him whether he was not after something merely verbal. He denied it firmly, but without heat. I keep wondering whether besides the physical state produced by highfalutin words there is really anything else in believers. During the Dreyfus war, it was fashionable to boast that one had *la foi du bûcheron*. Did they stop to ask the *bûcheron* what he had to say about it, and if he could have found words, would these words not have been their own fulfillment!

May 9th, I Tatti

[Professor Lamanna], Rector of the University [of Florence], on giving me my diploma made a beautiful speech, free from rhetoric and adulation, yet highly appreciative, cordial, almost familiarly affectionate. No pomp, the least ceremony. What a gift Italians—and perhaps most Latins—have for making an occasion seem the perpetual mood of the partakers! You would think they always lived above the clouds, and above the mephitic atmosphere of our workaday life, so much, so nearly all of it, dedicated at everybody else's cost to our own animal interests and

433

cravings. Nothing could have been more gracious, more human, more friendly than the atmosphere we all seemed to breathe. It even seemed to include my arch-adversary, [Roberto] Longhi. He by the way composed the lapidary "motivation" for the honorary degree, and I thought it perfect. I dreaded the ceremony, but it turned out not only tolerable, but delightful, and something to recall with pleasure. It does not change my feeling of failure, of inadequacy, of incompetence.

May 14th, I Tatti

The hard frosts and harsh winds have killed many olives, damaged nearly all other fruit trees and the wisteria, killed the plumbago and other plants. No growing thing out of doors but has suffered, with one exception, the tulips. I cannot recall such a display as now. Colour from almost black purple to rose, through every shade of grape-purple, burnished copper, straw-colour, ivory, to pure yellow, and yellow as free from blue, and green, and too much red, as scarlet among other reds. Not the colour only of the flowers, but the movement of the drooping leaves, and their exquisite drawing. I confess that no painting has given me such joy, not even Chinese, or Quattrocento great masters of the North or South. At the table I scarcely could eat or converse for absorption in the flowers decorating it. If only I had the verbal skill to communicate to others what I see and feel!

May 16th, I Tatti

"The Ring" is being given here. How I enjoyed it, how it thrilled me with its tragic sense of the numenal based on the sacredness (in the Roman sense) of money. Gold to barbarians was divine and hoarded, to be approached with awe, as a potentiality of incalculable and unforeseeable and mysterious potency. Money still is, after food and sex, the one thing that possesses and haunts people. I doubt whether I know anybody, no matter how near and dear, how respectable, who can be trusted to be perfectly fair where there is a question of money. In Latin lands the money code is easier than in English-speaking countries, because money is still a hoard to be seized. In England the private attitude

434

toward money is fair but business is as predatory as suitable. I have been amazed to see English gentlemen in private relations change to their very looks and gestures the moment anything became a matter of business.

May 18th, I Tatti

Took Mary McCarthy to Gricigliano, back by the Sieci and along the Arno. Tuscany at its most enchanting moment, a wonder and a joy for my eye. But Mary scarcely opened her eyes to all this beauty. Yet she will write about it, and be evocative and give readers the longing to come and experience for themselves, as I never, never could. Such is the power of a gift for words, and the technique for using them. The accomplished writer need not feel, nor muse, nor think as much as I do, but he will make his readers do so, as I cannot. I am led to wonder whether successful writing and feeling and dreaming and thinking ever go together. Paradoxical as it may sound, I tend to believe that the great writer may be only a *"tuba mirum spargens sonum."*

May 26th, I Tatti

The super-rich Americans when not engaged in oil, politics, and directing foreign policy, enjoy a life ready-made for them by interior decorators. These have to be elegant, smart, entertaining, and efficient. They must amuse their wives—temporary concubines—take them shopping for rare bits of "Louis-Louis" at fabulous prices, and to the passing "art shows." Their paradise is a period piece of the eighteenth-century French, where every object is supposed to have been used by historical personages of the French court. As if French people of the Versailles period were always living as the super-wealthy Americans in their leisure are decorated by their interior decorators to live. These interior decorators take the place of the elegant worldly *abbés* of the eighteenth century, only much more *contre remboursement,* counting not only on being dined and wined, but on access to the wives, and percentages from dealers.

435

May 28th, I Tatti

[Harry] Truman and his wife lunched yesterday. Came at one and stayed till three. Both as natural, as unspoiled by high office as if he had got no further than alderman of Independence, Missouri. In my long life I have never met an individual with whom I so instantly felt at home. He talked as if he had always known me, openly, easily, with no reserve (so far as I could judge). Ready to touch on any subject, no matter how personal. I always felt what a solid and sensible basis there is in the British stock of the U.S.A. if it can produce a man like Truman. Now I feel more assured about America than in a long time. If the Truman miracle can still occur, we need not fear even the McCarthys. Truman captivated even Willy Mostyn-Owen, aged twenty-seven, ultra-critical, and like all Englishmen of today hard of hearing anything good about Americans, and disposed to be condescending to them—at best.

May 30th, I Tatti

History as she is writ. There lived in Paris a handsome (not dashing) middle-aged New England woman, dazzling white hair. Fascinating apartment on *quai* in Paris and romantic château on Riviera. Highly respected heiress of rich relations. Died and given solemn and expensive funeral at Notre Dame. The facts as I could not help knowing them were, she was kept by a very wealthy countryman, who had gathered and delighted in showing one of the most compendious pornos in existence. Also she was in the pay of Duveen and perhaps of other dealers. She asked a former mistress of D'Annunzio to procure her a night with that hero of the alcove. He asked in turn whether she was white-haired everywhere. It is my luck to have information about respectable people, that no proper person ought to be asked to know.

June 3rd, I Tatti

Learned Hand voted for Eisenhower and will vote for him again. His reason is that the centrifugal tendencies in the U.S.A.

are a menace, and that we need a man everybody loves to bring us together again. Hand is far from being a soldier-lover or militarist, yet he instinctively turns to the "Happy Warrior" to save the country. So even he, a great jurist, a passionate humanist, recourses to the Brass Hat when the country is in danger. What this goes to prove is that even for such a man, military values after food and sex are the basic values. And for the rest of us? The state is so indebted to them that it knows no better means of celebrating an occasion than a military parade. The overwhelming majority of us love military uniforms when we wear them. Uniforms, parades, brass bands, drums and fifes, exalt wars, and we greatly enjoy them. Yet pacifists and ideologers will go on believing and preaching that wars must stop. Will they? I doubt it.

June 7th, I Tatti

Experts in the history and criticism of visual art discover in my library publications they have not been able to find in the great libraries of Europe, not even in the British Museum. They seldom talk of an article, let alone a book, which does not find room on my shelves. These experts raise the satisfaction I feel in my library. Its gathering has been done item by item, and until months ago none entered that I not only ordered unaided, but perused, and to a considerable extent read. No longer. I lack the time and the strength, but I still order them unaided, and I give a good look at everything as it arrives. It is the only achievement of my career that gives me complete satisfaction. All that I have published means little, almost nothing to me, and I know is either destined to be *überholt* or go under with my name when this name no longer is more than a label. But the library has a chance of giving opportunities, pleasure, even happiness for generations to come.

June 9th, I Tatti

Yesterday, a pleasant Canadian who teaches art history in Singapore! While driving a camion [as a soldier] in West China, he encountered and married a Chinese girl. She came with him, the first Chinese female I ever conversed with. Took a second to

437

get over instinctive repugnance to all types not Nordic European, and especially not "Indo-European." Then I began to see what a fine forehead, what intelligent eyes, and what exquisite hands she had. Nicky reported that this young woman read at sight the inscription on my sixth-century Buddhist Chinese altar. Talking with her, I was enchanted by the quickness of her "take-up" and readiness of her answer. Quickly I forgot her race and nationality, and talked with her as for instance I used to with the Serristori. I could have urged her to *"verweile doch, du bist so" intelligent,* and I was sorry to lose her after so brief but so penetrating an encounter. She spoke excellent English, with almost no Chinese impediments.

June 20th, I Tatti

I do not remember which of the Old Testament prophets foretells that the palaces of Babylon and Nineveh will be the dwellings of hyenas. Yesterday we went to a villa that once had been decorated by Castagno. Hyenas do not dwell there, but humble families, unaware to what their demands on life have reduced these noble spaces illuminated by the frescoes of a great artist. So the world over. *Mors mia, vita tua,* as John said to Jesus. "Life" is indifferent when not hostile to what does not suit it at the moment. Besides, the beauty of artifacts has no meaning for all but a few. For which reason they hitherto have not stood in the way of the day's convenience. And even today, a given portable work of art may be saved, but not buildings that no longer answer the demands of comfort seekers and speculators. Before very long cities like Florence either will be completely sidetracked or entirely lose character.

June 26th, I Tatti

My ninety-first birthday. It has been a year scarcely worth living. So much alarming illness, such depression, so many aches, pains, and nauseas. Worst of all, fatigue. Yet moments of satisfaction walking, if only for half an hour, working, if only for three quarters of an hour, stimulating conversation. I enjoy drawing people out, listening to good talk, as well as talking myself. Above

438

all the surprise of hearing myself say things deeper and wittier than I expect of myself. I sleep heavily, and wake more tired than when I went to bed. All day long, when alone, I easily fall into a doze, not a refreshing one. I have given up speculating about the coming year. I am not eager but ready to defunct. Only Nicky makes me feel I must live on—and for her. How I hate to leave her!

June 30th, I Tatti

Somerset Maugham to lunch. Lined, wrinkled face, senile mouth, kindly expression (or is it of mere resignation?). Stammered. Utterly unaffected, and no trace of playing up to his reputation. Simplicity itself. Talked of writers, of novelists. Said he had had enough of fornication in the writing of today. Never read a word of Mary McCarthy. In general did not seem *au courant* with up-to-date novelists. Never liked Faulkner. American novelists lack substance. Writes about painters, e.g., Zurbarán, but displayed yesterday a fantastic absence of feeling for visual art. In so far as he praised anything here, it was the poorest stopgap paintings. In that respect his inseparable young secretary had better taste and more genuine interest. All in all, Somerset Maugham is an agreeable talker.

July 3rd, I Tatti

I suggested that what makes great fiction is the creation of character, of figures so separate from their context that one does not think of their coming out of a book, and indeed the majority who speak of them do not even suspect their origin, any more than that of most terms we use. To which Somerset Maugham objected that it would be difficult to find even twenty such creations in the whole of European literature. I should begin with David—surely a completer, more varied, less faked-up presentation scarcely exists. And are not Saul and Samuel characters? True, they are done with few touches. Does it require elaboration and length to evoke and substantiate a character? I doubt it. Perhaps it is there that Somerset Maugham and I disagreed. I wish we had continued the discussion, but he was tired, and began to stammer,

439

nor was it possible in the presence of Acton and [Arturo] Loria, particularly of such a soloist as Harold Acton.

July 4th, I Tatti

From cradle to grave life consisted in my youth of suppression after suppression of all the animal instincts and urges, of all "anti-social," of all anti-orthodox Christian thinking, of all that might dissipate the fog of puritanical premise and assumption. Yet to me the result at that time had a beauty of its own. Its disappearance has brought no satisfaction, no real freedom. The animal instincts now have uncontrolled expression, and love as distinct from lust has almost disappeared from society. No premises, no assumptions, withstand the "Why not" that arbitrarily challenges them. The notion of antecedent probability prevails nowhere. So "Me this unchartered freedom tires," and there is a consequent return to *pensée engagée,* to *art engagé,* either toward the Kremlin or the Vatican, each as blatantly dogmatic, as contemptuous of opposition, as ecclesiastics teaching seminarists Catholic theology. They long for suppression.

July 9th, I Tatti

In a charming talk about her youth as Asquith's daughter, Violet Bonham Carter says, "The spirit of the age was tumultuous. Looking back it seems strange that those days of peace and cloudless skies should have been an age of such ferocity and violence at home." I say because "violence" must out, and if not abroad then at home. How often have arbitrary and aristocratic rulers been accused of starting rows in order to get peace at home. Man is a fighting animal and will fight to the end, no matter what the consequences. Wars on the scale of the last one probably are ended. What kind of fighting will follow? Hard to foresee. Surely not local affairs as are threatening everywhere just now. It will be more serious than that, and possibly in the nature of the sixteenth-century religious wars. Possibly of the nature of what is now going on in Algeria and in Cyprus, but even more senseless and more destructive. Yet peace movements should not be discouraged. Perhaps they can slightly, faintly, be effective.

July 10th, I Tatti

Giovanni Papini * dead and given an all but state funeral. I met him once or twice at the beginning of his career, and thought him arrogantly vulgar, and provocative. Undoubtedly he had a dose of genius, was master of the word and used it when in middle years again and again to express deep feeling and to illuminate dark places. Then converted to conventional Vatican religiosity, exploited it (or so it seemed to many) and adhered to Fascism, advising Mussolini to turn the Italian Academy into a bribe for writers defending Fascism, and rewarding them materially as well. As I do not believe in mature conversion and cannot forgive sub-servience to Fascism, I never felt kindly to him, although ready to praise him as a master of the word. I cannot get over my amaze-ment over the way Italians condone their heroes and propagandists of Fascism, as if these had never done any harm.

July 11th, I Tatti

I do not doubt my own values, but begin to question whether in this horizon it is possible to stand up for them and to impose them on others. Partly no doubt the feebleness of extreme old age, but even more the growing conviction that there is no use in talk-ing, leads me to let others talk while I listen (or seem to), and do not put in a word of my own. Far more distressing is my increasing doubt about the work I have done in the field of attribution. Per-haps I have stirred the stagnant pools and helped to clear the water. I have in no way changed them. On the other hand I be-lieve more than ever in my intuitions and my aesthetic aphorisms. ✓ If only I had the energy to restate them in a far more detailed and persuasive way than hitherto. I still would enjoy the fervour of believing I was doing something worth while. The work on cataloguing paintings according to my own grouping does not satisfy me.

* Italian philosopher and writer (1881–1956); at first caustic opponent of Christianity and iconoclast; converted later (1921) to Roman Catholic orthodoxy; author of *Life of Christ*, etc.

July 18th, I Tatti

Exclusive cliques are groups of individuals who have the same gossip, the same references, the same shibboleths. If consisting of well-born and well-placed persons, we are apt to regard them as deliberately asserting superiority of station. Snobs may teach them to think of their rank and amenities. Really they are associations for very easy conversation, where everybody understands everybody *à demi-mots,* as no outsider who penetrated their circle could. This outsider will end by withdrawing silently, or cringing to play the clown, the worshipper, to amuse them, to make them appreciate and value the superiority of their clique to ordinary mortals. Of course if this clique is composed of gifted men and women, they can give a push to cultivated society as a whole, and even inspire creation—as perhaps was the case in Elizabethan and Georgian England.

July 22nd, I Tatti

Pistoia—what a lovely town, with spacious streets and squares, lined with Medieval skyscrapers (often hidden behind sixteenth-century façades), or with elegant late Renaissance palaces. Cathedral with its original tower composed of colonnaded storeys, and inside the altarpiece from Verrocchio's studio, that Leonardo may have worked on with Credi, and the silver altar. (By the way, silver like gold does not lend itself to representation in relief, and least of all to Medieval illustrations.) In S. Giovanni Fuori Civitas the Della Robbia group of Mary and Elizabeth meeting, almost as good as the best high reliefs in the Ceramicus of Athens. In Sant'Andrea, the most intimately typical Giovanni Pisano, where that great artist displays his qualities as nowhere else. In San Francesco, spaces almost as in Santa Croce in Florence, and remains of many frescoes by or close to Maso that still tell what they must have been! And much more that I recall for which we had no time yesterday. It was market day, and the crowd around the cathedral could have been painted by Brueghel and his spiritual descendants.

July 24th, I Tatti

Stewart Perowne * writes to me of Israel that when its fate is decided, "the Jews will be able to return to their eternal destiny, which is spiritual." But even Jews are nine tenths animal and, as Shylock already pleaded, like all other humans. Then why should they only be perpetually subject to persecution, to discrimination, to legalized or administrative annoyance, and—wholesale extermination as practised a few years ago by Nazis? Instead of being regarded as spiritual and with a spiritual mission, he is the money grabber, the cheat, the usurer, the bloodsucker, ready to do anything rather than fight in war and till the soil between wars. Now that he has proved his capacity as a fighter and as a tiller of the soil in the land of Israel, from which he regarded himself through thousands of years as an exile, you want him to return to his spiritual mission, to be rewarded as before with contempt, with condescension, with antipathy, with persecution, with extermination. *"Les Juifs aiment à être massacrés; les autres peuvent attendre."*

July 27th, Vallombrosa

Since "maturity" I have taken less and less interest in systems of any kind, and least of all in the subjects constantly preoccupying me, namely, history, politics, and art—art of every kind. If I still read about them, it is to find thinkers who feel and write as I do, the object being to allay the fear that I may be a solipsist, feeling, thinking, and concluding as nobody else, and thus mentally deranged. (My father used to say that when a man thinks he and he alone is right, they put him in an asylum for the insane.) In matters of the visual arts, I care little for what others write, and seldom read on the subejct. Yet I enjoy confirmation of my own way of thinking when I discover others I have never heard of thinking independently as I do. My real, my lifelong interest has been to find out what I really feel, what I really think, regardless of others. Hence I never felt the spontaneous wish to quote others,

* English Orientalist and historian, retired civil servant; author of *Herod the Great*; *The Later Herod*.

443

to whom I owe nothing. It is that, however, which exasperates "colleagues." *"Er hat mich gar nicht zitiert."*

August 3rd, Vallombrosa

Yesterday, my second cousin Robert Berenson, usually known as "Berri" in the ultra-smart society of which he is a favourite, and where he passes for my nephew. Spoke quietly, with no trace of boastfulness, of his chums that include not only tycoons like Onassis and Niarchos, etc., but important people in U.S.A. diplomacy and in the Eisenhower administration. Horrified by the good-natured way he recounted cases of financial corruption among high officials, and Republican party chiefs. Spoke also of his intimate relation to U.S.A. diplomats, and their urging him to take service with them. Hitherto I have thought of him as a partner in the wide-flung firm of "Charm Incorporated," and that only. Almost he persuaded me that he must be more than that, that behind the sure charm there is tact, conciliatory instinct, and perhaps worldly wisdom that counts a great deal in diplomacy. I urged him to accept any serious diplomatic appointment.

August 10th, Vallombrosa

I cannot recall a single dream (and I have a good many) that I could not trace back to its complex-free source. Generally connected with the day's occupation. When pioneering, a passion for Correggio and Giorgione led me to see in dreams Correggios and Giorgiones more beautiful than any I had seen when awake. And so, all through life, dreams were the continuation and once in a great while the transfiguration of the previous day's working activities. Of course, I had erotic dreams when very young, but rarely obsessive. Frequently dreamt of landscape, and I used in the dream itself to labour to identify it. I once dreamt of a marvellous one, and for the life of me could not trace it back to any I had experienced. Sure enough! I finally succeeded in discovering that I had not lived it, but realized it so keenly while reading in Loti's *Au Maroc* that it remained a part of experience that dreaming could recall. So it is hard for me to accept the Freudian "dream

444

book," and trace all, positively all dreams back to some erotic and frustrated complex.

August 13th, Vallombrosa

I could live comfortably the rest of my days, despite all the troubles flesh so aged is heir to, if I gave up work that required serious effort, people who do not stimulate or amuse, travel, the reading of newspapers. I literally suffer bodily when I read what is going on in the world. Perhaps easier for distant observers than actors to see and understand what the actors themselves are doing, and what the consequences will be. But I still want to learn, I still want to understand, and I still want to write. How shall I get rid of these lusts? Physical incompetence only will emancipate me from their slavery, but what kind of freedom will it be? The ante-chamber of the End. But how I still enjoy sunlight, nature, and stormy skies, and sunsets, and trees and flowers, and animals including well-shaped humans, and reading, and conversing!

August 23rd, Vallombrosa

Georges Salles yesterday, from one to four in the afternoon. Had not seen him in six years, found him changed from a still youngish Frenchman to a white-haired elderly Jew, fine distinguished type of Jew, but Jewish enough to pass for any of the great Israelites of the past. Member of "Charm Incorporated," like Johnnie Walker, like Robert Berenson, *alias* "Berri," and thousands of others, who no doubt have capacities, and even merits, but nothing like (equal to) the rewards they garner. Mystery how this Jew weathered the Pétain regime in France, not only, but to become, or to remain, Director General of Art—all art—in France. Rather winced when (by inadvertence) we talked of his grandfather. This was no other than Eiffel, who designed and constructed the steel tower named after him, for Eiffel was an Alsatian Jew. His mother, Eiffel's daughter, complete Jewess. Have not met his, Georges's, father Salles, but so far as I have always understood, he too an Israelite. Georges a sugarplum for hungry but beautiful women his life long, and still so, I dare say. What a successful career.

445

August 27th, Vallombrosa

I long to travel, to see so many places I never have been to, India, Japan, Java, Angkor Wat and Angkor Thom, etc. I know it is impossible. Equally I long to read ever so many books of the past, and so many that appear at present. These I can and do buy, expecting to read them. The fact is that after I have half done with the week's periodicals I receive, the leisure for reading books is reduced to minutes rather than hours. I gather a harem of houris, each of which looks reproachfully at me for not embracing her, till finally I sweep them not into the Bosporus, but into the Black Sea of a library that has got beyond my intimacy, where I no longer find my way, where books are shelved till rediscovered by students, not to be enjoyed but studied. I buy books as brainless hens go on pecking corn. Almost a reflex act. And many of them are only good while young—like harem houris.

August 28th, Vallombrosa

I no longer feel a call of nature to chatter. Chatter wants relief, like sex, like the intestines, like the bladder. In the case of chattering, people with a gift for words that mean something, and are at the same time winged, enjoy it almost as much as sex relief. At my age I know that my words are no longer winged, and that there is little profit in trying to correct the nonsense, the absurdities, the malice, the calumnies, the self-assertion, the challenging dogmatism of one's young fellow bipeds, even if these belong to some degree to one's own world. So I now sit in the midst of others, listen, but feel no call to join in and chatter with or against them. So I munch my grapes, as Carlyle reports seeing Wordsworth do, and say nothing. My wife Mary as a young girl tried to get Walt Whitman to join in the chatter of her young friends. "No," he said, "I love to hear your voices and your laughter, but I could not enjoy your talk."

September 2nd, Vallombrosa

As a valuer, as a critic, as an interpreter, as a writer, I always had in mind what I regarded as the permanent relation to the permanent elements in the human heart, mind, but above all physiology, or if you will psychophysiology. I can still be amused (as hitherto) by all sorts of artifacts, including all the aberrations of the last thirty or forty years. No exoticism escapes my interest. But I do not rush after *le dernier cri* as is universally done today. Today art is reduced to mere means, discoveries, exhibitions, fantastic interpretations. They come and go almost like the afternoon newspaper. My attitude toward the work of art produces more permanent results. What I wrote between sixty and fifty years ago is still current, and there are complaints if new editions contain omissions or serious changes.

September 3rd, Vallombrosa

Israelites and even the Judeans took so much from Mesopotamia, as did all other Northern Semites. But they humanized every personage, every situation, as no other Semites, nor indeed the Greeks. They did not heroize. Their prominent personages remain altogether too human. Saul is a tragic figure, but only too, too human, and David even more so. Samson the Strong Man down to Jewish fable of my own childhood a ridiculous fool. Surely Israel as a people were a sport as is any individual genius. I can descry no "historical necessity" for the ultimate emancipation of Judeans from the horrors of human sacrifice, and other monstrosities practised by all other Semites down almost to the Christian era. No gross exaggeration in the Old Testament. Moses remains very human even in the presence of Jahve; the most beloved of all, David, could not be more human, and so with all the favourites of Israel in Jewish history through the ages. Not one heroized beyond natural size and capacities. Indeed, Jews are anti-heroic. And still more—indeed like nearly all Semites—incapable of divinizing, of turning human beings, as the Hellenistic Greeks did, into gods. "Incarnation" was abhorrent to them, and still is, for which reason they cannot now and never could be Christians, or indeed conceive how one could become a believer in the transubstantiation of a man into a god.

September 15th, Vallombrosa

One of my principal nonagenarian conclusions is: No matter how objective we try to be, and even succeed in being, our feeling

447

and even thinking is seasonal. The child's eject of a world is not the adolescent's, nor is his like the one of early manhood, nor that in turn of full so-called maturity. As we begin to decline, our cosmos gets thin at the elbows, the knees, and the seat, like an overworn pair of trousers. Later holes appear in them, and finally we are left naked. Happily, few are aware of this, because they are clothed by their "religious" beliefs in the "Emperor's clothes," and there is no telling them that they are going naked. For me it is not so. I face actuality. My problem is now to resign myself to it, instead of vaticinating and raging like Hebrew prophets of old against a perverse and suicidal generation. I too would like to believe in a Good Time coming. But—

September 16th, Vallombrosa

My nonagenarian conclusion about people is that essentially they will act according to their nature because they must. They may be constrained, they may be obliged to seem to conform to the values entertained by the umpires of the game. In hidden ways they will go their way, and only *force majeure* will stop them. I have seldom if ever encountered a person whose fundamental nature I could see modified. Wherefore one should avoid individuals whose ego is invincibly opposed to ours. No matter what their intentions may be, they act up to their own nature. To a sensitive person they ooze and smell and look what they are—I mean really that we all do—and we should avoid those that at first sight repel us. My worst troubles have come from trying to conquer instinctive antipathies, alarm signals.

September 18th, Vallombrosa

Satisfactions are what we crave for from our earliest to our latest days. They come in answer to wants. If not wanted, things give no real pleasure. Children don't know what to do with expensive and elaborate toys until they are old enough to crave the joy of using them. Grownups do not know what to do with suddenly or too quickly acquired great riches. Alexander was bored when he had no more worlds to conquer. Caesar at the end of his tether when he became master of the *oecumene*. When they do

448

not have an object to crave for, people yawn, are bored, and either resign to mere existence, as Hindus are apt to do, or go in for any and every kind of adventure, no matter how risky, how unremunerative. The intrinsic value of the object craved for has no importance. It may be a rag baby, or an empire. The telling thing is that it should be wanted eagerly, and for no matter how brief a moment. Life is one satisfaction after another—if lived happily.

September 19th, Vallombrosa

Yesterday an Italian couple brought their little girl, just two years old. She wanted to sit opposite her mother, and brought across a chair entirely made of wood. Then realizing it was too hard for her to sit on, she put a cushion on it. This awareness of means to ends, and knowing what she wanted exactly, is very different from the so-young of my own earlier years. Again and again in recent days I have encountered similar precocity in little ones of today. Then there is Francesco Colacicchi,* a boy of fourteen. With him you can discuss any subject, concrete or abstract, as with any intellectual grownup. What will a world be like in which "maturity" begins so early and lasts so late, where the very aged are going to increase, when at the same time the younger and stronger will want their turn earlier, pushing out their seniors, leaving them with precarious if any occupations, and inadequate pensions? The future is unforeseeable, unimaginable even. I fear solutions that now seem horrible, but that may be adopted—as they are almost universally in primitive and early societies.

September 20th, Vallombrosa

Brilliant, creative, even fascinating as I may have been in youth and manhood up to the First World War, it is only since that little by little I have found my deeper self, and most since the last war. Partly owing to increasing economic security and ease. My adversaries might say "like the Greek Sophist, who first would enrich himself, and then practise virtue." Perhaps a more adequate reason is that at last after all the heartbreaking betrayals or de-

* Son of the painter Giovanni Colacicchi; godson of Nicky Mariano.

449

sertions of friends and followers, as well as of my wife, all exploiting but none serving, even turning against me to set up as superiors—at last in Nicky I have found a person whose affection, whose attention to my needs and wants, whose indefatigable helpfulness, whose loyalty, have convinced me that goodness has not vanished from my world, that there is one on whom I can rely to understand, condone, love generously, through thick and through thin.

September 24th, Vallombrosa

Leaving this afternoon for Bologna. The summer has passed swiftly, and compared with the former ten years more quietly. Fewer and fewer to lunch or tea, and for the evenings often by ourselves, Nicky, my sister Bessie Berenson, and I. When alone listening to the radio or recorded music, I never read, but abandon myself to the sonority, to the rhythm, the cadences, and to the wisps of feeling and reflection and reminiscence, evoked or liberated by the music. For me music is a realm of being, and like art primarily to be enjoyed and absorbed, not to be scalpelled, anatomized, cross-questioned inquisitorially. But to come back to our sojourn here, I have felt feebler and more dispirited, and been without the care of my physician, himself ill and unable to come till yesterday. Also serious trouble with teeth. Nevertheless enjoyed walking, reading, conversation, and above all "nature," and the apocalyptic sunsets. So I can still lick the honey of the well,* as I perch on the precarious twig, which a dragon is gnawing at the roots.

September 30th, I Tatti

Left Bologna with regret. Such a living town—not as Florence depending on tourists as chief industry—and preserves its Medieval but chiefly Renaissance and more still Seicento and Settecento aspects almost intact. The great Piazza full of character, although oddly suggestive of a certain rusticity. Works of art still out of

* "Honey of the well" refers to the Oriental legend of Barlaam and Josaphat.

doors like Jacopo della Quercia's portal of San Petronio, and the matchless composition of the fountain by Giovanni di Bologna, and the Niccolò dell'Arca *Madonna* on the Palazzo Comunale. Struck by the abundance of noble palaces with inviting courtyards, all looking like residences of people who live in the grand style of a highly organized, opulent, and hierarchical society. Street after street of fine houses. Only drawback the crowd, the traffic, the noise. Crossing a street one risks life or limb. Too many inhabitants for the space a problem to be solved only by submitting all to traffic.

October 1st, I Tatti

Returning to I Tatti after absence of nine weeks, delighted with first impression. It is of harmony, of direction, of good spacing, of pictures, sculptures, *objets d'art* living happily together, though of such different schools and epochs. How has this come about? Not by planning ahead. By finding, little by little, what I could live with, what gave my eye, and lungs, and viscera greatest satisfaction to be with. How different from the "premasticated" ready-made dwelling of the poor billionaires! They can only have a say about their chequebook. No other relation to the museums, generally "Louis XV," they occupy, interiors that never become houses, that express nothing but their aspiration to be considered richer, and more chic than anybody else. I dare say they get their money's worth. Serves them right.

October 2nd, I Tatti

S. S. a couple of days ago had never heard of Prato, yet she insists on writing *my* "official life." She has not the remotest notion of what a person like me has read and seen and "contacted." Little of human concern that has not interested me, history, all literatures, all phases of art, no end of contacts with interesting individuals. Impossible for her to conceive of my life except as a vulgar success story, the high lights of which are Mrs. Gardner, and "Lord" Duveen, a personage who affected me negatively, if at all. She has no curiosity about those who really influenced me and contributed to my formation. While at college besides William James there was Barrett Wendell, Professor Toy, the Tom Perrys. Later on Sedgwick and Henry Adams— and all my reading since my eleventh year at latest.* The Old Testament, much of which I knew by heart before my fifteenth year, and from my sixteenth year at latest Goethe and Heine and German Romantics, later Burckhardt and Nietzsche, and French Classics, and contemporaries. Profound the influence of writers like Matthew Arnold, Wordsworth, and above all of Walter Pater. How can she who has never heard of Prato write of me as interpreter, appreciator, and historian of Italian art, and what has been my speciality, namely to see it, and feel it, in an ever present sense of universal art?

October 5th, I Tatti

Countess Serristori defines love as the idealization of desire, and lust as its degradation. True enough. Yet idealization can lead to too rigid self-control, to the cult of Chastity, to puritanical ignoring of despised natural urges. These then can fester and stagnate into the attitude toward sex in which I was brought up in Boston. It played a great part in my attitude toward women, nor have I even at ninety-one completely liberated myself from it. But I never revolted against it with puritanical, "Roundhead" zeal, zest, and thoroughness, the way so many Americans have, going to extremes of exalting sex, talking of nothing but sex, and acting as well as vociferating as if their whole vocation was endless fornication. A great deal of American contemporary literature (and its European imitation) is but a roundabout way of getting a male and a female to bed. Surely sex can take care of itself, and does not need propaganda.

October 18th, I Tatti

To tea yesterday, a guest from Catania, keeper of the archaeological museum there. Looks like a faun from the forest, with

* Barrett Wendell (1855–1921), American man of letters, author and teacher.—Crawford Howell Toy (1886–1919), American Orientalist and teacher. B.B. studied Arabic under him.—Arthur George Sedgwick (1844–1915), American lawyer, journalist, and essayist.

his rough chiselled face, his huge nose, his tousled black hair. Talks thunderously, but turns to me tenderly, yet slightly upsetting me by calling me *"Maestro."* How I shrink when addressed that way, or "Professor." Why? Must be because I never have taken myself professionally. On the contrary as a dilettante only. To return to Maganuco: * he talked without the slightest self-consciousness to all gathered for tea, Italians, Russians, English, and held attention. Talked of his beloved Eastern Sicily, of possible Antonellos, of work he hoped to do, of eagerness to engage my interest, my authority. I cannot believe I have any. I cannot recall anything that was in any way decided by my authority or influence. Yet people will go on expecting me to do miracles for them.

October 24th, I Tatti

Joan of Arc heard voices. So do I, but I know that they are not from without. I know that they are due to my hearing apparatus. I hear twittering and chirping all the time. Again and again I wake at night and hear a cataract of water, and rush to the window, to look at the serene night sky. No rainpour there. It was all in my hearing machinery gone wrong. As I wake from sleep, before realizing where I am I see shapes easily taken for ghosts, if I were not so on guard against flitting misreadings. Often as I lie in bed I feel as if I were rocking, the coverlets moving, and caresses on my face. Of course it is only whiffs of air from open windows. How easily taken for visitations of loving Dead! I am constantly fighting against sights and sounds that seem genuine enough to one who is not so armed with self-awareness and self-analysis as I am. Next to impossible to induce others to do likewise. How they cling to the supernatural!

October 28th, I Tatti

Except at meals and a short walk at noon, I spend most of the twenty-four hours sleeping heavily, unrestfully, or dozing. At the table I catch only a word here and there, and when more than six

* Enzo Maganuco, Professor of Fine Arts at University of Catania, and Director of the Castello Ursino Museum. Met B.B. in 1926 through his teacher, and B.B.'s friend, Pietro Toesca.

453

give up and do not listen. Anglo-Saxon women to right and left of me expect a *tête-à-tête* chat in the midst of the to me confusing uproar. There are voices that crush the words meant to reach me, and I cannot distinguish one word from another. I almost never feel comfortable. Instead, disgust with my body dripping from nose and bladder, and exploding from intestines. I become alive only when absorbed in conversation with stimulating and responsive persons, when I walk, when I listen to music, and when I write, but only for the half or three quarters of an hour before fatigue overpowers me. Is it worth while? One clings to mere keeping alive with an instinct stronger than all reasoning, even fearing as I do that if I go on living it will be more and more as a vegetable.

October 29th, I Tatti

The Trevor-Ropers left after a week's stay. She looked older than Hugh, but very well dressed, and not by any means stupid. He in the first flower of his years and career. Handsome in a Nordic way though not particularly distinguished-looking. Angular Pinocchio-like gestures, sawing up and down, and finishing argument with clenched fist. Cocksure, arrogant, but without insolence, and no effort to assert himself, seems to think it is not worth while. Seldom starts, but when cranked up goes on endlessly with infinite detail, and detective awareness and marvellous capacity for taking trouble to convince himself, and to convince his hearers. Seems to have known everybody, or at least everybody who has known anyone who has counted in the last thirty years. Can recite entire sagas about them. A fascinating letter writer, indeed an epistolary artist, brilliant reviewer of all sorts of books, very serious historian, and formidable polemist.

October 31st, I Tatti

Vanitas vanitatum, yes, if you look at the failure of the purpose, at the deviation of the intention only. I have made a home for myself, furnished it for my comfort and pleasure. Some supreme pictures, some real works of art from China, and odds and ends from everywhere. I have got together a library that within its limits can rank with great ones. I have built up a garden that is delightful to walk in. If I had a deliberate purpose it was to enjoy it all with a sense of timeless leisure in my old age. Now I am very old, scarcely ever browse in the library, seldom consciously enjoy the works of art, overwhelmed by all the publications I receive and want to master, baffled by lack of strength to cope with ever more demands on my writing, on my authority, on my patronage. I am like the peasant in one of Pearl Buck's romances, *The Good Earth,* who owing to his passion for tilling the soil, his intelligence and zest in doing it, becomes a great landowner, and deprived of the one occupation that gave him satisfaction: digging and tilling with his own body. Now, what is to happen to I Tatti and all its contents? I leave it to Harvard, feeling anything but confidence as to what Harvard will do with it. All vanity except the fact that purposes and intentions were vague. Real was the pleasure and satisfaction I found in building, furnishing, collecting, accumulating, from hour to hour, from day to day. This activity was its own and ample reward, and filled my hours with small (if you will) satisfactions for momentary desires, and tiny triumphs. Of these I have had an abundance, and what is more I was always more than half aware it was that that counted, and not some remoter purpose. Now I must try to stop worrying about what will become of I Tatti after I am gone.

November 7th, I Tatti

The trouble with the Jews today is that in no matter what walk of life, from the meanest and vilest to the *all but highest,* they are more intelligent, quicker, abler. They cross the interests or the vanity of gentiles, and are resented accordingly—the way Roger Fry resented my authority in Bond Street, and as good as declared war against me if I did not leave London to him. It is not for his too-universally human faults, but for his superiority, even as a cheat, as a disloyal competitor, that the Jew is resented and disliked. Except in the highest height of political and perhaps musical creativeness, in what intellectual, scientific, learned pursuit is the Western Jew not as good as if not better than his gentile competitor? True, he may be pushing and indiscreet, and a snob, but surely that is the fault of a world which persists in boycotting, ostracizing him, so that he never feels at home, is never wholly accepted.

455

November 13th, I Tatti

Why am I so opposed to the present-day preoccupation with the artist rather than the work of art, or with using the work of art as a mere illustration to the events of the day when it was done? The answer is that it drives interest and attention away from what the work of art and the work of art alone can give—a certain exaltation of all one's faculties, a certain vision of the way the world and things in it should look—and thereby inspire, encourage, and exalt. All this is now ignored by writers on art. They confine themselves to attributions, to using the work of art as a mere document, or to so-called philosophical, psychoanalytical investigation of why the artist did what he did, and how the average art-blind and art-deaf person reacts toward it. Hence my *vox clamantis,* and I seem almost alone, and for that reason perhaps really am driven by despair to exaggerated and even too violent protests.

November 17th, I Tatti

How beautiful has been this autumn, and in a different way still is. The colouring, rusty-red, scarlet almost, pure yellow, straw-colour, has gladdened my heart. A veil of mist, just thick enough to blur what is ugly, transfigured Florence with its suburbs, not an eyesore but shimmering through the mist. Just out of my bedroom window in the inner garden a persimmon tree. Its golden fruit peeped slyly through the bronzed leafage. Then the leaves began to fall, uncovering the paled fruit. Bassanesque distances, grey-blue, murky, but appealing. In this small park, every tree has its own individual foliage and colour, nearly every colour except those of the rainbow. The rivulets begin to run with water again, instead of showing their bone-dry summer channels. All along buzzes in my brain the old, old cry: How can man be so brutal, so bestial, suicidal, in the midst of all the beauty that the perceiving sense sees to enjoy?

November 19th, I Tatti

I never have had a technique, except as an "attributor." I never knew a language grammatically enough to be a philosopher—have never been able to write in any language but English—if that. I have had little ability in any field, although I have entered many. Willfulness has dominated me, and blinded me to reason. My spontaneous savage reactions are happily controlled, so that I seldom have given way to evil impulses of any kind. At bottom I have a deal of contempt for myself, and disapproval when not contempt. There remains a certain universality of interest, an unquenchable eagerness to learn and understand, to get to the bottom, to free myself from current catchwords and accepted premises. So in some ways I seem to myself more intelligent than able technicians, famous scientists, and political people. There is something of the prophet about me, but with no honour. Nevertheless I am puzzled by the stir I have made in the world, and wonder how little is my doing, and how much due to people who advertised me for their own purposes.

November 26th, I Tatti

My greatest remaining pleasure is reading. Reading for information of every kind, from the news of the day, to novelties of every kind in almost every field of knowledge, to which my mental preparation is accessible. I peruse rather than read. In my own narrow field, the field of Italian painting, the caption of a reproduction, a glance at the text, tells me all the author has to say. In other art and archaeological realms, I wander more cautiously, and above all I lap up information about new discoveries of artifacts, building, carving, painting of the remote past. I still enjoy narrative, whether declared fiction or the undeclared fables of history. In both cases, it is the movement, the contacts with human problems, the evocation of experiences I never have had, that carry me on and on, and even fascinate me.

November 29th, I Tatti

Serristori to tea yesterday. A good talk, and as usual in connection with questions of the day she wanted to clarify. We embraced again and again as she left, going to Rome in a day or two for the winter months. Each of us had a feeling, too resigned to be a fear, that we never might meet again. The first all but twenty years of our friendship were intimately happy. Then came the First World War, and to my distress it came out that she was a

457

violent pro-German. We kept meeting but in tears. Then came the troubles in Spain, and she was madly pro-Franco, and remains so till this day. Even in the last, the Nazi-Fascist, war, she seemed to lean more to them than to us. Our friendship has weathered all those storms, and we are more attached to each other than ever, although I do get bored when she repeats again and again the wonders of her granddaughter and this granddaughter's offspring.

December 9th, I Tatti

At what moment of the past should I, the I that I am now, have felt most at one with my fellow creatures? Perhaps in the years after the Napoleonic Wars, and in Germany, and in Goethe's Weimar in particular. Passionately devoted to Hellenism, but at the same time more and more aware of other outwardly spiritual climates, Middle Ages, Persia, Islam, India, in short the adventure of discovering a past hitherto ignored or avoided. Also the Biedermeier modesty of living, no luxury, scarcely comfort, but quiet, unhurried enjoyment of accessible things, ample time for thought and conversation, delight in each other's personalities, and aspiration, in quiet awareness, in contemplation. In Boston as a boy I had a taste of something similar in the way life was lived by nearly all the cultivated and by all who counted, except the few "world's people."

December 10th, I Tatti

Meanness—malicious, malignant meanness in literature, how common? Is Thersites* already a case in point? How often do characters like Uriah Heep, so frequent in Dickens and elsewhere in the English novel, appear in France and Germany and Italy? I doubt whether as often as in the English, not even in Balzac. The Russian novel seems almost entirely free from it. Brutal, bestial, but even in Dostoevski rarely out-and-out mean. Never at all in Turgenev and Tolstoi. I find it in Shchedrin † only, in *The*

* Thersites, loud-mouthed and quarrelsome character in the *Iliad*.
† Mikhail Saltykov Shchedrin (1826–89), Russian novelist, author of *The Messieurs Goluvlev*.

Messieurs Goluvlev, even there more sordid than hypocritical meanness. Why so much more in England? Is it that Uriah Heep comes up more often there than elsewhere? In my experience it would seem so. Elsewhere it is self-aware. In England only can a person be a sneaking hypocrite, deliberately mischief-making, and go on believing that he is a just man made perfect. I for one have never encountered it so frequently elsewhere—not even in kindred America.

December 22nd, I Tatti

Once I get on my legs, and for as long as the rest of my body will stand it, they work as well as ever, same brisk, secure walk as of long ago. My legs seem, unlike the rest of me, to have remained young. Lincoln would not sign death warrants against soldiers who ran away. He used to say, "A man is not responsible for his legs." During the First World War after Caporetto severe measures were threatened against runaways. The gardener's wife of Villa Medici at Fiesole came rushing to the proprietress, Lady Sybil Cutting,* imploring her to save her son. Lady Sybil asked why she was so terrified for him. "Ah, he has such fine legs for running." The doctor tells me I am "cured." Perhaps, but certainly on a lower level of vitality, and of free energy. Every serious illness (like the bronchial trouble I am cured of) pushes me down to a lower level of living. I have to vegetate more and more. *"Aber ist das ein Leben?"*

December 23rd, I Tatti

Anna Maria Cicogna Volpi burst out yesterday with "God knows what would have become of me if I were not born with plenty of money!" Promptly I answered, "You would be a much happier person. You have inherited your father's talents for business, for great affairs, for organization, for handling events. Born and brought up to huge wealth, you do not really enjoy it, because it has not and does not give scope and issue for your inherited gifts. You suffer from suppressed activity, and vainly try

* See p. 41, note.

to find a scope for it in all sorts of over-occupation with futilities, like the management of your house at Tripoli, furnishing and letting dwellings in Rome, etc. What you need to make you really happy is scope for the completest exercise of your inborn functions —not for elegant living, not for maternity, nor society, but for serious creative affairs." She agreed.

December 29th, I Tatti

I am irritated by people like X., whose talk consists entirely of *le dernier cri* in matters of painting first, and then of literature, and finally of music. Never a word about anything of the past, unless for a flitting moment it is conjured up to be the subject of chatter. His talk begins and continues with "Do you know," or "Have you seen," or "Have you read," or "Have you heard," and a word of answer leads him to another question. Yet X. is not born stupid or frivolous. He takes himself very seriously, indeed as if he had a mission. After all, he only exaggerates and makes a profession of the kind of interest and chatter that passes for conversation in polite society. Chief reason why I avoid it, and should even if I still was able to frequent it. How deadly bored I get with gossip, and exchange of catchwords about exhibitions, the last play, the last cinema, the last book that everybody is reading! I have outgrown all that, and am so much more serious!

December 30th, I Tatti

All my thinking and the depths of my feeling are based on an ever present sense of the Mystery of our existence, and my incapacity for coping with it, for understanding it. Whatever has made us, whether merely material processes or Divine Purpose, has not endowed us with any instinct for understanding Beginnings and Ends. I feel humble, and in awe before the Mystery, and can never get over my amazement that so-called theologians discourse about it so glibly, so eloquently, so fervently, and with such conviction. They intoxicate themselves with their own salivation and certitude that their verbiage defines and delineates Reality. For them there is no Mystery.

460

1957

No resolutions or prophecies for 1957. I may not live through it. While I live on, I could wish to be more comfortable in my body, and stronger, and abler to work. As for the world at large, I scarcely expect Russia to be less of a menace first to the rest of Europe, and then to other continents. Silly of me, a helpless ignored outsider to the political world, to be passionately excited over what is going on, and my distress of U.S.A. incapacity, unpreparedness, to carry on against an adversary so disloyal, so unscrupulous as Russia always, and Soviet Russia in particular. If wise, I would stop reading papers and withdraw to the Classics, in literature and all the arts, instead of wasting strength in kicking against the pricks, and worse still because the oceans of ill will, stupidity, and bad taste will not retire. I long for quiet, for harmony, for serenity. I long to be free from worrying about what no one can remedy.

I fight shy of Jungian, meta-fussical, aesthetic explanations of the origins of art. From my biological and anthropological standpoint, art in man is what it is in all other living things, only, as in all other things, more so. The structures of ants and termites and bees, the dams of seals and beavers, the song of birds, the chatter of apes, all continued by man, only very much more so. We humans simply carry on with these activities. The urge to carry on further and further and further results in all the inventions that have helped to humanize man, and make him more comfortable, but now threaten to destroy him. Our nature drives us along the path of innovation, *pereat coelum,* let alone all animal life. Useless any attempt to stop it.

January 5th, I Tatti

Conceit, vanity, pomposity, the urge to impose oneself on others, can spoil the pleasure of being with individuals of merit real enough to impress and win over others without any deliberate effort to do so. My neighbour R. has many qualities as a man of action, as a scholar, as university professor, as writer. So has V. as orchestral conductor and musical critic. Their qualities would manifest themselves and meet with friendly appreciation if only they did not overwhelm one with their bursting pomposity, their boasting, their loud expressions of self-glorification, etc. Vanity can spoil a career. Take Anthony Eden. He surely has an abundance of qualities to his credit, but he oozes conceit and vanity, and looks it, making it difficult to do justice to his real abilities. "It has been cared for that the trees should not pierce the heavens."

January 9th, I Tatti

Why do I still go on writing a page of this diary every morning? I dare say I repeat myself, and if I do not, I am sure that I have nothing to say that has not already been said by thousands, with a far better pen than mine. I write as I dress for dinner, as a matter of personal discipline. As I dress evenings to divide the working hours from the leisure ones, so I write in the morning as a good start to the day. It is mental and even more moral ritual, with no touch of production about it. Indeed, most of my remaining activities are of that nature. Books or articles appearing or being prepared, all to give me the illusion that I still am paying for my berth and board on the ship of life. I have small belief in the value, or indeed the necessity, of what I am doing. Like the Medieval juggler who had no other way of pleasing the Virgin Mary than by performing for her, I do my stunt—to whom? To satisfy my own self-esteem surely.

January 21st, I Tatti

How I should like to enjoy this sunny, almost windless weather, but at zero or below, instead of fearing, dreading what it will do to my carcass if I go out for even a short walk. I recall not only how I used to love far more wintry weather when I was seven to fourteen. I recall in Lithuania smoke from wood fires going up vertically because of the windless air. And how there too I used to stare and gape at the aurora borealis and a little later the copper-green ferment of the Boston skies! Winter used to be full of events, and I used to revel in the buffetting, icy, wild wind, as I crossed the long bridge between Boston and Cambridge-port with the thermometer 18 degrees below zero. Lightest of overcoats. Nearly blew over, and face burning with the blows of the storm, but such a feeling of getting the better of it! Boyhood —how unaware it is of what it is worth, even to such a pre-cociously self-aware creature as I already was. If only one could have felt it as I feel it in remote retrospect now!

January 22nd, I Tatti

News of Ralph Barton Perry's death. Had been for several years seriously ill with arteriosclerosis of the brain. Began by court-ing my eldest sister Senda, but was snatched away by youngest, Rachel, whom he married and lived with happily till she died of pernicious anaemia some twenty years ago. At first too puritanically severe for my taste, he ended by being far more to the left po-litically. Considered a good teacher, was head of philosophical faculty of Harvard. Wrote many books, including an encyclopaedic one about William James, all readable, active in politics during the last war. Loved and beloved by the ladies. Cheering talker, witty, delicately ironical, entertaining—in short, the best of com-pany. Read aloud most agreeably. I enjoyed him, and admired him, but some years ago he distressed me by seeming to favour, or at least to condone, the Soviets. Excepting perhaps the bulky volumes on James, who will read his copious works, who will re-call him as a human being, not merely as a book, even if as much? *Spurlos verschwunden*, the last of all but four or five of us.

465

January 26th, I Tatti

Listening to Schubert's Unfinished Symphony, I was carried back sixty years at least to the tramp Charles Loeser and I took from Buonconvento to Monte Oliveto Maggiore. This occurs every time I hear that symphony. *Per contra* every time I drive over the same ground (as I used to fairly often), I would inevitably hear this symphony. That was auditive association. The other visual. Every time I see the distances to Siena, to the sea almost, to the Monte Cetona, as I listen. Music shoots back, bolts into the chambers of heart and mind, conjures up moods, states of mind, memories, transports one on wings as huge as clouds, no matter how much I try to follow note by note. I am told this does not happen to professional musicians, and least of all to performers, to executors. Music is the most nonrepresentational, and yet the most expressive, the most evoking of all the arts. The visual attempts at deliberately nonrepresentational art achieve nothing that appeals to my sense and understanding, nor can I believe that it does to others. I believe it is a mystification of an hypnotic verbal kind, on the part of those who pretend to master it.

January 29th, I Tatti

Extreme old age finds leisure for grudges—perhaps because so much of it is passed in sleep-waking, uncontrolled by the fully conscious mind. The grudges are not all about others. They begin with myself, and never end, and indeed are the bitterest. The first I recall is how miserable I felt when I alertly ran errands for others, but would not for Mother. Against others for taking every kind of advantage of me and ignoring indebtedness—indeed, going so far as to credit others with what they owed to me. As I grudge I seem to imagine—is it only imagination?—that so much that has been written and done in the field of art has happened in opposition to me, or in restating in murky terms what I said only epigrammatically, yet clearly and suggestively. Of course when fully awake I down these yelping grudges. I am sure that my words have affected thought and writing on many art matters, and connoting my name with it is a private affair of my own, to which in better moments I give little importance. Yet the grudges keep fuming.

January 31st, I Tatti

Delightful walk with ex-Queen Helen of Rumania. Took her on what I had believed to be paths trodden only by myself and companions. She was familiar with them, and many others I asked her about. I enjoy Queen Helen's warm friendliness, and the pleasure she seems to take in my company. She walks as lightly as if floating. Fascinating eyes, cannot make out their real colour, look like dark amber. Talks freely about her life as Queen, and her horrible share of what she witnessed of Soviet atrocities when they arrived to "liberate" Bucharest.

February 2nd, I Tatti

I am convinced that the human mind cannot cope with the problems of the How the Universe came to be, and the Wherefore. I remain obsessed by the Mystery, but am convinced that we must not spend energies and lose time trying to solve it. I believe in using rational processes in treating the irrational. Yet here I am subject to the absurd superstitions of Friday and the number 13, doing the least those days, and starting nothing in them, not seeing the new moon through glass. When and where did I pick up those follies? I certainly did not get them from my Jewish childhood. Now they haunt me. I feel uncomfortable a whole month if it begins with a Friday, and so if a year begins with that day, and worse still if my birthday happens on a Friday. In all these instances, I cannot shake off dread, vague fear of what may happen to me—me, proud of being a reasoning animal, free of myths and anthropomorphic interpretations of things beyond and outside man.

February 6th, I Tatti

My fear: not of *dying*, but of existing without living. Already doctors forbid me to go out of doors even at noon on sunny days. *Post hoc* if not *propter hoc*. It is a fact that after two or

467

three outings I get a bad attack of bronchitis. So I fear becoming an indweller of a villa-tomb like those of Ti for instance at Saqqara. Memory of names sunk so deep that I cannot conjure them up. Sometimes even the most familiar disappear. I begin a letter to friends so intimate that they sign with first name or with nickname only, and suddenly I cannot recall their family name. Places I have been to in distant travel I no longer can locate without difficulty. I dread in consequence being cut off from possibility of talking or writing about them. I already am very deaf—I cannot understand what persons with resonant or roaring voices have to say. I do not altogether follow when Nicky reads to me, and I fear my eyes may give out, and shut me out from close, intimate contact with reading matter. In short, I dread being imprisoned almost in the solitary confinement of a body worn out with age. No joy in myself, *keine "Freude an sich selbst,"* a burthen to others, even to the two or three who love me most, who would dread my end, and yet subconsciously lose patience with my lingering. I dread, too, all the confusion that will follow the end of my bodily existence. How it all will be inventoried, correspondence locked away from prying eyes, rooms reduced to offices, works of art packed in a gallery, and occupants who will have no understanding, no feeling for the life I have lived here, and would wish to be continued. What a horror is the translation of a house that always has been the outer garment of one's spirit into an Institution! Nothing I dread more, but how irrationally. I shall not be here to be made unhappy by the change!

February 27th, I Tatti

Ever since I can remember, I have never lost a sense of the whole, no matter what absorbed me, and how minute. At my back I always heard or rather felt how much, how little, how very little what then occupied me, was compared with the *whole.* Where did I get that unfailing feeling for the whole? Does it go back to the scheme of universal history I imbibed so deeply before I was ten years old? Possibly. No other explanation, unless we recur to some such notion as a gift of birth. As I look back on my past, I recognize that this feeling for the whole is manifest in the first book I wrote. It is the *Venetian Painters.* At the same time I was absorbed deeply in the study of and writing about Lotto. Yet in the general discussion of Venetian painting, I dismiss him with little more than a bare mention. And so today, I never see a work of art or its reproduction without a feeling for universal art of all climes and periods behind it. That possibly is what distinguishes me from all contemporary writers about art.

February 28th, I Tatti

As I attempt to look back on life and try to recall what influenced me in my formative years of boyhood and youth, I recall at the very start Emerson's insistence on becoming, on being, rather than doing. I discovered my adolescent feeling toward women in Dante's *Vita Nuova*. It has played a great part in my life, and still does. Here, however, I want to note how much through the whole of life I have thought of becoming, of being, rather than of doing. In the vocabulary I use today, I wanted to become and be a work of art myself, and not an artist. That is why my standard unfailingly has been to ask of an object, of an event, of a person, what they meant, what they did to me. I could lose myself for a while in research, in connoisseurship, but at bottom I remained a dilettante, I mean I wanted to extract only what helped to sharpen my senses, and my wits, and I seldom lost myself in the pursuit of a subject to its very end, to its dregs. Instinctively I stopped short as soon as I became aware I was straying from my prime object, namely, to make myself. Yet I suppose sooner or later the urge to write would have possessed me, even if Mary soon after the beginning of our relation was not ceaselessly urging me to it. I started writing but have never cared for it, as distinct from what it did for me, namely, liberate me by delving deeper and deeper into myself, and to make sure that I was touching bottom, if only a momentary one. To this day, the only writing that counts, and is not a mere chore, is always to help me discover my own attitude, my own feeling toward something, and thereby to become, to be more lucid, more crystalline, in short, more of a work of art.

As a youngster I was sociable, and enjoyed reading aloud to a number of people, and discussing with them. How is it that

469

I became so shy of opening my mouth to more than a few at a time? It must be partly due to language. I was seeing men who could only converse in Continental languages rather than English. I felt that I could not in their languages say what I really meant. So I got into the habit of saying next to nothing, or only enough to make them feel I was not stupid, if mute. Then more and more I learnt to feel that discussion was useless, and one discovered the dead wall in each of us. Then there was the fact that the furtive life Mary and I necessarily lived for ten years before we could marry encouraged a habit of isolation, except with the very few who accepted our situation, and with whom we felt free of concealment. Later, too late, I discovered that I was everywhere, and with all groups, an "outsider." I could not wholeheartedly abandon myself to their ideas and ideals, to their cries, their enthusiasms. I was very seldom touched by them, and after rare occasions when I did get crowd-minded, I recovered quickly, and indignant with my lapse. To this day, excepting Nicky in most things, there is certainly no society, no small group, no individual to whom I could abandon my whole, my entire self. While young, I had but the vaguest idea of how I should live. I assumed I would go back to America and teach somewhere, living a very quiet life, making few demands. It has turned out so very different, so different that I am "in the news," like a cinema star, and find it difficult to avoid invasions of privacy from all kinds of quarters. I have been bothered with possessions, responsibilities, etc.

Yet I remain the outsider, not only to all not me, but to my animal, to my emotional, to my public self, and thereby saved from *solipsism*. I am more than ever the dilettante who comes to care only for what helps him to know himself better and better, to purify, to disengage his real soul from all impurities, who cherishes only what contributes to his getting near to a perfect work of art.

March 1st, I Tatti

I feel as Hans Sachs in the *Meistersinger,* as he reflects on the *Weltchronik, "Web, und immer Web."* Not a single item in daily press to give one comfort or even hope. Reading it spoils

Count Umberto Morra di Lavriano. *Photo Guglielmo Alberti*

Raymond Mortimer and Nicky Mariano, 1951

H.M. the King of Sweden and B.B., 1952. *Photo Locchi, Firenze*

Harry Truman and B.B., 1956. *Photo Levi, Firenze*

Princess Shams Pahlavi, 1950

Katherine Dunham

B.B. with Rector of Florence University and Roberto Longhi, 1956.
Photo Locchi, Firenze

B.B. and Yehudi Menuhin, 1957

my day. If only I could fade away, forget the present, and take refuge in the literature and art of the past, as known to me before the last century was over. Unimaginable the world that will come out, if indeed ever it will, from the whirling, cheering, mephitic, asphyxiating chaos of today. I fear something like the Soviet system at its worst may be the outcome. The individual will vanish, or rather be abolished. He, no matter how gifted, how obedient, as soon as he "deviates" or happens to be in the way will be liquidated. A more elaborate and colossal polity of termites will result. I dare say those born and grown up in it will be completely adjusted and happy—though in Hell!

March 5th, I Tatti

If I had the strength I could write about the propaganda against the Turks, as shown in Italian painting of the decades following their taking of Constantinople. It furnished subject matter for Piero della Francesca's frescoes at Arezzo, and for a like series by a local painter at Volterra. Continued in pictures down to the Cinquecento, by followers of Giorgione. Explains the cult of Constantine and his mother, Helen. The connection between art and propaganda goes back to early Egypt and Mesopotamia, was probably current in Greece, and certainly in Rome, in coins and medals and even buildings. The great master of showing the connection between painting particularly, and celebration of events and propaganda for them, was Emile Mâle.

March 7th, I Tatti

I almost am forgetting how to read with any concentration. I receive so many periodicals, from dailies to annuals, treating of all subjects to which my mind has access, that I seldom can do more than glance at the contents, and pass on. Partly due to being too weak to concentrate on anything for more than a few minutes at a time. Oh, for the leisure of spirit to read without "Time's winged chariot drawing near." I can scarcely recall the state of mind that enabled me to read *belles lettres* of every kind, anthropology, ethnology, any and every history of events, and of arts and sciences. I used to lose myself completely in what I was reading. Enjoyed it almost sensually, cosily, fretlessly, from my earliest years. What remains? Only as it were a colouring of the container that I am, and that colours all that momentarily it contains. Perhaps real culture is what remains after all one has learned is forgotten.

March 12th, I Tatti

Rosamond Lehmann arrived yesterday to stay a week. Had not seen her in eighteen months. As magnificently beautiful as ever, even if a trifle stouter. Only her eyes begin to have the rusty look of age. Wonderfully, harmoniously grand features, dazzling white hair, beautiful throat and arms, untouched by the years. Predatory, a Valkyrie. At the same time a work of art in herself, an artist. What an artist in words. Yet this marvel of a woman was distraught with grief when a lover like X. abandoned her. Perhaps she has the imperative need of a lover who at the same time is a child to protect. No doubt the combination can be oppressive, and I am glad that she and I met when I was beyond danger of walking into her parlour. As a spectacle, as a talker, as an artist, I know nobody so life-enhancing.

March 17th, I Tatti

Mr. and Mrs. Irving Stone here to write a *vie romancée* of Michelangelo, knowing no word of Italian or any other foreign language. No sense of the past, yet will end by producing a vastly popular book that will be at the same time a caricature of the present way of teaching and writing about the art of the past, ignoring the art and concentrating only on the artist. Mrs. Stone brought my *Sketch for a Self-Portrait* and *Rumour and Reflection* to autograph. She pointed to my photo, done in my twenty-second year, before leaving Harvard. She was wreathed in smiles. I believe she had never heard of my writing, and feared some sinister influence on her husband's activities. The abysmal ignorance of the present average American is hard to believe until one encounters it. Curious that Jews (like the Stones) get as bad as non-Jews. Assimilated indeed! And to use the all-justifying phrase, "They get away with it, don't they." The one and only test! How different from us!

March 26th, I Tatti

Has an author the right to ignore all arrangements, to go back on all engagements, because he feels he (or she) must write, suffers a *crise de travail*? Again and again I have been left in the lurch by scribblers. Of course the *crise* may have been an excuse for getting rid of me. The worst sinner was Edith Wharton. In the midst of a program of travel she would announce that she must stop and write, upsetting all our plans for days, even for weeks to come. Nothing could persuade her to go on with us, even if assured we would try to shorten the trip to the utmost. Possibly she could not stand our chatter any longer. Possibly she had a "date" with Walter Berry. I doubt it. I believe it really was as irresistible for her as what is known as a "call of nature." I used to resent in less creative writer friends the supreme importance they gave to their work, as if a sacred, sacramental function, of which they were the priests and protagonists.

March 28th, I Tatti

Nearly every other day there is a change of flowers on the dining table. I devour them with my eyes, the beauty of their drawing, the grace of their movement, the intensity of their colour. Yet withal a delicacy of touch, as of dew falling on them in the open air. As I gaze at them ecstatically I ask, "Why art?" Never have I seen any attempt at reproducing flowers, not even in Gentile da Fabriano, Fra Angelico, or Van der Goes, that remotely compared with them. As for later, say seventeenth- and eighteenth-century flower paintings, they simply disgust me, knowing as I do what real flowers are as works of art. Then what is the use of painting? Surely to teach us to appreciate the beauty of things that painting cannot touch. Not in flowers alone, but in all objects natural or man-made, as for instance Chardin's *natures mortes*, the visual arts lead us to become artists ourselves, needing nobody to tell us what and how to see as artists.

473

April 1st, I Tatti

Perhaps, though I am nearly deaf, my hearing of sounds has grown too sensitive. I am continually startled by banging, slamming, no thought of trying to put things down on tables gently, to move a chair without horrid scraping of floor. Perhaps, owing to the street noises of every kind of vehicle and their trumpets, nervous hurry and flurry, people have lost the capacity for being gentle, for doing things quietly. At my own table I have to hold myself down, might and main, not to jump up on hearing an even more than ordinary bang, or even screech of crockery, or of knives and forks. Guests seem perfectly used to these sounds. I repeat, I may be abnormally oversensitive owing to the nervousness of extreme old age, and all the bodily discomforts that go with it. Yet I cannot help feeling that we now live in a louder, more violent world.

April 3rd, I Tatti

The moment I begin to recall this or that episode of my past, out comes reminiscence after reminiscence, and in more and greater abundance, in detail, each detail summoning another. It would take another lifetime like mine to record all I seem able to conjure up from the Sheol of my own past. That reminds me that when very young, I seriously thought of writing novels, but could think of the novel only as an "ocean-stream-of-story," something like what decades later was realized by Proust. I fear it would have turned out more like Jules Romains, or even Galsworthy, than like the divinely gifted and perverse Proust. Of course I ought to make an effort, considering I have the bad luck of being "in the news," to give my version of my career and character, rather than to leave it to people who cannot possibly know who and what I really am. After all, what does it matter? Oblivion a day sooner or later, for all is destined to a *nox est una dormienda*. So let me live in present and future while still alive.

474

April 21st, I Tatti

In all realms of life, thought, politics, actuality, literature, all the arts, I am sufficiently competent to draw out individuals who each in his own field knows more than I do. They are happy being pleasantly drawn out, milked, helped to deliver what they gladly say. Invariably they leave convinced it is I who have been the brilliant talker. I recall a visit of Santayana's at Logan Pearsall Smith's during the First World War. For days I kept drawing him out on all subjects within his horizon—vast enough. As he was leaving he turned to my wife and said, "How brilliant B.B. has been, as never before." Yesterday it was Mattioli, the head of the Banca Commerciale, and a great patron of learning and literature. I asked him question after question, one leading to another. He answered copiously, and I could feel he was enjoying himself. I certainly did no more. Yet I am sure he left me believing I did all the talking, and was inspiring as never before. The truth is that he was as never before—often tongue-tied.

April 22nd, I Tatti

I do not miss the magical, the faërie world of popular Christianity (perhaps because I was not brought up to it), nor actively its ritual. I love them nevertheless, and am deeply stirred by them, particularly by Roman and even more by Orthodox ritual. Not only do I enjoy them as art performances, but I feel enlarged, exalted, inspired, freed for the moment from all that is sordid—as so much is sordid—in myself. Yet I make little effort to indulge in them. Partly due to physical, senile debility, but also to the fact that here in Florence there is small chance of satisfying a craving for them. In Rome I could not resist frequenting them, even if I had to be carried there. How happy I used to be, long ago when the Tsars supported it, in the Russian church in Paris, where the beadles always took me for one of them, or afterwards in the new church of poor Russian exiles on the Avenue Sébastopol, pathetically reconstructing all the iconography and paraphernalia of Orthodoxy.

475

April 25th, I Tatti

So uncomfortable, when not in acute pain, or sickening nausea and dizziness, that I long for easeful death. Yet underneath all that, part of me clings to life at all costs, even as La Fontaine's *cul de jatte*. I wish I could die in my sleep, or even in any sudden instantaneous way. What I dread is seeing the end, and far enough away to allow of every kind of intervening worry and figment of a disturbed imagination. I fear as well wearing out Nicky, and leaving her a wreck, yet having to cope with all the confusion that will occur the moment I die. I fear most of all being both deaf and blind, unable to communicate with anybody or anything, and *broyant le noir* as the chief occupation of the surviving mind. Haunted by recollections of all the meanness, furtiveness, snobbishness, dishonesties of one's past, no matter how distant, indeed all but from infancy—censoriousness besides, vindictiveness, unkindness, calumnies.

May 5th, I Tatti

Yesterday's visitors. First to my bedside, two American Jewesses from Boston. The elder still handsome and distinguished, born in U.S.A., but of highly cultivated parents from Königsberg. The younger, her daughter, an exquisite creature, delicate and lovely, a professional pianist. To lunch, our intimate Kiki Ritter, with her Kurdish lady friend, as European and Mediterranean as possible. To tea, a Florentine couple. He a lightning auto addict, responsible for more than one death. Very mild. The wife a masterful-looking person, handsome in a hard way, eloquent, explaining how she is descended from a Medieval family, and still owns the town house where they lived. Both eager (I wonder for what reason) I should go soon to see how they have dealt with a famous villa that now belongs to them. While she was elocutioning, telephone calls obliged Nicky to go away, and when she returned I was distracted with curiosity to know who and what. A sample of a relatively quiet day, with only two persons at a time, yet how kaleidoscopic! I wonder whether I could get on without it!

476

May 6th, I Tatti

At my age what is it to be happy? Nothing spiritual or even mental. I fear it consists in one's bowels not troubling, but being warm, quiet, and comfortable. That first and foremost. Then of being relatively free from burning toes and finger tips, from a feeling of bloatedness, from stabbing aches and pains anywhere, from nausea and a disgusting taste in the mouth, from difficulties with bladder and intestine—in short, to be free from every kind of physical *malaise*. All negative, except perhaps the peace of the bowels, which does seem positive, and not mere alleviation, or even removal of pain. Shall I end that way, happy in my bowels and satisfied, all else of the infinitely detailed universe forgotten, ignored as in infancy—to which indeed extreme old age may be the complete return?

Why, what, whither? The mere joy of living, of having enjoyed bodily pleasure, satisfaction of the intellect, ecstasies, and transubstantiation of erotic impulses into visions, distant prospects of a freedom from animality that would transfigure. Is it not enough? More is unconceivable, mere verbiage.

May 7th, I Tatti

First impression of Steinbeck. Bulky, heavy, seeming to have to work hard to give utterance to words. In that way a curious parallel to Silone. Probably it is my fault, although neither deliberate nor even conscious on my part. Neither feels at ease with me. Steinbeck was set up by my appreciation of his work, and before leaving said I "had given him a shot in the arm." He is not a dainty stylist, to be sure, but the reason for his being so little appreciated at home lies not there. Rather in the fact that he does not howl against persons and systems supposed to be responsible for the evils of the day, but attributes them to unavoidable as well as invisible forces and movements, as is the case in his *Grapes of Wrath*. But he is hard on agitators who make a profession of stirring up trouble, with bad results to their victims. For my part, I fear that like Faulkner, like Hemingway, he has come to the end of his tether, has written himself out and does not know what next. As he has written no verse or criticism, he is not likely to take to them now, as some hitherto successful novelists are doing. I look forward to getting more out of him.

May 12th, I Tatti

With the eyes I live and enjoy more than ever before. The road sweeps in living curves before me, and helps me on like a rolling platform. Distance fascinating beyond possibility of art. Near at hand everything alive for me. Middle distances with their paths and tracks call up poignantly the hazardous climbs I used to make, and that now with *Wehmut* I can enjoy only with my eyes. But as I look far and near, I recall the friends I have had as companions on my strolls. Their number would be great if I attempted to enumerate them, and their individuality and qualities of nearly every possible nature. Loves, bedfellows, of all European nationalities, companions of an hour whom I never saw again, or intimates of a lifetime, loyal or enemy-friends, exploiting me, journalists, writers of every kind, politicians—in short, members of nearly every profession. None survive, except much younger, forty years younger, than myself. Not only gone my near contemporaries, but forgotten like the leaves of the Man tree that they were

May 15th, I Tatti

Yesterday amazed at Goldscheider's * breadth of information, and up to a point even depth, also by [his] brilliance of talk about all subjects in which I myself am interested more or less deeply. At the same time I kept wondering how anybody can be so sure of himself, feel so "in it" with everything and everybody. Then all of a sudden it seemed as if I was looking into a mirror, and saw there a somewhat distorted image of myself, and the way I must seem to others. Has G., however, my humility before cerebral, mental, intellectual superiors, that I always have had, the reverence, the awe even I have felt and that now more than ever fills me toward them? That will be my plea before the "Great

* Ludwig Goldscheider, Austrian-born English art historian and critic; partner in Phaidon publishing house.

White Throne," when I come to beg for salvation, and the right to be one who on the whole has always been on the side of the angels. Any rhetorical appearance of dogmatism, of superiority to others, has been followed by restless doubts about myself, my convictions and self-assertions. Surely my writing gives glimpses of all this, and my more than readiness to reconsider, and to ask forgiveness for, my errors, even if made only yesterday.

May 16th, I Tatti

Yesterday with Goldscheider of Phaidon Press examined illustrations for two-volume edition of *Venetian Catalogue*. I expected to fall out after half an hour at most. Instead I was at it for an hour and a half, and he gave up before I did. He is reported to have been amazed by the quickness of my decisions, and their acceptability. Walked in inner garden for fifteen minutes talking to Willy [Mostyn-Owen]. Lunched, and talked to U.S.A. Consul Fisher,* still feeling alert. Siesta followed by Serristori for tea. Either I already was played out or her enunciation was so unusually indistinct that it was a serious strain to understand her. After she left perused papers and illustrated art publications. By that time I was *kaput*. To dine, Marina Volpi-Luling and her niece. Was dullest of hosts, half asleep and trying hard to hide it. Felt ashamed of myself at such an exhibition of senility. It was a stunt of a day for a frail body of ninety-two. Must beware of repeating it, and of illusory *regagne de jeunesse. Entbehren sollst du, sollst entbehren.* How hard to have to give in!

May 22nd, I Tatti

The work done by young men, yet as old as Kenneth Clark, seems to me miraculously superhuman. Yet historically, I know that I worked as hard up to that age, and harder perhaps until thirty-five, and kept on fairly well till seventy. I now cannot believe it, picture it, understand it. A day full of work and play, and not of gingerly attention to aches, pains, and nausea, is now

* Dale Fisher (1919–61), U.S. Consul in Florence, 1956–58; killed in airplane accident in Abyssinia.

beyond my imagining. Of course, I know it exists, I see what is done all around me, but I do not, cannot, translate it into terms of my own present so limited capacities. It is a curious instance of knowing but not believing, as we know that we are going to die but do not believe it. Nor can we, although knowing that it is not so, really believe that we shall be as dead as the fallen leaves of autumn. We always think of ourselves as seeing and feeling over what will be going on in the world we have left with our bodies only, but not with our continuous awareness. Knowing seems to have little influence on believing. One of the reasons why arguments are so useless, so unconvincing.

May 23rd, I Tatti

Stupidly ignorant review in penultimate *New Statesmen* of a very poor book on Sargent. I would not agree with Boston and then London that he was one of the great painters of all times, and by far the greatest of contemporaries, and got myself disliked everywhere for standing aside. I did not fail to appreciate his draughtsmanship, his technique, his arrangements, as well as his sensory revelation of character. If he degenerated in London, it was due to sitters who would be done by him. As a man he was good company, although not overexpressive. A musician, a great and selective reader, an appreciator, a loyal friend. Was he a lover of women? To return to his art, his water colours always delightful, particularly those of Venice. Failed utterly as decorator. As "murals" I know nothing less appropriate to their walls than his in the Boston Public Library. The contemptuous indifference toward him is sure to pass, and I prophesy that he will be appreciated at his value.

May 24th, I Tatti

Even greater than for Sargent was the mass enthusiasm over Burne-Jones. On his death the contents of his studio fetched fabulous prices at auction. Then a flop. Nobody deigns to look at him. Pictures of his scarcely find buyers nowadays, and not long after his demise could be had for a song. But I still appreciate his combination of Mantegna's contours with Fra Filippo's wistfulness. I still admire his ornamentation of furniture, as I lived with it in Lady Horner's house in Fitz-Harding Street, London. I have seen a sketchbook filled with rapid, veristic, human, almost improper drawings of his. Indeed, I may be his last admirer, although never joining in the mass cult prevailing in England (and to some degree in U.S.A.) during his own later years. So in my career I never could join mass enthusiasm over writers or composers, but I still retain my measured admiration and pleasure in their work. In short, I am not subject to contagion, to verbo-intoxication. Never has the crowd wrenched me off my bearings, except perhaps for Wilson's proposal after World War I of a League of Nations.

May 28th, I Tatti

Am continuously asked if I know young and youngish men, to fill different posts connected with art directing or teaching. John Walker of Washington National Gallery in search of under-director. Harvard in search of a professor to replace Meiss,* dealers want people I can recommend as advisers. No American or British available, and even German Jews, who still hold the field of art "teaching" and administrating, are beginning to give out. What is it due to? No diminution of mere curiosity about the arts of the past. There has never been so much of it as now, thanks to countless publications reproducing every phase of them, although more particularly the decadent European or the pre-Classical arts, and all barbarian *primitifs*. Idle curiosity, leading nowhere, merely listless turning over of picture books. Tending if anywhere only to justify every type of contemporary "anti-art" as I call it. Understanding little, students turn to an interest in the life stories of past artists, and almost altogether away from art (as I understand it) and artistic personalities.

* Millard Meiss, American art historian and critic; Professor of Fine Arts at Harvard; since 1957, Fellow of Princeton Institute of Advanced Study.

May 31st, I Tatti

I leave today for Naples, dread the train and hate to leave home comforts. Too weak to put order before leaving. So piles of books remain everywhere, and all sorts of papers and magazines, still unread, presents of books I ought to thank for even though sent by authors, hoping a word that their publishers can cite in advertisements. Hard to believe I shall be able to get out and about in Naples, where I love to roam on foot, and where there is so much I long to see again. I dread still more all acquaintances in Rome, whom I want to see. Knowing as I do how quickly I give out, and the humbler ones may take offense and turn sour if I do not see them. Strange how little I look forward to seeing pictures—excepting Villa Borghese. Classical Antiquity still grips me as no other phase of art, and Classical ruins, even down to latest period, as in very early Christian mosaics. Of later periods I scarcely think, excepting the one artist I love beyond all others, Botticelli, and him only in his middle phase, neither embryonic nor decadent.

June 1st, I Tatti

I leave home and *a fortiori* other places with no wrench, and once gone would never return unless indeed I want to revisit them for their works of art. What I mean to say is that I am not a bit sentimental about places, and coming to think of it, about friends. I leave them without pangs of any sort—unless of course they are absolutely necessary for my existence, like Nicky or, in the merely hygienic sphere, Emma. Others, no matter how affectionate I feel toward them, I can take leave of easily, perhaps with some relief in many cases. For most of my relations with people after eighty years of living with them are based on "making a noise as if" one cared for nobody else but the one present or to whom I am writing. In other words, except for Nicky, I take all contacts with others as part of my very extensive play-life, and as not indispensable. How much of *als ob*. If I have Nicky, reading matter, writing material, and creature comforts, I easily get on anywhere. I prefer places where I can enjoy walks, and things to see, architecture particularly.

June 2nd, Naples

Left Florence little before 5 P.M. To see us off, William Mostyn-Owen and his girl friend, obviously destined to be a *femme fatale*. Pullman car not crowded. Across the aisle a very brainy-looking man reading in a book, and smoking, eating, and drinking all the way to Rome. A superior person, a business lawyer perhaps, yet nibbling and munching like any beast of the field. How like most of us, and how much of us remains beast of the field, the best of us like sheep and cattle, nibbling and munching and drinking all the waking hours. My ribs ached from keeping same position. Relieved somewhat by pacing up and down. Excellent dinner, very tender veal such as I never get at home, and vegetables all served piping hot, and of course not warmed over. After feeding, Nicky got attendants to make a sofa out of two easy chairs, where I dozed comfortably till we reached Mergellina. Met by flunkeys of Excelsior, "making a noise as if" ever so happy to see me. Bakshish ennobled to a real feeling. Then drive along Chiaia, brilliantly overlit, but few people sitting or walking. Hotel, given royal reception, and found Emma, who had come in the car with Parry, luggage upstairs, and my room looking exactly as it did when I occupied it two years ago. I confess I enjoyed the warm reception as to a home-coming.

June 3rd, Naples

I did not believe in the possibility of a great museum at Capodimonte. I did not count with getting across to the money-bags, even the *Cassa del Mezzogiorno* existing, I fancied, solely for the improvement of the most indigent South. This capacity for organization even has taste. Every room carefully coloured down to pavement as best suited for the pictures exhibited. Behind screens serving the lighting, access to views of pell-mell Naples. I was speechless with admiration, and every preconception against it, and I had many, vanished so completely that I cannot recall

483

them. I dare say this or that trifling criticism could be made here and there, but only after recovering from the shock of the general impression. I first met Molaioli * in his native Fabriano, where he was connected with the trifling local museum. I had not the faintest idea that I ever would see him again, still less hear of him. What fertility of talent and even genius may spring up in any village of Italy. History is crowded with them. Even today the man who is said to be one of the most powerful businessmen in Europe "stems" from a tiny place in a rarely visited province, a certain Mattei.† One could compose actually a gazetteer of genius on the Italian peninsula.

June 4th, Naples

Saw this morning at the Museo Nazionale an Alexandrian obsidian cup some six inches across, adorned on the outside with Isiac episodes in traditional Egyptian style. Incrustations of gold, amethyst, lapis, enamel, technically so perfect as to achieve an effect of splendour, of gorgeousness, yet of fabulous good taste. Glanced here and there at treasures of silver, gold, crystal, glass, ceramics, with their ever so inventive patterns all based on anthropomorphic or zoomorphic elements. The invention, the variety, the achievement took my breath away. I panted with eagerness to indulge my appetite for them, to live with them until I had memorized every one of them. What artisans they were in Antiquity, each artisan an artist. What has been done since in the West is crude and heavy and unimaginative in comparison. Not even when done by the most refined Italian or French or most inventive German. With rare exceptions they owe their best to attempts to copy Antiquity, even when least aware of how much they owed to its traditions!

* Bruno Molaioli, Italian art historian, on the staff of the Fine Arts Service; since 1958 Director General of Fine Arts in Rome.
† Enrico Mattei (1906–62). One of the most outstanding figures of postwar Italy. Leading Partisan during World War II, founder and President of E.N.I., founder of the city of Metanopolis, killed in an air accident in October 1962.

June 8th, Naples

Goethe horrified his world by marrying the widow of a humble parson. He knew what he was about. He knew how strong in him was the mere animal. Frau Vulpius could satisfy the two imperious animal demands, food and sex. We know she fed him to his satisfaction, and we may be sure she afforded him complete sexual relief. Free from this sexual preoccupation, he not only could work better at his numerous and varied tasks, but enjoy real friendships with women. Friendships with women are never sex-free, but sublimated into an atmosphere of delicate, subtle tenderness. It is an exquisite relation, and perhaps the inspiration of much of the very noblest painting, music, and above all of poetry. It has played a great part in my own life, ever so much more than mere animal sexuality. Disguise this as you will, it ends in lust, and lust lasts but a time, unless the woman is, as no doubt Frau Vulpius was, expert at keeping a male "happy." Sublimated sex can last a lifetime. It certainly has in mine. My friendship with the Serristori began sixty years ago, could easily have degenerated into passion. I had the sense not to let it, and now that she is eighty-six and I ninety-two we are sweeter to one another than ever before. Sublimated relations with women can last forever. I fear that is seldom the case with friendships between men, even when not homosexual.

June 14th, Naples

Looked out this morning to see the dawn over Vesuvius. Exquisite harmony of tone and colour, quiet, silent, peaceful sky, brightening, but far from presaging the garish light of common day. For me it was a work of art beyond any painting done by human hand, yet as much an art product, but reaching far beyond its goal. Thousands of poets have described it. Who of them asked how it was done? Even Ruskin, who attempted to drag in geology to explain our love of nature, would not have attempted anything but an ecstatically lyrical account of what I saw this dawn. Nature as mere visibility carries us away captive, and we never ask how she did it.

485

June 16th, Rome

Via dei Tribunali, and all that centre of Angevin Naples, can only be seen on foot, and I can no longer dart about tirelessly to ferret out this and that church or cloister, or gallery. So farewell to my Naples of old, which from my twenty-third year I know inch by inch as it were. In this case I must say, *"Fontaine, fontaine, je ne boirai plus de ton eau."* I shall confine myself, returning to Naples, to what I can approach in the car. Even in museums I shall be able to do less and less, if not in a wheeled chair. Not of course in Naples alone, but everywhere—a *Farewell to Arms*. Cultivate resignation. *Ergebe dich in deine Pein,* and you will be rewarded with the peace of a vegetable.

June 17th, Rome

Very often American friends never write. You conclude they have forgotten you. You regret and think of the transitoriness of human relations. One fine day they bob up serenely, are as cordial, no, more affectionate than ever before. The Dunns today were an example. Could not have been more loving, more tender to my senility. Could have listened to him from dawn to sunlight touching on his various ambassadorships. Most interesting on Spain and France and then on Brazil. Now settled for good in most attractive apartment at top of Caetani Palace, with fascinating view of Ara Coeli, and all that is under it. Seem very happy to be retired, with nothing to do except enjoy the day. How I envy people who can retire, because their job is ended. For my kind there is no retirement. One is driven by a demon till he too is too weak, too near the end, to carry on. One stops but does not retire.

June 21st, Rome

Museo delle Terme. How freely I breathe in the midst of all that is exhibited there. Scarcely an object, a fragment, that does not excite zestful interest. As for aesthetic delight, few works of art give me more than the *Dying Niobide,* the youth from Subiaco, the "Ludovisian throne," the murals of Villa Livia

486

from Prima Porta. Hundreds of works inferior to those just named, yet attractive and enjoyable even if only copies—but what copies!— of great originals, as for instance the rather slack *Lancellotti Discobolus*. The paintings make me feel as if in an enclosed garden, with luscious fruit on the branches, birds singing, a "paradise." So my appetite now is ever so much more for Antique sculpture than for any other phase of European art. Except for the greatest and most rustic, homely painters—wild asparagus— I care less and less for the "Old Masters." I really prefer the French of the so-called Impressionist period, or even from David down to the death of Degas. Minor Trecento painters, mere artisans, bore me, unless indeed I take them as handicraft. I still keep asking how much of Italian painting would affect me if I were not interested in attributing and dating them. Little, I fear!

June 22nd, Rome

With Vittorio Cini to the Vigna di Papa Giulio. As architecture every prospect pleases, nothing meets the eye that is vile. The museum admirably arranged, perhaps a little too didactically. As always in a museum, I say nothing, or next to nothing. Yet in going out, Cini said that seeing with me made him feel as if he were seeing with my eyes and not his. I first heard the exact words on the lips of Isabella Gardner, nearly seventy years ago, leading her to ask whether, as I accompanied her through the London Gallery, pictures like those I took her to see could still be had. Fatal moment, destined to have such an effect on my career—although not on me. Well, what is it that makes people say that they see with my eyes, although I say next to nothing? Is it *osmose*? I try to find more manifest explanations. Perhaps it is the way I pass by so much and stop to look only when something interests me, and the way I look at it, with concentrated attention, and perhaps a few movements of my hands, as if to caress the object, perhaps a word or two. They go away feeling as if they had enjoyed an artistic experience.

June 24th, Rome

Yesterday to the Pantheon. Nothing I have seen anywhere comparable to its grandeur, to its splendour. Down to fifth or sixth century A.D. no edifice elsewhere but finds its origin in structures like this Pantheon. Pity the bronze tiles of the ceiling have disappeared. In other respects it is miraculously well preserved. One travels far and wide, and comes back to Rome, amazed to find the best is there. It reminds me of Hawthorne's story of the man who wanders the world over to discover a treasure, and returns home empty-handed. But as he treads on his doorstep the stone gives way, and there is the treasure he is looking for. Rome gathered to itself not only the wealth of the empire and all its resources, but the best talents, and among them the best artists. What they did here no doubt surpassed what with more limited resources they could achieve elsewhere. We need not attribute to the Latin population of Rome all the affluence, any more than what now is produced in New York is due to the descendants of the Dutch who settled there centuries ago. Like New York today, but on a grander scale, Rome absorbed and used all that was most talented in the empire.

June 27th, Assisi

I start my ninety-third year with no fear of dying, but dread of getting blinder and deafer, cut off from the outer world, from reading and seeing with my own eyes—the greatest joys of my past, and reduced to what surges up from the depths of memory. What does surge up is seldom recollection of happiness, of good doing, of what others owe to me, but of the meannesses, pettinesses, nastinesses, dishonest actions committed by me in the past, even the distant ones of my childhood. I fear that sort of survival, or even worse, being reduced to a mere vegetative condition, feeling nothing, let alone thinking anything, just remaining alive, because heart and arteries still function—in short, no bright prospect—neither alive nor dead, tiring out even and particularly those who haved loved me most, and devoted their whole living to me, like Nicky on the higher level, and Emma in the care of my body. Is there a ray of hope that I shall survive spiritually as well as physiologically? Is there?

June 30th, I Tatti

After a beautiful drive through the Upper Tiber Valley, stopped at Monterchi to see its famous *Madonna del Parto* by Piero della Francesca. The taut curtain which two sturdy wenches are working hard to pull apart is realized spatially as figures are in tactile and movement values. Inside in poor condition. The Madonna a birth goddess, but not the least Antique or indeed idealized. Only a woman big with child. Nothing less spiritual here, as elsewhere in Piero. Yet because for purely artistic reasons he is so admirable, and admiration of him obligatory, he is being endowed with all the qualities most admired today—spiritual, metaphysical, psychological, transcendent, *toute la lyre*. Well illustrates Ibsen's saying that by the time the crowd discovers a truth, it has become a lie. Strange that it should happen to him and not to another great ineloquent, Velasquez. I dare say he is spared such a fate because everything nearly that he did had a clearly ascertained historical connection. Paul Veronese is too obviously decorative. Andrea del Sarto too ignored today, although much spiritual nonsense could be written about him too.

July 1st, I Tatti

For once let me boast. I have paddled my own canoe. A very tiny one, yet its wake was wide and even deep. Little has been written about Italian painting and even on art in general that was not done under my influence, or in deliberate opposition to it. The most perfidiously hypocritical of my enemies, like Roger Fry, seldom published anything not inspired by the wish to assert himself against me. Roberto Longhi knows my writings so well that he could reconstitute them if lost. Twenty-five years ago Ugo Ojetti in an article for the *Corriere* wrote that nobody who wrote on art but follows me, without ever naming me.

On the positive side let me boast of the persons who would not be what they became if I had not helped to start them. Not only in my own field, but even others. For instance it was I who

489

urged Sirén to take up with Chinese art. In the field of Italian in particular, and even art more universally, I had my hand in starting Harold Edgell, Kenneth Clark, John Walker, etc., as gallery directors, Kühnel as writer on Islamic art, Yashiro on Botticelli, even Lazareff on relation of Byzantine to Western art.* I could enumerate by patient drawing on memory many other cases. My worst adversaries, cryptic or declared, valued nothing more than a word of approval from me. Fry was always eager for it. Last time I saw him, little before his end, he literally during a party I gave cornered me to persuade me of some discovery of his. Thus far I never in print have uttered a word against my enemies, nor shall I. I am prepared for *history* to be unaware of what others owe to me, how much they parade in my clothes. My own colleagues are the least generous toward me. I have been ever so much more appreciated always by "laymen." They were not competitors, and therefore free to understand me.

July 3rd, I Tatti

A curious phenomenon is what happens to Central European and Italian Jewish scholars in America. Refined, modest, even shy before, they become blatant, slangy, with sweeping arms and positive enunciation, adopting the most unattractive American society manners. This does not seem to be the case with German and Italian gentiles who go to the States. So I am led to ask what it is that makes the Jew in the U.S.A. become the vulgarian he so very frequently is. Can it be that in Europe he still feels that he must be on his best behaviour if he is to get on? Does he in New York for instance feel that he must get assimilated as soon as possible, and that assimilation to the vulgar is so much

* Osvald Sirén, Swedish art historian, author of numerous articles and treatises on Chinese art; began by studying Italian art in Florence.—Harold Edgell (1887–1954), American art historian, Director of Fine Arts Museum, Boston, 1935–54; prepared his first book on the Sienese school of painting in the Tatti library.—Ernst Kühnel, German scholar of Islamic art; began by studying Florentine Quattrocento painting, and was a frequent guest at I Tatti at that time.—Victor Lazareff, Russian art historian, special field Byzantine art, Member of the Academy of Science, Moscow.

more natural than to be assimilated to the quiet, the unassuming, the refined? It is a phenomenon worth study. The result cannot be helpful to any but the increasing number of anti-Semites in the U.S.A.—to some extent encouraged by the Arabophile U.S.A. State Department.

July 6th, I Tatti

Italy should be seen at this season. A couple of days ago I had a glimpse of the Baptistery, Cathedral, and Giotto's Tower. They looked radiant in their splendour, as indeed I recall every building of note in Italy looks at this season. Yesterday took "Morgan Walk" for the first time in two or three years. Close at hand, a carpet of gold-flowered broom. Sky pure as crystal, distant horizon exquisitely drawn, and in between landscapes as seen by Fra Angelico. Saltino over Vallombrosa gemlike. Recalled a long stay at Siena thirty years ago at this season, and how Nicky and I enjoyed colour and shape despite melting heat. Was told decades ago that to enjoy Jerusalem, you should see it at midday in midsummer, when contrast between sun and shadow is beyond words fascinating. Senses curiously receptive when one is languishing with heat, and readily stirred erotically. I recall how much I enjoyed love-making afternoons on boiling summer days, long, long ago.

July 21st, Vallombrosa

Walking yesterday forenoon in the nursery garden between here and church, suddenly collapsed, could barely drag myself to the top. Felt as if spine was ready to double up like a pocket-knife, and shoulders detached from each other. Was taken to a sort of shed where workmen were having their luncheon. They not only let me sit down, but opposite a fire, were touching in their readiness to do all possible for my comfort, as Italians always will in presence of physical pain. I could scarcely sit, and felt as if I must stretch out on no matter what. Nicky asked one to run and get the car, for I could not have walked back. It came in a jiffy, and they tenderly put me in, and in a few minutes I was in bed with high fever and alarming pain. Everything done to

491

make me comfy, but with no results. Doctor came this morning, and found fever abated, and followed by deadly weakness. Better as day advanced. Fever not returned. "Walking in the fear of the Lord" but yet aware that "His mercy endureth for ever." Life now is exciting enough, suffering all the caprices and tricks of my body. Incalculable and frightening, and one wonders how long it can go on.

July 24th, Vallombrosa

When Job appeals to Jehovah to explain why he who fulfilled his part of the contract, and was in every way a just and good man, was so badly treated, all Jehovah did was to jeer at Job, and to refer to His own almightiness, rejoicing in His power and jeering at His victim. He, Jehovah, behaved like a cannibal demon, rather than an all-merciful deity. He taught poor humanity fear, fear, and only fear. Gods laughed at the humans they were torturing or making fun of, before driving them to suicidal madness, as did the Bacchus of Euripides, and indeed for most part Homer's gods, not ferocious perhaps, but vindictive if in the least offended, and amused by human discomfiture. How did the grim, jeering, sneering God of Job become "the Lord is my shepherd" of the Psalms? I know of no historical process by which this change came about. Surely nothing known to us that Israel could have picked up during the seventy years' exile in Mesopotamia. Rather perhaps the ripening of the species Homo. Why this should have happened in Judea as nowhere else, and produce songs that as psalms are still sung, chanted, recited all over the wide-flung Christian world, probably will never be known. Plato may have had the idea of such a God even before the Judeans, but did not make it effective as they did. It has been carried further by Christianity, first in the East Christian world, then from St. Francis on, and sentimentalized and dulcified by the Jesuits. All in all, it has never found more genuine expression than in the Psalms.

July 27th, Vallombrosa

After tea yesterday drove out to Saltino and beyond toward Reggello. View over badlands and the hills beyond veiled and suggestively mysterious. Drove back toward sunset, and clouds took on Tintoretto twilight colours, golden brown streaming out of crystal blue, and bordered with plum-colour. More and more gorgeous every minute, and as we drove on where thick woods shut off the landscape, diamond glints reached us. When we got to open again, sky was clear and sun refulgent, and I could descry the distant Carrara mountains stretching toward Modena. From my bed, I enjoyed the *rose Du Barry* afterglow, until it too paled and died away. Dramatic sunsets here almost every evening, and *vivaio* between Casa al Dono and church, as if made to be a theatre for the spectacle of the sun going down, transforming landscape before us into a magic land; cloud and reflection on Val d'Arno toward Fiesole, and Florence owing to light thrown up from its windows, felt rather than seen. Clouds above, of all possible shapes, forming and melting.

August 2nd, Vallombrosa

Beyond, *jenseits, au delà* in all fields, but particularly in personal feeling. I recall vividly how as a little boy I wore out my thin legs running as hard as I could to get beyond the horizon. Even now at ninety-two I never face a distant prospect without longing for the *Beyond*. I shall never forget how some miles out of Konia eastward, I saw the Sultan Dag and yearned to get beyond, and beyond and beyond. In all realms of knowledge, "Yes, but what then and then and then?" Almost from infancy I have been obsessed by the Beyond, the still to be experienced, chiefly in the world of space, and what exists in visible space and all that thereon is. I never go to Naples without hankering for Sicily, and there for Tunis, and at Tunis for the Sahara. Not quite the same in the North. At Stockholm I had no desire to go beyond Upsala. Nor does the west of the U.S.A. attract me. Always rather the South, Yucatán for instance, Peru, never the tundra and ice of Northern Canada or Siberia. Beyond the *"flamantis moenis mundi,"* always, at the faintest suggestion, *Dahin, dahin!*

August 3rd, Vallombrosa

From being an author taken seriously, although seldom too keenly, I have declined to the role of *bénisseur*. Writers and publishers want introductions and prefaces to books on subjects even that I have never written about myself. Nor can I pen a few lines about a book sent to me without its being used at once in reviews and advertisements. The more unable I get the more is asked of me, as if I could still do the work of a young man. They seem oblivious of my extreme old age, while it is that which gives me the authority to commend their publications. How much I could now write if only I could work as I used to, hours at a time, day after day, week after week, month after month. Now I am glad and happy if I can do half an hour of real writing, not scribbling of letters in a devil-may-care way. I see clearly now what seemed murky before. I can bulldoze through walls of piled-up pedantry and irrelevancy, get straight at the significant—if only, if only!

August 11th, Vallombrosa

A few days ago I read an article on Malraux. It compared his breadth of interest in art with mine, confined to a couple of centuries of Italian painting. As a matter of fact, my curiosity has led me further afield than Malraux. Whatever has been found dating from the earliest period to the art of today, I am acquainted with. The library of I Tatti is my witness. No publication there I have not read, or at least perused. It covers the whole world's art not only with printed matter, but with photos, including Chinese, Japanese, all the Indias, etc. But I have never wanted to write except of what I knew as much of as at present can be known. With that in mind, Italian painting from 1300 to 1600 has been more than enough to absorb the last seventy years of my life. However, I have always written with a sense and feeling for the whole world's art in the back of my mind. The sober fact is I have not failed to recognize quality in every phase of visual art while it was art, down to circa 1900.

August 12th, Vallombrosa

The Menuhins * to stay. She over-talkative, pirouetting like the dancer and actress she used to be, and more Jewish-looking than he. He not at all. Possibly short hairs on limbs and chest, whose colour tends toward rusty red, may be Semitic. He is beautifully built, complexion pale ivory, characteristically Russian. Angelic temper and talk. Quiet, modest, keen nevertheless not only in music. Interested in Israel and Zionism, distressed by U.S.A. Jews attacking Israel. Showed photos of his mother, reading. Looks like any Daughter of the American Revolution. Played Bach, a joy to hear, gave me the feeling his violin needed no accompaniment, as if it had its own. Great lover of Indian music, which he finds subtle, delicate, varied, and always fascinating. I perceive in him no sign of that aloofness of feeling above and beyond all other musicians, of which Igor Markevich accused him the other day. My body servant Emma indignant at his coming in shorts to the table of Mr. Berenson. For lunch only, dressing for dinner. I have seldom had a more satisfactory and stimulating visit. Yehudi is the sort of person I could wish to have access to every day. I was deeply gratified that they came from Gstaad on purpose to see us and turn back.

August 25th, Vallombrosa

While with Catholics I can sympathize with them, and even share their point of view. The moment I turn my back on them I begin to doubt, and soon recover my equilibrium. The most flagrant instance was my becoming at twenty-six a Catholic, owing to sympathy with and pressure from my future wife, then a fervent Catholic. The ground had been well prepared by my enjoyment of Catholic ritual, not only in the grand manner of St. Peter's or Sant'Anselmo, but even as bawled out at vespers in humble village churches. No sooner received than I began to doubt, and before long resumed my normal attitude, one of delight in the Church as a work of art, from every point of view, and

* Yehudi Menuhin, the violinist, married to Diana Gould; lived in the Tatti Villino, 1958–60.

495

another of great disapproval of the attitude of its highest prelacy toward the laity. These regard the laity as clay in their potters' hands, or to be got rid of. Far from conceding that they exist for us laymen, they insist that we shall be their sheep and little lambs. Their pride, their arrogance, their lust for power, their greed for money, their institutionalism, "met with my highest disapproval." But I feel more or less the same about all institutions. Intended to carry out an ideal, they almost invariably, given human nature, become their own end, all for their own advantage.

August 31st, Vallombrosa

Vorrei e non vorrei. How much that is the state of most mortals with regard to almost everything that requires a thoughtful decision. Of course we all obey physiological instinct, and no doubt most people carry mere instinct into all their activities, like all other animals in fact. But like "the woman who hesitates is lost," the moment we begin to reflect, to question, to hesitate, we too are lost. But the Siegfrieds of the Nibelungen, the Alexanders, the Caesars, were they, the last two I mean, incapable of hesitation until indeed they had conquered the world, and then and then only hesitated not knowing what to do further, saved from who knows what follies by Alexander's death at thirty-three, and Caesar's by his assassins—and let us add Napoleon by his defeat at Waterloo. Indeed, one may add as an axiom that conquering is easy, but to know what to do afterward—there is the rub. What an interesting question, whether there have been in history conquerors who knew what to do when there were no more worlds to conquer. Perhaps outside our "Latin" world, Asiatic conquerors, Akbar and his like. In our limited private life *Vorrei e non vorrei* takes comic shapes. For instance I feel worried, harrowed, besieged by people who want to have a look at me, who ask me for articles, and even books, for prefaces, for recommendations, etc. Yet I am sure I should feel neglected and forgotten if I really was left alone. I feel for instance an infinitesimal moment of resentment against anybody of mark, or any budding art historian, who comes to Florence and does not "ask for an audience." My wife as a young girl befriended Walt Whit-

496

man, and when she went to England brought an introduction from him to Tennyson. Was invited to lunch, and during the meal the poet kept complaining of Americans who besieged his place so as to get a look at him, and of others who, invited to the house, would not go away without insisting on carrying away an autographed photograph. My wife, determined not to ask for such a gift, was approached by the poet's eldest son, who whispered, "Be sure to ask him for an autographed photograph." Likewise, we feel left out if not invited to parties we would not go to, and feel an instant of a twinge of pain when finally, knowing we would not go, people stop asking us. Let me add that I never committed the sin of taking pleasure in boasting that I had been asked but knew better than to accept.

September 12th, Vallombrosa

I do not recall taking an avid interest in politics in my early years. Nor was I a newspaper reader. I was merely convinced that the U.S.A. and England always acted up to their ideals, and that other countries seldom did. The Oscar Wilde trial in London gave me a shock I never got over, and habituated me to newspapers. What do I now get out of them, but despair at the crumbling of my Judeo-Greco-Roman-*founded* universe? The only possibility of preserving some of it is through Roman Catholicism. Yet that too may give up Latin for the laity and confine it to the priesthood, nay to prelacy only. I read reviews so as to learn what to add to my library, and what is contained in books that I shall not find time to read. I get sick with despair over the neglect, if not utter contempt, of common sense, of reasonableness. These always have seemed to me like a match lit in a pitch-black night, that we should do all we could to keep going, instead of blowing it out deliberately or through stupidity. I should be ever so much more comfortable if I could stop interesting myself in the present, a present no longer mine, and confine myself to my present, which begins with the beginning of history, and ends with the First World War.

497

September 22nd, I Tatti

Moses on Pisgah looked toward the promised land which he was not to tread. At the brink of the grave, I do not look forward but backward. Much as from books and photos I am acquainted with the arts of Further Asia, I do not hanker for them. I do for all that in the last seventy years I have seen myself, from Upsala to the Sahara, from Gibraltar to the Euphrates. Seldom a day when I am not filled with longing for some place I already am familiar with. One day it may be Kairouan and another Salamanca, and all that is near them. And how I should yearn for Florence and Italy, if I was stuck as I am here in any other place. Yearning, longing, *Wehmut,* are not negative, but positive states of being. One lives more by them than by merely animal actuality, so easily identified with happiness. "A divine discontent" is the condition of life for one like me. Not only would I see again all I have seen, but read again all that I have enjoyed, all that has fed my spirit, all that has formed and shaped me. And of course, I long to hear again all *die alten Weisen.* Infinite yearning.

September 27th, I Tatti

Never in my long life so courted with every kind of appealing, languishing, hypnotizing looks, as yesterday evening by a beautiful, magnificently evening-dressed young Israeli woman. Apparently came all the way from Israel to get me to do—what? Transfer I Tatti and all its contents to the Holy Land? To establish there as she suggested a Berenson House alongside of other great Jewish establishments for science and learning? To emigrate to Israel myself, and grace and enhance its coming *decennalia* with my presence? She did not quite dare to make it plain. Parried my severe criticism of Israel's submersion to rabbinism, to using Hebrew as current language, etc. Had she read a word of my writings? Did she realize my deep feeling for Catholicism, and that I regard it as detribalized Judaism, as affected by the centuries? Of course that is just what Israel does not want. It wants to persecute and isolate, and act as container for Jewish blood. To return to my bewitching Israeli lady, she left my head

498

unshorn, despite all her Delilah beguilement. I wonder what she makes of my stupid obstinacy, and the failure of her mission, if indeed mission it was.

September 28th, I Tatti

Yesterday to lunch, Louis A. Turner,* nuclear physicist. He did not know where "science" was going and said I asked him the very question he could not answer. Science as conceived by young Renan and contemporaries was going to serve strictly the purposes of a humanistic ideal of society. Could not conceive a time would come, as it now has, when it would run amok on its own, careless of mankind. As a matter of fact, the various arts as well have ceased to serve man, and each runs as far as possible from any human interest. Turner recounted that when the press was announcing that Einstein had found the "secret of the universe" this great man gave them a talk in which he tried to explain what he really had discovered, and said, "It may turn out to be of some interest. If not, it will have wasted very little of your time listening to me." How modest are the rare scientists that come to see me, and how puffed up with pride the philosophers, aestheticians, and abstractionists in general. How I envy the scientists, and how I wish I were one of them, and not the magician I am taken for because of my disreputable profession!

October 2nd, I Tatti

Spent whole hour between four and five this morning coughing up phlegm, sneezing, spluttering, in utter physiological discomfort and distress. Nicky sat by and held or at least touched my hand. Her self-controlled look of cheerfulness, her caressing smile, the love she radiated made me as happy as I seldom have been, despite my troubles and self-disgust, and the despair I should have felt if she had not been sitting by me. How I love her face. I have been looking at it for nearly forty years, and every time I find it *herrlich wie am ersten Tag*. Never has one person

* American scientist, son-in-law of B.B.'s lifelong friend, the art historian Frank J. Mather (1865–1953).

served another with greater zest, devotion than she, always ready for new tasks, for answering more letters, for doing more research, for reading aloud, as if she had nothing else to do. Truly a miracle of a woman. How I depend on her, how I tremble for her health, how I worship her. I have never known a less self-regarding, a nobler creature. I feel religiously humble before her, and utterly unworthy of her. There is "no damn merit" in life, and Nicky gives me endlessly more than I deserve, almost makes me feel that I do deserve her.

October 21st, I Tatti

Anxiousness troubles many people, for no specific reason, no event. They will feel anxious anywhere, and in all safety. They may know and recognize the satisfactory conditions they enjoy, but spoil them for themselves, through quaking fear they won't last. People subject to anxiety will be anxious lest they fall ill, every symptom may be of cancer or another dire disease. If they have no material, serious cause for anxiety, they will invent them, just as the stomach when not supplied with food to digest will digest itself. I wonder whether the recent (if already diminished) cult of *angoisse* may not have been due to having nothing serious outside ourselves to worry about. So the *angoisses* had to scratch and dig, and invent all sorts of reasons, most of them fictitious, for worrying, for anxiety. Nor do people in troubles they are working hard to master have leisure for *angoisse*. May it not be brought about by so much welfare and consequent boredom, that they find relief in *angoisse*? It becomes serious on its own account when it succeeds in making song and story out of it. Then it can take the aspect of *Leiden wird Gesang*—the result hitting back and replacing the cause. *Eine alte Geschichte.* "It is worry that kills the cat."

October 25th, I Tatti

The Bible all in all is the most fascinating book of my world. I could spend a hundred years on studying it, all that it tells, all that it reveals, all its implications. In a way it is a history of the humanization of Man. It ends with a tender, loving, almost caressing relation to Deity, almost as, in many representations of the Last Supper, John hides in the bosom of Jesus. Scarcely a word, whether in Old Testament or the so very Jewish New Testament, that does not stir me to investigate, to speculate, to dream about it. No wonder it won the hearts of the *oecumene* as nothing in Greek or Latin literature had done, and that the Psalms became the most popular because the most comforting of chants, replacing everywhere what had been sung previously, and that all new hymnals were but literary versions of the Psalms. What a progress from the furious Jahve of the Pentateuch to the Lord who is my shepherd. Yet always severe, genuine, free from rhetoric. And adventurers like David, unscrupulous, vicious, vindictive, lecherous, yet endowed with a charm that makes him a man according to his God's own heart. Perfect example of truthfulness.

October 27th, I Tatti

Surely the world was ever so much more cruel, brutal, bestial in the past. The first object as you approached a town used to be the gallows and hanging victims. But one was not pelted with news of crimes and horrors from all the world, as we are now. Compared with what used to happen the world over, these incidents are few and far between. Partly we all have become more shockable, and partly newspapers do their utmost to make our flesh creep. What a mistaken tendency in human nature to fancy and fable of a golden age behind us. It has always been a bestial world, but it used to be taken for granted. Now we rebel against it, and will allow none of it, not even the few (relatively) private crimes, let alone general massacres. The last also used to be taken for granted. True, they were on an ever so much smaller, minuter scale than now, when Nazis can exterminate hundreds of thousands. But even these massacres have to be justified by the pretence that it was all for the future advantage of a race, or (as in the case of Communism) for humanity as a whole. Massacre for the mere fun of it, as in the past, is no longer allowed.

October 31st, I Tatti

A day or two ago to tea, a heavy-browed young woman with hair tending to brownish-red, great-granddaughter of John La Farge, reminded me of my meetings with him, his progeny and his art. Of Southern French stock, completely assimilated in U.S.A. A bosom friend of Henry Adams, accompanied him to the South Seas. Painter—I recall a stained-glass window in New York which used to impress me as illustration and colour together. When I knew him, he was already elderly, but tall and physically impressive. Something of a Chinese sage about him. Did he not go to Japan, and partake in the enthusiasm of Bigelow,* Denman Ross, and other Bostonians for Japanese pictures? My most vivid recollection of him is of a dinner party given by Sir William Van Horne. This Yankee builder of Canadian Pacific, and naturalized Canadian, happened to have a certain taste for Italian pictures, owing perhaps to the fact that he almost never slept, and spent hours drawing and daubing. Had invited me to stay with him at Montreal, which I did to satisfaction of both. By the way, he took me to see other collectors of the same town. All had faked Tanagra and little else. I loved the winter landscape, and a sleigh ride in the city park heaped with dazzling untrodden snow. Well, to come back to the dinner given by Van Horne in New York, I had the honour of being present. There were a number of distinguished guests. The host put me on his left. Still at the table, he began to show us his drawings. I looked and without a word passed them on to La Farge, who sat on my left. He looked and looked, and finally said, "Sir William, would you mind letting me take them home? I want to give them the study they deserve." I could have crawled under the table with shame at my dumb boredom. Yet I was enraptured with admiration of La Farge's diplomacy and tact. It was a lesson I never forget, although it is not in my nature to profit by it. I often recall it, and always with the same admiration. La Farge died soon after, and his descendants male and female highly respectable, but less and less interesting. However, the young woman of two evenings ago came to Italy to see works of

* William Sturgis Bigelow (1850–1926), American physician and Orientalist.

502

art after a surfeit of photos and black and white reproductions. Some promise!

November 8th, I Tatti

To tea yesterday by my bedside, Hortense Serristori. Lucky creature at eighty-six still sees and hears normally, and digests well. Only circulation is a bit alarming. Touching to see how she clings to me now, after full sixty years of friendship, except in politics never disagreeing. It has with the exception of those storms been a glorious voyage, and how we love to be in the same room, sitting close, even without saying a word. No greater sign of deep affection—when it is not routine indifference—than to be without fear of being together without talk. *Lieder ohne Worte.* She was in ecstasy yesterday hearing Nicky read the story of Sharkan and Abriza in Mardrus' version of the *Thousand and One Nights.* Then we recalled with what enjoyment we read these volumes as they kept appearing, one after the other, and how once she exclaimed, "What shall we do without further volumes of Mardrus!" She has been a great stimulus, and has drawn out my still unshaped thoughts, and given them form—but in a French way, oversimplified, overcrystalline, with nothing left to brood over, to try to puzzle out; Spanish temperamentally, but ultra-French mentally and linguistically. Nothing she cannot express in the most elegant French mode. Indeed, France has given her the Legion of Honour for it!

November 10th, I Tatti

The other day the King of Sweden asked to see reproductions of the Shi Shoin [Treasure] Magnificent. I looked around the library (which I now frequent so seldom), and a gripping eagerness seized me to "world-forget" and be "world-forgotten," but with good enough eyes and enough strength to be able to browse all day long. What treasures in every field of art. Scarcely anything missing that really counts, from the whole earth, illustrated books from the most luxurious to the horrid Soviet publications on the prehistorical art of Siberia. Photos and magnificent reproductions of not only Italian and Greek and Roman art, but of every province of Antiquity, or Far Eastern, or Indian, or pre-Columbian American. They give me the only real satisfaction that my so-long and so-varied past can still offer me, and I cannot help returning to my library and boasting of it. If only my boundless curiosity for information and my delight in looking were not crossed by my increasing blindness, my feebleness, my bodily misery. If there be such an unimaginable thing as survival, may my spirit haunt this library, and enjoy it physically as I can no longer.

November 22nd, I Tatti

After nearly sixty years of habitation and subsequent arrangements, enlargements, etc., none much later than fifty years ago, this house is getting old and shabby itself, and disagreeable for elderly people to live in. Impossible to heat equally. One has to go through long corridors, for the most part very chilly. The house attendants I need most are nearly seventy, and feel the change from one part of the house to another. I myself no longer visit the libraries, partly for lack of time, but more because of the unequal heating. "Grow old along with me! The best is yet to be," sings Browning, but Mark Twain belches out the truth, "Cheer up, old cow, the worst is yet to be." Seeing every near one getting greyer, stouter, unattractive, coughing, hawking. Every inanimate thing mouldering, crumbling, peeling. If one were wise, one would change abode, and get attendants, fresher, younger. But would they give one the affection, the tenderness of those who have grown old along with one? Certainly not. Nor could I fail to hunger for the feeling of home, that nearly sixty years of living in the same house gives one. So the insoluble paradoxes of life go on, and will till the end of awareness—if not of life itself.

November 27th, I Tatti

We are sparks of the Sun made flesh. But how has this flesh become aware of itself! Awareness of the outside is necessary to preservation. But awareness of the inside, not as pain or pleasure, vaguely, but disinterestedly aware, curious, inspection of how (so to speak) one's own mechanism works as if a timepiece were able to do so. And will this go further and further in the course of time? What will it lead to, assuming that it is not suddenly snuffed out? I for one cannot conceive, cannot imagine, and end with a bump every time I try. Yet it absorbs, preoccupies me, as nothing else. I am haunted by it, cannot shake it off, possessed like a Central African devil, shouting "Allah, Allah" every waking minute. Always behind every thought, what I look at, what I read, what I hear, most of all when listening to music. Yet with my mind I remain an agnostic, who cannot accept what he cannot understand, except in fields of material pursuits, where however the methods are even more empirical and rational than my own. So there remains the mystery of mysticism and one's Self, the question of its Future, if indeed it is to have one.

December 7th, I Tatti

In memory I see thousands of towns and landscapes I have enjoyed. How I wish I could see them again, but I know I shall not, and with a certain wistfulness I am resigned to it. Resigned even to my walks' getting shorter and shorter. On the other hand, what I still cannot resign myself to is not writing again. My mind is full of things to write about, as memory is full (although dimly, vaguely) of what I have read and thought. I feel humiliated, crushed, angry that I no longer can even hope to write again about current matters, let alone remoter ones. Not even letters to friends. Brilliant, witty, illuminating answers occur to me, but scarcely any will ever be written. This impotence I cannot resign myself to, although I am never troubled by my sexual impotence. Indeed, I never think of it at all. But the creative lust torments me, savagely, and is the greatest source of my indifference, my despair, my utter discouragement. And ever so much more than my so numerous and so disgusting physiological disabilities and troublesome discomforts. I can't get myself to accept the conclusion that mind cannot compel the body to do its will. What superstition, but like all superstitions invincible.

December 9th, I Tatti

How I enjoy, as I look through the window and see the reflection in the mirror at bottom of bed, the wild dance of branches and twigs of the stone pine. Does each of them join the dance with the feeling of the dervish in his hypnotizing gyrations? The change of colours in the spotted sky. The distant horizon line of subtle delicacy. When I walk, the leaves of the olives dip into the air like tiny oars, and leave tiny wakes behind them. The sky itself seen over the green of pine and cypress is of an intense crystalline blue. I enjoy the humble field flowers, and regret that I cannot address them by name. Every pebble and splinter on the road is alive for me, and so the lordly sweep of the road itself. Then why can I not enjoy machine-made objects? The life has been pressed, squeezed out of them, and they are cold as rubber hoses. People too. I can enjoy them to the full and of all ages, provided they have preserved spring and vitality, elegance or grace, or indeed perfect naturalness. They too can look as if all had abandoned them that could have been life-enhancing about them, and not as Rembrandt's old women, who when they lend themselves to it, I can visualize as endowed with the vitalizing qualities of great art.

December 12th, I Tatti

I scarcely open a periodical of art or literature without discovering announcements of another encyclopaedia of all the arts. What does it mean? All richly illustrated with coloured plates. I fear it is these and these only that will attract buyers. They act as do the cinema and television. I cannot account for this appetite for visual merry-go-rounds. The result is no more than riding in one of them. What does the public learn, what does it get out of it? Information, not knowledge, still less feeling, losing oneself in the work of art. Let us hope that among the hundreds of thousands who look without seeing, at television speed, there is one who is ignited, in whom it becomes positive, creative, and fecundatory. Comes high, but still! I wonder how it came to me. Surely not through reproductions. There were none in my youth that gave the touch of the original, only the composition. Nor had I seen

many of them, when I first visited the Louvre, and I discovered
and loved almost all the works of art I still admire and love.

December 14th, I Tatti

Nicky's birthday yesterday, her seventieth! Beautifully staged
[by Alda], well attended, lavishly drenched with champagne.
Nicky looked beautiful, and anything but septuagenarian. I was
settled in the little French library, and guests were brought one
after another. Among them people I had not seen for ages, so that
those formerly young now looked middle-aged, and those formerly
middle-aged old and wizened. I was reminded of Proust's *Temps
Retrouvé*. The least interesting cling, with difficulty making place
for others. More and more they came. Unique Nicky. I can't
imagine a more loving, more devoted, more selfless, more eagerly
helpful, more patient, more comforting woman. What would my
life the last forty years have been without her? A dreary desert at
worst, a doubtful series of loves—at best.

December 20th, I Tatti

I ought to consult an aurist, a urologist, an eye specialist, an
up-to-date dentist, etc.—in fact spend most of my time and money
in an effort to prolong life. Why? Living at my age with all my
disabilities is anything but a picnic. So why cling to it? Partly
out of mere animal instinct. Partly out of curiosity about tomorrow
and day after tomorrow. Partly because I am not resigned to giving
up, and still am eager to achieve, if only as inspirer. Most of all,
for Nicky's sake. I am still the spool, the reel around which all the
threads of I Tatti are wound. When I die all these threads will fall
in a tangle on the ground. It will be for Nicky to try to disentangle
them, and wind them around a new reel. Who will succeed me?
Who will be proprietor? Will they leave Nicky free to carry out
my wishes, to make of I Tatti a cultural centre for all arts and
humanities? Or as I fear reduce it to a research centre for "more
and more about less and less"? For all of which reasons I can't
afford to die, although remaining only physically alive may be
anything but pleasant for me, and very tiresome even to Nicky. I

507

foresee all sorts of difficulties and troubles if I live years longer. I foresee them, but dare not enumerate them.

December 22nd, I Tatti

Always *Vorrei e non vorrei*. I loathe the ghetto and the rabbinists in all their phases. I shun it, and want to have nothing to do with it. Yet do I really want the Jew to be dissolved in the Western world, leaving no manifest, even obvious trace? Will they go on affecting the rest of the world, as Jews have in the past twenty centuries, while they were self-immured by their taboos, and immured from the outside because they could and would not submit to the totalitarian regime of the past, like Medieval Christianity, and hang-overs of it till nearly our own time? However, if the Jew wants to act as if a non-Jew (as was my case before Hitler) he still is uncanny to others, even to the most civilized and advanced "gentiles." It is the non-Jew who remains Jew-conscious, except perhaps males toward females, and females toward males. I recall Adolf Goldschmidt * saying it would take a thousand years before the feeling about the Jews as outsiders disappeared entirely.

December 31st, I Tatti

Time as days, weeks, months, almost ceases to exist. All a blur. To know what day it is, I have to consult others, or to look into this diary. Day follows day, does not follow, swishes by, so that it scarcely seems worth while to button and unbutton. I have time for nothing creative. Thoughts whirl through my head, but I cannot bring them to book. I cannot resist reading dailies, weeklies, monthlies, trying to keep abreast (if superficially) with what is being done in all fields accessible to my intelligence. I go down to meals, and often, but far from always, enjoy talk, talking myself, but more the real talk of others. So much is mere gossip, or "Do you like." "I don't." If only one could shelve old friends, let alone acquaintances, the way one does books that no longer

* Eminent German art scholar (1863–1944); professor at Berlin University, guest professor at Harvard, emigrated to the U.S. in 1936.

stimulate one, retaining good memories of what they used to be, and not being bored by them as they are now! Perhaps a great mistake to have lived so very long in the same place. Too easy for bores to find one, too difficult to refuse their entrance. "Oh for a lodge in some vast wilderness." How long could I stand it?

1958

January 3rd, I Tatti

This winter the scrub oak that makes up the underbrush of cypresses and stone pines has at first been golden amber, later and still later a dull and duller brown. All under crystal skies as I tramp high over Vincigliata, and enjoy what meets my eye far and near. The distances with exquisitely delicate sky line, remote sunny peaks, the city shining in a silvery haze, with the cupola dominating as if crowning the whole town and not one building only. Now the glitter and shimmer on each olive leaf, and seen together like so many diamonds. Then the road itself as it sweeps and curves affects me as if carried along on a rolling platform, while enjoying every line as if a work of art. The bitterness at the bottom of the cup is that I cannot inoculate others with my enjoyment. When young I could salve my conscience with the hope that mystically my delight reached others. No more. I doubt whether my own writings have led to my purpose, namely, ideated pleasure from the visible. Now art publications are a heavy industry, and furnish endless information, visual and verbal. "Knowledge comes"—information, that is—but enjoyment of a specific kind sadly wanting.

January 5th, I Tatti

Yesterday to tea, an important Swiss diplomat, so flattering, so obsequious, so fawning almost that I wonder whom he takes me for. An American secret agent, a sort of Holstein, an *éminence grise*? How often I have been taken for what I never was, and never in any way pretended to be, a Russian prince, heir to an English duke, a dispenser of endless wealth too cruel to share it with others, a versatile lady-killer. I never pretended to be anything but what I was. I could not go about like a sandwich man, crying, "I am only a child of Jewish parents from an East European ghetto." When men began to suspect that I was not the important person that they imagined, or being one that I would not play their game, they turned against me, and women because I did not comply with their languishing appeals. Now as I try to understand my past, I must assume that from childhood up I had a certain mana, something fascinating that attracted or repelled, but never left indifferent anyone who came near enough. What is a fact is that I was utterly unaware of there being anything extraordinary about me. Always considered I was an *ordinary* person with a passion for learning, for understanding, for friendship, and most of all for enjoying *Freude an sich selbst*. But I never dreamt there was anything unusual about this. I assumed all educated people were like that.

January 6th, I Tatti

Yesterday Staude,* himself a painter of talent, brought photos of portrait heads done by a German sculptor he (and Jean Rouvier) admired. They were charming, winning, delightful as photos, but not sculpture. I tried in vain to say why I thought so. Talked and talked, and saw they were more and more puzzled, and unable to understand why not sculpture. Were they not in a solid material? Yes they were, but solid material in itself is not sculpture. To be sculpture, material must like any other representation make us feel the structure, the vitality, the *push* from within; if not, it is mere photography. It may sound paradoxical, but "tactile values" are not communicated by solidity of material, although most of my readers have thought so, including such a scholar and writer as Kingsley Porter. It must strut with vitality and energy, and make us feel that it is embracing us, before we return the embrace. Hopeless to try to make others feel what I do. Perhaps if I had the energy and staying powers to write about it at length, I might discover a way of making it more graspable, more intelligible, for the *pen* has its own way of suggesting solutions that talk seldom offers. All so deeply felt by me, but how to find

* Hans Joachim Staude, German painter established in Florence; a member of the Tatti circle from 1933.

the *open-sesame* of words, of phrases, of arguments that will convince others, even when they do not understand.

January 7th, I Tatti

Ideas—*Einfälle*—flash through my head like lightning, and vanish as suddenly, seldom leaving a trace in memory. How many unborn ones are tucked away in the brain, waiting an occasion when they can come to light. While dozing, my head is like a cage with whirling little beasties skimming round and round. In my case they are apt to be archaeological, etymological, Biblical, historical, particularly with regard to Ancient history, etc., continually asking questions, proposing problems, trying to discover solutions. Of course there also are anguishing preoccupations with questions of health, of money, of all kinds of personal relations, from deepest truth to doubts and suspicion. Never anything preoccupyingly erotic. Of such are the contents and preoccupations of my—shall I call it mind?—little beasts, whirling round and round, and useless, mean, sordid, remote, impersonal, disinterested, kindly, adoring, affectionate—what a jumble, yet making up the uncontrolled life of my mind—or whatever we call it. I am overwhelmed with doubts and going on living as a make-believe—*"als ob."* What else at my time of life—perhaps at any time of life!

January 17th, I Tatti

It is depressing to be so out of step with opinion, ideals, ideas, and activities of today. It is my lot to have outlived zest, delight in mere exercise of function, no matter what. We cannot escape feeling, and seeing, and thinking according to the sense of our own lives. I had my childhood brimming with wonder and joy. My glamorous youth full of eager hope. My early love affairs and money worries soon began to make trouble, and less and less ability to cast them off, be carefree, as my age increased. I still could hope when the First World War broke out and we of the U.S.A. came in, was young enough [to hope] still that it, the war, would bring about universal peace and possibility of contentment and even happiness for everybody. The failure gave a pessimistic turn, a twist, that I have never got over. I am in the deepest

515

winter of discontent. I see everything as frosty, uninviting, ungenial, and myself as a pillar of ice, the ice of a moraine, not of a high glacier. No balm in Gilead, all dreary ways, used up. "Out of the day and night, A joy has taken flight." I cling to life out of mere animal instinct. The future has only worse to offer.

January 18th, I Tatti

Two kinds of agnostics, and no wonder. The gnostics, i.e., the people who pretend to know all about God and His purpose, are so arrogant, so positive, that they drive the agnostics to oppose them. These agnostics pretend not to know anything, but are really dead sure that there is nothing beyond "sense" and "reason." I certainly am not one of them. I really believe that I have not been endowed with the faculty to see beyond my sense and reason. On the other hand, I am humbly aware that these are pathetically limited. I gladly admit possibilities of realms of being that may be revealed to us, or that exist and deeply influence us without our becoming more than very vaguely, dimly, although perhaps hauntingly aware of them. So I welcome any S.O.S. in the shape of ritual, of song, of story, that helps our cry for understanding, beyond our present so earth-bound possibilities. Wherefore I would call myself a tender, not a "hard-boiled," agnostic, humbly confessing his incapacity, and therefore refusing to inquire, but far from excluding what is beyond his ken. On the contrary—hopeful.

January 22nd, I Tatti

Sixty-five years ago I wrote that when we can do everything, we no longer know what to do. I will not say that Picasso can do everything he wants to do. Perhaps all his absurd experiments are inspired by an urge of which he is but dimly aware, the urge to be up against something beyond his reach, to discover a real problem based on a real conviction. If, as implied in his recent encyclical, it is the absolute reproduction of actuality, then he is no artist at all. As a matter of fact, all through his career up to date he can go back to painting "materialistically," or to patterns inspired by Greek vase painting, thereby confessing that in the rest of his output there is nothing compulsive, nothing imperative, but only of tossing about, attitudinizing, etc. To me it is sardonically comic that the *grands bourgeois* of the U.S.A. and their like patronize him. Catalogue of Philadelphia exhibition just now fascinating. Scarcely a well-known name of the American plutocracy who is not there. One wonders what these "pictures" mean to them. As for the "critics," they have to put all sorts of mysterious meanings into them to justify their verbal admiration and rhetorical froth. "O trumpery." "O Moses."

January 27th, I Tatti

Nature's behest is "Eat and be eaten." Wherefore nothing seems more miraculous than the sense of beauty, particularly a feeling for nature. We have it already in Homer and the early Greek poets. Rosy-fingered dawn, the wine-coloured sea, forest silences, etc. That has nothing cannibal about it, is already a preparation for not considering things and people as mere edibles (so to speak) for one's self. Nature then made a leap beyond itself, to the supernatural, to what was called the "spiritual." Will it stop where we grope in the twilight, or will a day come when we shall see that the universe as a whole is tending toward Spirit? But what notions are these, and how can we entertain them except verbally, with no definite meaning behind our words? We are blind and deaf to all but an infinitesimal segment of the Circle of Being. Yet the sense of beauty of nature does seem to promise more than a humanity that with all other living things exists only to eat and be eaten. What a mystery it all is, and how I blunder about trying to understand—all in vain.

February 1st, I Tatti

The Man on Horseback, *l'homme à cheval*, still counted as late as the end of the nineteenth century, when Boulanger was expected to take that role. Always an apocalyptic figure, from the one appearing in the Temple of Jerusalem to annihilate Heliodorus, to Constantine. This dubious genius fulfilled all prophecy by Christianizing the Mediterranean world, and therefore counted as the expected messiah. That is why we have him on horseback in arches outside churches, all over the remoter parts of France, and

517

still see him in a Baroque version in the atrium of St. Peter's in Rome. Only in our day has the Man on Horseback ceased to count. Who ever saw a Hitler, or a Mussolini, or a Lenin, or a Stalin, or even an Eisenhower on horseback! Does that kind of *panache* count no more, has our world become so drab? Not so long ago we had in the U.S.A. Sam Sherman on horseback by our greatest sculptor, St. Gaudens himself. Yes, a drab world. Will it go on like that, and is the feeling for glory and *panache* and magnificence reduced now to mere processions of military in workmen's clothes, and with braying brass music?

February 22nd, I Tatti

[Paul] Cabot of Harvard Corporation bowled over by I Tatti, says at Harvard they have no idea of what it is, what it stands for, what it should be. But even at Harvard people of universal curiosity scarcely exist any more, certainly not among those connected with the visual arts. Vertiginous exhibitions seem only to confuse, and conclude that one kind of art is as good as another, and only better if latest and most extravagant. Universities and public galleries lay themselves out to excite, to amuse, to entertain, rather than to promote any feeling, let alone understanding of art that humanizes, breeds conviction, forms the will to prefer the life-enhancing to the depressing or nothing at all. That is the siren's song, or rather that which goes "I am a cook and a captain bold, and a mate of the *Nancy Brigg*," etc. Scarcely anyone listens to my sad lay, or to my shouting in the wilderness of today. No hope in sight of betterment, although I am sure it will come, and have its day. All this I have written scores, hundreds of times, and keep grinding out, as on a hurdy-gurdy.

March 2nd, I Tatti

The Berenson myth and my longevity hypnotize people into approaching me with defences of every kind. They try to bluff, to be bumptious, pretend not to care a damn. The only ones who act naturally are those who have no use whatever for my values, and consequently are unimpressed, but come only to gorge a brainless curiosity. I am consequently in the position of royalties who scarcely ever see and hear people as their peers see them. I deplore being thus deprived of the natural approach of most people, and of the possibility of feeling and seeing and appraising them for what they really are. I see no remedy, seeing I have done nothing to produce this condition of things, and am never rude to people unless they provoke me. At worst I can be distant. So all bores and pretentious individuals have to do is to go away with the least ceremony and greatest all-round convenience.

March 7th, I Tatti

Once in a while I wake from a nightmare hearing myself cry "Help, help, help," because assassins have come to kill me. I do not cry Harry, Tim, Willy, or any other individual to serve me. The instinctive cry is impersonal, abstract. And that is my cry for help. I know not for whom, for what. For nothing material, for release from the murky cell of my infinitely limited understanding. It can comprehend, at best, its limitations only. Nothing of reality. Indeed, so limited as bound to question whether there is anything outside its narrow cell, barely wide enough to hold me. I cry for help, but who hears? All sorts of religions through the ages acted and still act as if they knew. I can condone and even love them as part of human history. Today their claims seem blasphemous, and their efforts to impose them revolting—particularly on the part of the Vatican. In exasperation I all but prefer the Vatican's *vis-à-vis*, the Kremlin. It has the merit of not pretending to know the answer, not to claim to be on familiar terms with the Mystery of the Universe. Of course I do not yield, for with all its faults the Vatican favours human values, and the Kremlin does not.

March 8th, I Tatti

I cannot help wondering how a Socrates as an old man kept clean, and did not stink. I mean the Socrates of Platonic Dialogues. Did Alcibiades hold his nose while embracing him? If there were perfumes, Socrates was too poor to enjoy them. The ephebes kept sweet of course, but even they, how, with what, did they wipe themselves after stools? From my own childhood in Lithuania I

519

recall rabbis with wonderful mien, who certainly never washed, and used to wipe their noses on their sleeves. Perhaps the relative brevity of life was due to so much less cleanliness than nowadays. Even now, however, the greater part of the world still is as filthy as ever. Do they not partake of our European longevity—the Chinese, for instance? I have read that under their magnificent robes, mandarins felt lice running over their bodies, and would scratch themselves, and even try to catch them and crush them. So my idle thoughts wander to and fro through time and space, asking questions, yet leaving me humiliated often because questions come up it had not occurred to me to ask. Except in a world based on mathematics, my curiosity wanders and wanders, to no purpose. Idle amusement, but how entertaining!

March 9th, I Tatti

I remember the Franco-Prussian War of 1870, and the rise of Germany to a world Power. Her provoking England to war, and England's suicide in using herself up to defeat Germany, in two wars, and thereby declining to a humiliating position between the only two great powers in the White Man's world, U.S.A. and U.S.S.R. The almost simultaneous collapse of German, Austrian, and Russian imperial Houses, and how I felt as if the tripod on which our world rested had broken down. (At the same time, the successful splitting up of the atom affected me as if my world, my material world, could no longer be trusted.) The Communist and Nazi onslaughts on our way of life, and their murderous ferocity to establish their power. The devastating folly of the Hitlerites, and the complete triumph of Stalinite totalitarianism. How can a Christian Providence be accused of a purpose, a purpose to achieve what? Termite-like totalitarianism? Is that the divine purpose of man's trajectory across this planet? That is where under no matter what name of regime we are tending, nay, running, and we scarcely dream, let alone plan, to oppose it.

March 11th, I Tatti

Snowed all night, and translated an Italian landscape into a Chinese one. Only that instead of spots of russet here and there,

520

it is the deep green of the cypresses that resists the greyness of the rest. Why did the Chinese rejoice in that kind of landscape? For technical reasons, unable to do better? Or did they prefer something that reflected the drabness of their monotonous, dull lives? If not that, then why? Or was it for a suggestion of infinity, of the stream of existence toward the infinite sea, as seems to be the case with most of their monochromes? Chinese landscape seems autochthonous, that is to say I cannot descry to what foreign influence it owes anything. Surely not, as in its figure arts, to remote Greek, for the Greeks (to my knowledge) down to Byzantine never developed more than a strictly confined landscape, and with no background even, never a Chinese suggestion of endlessness, and of wilderness, rocks, streams, mountains, glades, rivers! One of the many problems in art history that seem insoluble, yet that keep on gnawing the teeth of curiosity. Better to enjoy as happily as I can, and not bother about "how" and "why"—if only I could master my eagerness to know as well as to feel, and through feeling to understand.

March 13th, I Tatti

Most of the mistakes I have made in my career as attributor of pictures have been due to a far too narrow and dogmatic concept of the painter, excluding everything that did not fit into this idea and even ideal. From Giotto to Giorgione! The last I already have rectified in the Phaidon edition of Venetian painting. The Giotto nut is hard to crack, for I must admit that in mid-career his vocabulary (so to speak) changed over from Romanesque to Gothic. Scarcely one of the painters I dealt with whom I treated according to evidence, and not according to an ideal of him, even Botticelli, perhaps even Raphael. Yet if there is a person meaning always to be *sachlich*, it is I. I never publish to vex, although I may to anticipate being filched. On the whole I can assert that my mistakes always have been due to idealization. Nothing harder to get rid of, and few things give me more pleasure than to emancipate myself from error, particularly when I am the first to do so. Indeed, fifty and more years ago, Salomon Reinach accused me of showing off my changes of mind, and others less friendly have

521

been loud in proclaiming how unreliable are my judgments, and how frivolous I am in changing them.

March 19th, I Tatti

An English eye specialist announces that so many painters of today and El Greco in the past suffered from eye troubles which made them see things in the queer way that they painted them. But why do such maladies of the eye occur in moments of disintegration of an accepted style, or to individuals who try to adopt a style entirely different from the one they were brought up to? That was the case with El Greco. He did his best to become a Venetian, and I believe had he remained in Venice he would have become one, casting off entirely his Byzantine training. In Spain he was free to let himself take the easiest way, and that was to give up trying to be a Venetian, and to return to his Creto-Byzantine technique, as foundation, with Venetian reminiscences superposed. Why not take in all the Mannerists? Why never in Classical periods, neither in Florence nor elsewhere in Europe, before disintegration, not even when Flemings tried to be Raphaelesque, or Michelangelesque. Of course, there may be a minimum of truth as applied to individuals of today. What by the way of Claude, let alone Turner? And Wilson Steer? And what of Magnasco? A little array of facts is a dangerous thing, the source of misleading generalizations.

March 20th, I Tatti

Giotto—what a problem. Procacci * brought photos of the St. Francis frescoes in Santa Croce—so shamelessly made over a hundred years ago. Perspective more admirable than any in Italy till Alberti and Piero della Francesca. Magnificently manly the Sultan with his wonderfully wound turban. Genius if ever—but no followers to take up his teaching, and follow his example, not even the greatest of the Giotteschi, Andrea Orcagna. In his own career he owes nothing to Cimabue, perhaps something to Cavallini. Dif-

* Ugo Procacci, Italian art historian on the staff of the Fine Arts Service; at present Superintendent of Monuments for the province of Florence.

ficult to get an idea of his successive phases. Then in mid-career he seems to have suddenly changed over from a Romanesque to a Gothic style. After which it would seem that he was more of an *entrepreneur* than executant. Of course he must have designed all (or nearly all) the frescoes and polyptychs ascribed to him, but in the frescoes particularly there seems little convincingly his own, except at Padua, and much in Santa Croce of Florence. A central figure in universal art history, who yet remains a problem, and to me an insoluble one, more than any other in my range of continuous study. I feel baffled, and humiliated, and ready to say "Enjoy him" and leave the problems to others.

March 21st, I Tatti

I have lost grip in almost every way. I no longer can recall the reasoning by which I arrived at my convictions, particularly in questions of art as experience, and even of attribution. I go on with them, but can no longer discuss them with myself, let alone with others. I accept them by rote, and that makes me feel ever so diminished, so superfluous, so unworthy of all the alarming expenses and trouble to others of keeping me alive. And why do I cling to life, despite everything? First and foremost, for Nicky's sake. Then the hope of a younger generation at Harvard that will be better than the present "art teachers," and will appreciate what could and should be done with all I Tatti offers them. I continue piling books and periodicals into the library, so as to serve as models for what is to be continued. Of course I cannot hope it will be kept up, as I could afford and my successors may not, even if they had my instinct about books, the fruit of eighty years of experience. One must give oneself reasons for what one does, instinctively or by intuition. How I miss my capacity for justifying my tasks, my convictions, my axioms, my assumptions! I gasp and yearn, and fall back humiliated.

March 26th, I Tatti

In U.S.A. the universal answer to "How are you?" is "Fine." Meant to stop further inquiries. On the right assumption that self-protectively nobody cares too much to know and feel what others do. Impossible, if one wanted to, to imagine exactly what annoys, what troubles others, what aches and pains and collapses others suffer from, not even those we love most. I already have noted in these pages what remorse I feel over my impatience with my wife's lamentations over her bodily distress, and how much I wrote them off as imaginary. Each time I now feel a twinge I recall her complaints and how she asked for sympathy, and I turned a deaf ear. How learn to suffer and say nothing, not to ask for sympathy with a feeling of resentment that others are not suffering as we do, ejaculating *Non est dolor sicut dolor meus.* How invalids are admired for not complaining, not groaning even at the creaking of wheels over rough roads, how heroic they seem and how admired! How I should enjoy such admiration, but I am no Stoic. I have no control of my nerves. It would be against nature for me "to consume my own smoke," to play the suffering but silent "hero."

March 29th, I Tatti

Romanesque architecture, particularly in the Southwest of France. How stately, how convincing, how beautifully designed! Truly life-enhancing. And in contrast with the structural vitality, the exquisite, playful carving of the capitals—same idea as initials in Medieval illumination, only endlessly more exquisite in execution, more lovely. Yet destined to disappear before the logic of the builder's exigencies, and the onslaught of St. Bernard. So that where there was money enough, Romanesque disappeared before Gothic, all over the Western world. Holy poverty is responsible for the preservation of the Romanesque churches in Aquitaine as well as in other regions. Even in neglected spots near Paris, for instance, they have remained, humble structures, yet pleasant. But so it is with every style. It is always *"Cimabue tiene il campo, poi Giotto ha il grido."* Pity Dante does not say which he preferred. The cry for change, for *otherness,* is in itself a human demand, and explains much that today gives me the creeps. Would I like a changeless world? Yes, if by itself as wide and varied and full as I know it can be—and mine has been.

April 4th, I Tatti

H. F. M. Prescott's * *Once to Sinai,* based on the pilgrimage of Father Felix Fabbri. Seldom read a book that kept my fascinated attention so much, that made me think so much, and understand so much better what I already knew. I have read no end of Venetian history. I knew it had a real empire southward from Venice, and eastward to the Aegean, and in a way overshadowed what remained of the Byzantine Empire. I never realized before how much it was like the Hanse, rather than Britain. The captains of its galleys, all the famous names, were themselves tradesmen, merchant princes, and not at all feudal barons, although they became so later when their empire crumbled and disappeared. Their pride was generated by having to fight for consideration, while everybody took the feudal nobility for granted as unassailable, and it was therefore much more easygoing. Started me thinking of how German pilgrims and merchants travelled from Venice to their homes. Gave me an idea of the physical hardships of travelling to Sinai, and then in Mameluk Egypt, all the greed, hostility encountered, and the arbitrary exactions, and caprice and even cruelty of officials, as well as misconduct toward pilgrims of the mob, and inability of Venetian captains to protect them, and then their discomforts in the galleys where they only could crowd between bales of goods.

April 5th, I Tatti

Santayana's mother was once asked what she did with herself. "Oh, it is very simple. I try to keep cool in summer, and to keep warm in winter." If, like her, I did nothing but devote myself to trying to relax comfortably by keeping all the particles of my body from quarrelling and snarling and kicking, and to avoid any move on my part to encourage this warfare . . . But I am possessed by a demon who rides me and whips me up to attempts to write, to organize, and to produce beyond any possibility of concluding anything. So I feel frustrated and despairing. My mind still so active, handicapped by lack of memory, i.e., inability to

* English writer, author of *Man on a Donkey,* etc.

call up names and images of all kinds when I need them. How often writing to dear loves and intimate friends, I begin to write "Dear," and then cannot recall the name—not at the moment. Then I see less and less when I try to read, and my handwriting I myself cannot decipher even the moment after writing. Yet eagerness to do, to create, to organize, does not diminish. I keep trying, and failure does not down me.

April 9th, I Tatti

John Walker, his contagious laugh, his appealing look, his endearing smile, and now his greyed hair make him irresistible. One of my earliest pupils (although long after Kenneth Clark), and so affectionately devoted that I urged him to step in at I Tatti, the moment I disappeared. This was accepted everywhere, and militated against his appointment as Director of Washington National Gallery. He asked to be released, and of course I did, and he promised to take up I Tatti after ten years. Did he expect me to live well beyond a hundred, or did he not stop to consider what was against his will, against his ambition, against his interest? I suspect that he is unconscious of his own *tropisms*. All in all, a radiant creature, irresistible, and the best of company. He himself is the adequate return for all one does for him.

April 13th, I Tatti

When young, I did not conceive of being a life-enhancing work of art to older people. So I never tried to approach the great or the merely important of the moment. I had access to Samuel Butler, and never took advantage of it, and almost never presented an introduction, so convinced was I that it could only be a nuisance. The more I admired, the more I abstained, as was the case with Matthew Arnold. I did meet Pater, although against my will, and it was very disappointing. There can be no personally satisfying relation unless reciprocal, or the thankfulness becomes a burthen and turns to revolt. That is so easily the case between parents and children, benefactors and beneficiaries (as in the classical instance of Petrarch and his favourite secretary and pupil), so often between wives and husbands, between class and class. So I always urge ac-

526

cepting presents, even relatively costly ones, from humblest dependents. It takes the burden of gratitude from their shoulders, and gives them a sense of giving as well as taking and of feeling for the moment our equals. So never refuse a gift from those who work for you, depend on you, really live off your largess. Few understand this, and so fail to avoid trouble.

April 14th, I Tatti

Since I have fallen into the ocean-stream of the news, since my capsulation like Merlin in the deforming glass case of legend and gossip, thanks to my longevity, my career, and to some trifling degree my achievements, I have become an object of curiosity, of boasting that *they* have seen me. People I have not met before, seldom ever are natural on first contact with me. Either spreading the butter of adoration too thick or, if young, too squirming, and wriggling provokingly. It took me till quite recently to realize what was the matter, that it was funk and not disrespect. So instead of doing my best as at least I now try to do, I took their behaviour as a deliberate challenge, and sent them away hating me, I am sure. It has been hard to learn this lesson, and proves that I am not good at understanding and penetrating others. On the other hand, it has saved me from women who, as I look back, I now realize were after me to have me for a while, and then to throw me away. This was better than insistence on having me for keeps.

April 15th, I Tatti

Yesterday saw a woman who evoked memories of fifty or more years ago. I was upset and have not got over it yet. Partly because I could not help trying to give them more substance, and in part because of people and events despicable in recollection. So much in my past that I hate to evoke. Short of violence, I have been capable of every sin, every misdemeanour, every crime. With horror I think what I should have become if I lived the life of an ill-paid professor, or struggling writer, how rebellious, if I had not lived a life devoted to great art, and the aristocratically pyramidal structure of society that it serves, or worse still if I had re-

527

mained in the all but proletarian condition I lived in as a Jewish immigrant lad in Boston. So I remain sceptical about my personality. It really seems to have reached its present integration in the last twenty years, with the wide and far vision I now enjoy, with *tout comprendre, c'est tout pardonner*, expecting little and trying to be thankful for that, the serenity for which I am now admired. But I keep hearing the Furies, and never forget them.

EPILOGUE

During the first months of 1958, B.B. was laid low twice by an attack of severe pain in his back and both times recovered after a few days in bed. The third attack, about the fifteenth of April, was so serious that from one day to the other his still fairly normal life was changed into the existence of a helpless invalid. Accustomed to his almost miraculous recoveries, we went on believing firmly (and perhaps he himself did so too) that his frail but surprisingly tough body would again get the better of the onslaught. It was not to be. The process of decalcification of the bones—osteoporosis—extended to his ribs and he could hardly move without intense pain. Then several other complications arose and gradually wore out his strength. The brave effort he had made to keep up a semblance of his former daily schedule by dictating letters and attending to the revision of his "Lists" of Florentine pictures could not be sustained for long. More and more frequently he had to stop after a few minutes. Finally it was only at his best hour, after his breakfast, that he was now and then able to concentrate on a problem of attribution, dictate a short note, look at new books.

Fully aware of his condition, he accepted it without any fuss or complaint. Undoubtedly his lack of any false pride made his being suddenly utterly helpless easier for him. When I decided to get a Bath chair for him his Emma was almost in tears because she expected him to be *mortificato*—humiliated—to go about in it. B.B. was on the contrary pleased to be able to see some of his favourite views at Casa al Dono and in the Tatti garden so comfortably. "To become as old as I am," he would say, "is not an adventure to be recommended." A great consolation for him was the tender and watchful assistance he got from his nurse, a strong young woman who could lift and carry him like a baby. She became so utterly devoted to him that I frequently had to force her to

529

take off a few hours for her own relaxation. One day I said to him, "B.B., do you realize that you have made another conquest? This young woman worships you!" He smiled and said only, "Of course." Later on, a night nurse became necessary. At first he would not hear of it but then grew to be very fond of her too and called her *l'angelo custode*—the guardian angel.

Toward the end of 1958 he seemed no longer interested in current events. One morning as Emma was handing him the daily paper he said, "No, take it away. I have seen it already. It is yesterday's paper." From then on he never looked at a paper again. And yet I was surprised to hear him talk with Walter Lippmann—who came for a short visit a few weeks later—about Walter's trip to Russia and other political matters as if all the information on the subject was at his command.

All through the last year it was a continual up and down, happier and clearer days alternating with more difficult ones. Spurts of his former mental energy would suddenly dart out like a bright flame from a smouldering fire. When the notes for *One Year's Reading for Fun* were being prepared an essay by Matthew Arnold on Wordsworth could not be traced. When I asked B.B. about it his eyes lit up. "It is not an essay," he said, "it is the introduction to a collection of Wordsworth's poems." A few days later I inquired about a quotation from an obscure late Latin poet and he told me in what section to look for the book containing the quotation and what its binding looked like. B.B.'s recollections of D'Annunzio inserted in this volume at page 33 he dictated to me on one of these auspicious mornings. They gave me the momentary illusion that all was well again.

"You cannot imagine what a confusion I have got in my head," he would say on his bad days, and then look with such a wistful expression at the new books from the library I had spread out for him. "I used to know a great deal about this subject but now I cannot co-ordinate things any longer." Never did I hear him babble or ask the same question over and over again. The moment he felt that he was not registering clearly he would keep completely silent.

To my reading he went on listening, sometimes for a short time, on better days for longer. He wanted only what he called "timeless" books: the Bible, *Don Quixote,* Boccaccio's *Decameron,* the *Thousand and One Nights* in the translation of Mardrus, his

favourite Trollopes and Thackerays. *Vanity Fair* was the last book
I read to him.

Listening to records had been for a number of years a joy
and a relaxation for him. A few months before his death something
happened to his ears that distorted the sounds and he had to give it
up. Not long before this happened he had been rapturously enjoying the small concerts arranged for him by Yehudi Menuhin,
his neighbour at the Villino and among the friends of the last years
one of B.B.'s favourites.

What went on giving him pleasure even at the expense
of getting thoroughly tired was seeing his friends again quietly,
rarely more than two people at a time. He even made several new
links. When young John Carter Brown came to spend a fortnight in Florence in the autumn of 1958, B.B. saw him almost
every day and found him most congenial, also promising as an art
student and future museum director.

He was delighted to welcome Miss Helen Frick and her
charming young grandniece and to discuss with her the plans for
a new museum in Pittsburgh.

A great event for B.B. was Adlai Stevenson's visit to Casa al
Dono in the summer of 1958. Although unable to sit up at the
lunch table with us, he had a good talk with his guest afterward.
Stevenson was delighted when B.B. told him that a new war cry
should be launched: Intellectuals of the world, unite!

Other meetings and talks I remember vividly, some at Casa
al Dono, others in the small French library at I Tatti where B.B.
had his meals and where he would receive guests, seated in a deep
armchair, clad in his burgundy-red velvet dressing gown and cap.
I see him before me listening to Iris Origo's account of her lectures
at Harvard, of her contacts with teachers and pupils; looking at
photos of Renaissance bronzes with John Pope-Hennessy and discussing them with him as he would have done in his best days;
Doro Levi explaining the latest discoveries in Crete to him; Robert
and Mildred Bliss showing him a rare Byzantine coin, the gift
of friends for their Golden Wedding anniversary; Lawrence Berenson, his cousin, describing his trip to Israel and his impressions
there; Agnes Mongan, Sidney Freedberg, and John Coolidge each
in his turn entertaining him with gossip from the world of art
studies. As particularly happy and gay I remember the evening
when Harold Acton brought his friends, the Chinese scholar

531

Chen Shi-hsing with his young wife, so graceful in a white embroidered satin dress of modernized Chinese cut. B.B. enjoyed looking at her, talking to Chen about Chinese literature, and listening to his chanting Chinese ditties.

When my nephew Cecil Anrep introduced his lovely bride to B.B. he received them charmingly and said to them, "Remember one thing: you can quarrel as much as you like but never sulk."

On B.B.'s last birthday McGeorge Bundy—at that time Dean of the Department of Arts and Sciences at Harvard—came to see him and spoke most encouragingly about the future of I Tatti. He begged B.B. not to worry and assured him of Harvard's firm intention to carry out his wishes. Although Bundy's promise has been so far fulfilled only partly, I feel grateful to him for having given B.B. a moment of real happiness.

Other last birthday guests were John Walker and his daughter Gillian—a special pet of B.B.'s—his beloved friends from Cleveland Henry and Frances Francis, Umberto Morra—who was like a member of the family for us—and Freya Stark.

When we went to Casa al Dono for the last time in the summer of 1959, B.B. insisted on my taking along the photographic material for all the great Quattrocento Florentines. Each day for about twenty minutes he made the effort to look at them, lingering over his favourite pictures and making small corrections to the "Lists."

Toward the end of our stay at Casa al Dono the swellings in his face and mouth had become so severe that it was difficult, sometimes almost impossible, to understand what he was trying to say. While he was still able to talk clearly it happened one day that his doctor, Alberto Capecchi, whose wife had died a month earlier after years of suffering, came up for his usual visit. In a fit of utter despair over having lost his companion he broke down and asked B.B. for a word of comfort. "You do believe, don't you," he said, "that I shall see my Elena again, that we shall be reunited in a better world?" B.B. kept silent for a moment and then said, "Dear friend, you certainly deserve to be granted such happiness, but I cannot help wondering whether many husbands might not want to be assured of the contrary."

It was the same faithful, devoted Capecchi who on the morning of October 6th told me that he did not expect B.B. to outlive

the day, and what was I going to do about his duties as a Catholic?
I did not know what to answer. B.B. had been converted to the
Church in the early nineties at Monte Oliveto but had stopped
being a practising Catholic a year or two later. His attitude was
one of tenderness, of sympathy toward the liturgical and ritual
side of the Church and of animosity to the theological and dog-
matical aspects of it. While he was still able to express himself
clearly he had never said a word about his death or his burial. But
I remembered that he had fully approved my asking Mary a few
weeks before her death in 1945 for permission to disregard her
wish to be cremated. "The feelings of the humble people around
you," I said to her, "of the women who have nursed you with so
much devotion, are much more important than a whim of yours.
Do not offend them by not having a proper Catholic burial."
With this precedent in mind I knelt down by B.B.'s bed and told
him that his doctor felt very anxious about the saving of his soul.
"I know," I said, "that you are not anxious, but would you allow
me to call in the parish priest to give you his blessing?" B.B. had
opened his eyes while I was speaking and I could see that he was
following my words with all his attention. He nodded his head. I
repeated my question to be quite sure and he nodded his head
again. When our parish priest—the son of peasants from the upper
Val d'Arno—approached B.B.'s bed I was deeply moved by the
tact, the dignity, the simplicity with which he discharged his task.
It made me think of Edith Wharton and of how she used to speak
of Catholic ritual and of the sublime "frame" it gave to the three
great events in human life: birth, marriage, and death.

When I now take friends to B.B.'s tomb in the small chapel
at I Tatti they frequently ask me whether it had been B.B.'s wish
to be buried there. He never said anything about it. When starting
out for a journey, particularly to more distant shores—as in 1938
to Asia Minor—he would say to me, "Remember, if I should die
on this trip I do not want my earthly remains to be trundled about.
Wherever I die, there let me be buried." And thus his wish has
been fulfilled.

NICKY MARIANO

San Martino a Mensola
February 1963

533

INDEX

Abano, Italy, 83

Abbott, Senda Berenson, 169n., 465

Acton, Harold, 409 and n., 440, 531

Adams, Charles, x

Adams, Henry, 407, 452, 502

Aix-les-Bains, France, 173

Akbar the Great, 496

Aksakov, Sergei, 303 and n., 426

Alassio, Italy, 184

Alazard, Jean, 381 and n.

Alberti, Guglielmo, xi

Alberti, Leon, 522

Albertini, Alberto, 267 and n.

Albertini, Luigi, 5n., 79n.

Alcibiades, xiv, 141, 519

Alcinoüs, 41, 338–339

Aldringen, Prince Alphonse Clary, 254 and n., 311

Alexander, King of Greece, 86n.

Alexander the Great, 138, 326, 448, 496

Alliata, Prince Fabrizio, 313 and n.

Alliata, Princess Iana, 313 and n.

Amalfitano, Italy, 264

Ambrosiana, Biblioteca, Milan, 132

American Cathedral, Paris, 178–179

Amiens, France, 192

Andrews, Henry, 290

Andrews, Mrs. Henry, *see* West, Rebecca

Angelico, Fra, 473, 491

Angelo, Cardinal Roncalli, 346 and n., 347

Anrep, Baroness Alda von, 103 and n., 315, 507

Anrep, Cecil von, 118 and n., 532

Anrep, Baron Egbert von, 103 and n., 375

Antonello da Messina, 385, 453

Arezzo, Italy, 44, 471

Aristotle, 216, 422

Arnold, Matthew, 185, 348, 452, 526, 530

Art Institute of Chicago, 25–26

Ascoli, Max, 232

Asolo, Italy, 134–135, 321

Aspasia, Princess of Greece, 86 and n.

Asquith, Herbert, 1st Earl of Oxford and Asquith, 256, 440

Assisi, Italy, 45, 83, 90, 196, 392, 488

Aubert, Marcel, 178 and n., 179

Auden, Wystan, 232, 421

Autun, France, 183

Auxerre, France, 174–175

Baccara (pianist), 34

Bacchelli, Riccardo, 347 and n.

Bach, Johann S., 11, 495

Bacon, Mrs., 150

Badile, Antonio, 84, 85

Bagazzano, Italy, 317

Baiae, Italy, 313

Balaam, 101

Balzac, Honoré de, 9, 458

Bandinelli, Bianchi, 390

Barbaro family, 83n.

Barber (B.B.'s), 6, 199, 201, 359

Barbey d'Aurevilly, Jules, 334

Bargello, Florence, 327

Barker, Helen, *see* Huntington, Helen

Bassano, Francesco, 211

535